W9-CBF-546

Communication SHARK™

A Human Communication Guide

SECOND EDITION

Penny Joyner Waddell, EdD

Kendall Hunt
publishing company

Cover designed by Cassandra West

www.kendallhunt.com
Send all inquiries to:
4050 Westmark Drive
Dubuque, IA   52004-1840

Published in the United States of America

"You do not have to be GREAT to START,
but you have to START to be GREAT!"

Zig Ziglar

LET'S GET STARTED!

"Human Communication is a process which involves verbal and nonverbal communication methods in your personal, professional, and public lives."

Contents

Learn about the foundations of communicating effectively with others and how to confidently deliver a message.

UNIT #1: FOUNDATIONS OF COMMUNICATION 1

UNIT #2: COMMUNICATION TYPES 21

UNIT #3: INDIVIDUAL AND GROUP COMMUNICATION 129

UNIT #4: WORKPLACE COMMUNICATION 311

GLOSSARY 381

**Logo and Book Cover created by
Cassandra West, Graphic Artist**

E-mail: Cwest@SpeechShark.com

Meet the SpeechShark App Team!

Penny   Marcus   Maurice   Cassie   Charles

Dr. Penny Joyner Waddell, author of *Communication Shark: A Human Communication Guide, SpeechShark: A Public Speaking Guide,* and designer of the SpeechShark app, has years of experience as a public speaking coach and a reputation for providing students with a practical step-by-step approach to communication.   Both guidebooks coupled with the SpeechShark app have just the right amount of instruction with easy to use guides and worksheets to help you communicate like a pro in record time.

Marcus Smith is the key coder and developer for Android versions for the SpeechShark app development team. As a software engineer and with a background in game development, Marcus has worked on several group projects creating mobile platforms and web APIs, as well as principles of software designs. He is especially talented with identifying software defects and recommending improvements.

Maurice McFarlane is the key iOS coder and organizer for the SpeechShark app development team. As an accomplished applications developer, Maurice also works with Tier 1-2 retailers creating the Point-of-Sale system customizations, building custom APIs for payment devices, and implementing P2Pe/EMV solutions.

Cassandra (Cassie) West is the graphic designer for SpeechShark. Her expertise includes brand identity, corporate presentations and campaigns, Web collaboration, UI design, package design, book cover/layout designs, and more. You'll see her beautiful design on the cover of this guidebook and she created the brand, icon, and page displays used for the SpeechShark app.

Charles Hardnett is the project manager and senior developer for the SpeechShark app. His career includes a vast array of experiences as a computer science professor and researcher, software developer, educational administrator, and software architect. Charles has worked on projects involving the development of compilers for high performance computing, access and switching for telecommunications, Web applications for a variety of domains, and mobile applications for entertainment, productivity, and education.

Preface

Several years ago, I had the inspiration to develop a speechwriting app that would help students and business leaders plan and write speeches. Through my many years as a speech instructor and speech coach, I learned that when people say they have a fear of public speaking, it is more a fear of not knowing what to say. Speakers who have a message and a plan for the clear points they will cover, take the time needed to rehearse and will incorporate trained tech support to make their presentations shine. Through this effort, they cure their own fear of public speaking. The SpeechShark app was developed to be a tool for speakers to organize thoughts and put content into a package that could be well received by any audience.

Human Communication figures into this same idea as we realize Communication Sharks are not like vicious man-eater sharks; instead, they are a focused species with a purpose to connect with others using verbal and nonverbal communication skills through personal, professional, and public interactions. Instead of an ocean, Communication Sharks navigate life in many different roles. Instead of sharp, pointed teeth, they use their emotional intelligence and problem-solving skills to strategize and create a calculated plan for success. To a Communication Shark, the world presents an ocean of opportunity for building strong relationships in every aspect of their lives.

Communication happens one-on-one, in pairs, groups, or to audiences of hundreds. It takes a Communication Shark to assume the sharky attitudes and strategies needed to make effective communication skills a reality. Stay out of the water? Not you, because you will put on your shark skin suit, better known as thick skin, and confidently move toward the life for which you have always dreamed. *Human Communication* takes a more in-depth look at the way we communicate with others. Using the SpeechShark app will help with public speaking opportunities that may come your way, but the content found in this textbook will help you navigate the turbulent waters that we often find when beginning new relationships, strengthening existing relationships, facing challenging relationships, and maintaining quality relationships that will last your entire life. The combination of using the SpeechShark app along with the information found within the textbook means that you will be a Communication Shark and this guidebook was designed just for you!

Communication
SH▲RK™

How Do I Use the SpeechShark App?

Did you purchase the SpeechShark app? Excellent! If not, visit our website at www.SpeechShark.com to see a demonstration. The app is available for Android users in **GooglePlay** and for iOS users in the **Apple Store**. Using the app means you are on your way to creating effective and exciting speech presentations for your audience! Click on your SpeechShark app and let's get started!

Here are steps to follow:

1. Open the SpeechShark app.
2. Select "Home" to see options to create speeches, manage speeches, or select preferences.
3. If you want to create a NEW speech, select "Create Speeches."
4. A page will open that asks about the purpose of your speech. Read through each type of speech and choose the type that works best for your purpose. If you need more information about each type of speech, simply "LONG PRESS" the speech type to receive a brief tutorial regarding the speech. A "SHORT PRESS" of the speech type will take you directly to the next step in creating a speech.
5. Answer each prompting question using a complete sentence. Use correct grammar and spelling as this information will automatically begin building a speech outline.
6. Take your time and work through each step—one at a time—answering each prompting question and when finished touch the "Continue" bar.
7. SpeechShark takes all of the guesswork out of crafting an effective speech, but it is up to you to answer the prompts, keep the purpose of your speech as your goal, and consider who will be listening to your speech. What does your audience need to know? What does your audience WANT to know? What can you do and say to connect with the audience and engage them?
8. As you have answered all of the questions, you will notice that SpeechShark will then deliver a full written outline that you can print, share, or e-mail. Additionally, you will see that SpeechShark will automatically generate three note cards that can be used for notes on your phone or tablet/iPad. This will make you a Card Shark because instead of standing in front of your audience with awkward note cards, your notes are easily accessed using your electronic device and are available with a simple swipe.
9. Once the speech has been written, you can always retrieve it by going back to the "Home" file on the SpeechShark app and selecting "Manage Speeches." Every speech you craft will be stored there in a file with the "TITLE" that you give to the speech.
10. You, too, can be a Communication Shark!

Acknowledgments

Oceans of appreciation are extended to the following: the dedicated members of the SpeechShark app design team (Charles Hardnett, Maurice McFarlane, Marcus Smith, and Cassandra West), personal editors (Ruth Rowell Joyner and Bonnie Smith), and the publishers and editors of Kendall Hunt. I am most grateful to God for the support from my husband, Bill, our children (Katie, Steven, Maggie, Marc, Halie, and Nick) and my grandbaby sharks (Will, Bailey, and Hunter).

Communication SHARK™

Unit #1

Foundations of Communication

History of Communication

Purpose of Communication

Models of Communication

Communication SH▲RK™

NOTES

Chapter One

History of Communication

Aspects of Communication from Classical Rhetorical Roots to Modern Social Science

© mindscanner/Shutterstock.com

In this chapter:

Timeline of Communication   History of Rhetorical Communication

One of my favorite books about Public Speaking and Human Communication was written by James C. Humes, who was a speechwriter for five American presidents. His book, *Speak Like Churchhill, Stand Like Lincoln,* contained twenty-one chapters of communication secrets that he learned from observing some of our world's greatest speakers. When I use the word—greatest—this didn't always mean they were the best leaders; however, they were the most powerful when it came to their communication skills and their knack for influencing others.

Through the years I shared his book with many of my speech students and, quite often, I've read passages from the book to my classes when trying to make a point about something I was hoping they would do as they were crafting and presenting speeches for the fundamentals of speech class that I teach. I've also shared some of his famous tips with my SkillsUSA speech competitors and wondered what James C. Humes would say to them as they won state competitions and then proceeded to win first place in the United States of America for a SkillsUSA speech competition. Although I've never met Mr. Humes, I can imagine that he would be proud of any young public speaker who was working diligently to speak in a competition that gains national recognition. While Mr. Humes is one of our modern rhetorical giants, I would also like to share with you a brief summary of the history of communication which began over 500,000 years ago.

TIMELINE OF COMMUNICATION

Oral communication, in the form of *storytelling*, is considered as one of the earliest forms of human communication and continues to be popular throughout the history of mankind. While this was important as a method of passing along information, it was also a social time as elders would gather around to share experiences and bits of wisdom. This week I was reading a magazine article that was giving details of storytelling festivals in the state of Georgia. I've made a mental note to be sure and attend one of those festivals just as soon as I have this book finished and posted to the publishers.

Primitive communication was evident as far back as the stories involving Adam and Eve. Several years ago, I spent the summer in Zimbabwe, Africa, and saw firsthand cave paintings that were used as pictorial communications. These were called *petroglyphs, carvings or paintings into a rock surface.* While these symbols were not detailed, it was clear to see they were communicating with others to share information. One carving we saw showed drawings of several people with spears in their hands in pursuit of an impala. Another picture showed the people cooking meat over a fire and wearing a hide from the impala. Some of the cave drawings looked like simple maps which pointed to certain areas where game could be found to provide food.

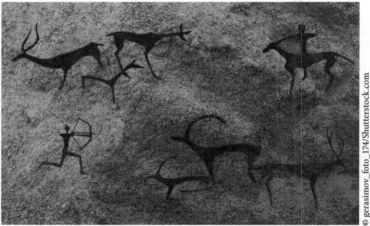

© gerasimov_foto_174/Shutterstock.com

We still use pictures as we communicate, but the *pictograms* (*graphic elements of uniform size and arranged in sequence*) and *ideograms* (*picture or symbol used in writing to represent a thing or idea*) of the past evolved into the formation of early scripts known as *logographs* (*a letter, symbol, or sign used to represent a word*), which was a combination of pictures and symbols. For example, a modern logograph is the dollar sign. When you see the symbol, $, you understand that it is communicating something to do with money. Here are some other logographs that you regularly use: %, &, #, +, =, and @. Numbers are also logographs when we use the number 2 when we are saying the word, two.

Those evolved into the alphabet introduced in the sixteenth century BC. Later as paper was developed and the quill was invented, writing became a more widely used form of communication. The **printing press** made its debut in the mid-1400s and this technology stalled due to limited paper and printing resources. The production of paper from wood pulp in the 1800s resulted in the development and mass distribution of **newspapers** and **magazines**. Imagine the communication breakthrough that happened as people were able to pick up a newspaper to learn what happened in the world the day before. Still there was quite a delay between the time something newsworthy happened until that same information could be shared with the public.

Have you ever heard of the **Pony Express**? This also came about in the 1800s and we usually think about this type of communication as we think about the Wild West. Mail became a way of sending written communication from one place to another. The stagecoaches that carried mail were not as fast as one man on a horse and that is how the Pony Express came to be.

Telecommunications involved *transmitting signals over a distance for communication.* Imagine the buzz that was made when the first long-distance telegraph line delivered messages tapped out or when Morse code replaced smoke signals, sounds made by firing cannons, or ringing bells.

The 1800s was a huge time in our communication history with the introduction of the long-distance electric telegraph lines, the phonograph, and then in the 1900s when we heard the first **radio broadcast**. This form of communication included the element of entertainment which truly took the world by storm. During this period, neighbors would gather around the one radio in an area to listen to news reports or stories that were told and broadcast music for the sole purpose of entertainment.

During the 1920s and 1930s as our country entered the time known as the Great Depression, economic history was made through the radio industry. The radio broadcast expanded to include advertisements and radio stations began popping up like daisies all over the United States.

I was a little girl when we got out very first television in our home during the mid-1950s. Many of you can remember using the Sirius satellite radio for the first time in the past twenty years. Although none of us can remember life without a telephone in our hands, my childhood included the use of a party-line where you could pick up your telephone and hear your neighbor down the street gossiping about Sister Better-Than-You from the neighborhood church. I can remember driving down the road with my three little girls in the back seat during the 1980s and letting them talk to my mother on our first cell phone. We called it a car-phone. That was HUGE and in more ways than one. The car-phone was kept in a suitcase that we might have trouble taking as a carry-on today for a flight to Italy.

Although we had computers since the early 1950s, I used a computer that was the size of my living room while working for WCWB Television in Macon, Georgia, in 1974. The temperature in that room was kept at a cool 62° and we had to wear heavy jackets in the control room up until the moment we went on the air to deliver the news.

The great thing about advancements made in communication technology is that at any given moment we can know what is happening synchronously in every corner of the world and at the click of a button. Yes, communication is evident in every area of our lives.

HISTORY OF RHETORICAL COMMUNICATION

Communication Sharks need to know something about rhetoric as both a practice and a philosophy built on the foundation of a rich history. As a practice, *rhetoric* is the use of effective speech and is the study of how we use language to share knowledge. This is where we place emphasis on the way such philosophers as Socrates, Plato, and Aristotle used persuasive speech as a method of representing truth and reality.

It has been said that our rhetorical background included three sources of persuasion: argument, the character of the speaker, and the emotions of the audience influenced by effective communication skills. Early history of rhetorical communication included an elite society of males who were privileged, literate, propertied, and had citizen status. In other words, to speak publicly meant the speaker fit into a narrow mold in which rhetoric reflected the beliefs, values, and culture of the speaker.

With radical shifts in social, economic, and intellectual thought during the eighteenth and early nineteenth centuries, the emergence of a middle class stepped into positions once held only by the elite. This phenomenon brought about a wider span of speakers who sparked debates about matters of local, national, and international importance. It was this public demonstration fueled by increasing literacy rates, printing materials such as newspapers, and available meeting places that catapulted the beginnings of discussions regarding philosophy, science, arts, and morals. This was also the time where others, such as women, working class citizens, and diverse cultures joined the arena to expand the rhetorical strategies previously practiced.

As a philosophy, rhetoric was the discussion of human sciences such as anthropology, psychology, sociology, and economics. During this time, philosophy was thought of as a genre which included inquiry, drama, and history. This extended the thought of rhetoric into a logical and liberal area which added a mixture of literature, theology, mathematics, and science.

Elocution became the new buzz word, which focused on the sound of language. This not only involved how words were pronounced but involved how words were delivered. Vocal passion, tones, and performance made speech delivery what we now think of as the art of communication. This is one reason why women or weaker voices were often eliminated from those who spoke in public.

Rhetoric and eloquence were primarily associated with power and masculinity. As a result, lawyers, politicians, clergymen, and business leaders were the occupations most represented as public speakers. Thankfully, the nineteenth century brought along women and men of diverse cultures who combined their powerful rhetorical and elocution skills to be included as competent communicators. Through social, moral, and political reform, these speakers influenced important issues such as the abolishment of slavery, freedom of speech, freedom of religion, and the emergence of women's rights.

Rhetorical practices and philosophies influenced politics, religions, and changes in diverse public cultures as more people were educated and learned ways to include speech as a method for communicating knowledge. Rhetorical style evolved over the years to accommodate the demands of the speaker as well as the audience.

A look at rhetoric's past means that we also look forward to its future. *Visual literacy* is taking its rightful place beside oratory literacy and brings in the nonverbal aspects of communication. Visual literacy is the ability to understand and make visual statements influenced through popular culture, mass media, and technologies. Social activist movements such as feminism, gay and lesbian activism, along with political activism use visual literacy as a method of rhetorical communication.

Eloquence in human communication will always exist. When one form of communication wears thin, another will emerge to express knowledge, beliefs, and values. Rhetoric will continue to change and evolve in ways that we might already imagine, but also in ways we cannot imagine. From the smoke signals of the past, we have progressed to the point where this book that I am writing for you is being constructed, produced, and delivered electronically; a fact that was not an option in years past. E-books have taken over the market of past archaic print versions, and to our benefit because they are less expensive. Blogs and virtual forums have taken the place of meeting halls. Music videos deliver a message that at one time were only sung in recital halls. At any given moment, at any time, and through multiple media opportunities, we are able to send, receive, and process information used for knowledge or entertainment.

With such a rich history of rhetorical giants, we find ourselves looking forward to what is to come and can count on technology influencing the rhetorical skills and paths with more increased fervor than in the past. At its very core will be the desire for accurate truth which expands knowledge and understanding.

© Life and Times/Shutterstock.com

KEY TERMS

- ► Elocution
- ► Ideograms
- ► Logographs
- ► Oral Communication
- ► Petroglyphs

- ► Pictograms
- ► Rhetoric
- ► Storytelling
- ► Telecommunications
- ► Visual Literacy

Chapter Two

Purpose of Communication

In this chapter:

When going into the ocean or into a business meeting, many things can go wrong. Sharks can be the changing business climates, creative investment strategies, communication opportunities, or problem-solving strategies. You might ask yourself, "Why do we keep swimming in spite of calculated risks that we can't always navigate?"

My plan to avoid a shark attack is to not resemble the seal! Understand your strengths and weaknesses. Become informed. Learn the difference between communicating and speaking in public. Just as sharks maximize use of the ocean, Communication Sharks maximize the use of communication tools and strategies in order to effectively maneuver the murky waters of communication breakdowns. Become an educated communicator, focus on your goals, and swim confidently toward your prize.

PURPOSE OF COMMUNICATION

The purpose of *communication* is to transmit, share, or exchange ideas or information. This is done through various methods that are verbal and nonverbal such as writing, speaking, art, music, movement, food, clothing, e-mails, videos, gifts, and the list goes on. Verbal communication is transmitted as we listen to hear content shared. Nonverbal communication is transmitted as we watch and establish meaning from cues sent and received.

Communication is a process. The success you achieve in your personal and professional lives will be a reflection of how effectively you communicate with others and can assist with the perception others have of you. According to the National Association of Colleges and Employers, there are several key attributes employers seek when looking for the perfect employee (NACE). As we cover human communication skills, we note that problem-solving, written communication, verbal communication, and interpersonal skills are high on the list of attributes employers want to see.

Problem-solving is the most sought-after skill with "82.9%." Next on the list are written communication skills with "80.3%" and verbal communication skills with "67.5%" of employers noting the importance of these attributes. Employers also rank Interpersonal skills at "54.7%," which means they are looking for employees who relate well to each other (NACE). As an employer, I also look for candidates who exhibit the soft skills needed to not only relate well to customers, but also to others within my organization. Effective human communication skills are good for business as well as other relationships. Learning to communicate more effectively will help you to improve your relationships with others in your private life and in the workplace. If you are wondering about your own skills for the workplace, please complete the evaluation on the next page. If you feel there are areas you need to improve, let's get started so that you can be a Communication Shark!

HOW ARE YOUR SKILLS?

Name:_____Date:_____

Complete the following evaluation to become aware of your own employability skills.

Skill	Excellent	Good	Average	Fair	Poor
Problem-solving skills					
Ability to work in a team					
Communication skills (written)					
Leadership					
Strong work ethic					
Analytical/quantitative skills					
Communication skills (verbal)					
Initiative					
Detail-oriented					
Flexibility/adaptability					
Technical skills					
Interpersonal skills (relates well to others)					
Computer skills					
Organizational ability					
Strategic planning skills					
Creativity					
Friendly/outgoing personality					
Tactfulness					
Entrepreneurial skills/risk-taker					
Fluency in a foreign language					

1. Where are your strong areas?_____

   _____

   _____

2. What areas need work?_____

   _____

   _____

THE COMMUNICATION PROCESS

Were you surprised at the results from the evaluation? Do you think an employer will want to hire you with the communication skills that you have? How well do you understand the communication process?

First, the speaker decides to send a message. Before sending the message, the **speaker encodes the message** and content to send. *Encoding* is a process by which a person derives meaning and understanding. It may involve finding a common understanding to develop a deeper understanding of the point or topic. Many speakers find that conducting research or speaking to someone with experience about the topic will help them develop a deeper understanding of the topic.

Once the speaker has a good understanding of the content, the **speaker delivers the message**. Each rhetorical situation is different; therefore, the speaker needs to consider many factors when deciding how to deliver the message. Finding common ground between the *speaker* and the audience (*receiver*), emphasizing the sharing of an idea, and determining an effective approach will help the speaker to achieve the intended goal.

As we speak about an audience as it pertains to the communication process, we need to realize that this may be one person or many people. Each rhetorical situation is different and the speaker must consider all factors involved. The **audience listens and receives the message**, but the message may come distorted according to distractions in the surrounding area or by preconceived ideas and opinions of the audience member(s). As the audience receives the message, they decode what they have heard and understood before sending verbal and/or nonverbal feedback to the speaker. *Decoding* is a process by which we translate or interpret the content into meaning. The decoding process can be altered depending upon "noise" in the environment. *Noise* is defined as distractions in the speaking environment, but also can include preconceived notions, opinions, and ideas. Sometimes *feedback* is verbal, but many times the feedback to the speaker is nonverbal. Feedback helps the speaker to know if the content delivered has been effectively decoded and received.

Here is a diagram to show how the communication process might look:

Source: Waddell and Obis

KEY TERMS

- ► Communication
- ► Decode
- ► Encode
- ► Feedback

- ► Message
- ► Noise
- ► Receiver
- ► Speaker

REFERENCE

National Association of College and Employers. *Job Outlook*. 2018, http://www.naceweb.org/career-development/trends-and-predictions/job-outlook-2016-attributes-employers-want-to-see-on-new-college-graduates-resumes/.

Chapter Three

Models of Communication

© wavebreakmedia/Shutterstock.com

In this chapter:

Action Model of Communication

Transactional Communication Model

Interactional Model of Communication

To help Human Communication students better understand the nature of communication, we often use communication models. Throughout this textbook, you will learn how models interface with the communication process. Since a picture is worth a thousand words, visual models and graphics illustrate how this works.

Our understanding of the communication process is in constant motion as communication continues to evolve and change as technology improves and increases opportunities for growth. In the beginning, the models used were simplistic and covered a basic sender-receiver approach. Now that communication has become more sophisticated, the models have expanded to include the interactive aspects of communication and demonstrates the process in which meaning is transmitted simultaneously among individuals and groups.

ACTION MODEL OF COMMUNICATION

This model shows communication as a motion or action sent and communication as its meaning is received. It is that *Aha* moment as we realize communication is a method of sharing meaning (content) from the sender to the receiver and is the basic sender-receiver approach mentioned earlier. This simple model answers the following questions:

1. Who is the sender?
2. What is the message?
3. What channel is used?
4. Who is the receiver?
5. What channel is used?
6. What is the end result?

A basic pictorial model is used showing the motion of communication going in one direction.

> **SENDER ENCODES** → Channel → **MESSAGE** → Channel → **RECEIVER DECODES**

Let's put names to this model:

Questions	Answers
Who is the sender?	The sender is Penny Joyner Waddell.
What is the message?	Communication models are used to help you understand the communication process.
What channel is used?	The textbook is the channel.
Who is the receiver?	YOU are the receiver.
What channel is used?	You read the chapter in the *Communication Shark* textbook.
What is the result?	You understand the communication process.

The model includes the names and information provided as the questions above were answered. The *sender* is the source or originator that **encodes** the communication being sent. The *message* can be written, spoken (verbal), or unspoken (nonverbal) communication and can be sent intentionally or unintentionally. The *channel* is the path through which the message is sent. The *receiver* is the person who decodes the signal and makes sense of the information.

Sender	Message	Channel	Receiver	Channel	Result
Penny	Model used to help YOU understand process.	*Communication Shark* Textbook	You	*Communication Shark* Textbook	You Understand
Communication Process					

TRANSACTIONAL COMMUNICATION MODEL

The second model we will discuss is the transactional communication model. Communication in real time is complex and simultaneous, as we are continuously exchanging verbal and nonverbal messages.

The **Sender** and **Receiver** have an important function in the model of communication, as they are both the encoder (sender) and the decoder (receiver) of messages. The communication source creates a message intended to produce a desired response. This message has no meaning until it has reached the receiver, who interprets and evaluates the message. This process of sending and receiving messages formulates communication. To communicate with others, you encode your ideas into verbal and nonverbal messages (codes) and send those messages to generate meaning. Decoding is the process of converting that message into information that can be understood. The **channel** is represented as the method we utilize to express the message. In this model, the concept of feedback and the elements of noise are explored as they impact the flow of communication. **Feedback** is defined as a response that can be seen, heard, or felt in either a verbal or nonverbal method. You provide feedback when you nod, smile, frown, or laugh. In addition, showing levels of interest such as asking questions or other types of appropriate behavior are important to ensuring your intended message was received. Expert communicators work to interpret feedback, to ensure they are achieving their purpose, otherwise they adjust the message. **Noise** is defined as anything that can prevent a message from being received. Noise can be either internal or external. External noise includes physical elements in the environment that interfere with effective communication. Examples may include traffic/honking, a difficult accent, high/low pitch, warm/cold environment, odors, or types of designs/colors used to communicate a message. Unlike external noise, internal noise is a mental distraction you experience while processing a message. Internal noise consists of thoughts, feelings, and attitudes that inhibit the ability to understand a message as it was intended. If you are preoccupied with your own personal thoughts, you can misinterpret information. This model reflects this process in a variation of contexts. ***Context is identified as the environment or setting in which the communication occurs.*** Choosing particular environments can determine whether or not an intended message is accurately received. For example, if you choose to deliver sensitive information in a context that is open, such as a classroom, you change the way in which the message is interpreted.

The *Transactional Model of Communication*, as you can see, is more complex than the Linear Model of Communication. Here is a diagram to help:

© Foxy burrow/Shutterstock.com

INTERACTIONAL MODEL OF COMMUNICATION

The *Interactional model* is used to explain how we use communication to exchange messages. During this process, we pay attention to the fact that there will be feedback to the message we encode and send.

Feedback is defined as a response to a message we send and is important because it helps us to know if the decoded message was received correctly. Sometimes feedback can be nonverbal in the form of a smile or a head nod. Other times, feedback can be verbal as the receiver will audibly agree or disagree with information sent.

You've heard people say that something they said was taken out of *context*. Because of this additional feature involved with interactions, we realize that context includes the environment where the message was delivered, the people who received the message, your experiences with the topic, and the receiver's experiences with the topic. It doesn't stop there. We can add to that the mood of the sender or the receiver and any distractions or biases on the part of the sender or the receiver.

© George Rudy/Shutterstock.com

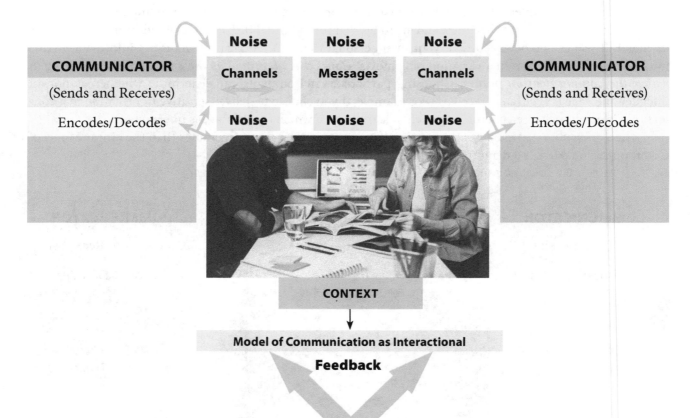

COMMUNICATOR	Noise	Noise	Noise	COMMUNICATOR
(Sends and Receives)	Channels	Messages	Channels	(Sends and Receives)
Encodes/Decodes	Noise	Noise	Noise	Encodes/Decodes

CONTEXT

Model of Communication as Interactional

Feedback

KEY TERMS

- ► Action Model of Communication
- ► Channel
- ► Context
- ► Interactional Model of Communication

- ► Message
- ► Receiver
- ► Sender
- ► Transactional Model of Communication

Communication SH🦈RK™

Unit #2

Communication Types

Verbal Communication

Nonverbal Communication

Intrapersonal Communication

Interpersonal Communication

Intercultural Communication

Communication SH▲RK™

NOTES

Chapter Four

Verbal Communication

© G-Stock Studio/Shutterstock.com

In this chapter:

ARE YOU WAITING FOR YOUR SHIP TO COME IN?

If you are sitting around waiting for your ship to come in, then you really should take another look at details involved with achieving success.

Some people think they will find success as they sit in their sturdy little rowboat, master of their own ship, and armed with a strong work ethic and perhaps a few well-chosen tools (oars would be helpful). These people believe that they will row, row, row the boat toward their goals and ultimately find success! And, they may find success eventually and with a great deal of effort! But, that is not YOU!

Other people think they can sit back on their rickety old raft in a nice comfortable lounge chair with a glass of sweet Georgia tea close by and just follow the wind until, hopefully, success finds them! These dreamers believe they are so wonderful that sooner or later someone will notice how great they are and will drag them and their raft directly into the success stream! But, that is not YOU, either!

On the other hand, YOU stand at the helm of your stately sailboat with well-chosen officers on either side and a crew of qualified mates helping you to chart a course and carefully follow the route toward success. YOU have the vision to see what is beyond the horizon. Your loyal officers are paying attention to all details required to set manageable goals and your crew is determined to help you reach those goals. Yet, all of you realize that without the "wind in the sails," your sailboat will go nowhere. The wind is the motivation that comes from within! This is the force that will move this stately sailboat toward the goal. This is the catalyst that is needed to propel you, your officers, your crew, and passengers to success! Yes, this is YOU!

How did you arrive at this type of thinking? How do we know this is YOU? We know this because YOU are the person who sees the value in making good choices regarding your support staff! YOU are the kind of person who chooses to use a great app like SpeechShark to help draft and create speeches intended to reach your goals. YOU are the kind of person who reads a speech textbook to learn about extra tools needed to help you become the speaker you want to be.

YOU are the captain of your ship and you don't have to wait for your ship to come in because you are the one who is navigating the ship toward success! Whether you are making a point during a speech presentation with an audience or you are communicating with your co-workers and colleagues in a board meeting, *Communication Shark* can help you verbally express your enthusiasm for things that motivate and move you! Yes, this is YOU!

NATURE OF LANGUAGE

Whether face-to-face, using Skype, telephone, e-mail, texts, Messenger, Twitter, Facebook, or any other version of technology, communication happens as we send and receive messages, interpret meanings, and respond accordingly.

Verbal communication happens through *language* and is actually the smallest part of the communication process. The Communication Model developed by *Albert Mehrabian* almost fifty years ago is still being used to illustrate that only 7% of communication involves words, 38% involves the way we say the words, and 55% involves what we see as body language (Mehrabian).

Language is used for communication but involves the meanings of words and phrases which scholars often label as semantics. When you are discussing the meaning of a word, you are talking about *semantics* and that is an element of *linguistics* also known as language. So, if someone asks you "What is language?" you can answer that by saying language is a system that we use for communicating that involves words. Not so difficult, right?

This next area may prove to be harder to understand as we cover denotative and connotative language. The truth is that words do not always have just one meaning. Actually, most of the words we use have many different meanings and are defined as either denotative or connotative. As we explore *denotative language*, we realize that this is a word that is defined exactly as it is shown in the dictionary. An English instructor I had one time explained that if a word is denotative, you could bet that it is found in the dictionary as a definition. Here is an example: the definition of an apple is a round fruit grown on a tree that has thin red or green skin. Yes, that is a basic definition and exactly the definition of an apple. However, if you say, "My daughter is the apple of my eye," you are not talking about fruit any longer. This is when the word—apple—becomes *connotative language*. When we use expression in language, the meaning of the word can change depending upon the connotation in which the word was said. One thing to always keep in mind is that you should use denotative language if you want to make sure there are no misunderstandings because negative connotations toward a great word can often result in disastrous results.

Language can be *verbal* or *nonverbal*. For example, the sending and receiving of language using a computer, reading it from a book as you are doing now, e-mails, texts, Facebook posts, and so much more involves the written language (nonverbal); whereas the spoken language is verbal. Understanding the nature of language is understanding that meaning is derived from so much more than the words used. Signals and symbols are both evident as sounds have meaning, just as much as meaning is derived from words. Verbal sounds include laughing, crying, sighing, and others which communicate meaning.

POWER OF LANGUAGE

"Sticks and stones may break my bones, but words will never hurt me." That is an old adage that has been repeated over and over through the years. Parents will repeat the rhyme to soothe the feelings of their child after hurtful words were exchanged on the playground. As a parent, I also found myself saying this to my own child who was hurt by something someone said to her at school. Even as I was saying the rhyme, I realized that the saying just isn't true at all and wondered why any of us ever used it!

The truth is, words have a power to heal, motivate, and encourage. Words also can be harmful. While they will not break bones, they most certainly can break a heart. Harsh words can break a spirit and they can break down dreams by lowering a person's self-esteem. Yes, there is a power in language. Speakers have a responsibility to use the power of language for good.

We cannot discuss the power of language without also recognizing that the power is in the use of language. Having a good command of language means that the speaker has a good understanding of how to use language effectively and how to organize meaning to share a message through language. You've also heard about the Power of Persuasion. Again, it is the effective use of language that can persuade someone to change the way they think of something or at the very least to be motivated to think differently about a topic for which they have developed an understanding.

Your instructor may use the power of language as she shares information regarding assignments due and testing to be completed. The power of language is not the sole responsibility of the speaker, but it is how the speaker uses language. This power can belong to anyone who has a good command of the language for which they are speaking.

**THE FUNCTIONS OF LANGUAGE

Simply stated, verbal communication has a purpose in our lives; it works for us, and it performs a role in our daily interactions. It enables us to express our own thoughts, feelings, attitudes, and beliefs, and it also helps us learn more about others as we gather information about a host of topics. In the following diagram there are several general functions of our language system: the cognitive function, group identity function, and social reality function.

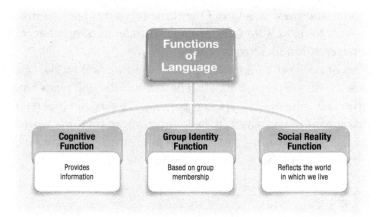

Each of these has a place in your personal, professional, and public lives. The *cognitive function* describes using language to gather information, to reason, and to make sense of the world. You experience countless examples of the cognitive function in your daily interactions with others. Examples of this include, on a first date, you and your partner exchange stories about childhood; during a performance review with your boss, you ask a question about the future of the company; or while giving an oral presentation, you provide statistics relevant to your topic.

The *group identity function* focuses on the use of language as a signal of membership or solidarity in a group. Often, individuals outside the group do not understand the unique meanings associated with the words used. Perhaps your family refers to you by a nickname that your friends don't know. As you begin your career, you may discover that there is a unique language spoken in your chosen field of work. For example, while attending a school board meeting, you may discover that attendees use language such as QEP (quality enhancement plan) that those who are new to the meeting may not fully understand.

Finally, the *social reality function* focuses on how language is used to reflect the reality of the world around us. Language changes and responds to the world in which we live. For example, you could assign a nickname to a romantic couple (e.g., "Brangelina" describes Brad Pitt and Angelina Jolie); during a meeting at work, you learn of budget cuts and begin to call the person making the budget cuts the "Grim Reaper;" or while describing the most up-to-date technology, you call the device by the name given to it by its creators.

As you can see from these examples, our language system provide us with information or knowledge, showcases our memberships and alliances with groups of people, and responds to the unique world in which we live. These three basic functions, and there are likely many more you could name, provide important information for our lives.

THE IMPORTANCE OF LANGUAGE

Not only does language serve a variety of functions, but it also has unique benefits for our personal, professional, and public lives. In the following sections, we discuss the importance of language in these interactions.

In Our Personal Lives

One of the most important qualities of our language is its unique ability to help build relationships. We can use verbal communication to learn more about a person and then use that acquired information as a guide to help us determine if we want to build a relationship with that individual. For example, while on a first date you and your partner begin discussing your respective families. Your date indicates that while growing up, if anyone in the family broke a rule, the family would gather and have "family talks." These talks included everybody discussing their feelings and establishing rules for future interactions.

Upon hearing this story, you immediately become excited because your family used a similar discipline technique, and you begin to share your story. This story-sharing is called *self-disclosure* and refers to the sharing of personal information with others in an attempt to build or maintain a relationship. During the self-disclosure process, individuals typically share meaningful information verbally (Derlega & Chaikin, 1977). We assign value, whether positive or negative, to self-disclosures. When we engage in self-disclosure, we experience positive outcomes such as increased physical health (Greenberg & Stone, 1992) and self-esteem (Afifi & Caughlin, 2006), as well as gaining insight about information (Kelly, Klusas, von Weiss, & Kenny, 2001). Based on our assessment of the self-disclosure, we then make decisions regarding relational development. These assessments are highly individualized. What one person regards as an "awkward disclosure," another person may deem as important information. Self disclosure is discussed in further detail in Chapter 7.

In Our Professional Lives

Not only do we experience benefits to build and sustain our interpersonal relationships, but we also experience benefits in our professional lives. Johnson (n.d.) has outlined several benefits verbal communication has in professional communication, including promoting diversity, building teams, and increasing morale. Previously, we discussed the idea of communication being bound to a culture. If we use language effectively and understand the unique cultural distinctions in our language system, we create an open, inviting atmosphere where all voices are welcomed and incorporated. Another benefit of verbal communication is its ability to help us build better teams. Verbal communication can be used to create bonds among individuals. It works to strengthen relationships as well as to clarify tasks and gather information.

Another benefit of verbal communication is its potential to increase employee morale. Have you ever received a positive message from a boss? Perhaps while giving an oral presentation you received positive verbal feedback as a result of something you said? These rewards have a positive impact. They make you feel good and, as a result of this good feeling, you're probably going to feel like a valuable source of information.

In Our Public Lives

Considering our language in our public lives is especially important. Oftentimes when we engage in public communication, our audience has little knowledge of who we are as people. They do not know us, the real us, and what we hold to be important. Consider giving an oral presentation to a group of people who had limited information about you. Before you begin speaking, you are introduced by name and job title. The audience only receives information about your professional credentials. They do not, however, know other, more personal aspects of your life. If while giving your presentation you make a verbal misstep and alienate your audience, they may be less forgiving of your mistake than if you had presented your message to an audience of people who know you and understand who you are as a person.

© Yuriy Rudyy/Shutterstock.com

As you can see, language is an important component of any interaction. Knapp, Stohl, and Reardon (1981) identified a key reason to focus on verbal communication. They argued, "Some interpersonal messages are reported to be remembered for a long time and to have a profound influence on a person's life" (p. 27). In thinking about your own life, you can probably recall several messages that had a profound influence on you. Perhaps you can recall the first time someone said, "I'm proud of you," "I love you," or "You're not attractive." Positive or negative, our choice of words matters and can leave a lasting impression. Not only are you likely able to recall influential messages, but you are probably also able to recall hardships, miscommunications, or conflicts you've experienced as a result of verbal communication.

THE CHALLENGES OF LANGUAGE

Our language system presents a number of challenges and considerations that we need to examine when creating the verbal message; that is, language is not a flawless set of symbols. In fact, a number of words or phrases we commonly use can create problems when used in certain contexts, talking with particular individuals, or addressing a given topic. More specifically, our language system is abstract, can communicate power and bias toward others, can be used to control the type of environment that develops while with others, and is affected by context and technology. As you read the next sections, consider how you may have experienced a situation with one of the challenges associated with our language.

Bias

Our language system shapes our view of the world and influences our perceptions. Biased language comes in many forms. When we describe language as having *bias*, we refer to the potential for language to convey stereotypes, insensitivity, or negativity toward a group of people or about a topic. Table 4.1 contains descriptions of the different biases our language may convey, a verbal example of the bias, and an alternate verbal message that can convey the same meaning without showing bias.

FIGURE 4.1

FIGURE 4.1
Types of Bias in Language

Type of Bias	Example	Corrected Verbal Communication
Stereotyping language – assumes an overgeneralization about a group of people.	"Even though she's a female, Mary exhibited outstanding leadership skills during the meeting."	"Mary exhibited outstanding leadership skills during the meeting."
Sexist language – does not account for both male and female experiences and instead communicates about ideas as inherently male or female	Fireman, policeman, mailman	Fire fighter, police officer, mail carrier
Ability language – focuses on the shortcomings of a person rather than emphasizing the person as a human.	Disabled man, handicapped woman, wheelchair-bound man	Person with a disability
Racist language – insensitive and derogatory language about a group of people.	Guido, Indian giver, Bible banger	Italian, person who takes back a gift, a religious person

The examples of bias in language in Figure 4.1 are just four of the main ways in which our words can communicate intolerance or negativity about a group of people or ideas. This language, while not offensive to all, has become, in general, negatively valued in our culture. The words can potentially elicit a negative evaluation, conflict situation, or even relationship termination. However, by reframing our language—into what is frequently referred to as "politically correct" language—we can communicate more neutrally and potentially avoid miscommunications with individuals.

Ethical Versus Unethical Use of Language

Words are used in the creation of messages that have the potential to be ethical or unethical. *Ethical communication* stems from your ability to be honest and uses a set of standards to guide appropriate or positive behaviors. What one person perceives as being ethical may be perceived as unethical by another. Some use the law as a standard of ethical behavior; that is, if it is legal, then it is considered ethical. If it is illegal, then it is unethical. Others use religion to determine ethical and unethical behavior. When considering our verbal communication and ethics, there are several guidelines you can use as you form your messages (Figure 4.2).

FIGURE 4.2
Guidelines for ethical communication.

One of our primary goals as communicators should be to share information that is truthful, honest, and representative of what we are currently experiencing. When constructing our verbal messages, we want to present information that is truthful. Additionally, we should always be forthcoming. That is, we should be prepared with answers and have the ability to provide an answer when needed. Next, we need to be consistent. We should use the same standards to guide our language choices across contexts and topics. Finally, we need to be clear. We need to select language that has a clear meaning to the receiver.

When we decide not to use the above behaviors, we could potentially create an environment where individuals feel mistrust, that we are not individuals with whom they can share thoughts. In response to those feelings, an individual may use a defensive style of message production as a result. Defensive communication (Gibb, 1961) can be a result of perceived differences in standards; that is, you and the individual you are interacting with perceive different expectations of appropriate behavior and communication. A *defensive message* is produced in response to some kind of threat (Gibb, 1961). The threat does not necessarily need to be explicit (e.g., "I am going to kick you out of the apartment if you don't tell me the truth"); rather, a threat may be more implicit in the message (e.g., "I need to know what is happening right now!"). When engaging in unethical verbal communication, you could prompt this reaction in an individual. An additional plausible reaction is *supportive communication*. This type of communication occurs when an individual feels as though he or she has little reason to have anxiety or concern about the communication being received. Supportive and defensive reactions come in many forms. For example, supportive communication can be an empathetic message. This would be a message that takes care of others' emotions or experiences. It can be conveyed in phrases such as "I understand your perspective" or "That situation would really upset me too." In these types of responses, the message is offering solidarity within the experience, communicating that he or she is sharing the experience. However, a defensive response could come in the form of a certainty message. *Certainty messages* do not account for others' perspectives or views; that is, they discount the others' stance on a topic. A certainty message would sound like "What you're saying is not correct" or "Your opinion doesn't even make sense." When these messages are produced, it seems as if the originator of the message only believes in his or her perspective. As you can see, the way in which we present information and how much information we present can create a number of reactions, both positive and negative. Using ethical guidelines for speaking can help get positive reactions and supportive communication from others.

Context

A second ethical consideration involves our word choices based on the communication *context* or setting. You need to consider "where" you are interacting with others in determining "what" to say. For example, where would you want to have a conversation when you're ending a romantic relationship? In a crowded restaurant? Via a text message? In a private setting such as a home? The setting in which you find yourself—be it at work, at home, or in front of an audience—provides useful information that should be considered when creating the verbal message.

Some strategies to potentially enhance the use of verbal communication in your personal life include the following:

- ▶ Creating verbal messages with the goal of building or strengthening relationships. Solicit disclosures from others, ask them questions, and share your own stories.
- ▶ Focusing on the dynamics of other people's relationships so you can incorporate that information into your verbal communication.

▶ Sending thoughtfully constructed messages when using mediated forms of interaction, such as a text message. The recipient cannot experience our nonverbal communication so messages sent electronically need extra care.

▶ Willingness to address sensitive topics. In comfortable, intimate locations, people tend to feel more relaxed and open to communicating about potentially sensitive issues.

In your professional life, your verbal communication style should include a clear, context-appropriate expression of what you think, how you feel, and what you would like from the communicative interaction. Remember, our workplace communication style is likely quite different than our interpersonal communication style. It is imperative that you not be demanding during these instances; rather, you should be sure to communicate that both people matter in the interaction. According to the Department of Education, Employment and Workplace Relations (n.d.), your communication should include:

▶ Expressing your own thoughts, feelings, and needs.

▶ Making reasonable requests of other people (while accepting their right to say "no").

▶ Standing up for your own rights.

▶ Saying "no" to requests from others at times, without feeling guilty.

Finally, when communicating during an oral presentation in a public setting, there are some key considerations to incorporate in the creation of your messages. Keep in mind:

▶ Determine if the topic is appropriate for discussion in a public setting.

▶ Take your audience into account. Try to gather as much information as possible about who is getting the information.

▶ Consider the size of the space in which you are presenting. Adjust your delivery to account for large or small spaces.

Technology

An 2012 article in *Entertainment Weekly* paid tribute to celebrities who passed away during the year. Each of the brief memorial statements was written by another celebrity. In one particularly interesting statement paying tribute to Dick Clark, Grammy award winning musical artist, Prince communicated how much Clark meant to him in the following statement:

> Dick Clark was always very generous and kind 2 us whatever the circumstance. He would call U personally and always speak with grace and candor that is rare in an industry that is rife with gamesmanship. That kinda class is sorely missed. Not sure why but Mr. Clark seemed 2 genuinely like me, and Eye liked him also. (2012, p. 43)

What is your reaction to the statement? You probably notice some abbreviations that you use in your own text messages, such as *U*, *2*, and *kinda*. However, in this format, an in memoriam statement written to convey meaning and emotional impact, the style is likely inappropriate.

Consider the following real-life example of a face-to-face interaction between two roommates:

Roommate 1: Hey, what are you up to?

Roommate 2: Not much, you?

Roommate 1: Nothing. Want to get out of the house and see that movie?

Roommate 2: Totes! That will make Kelly (roommate 3) so jelly!

Roommate 1: (*pauses*) Um, sure?

Roommate 2: It totes will! Kelly has been asking me to see it with her so the two of us going without her will make her mad.

Roommate 1: Ohhhhhh, yes, she will be jealous.

Perhaps you have experienced a similar situation in which your verbal communication style used when interacting with others via technology, such as abbreviations when texting, carries over to your offline or face-to-face interactions. What if the above example had occurred via text or email? The example of the conversation between two roommates seems appropriate in an online format but feels out of place in the face-to-face context. That is, some messages or phrasing are more appropriate or suited to mediated formats. In addition, you should consider the appropriateness of using mediated channels instead of an in-person conversation when discussing specific topics. Consider the following verbal messages and determine if they should be said via a mediated channel such as text messaging or if face-to-face communication is more effective.

- ► "We need to talk."
- ► "I love you."
- ► "Let's have pizza for dinner."
- ► "I'd like to offer you a promotion."
- ► "How about we go to the late movie tonight?"

As you can see from the above examples, sending some messages via text or email are appropriate. However, due to our limited access to tone of voice, rate of speech, or facial expressions, it is often easy to misinterpret the meaning sent via a text or email message.

Regional Differences

As we travel through the United States and internationally, we notice differences in language usage. When you go to the grocery store and need something to hold your groceries, do you use a cart or a buggy? Do you drink a pop, a soda, or a Coke? These examples represent regional differences in language usage. They also represent differences in *dialect*. Regardless of what you choose to put your groceries in (cart or buggy) and whatever you decide to drink (pop, soda, or Coke), you are using language that is specific to a region.

Have you ever thought that someone "talked funny" when you traveled to a new place or watched a movie that was set in a particular region? Maybe you have identified distinctions in how someone from Massachusetts, Georgia, or Minnesota speaks and thought they did not sound like you. This is due to our individual accents. In fact, we all have an accent. An **accent** refers to how we pronounce words. Accents differ by region and country and can impact how we perceive someone. In fact, you might hold perceptions about certain accents. For example, individuals with a Southern accent might be perceived as friendly. Individuals with an East Coast accent, such as a New Yorker, may be perceived as rude because of a more abrupt communication style. Collectively, accents are a common occurrence and inform our perceptions of others, be it positively or negatively. Verbal communication clearly has a large role in our lives and is something to which we need to give attention. With its potentially different uses, spending time carefully creating messages is an important component in developing competent communication.

MESSAGE FORMATION AND DESIGN

One idea to consider when thinking about your verbal communication is how the message is put together. Scholars call this idea **message formation**. When we focus on how things are said, that is, how the verbal component should be created, we can produce effective messages. One of the first ways we can work to produce effective messages is by considering the content (what the message is about), the context (the situation), and the relationship (the connection between the sender and receiver). What kinds of verbal communication would you create if you experienced the following examples?

➤ You need to break up with your romantic partner of six years. You feel as though the situation has gone from good, to poor, to bad. You constantly fight about money and the division of labor in the house. Your partner, while someone who does not enjoy fighting, does seem fairly happy in the relationship and does not want to break up. You, however, feel it is best to end things for your own personal sanity. One possible solution to this scenario is to select an effective context or location to talk with your partner. You would want to pick a comfortable location where you and your partner feel relaxed, such as the living room. When communicating, it is best to use "I feel" messages. For example, you may say, "I feel stressed when I have to do most of the chores." By doing this, you avoid blaming the partner. Saying "You do not help with the house," while true, could put a partner on the defensive and use language that justifies actions.

➤ Your boss has assigned you to lead a group of people on a special project. The company has lost money in the past on special projects but your boss thinks the current project is a revenue-making endeavor and believes in your ability to lead. You know, however, that if the project fails, you will experience serious consequences, such as a pay cut, demotion, or even termination. You would prefer not to lead the project and want to tell your boss your wishes but are nervous to approach the topic. A possible solution to this problem is to first arrange a meeting with your boss. This could be done by email or face-to-face, but you should communicate a desire to talk about the project and serve as the leader. You may even suggest that you and your boss get a coffee or lunch while talking. This makes the context seem more informal and could make you feel more comfortable approaching the topic. At the start of the meeting, you should use messages that showcase your appreciation for being asked to serve as the leader and your boss' perceptions of your ability. For example, you could say, "Thank you for the

opportunity to serve as the leader of such an important project. Having a boss that believes in my abilities is very important." After that, you could address your fears by using "I feel" statements.

► You have been asked to act as the master of ceremonies during a "roast" that honors your father. Attending the roast are your father's professional contacts as well as a majority of your family members. You want to write jokes about your father but because of the different types of people in the audience you are unsure about which topics to address.

You could start by gathering information from those who will be attending the event. You could ask for the anecdotes or special stories or information they would like to hear while attending the event. If possible, you could visit the venue in which you will be speaking. By knowing what others will want to listen to and feeling comfortable in the venue, you will likely feel more at ease with the assigned task.

Another technique used to understand how messages should be created is verbal modeling. Listening to how others speak, and then consciously using the same words or phrases they use, is called *verbal modeling*. By doing this modeling behavior, you are building rapport with that person and cultivating a positive relationship. One theory communication scholars utilize to understand changes in verbal communication is the *Communication Accommodation Theory* (Giles, Coupland, & Coupland, 1991; Giles & Ogay, 2007; Giles & Smith, 1979). In general, the theory argues that we change our verbal communication during the course of an interaction. This idea is labeled *accommodation* and is a result of perceptions you have of the people with whom you're interacting. Below are the theory's basic principles (Giles & Ogay, 2007).

- Communication is influenced by several factors, including the immediate situation, the individual's orientations toward the situation, and past sociohistorical contexts; that is, events that have occurred in the past directly impact current situations.

- Communication is also a way to share thoughts, feelings, emotions, and group memberships.

- People have expectations for accommodation. These expectations are based on social and societal norms and range from nonaccommodation to overaccommodation.

- Individuals use two types of accommodation: convergence and divergence. To *converge* means that individuals become more similar in their verbal choices and to *diverge* means that individuals become increasingly different in their verbal choices.

Ultimately, message formation is a skill. Creating messages is something that we can improve upon over time. Creating appropriate verbal communication is a skill that can be strengthened if you are motivated to assess each situation and consciously work to improve it. While a number of strategies and solutions are possible, the website *www.littlethingsmatter.com*, designed to improve different areas of your life, lists the following behaviors as ways to improve verbal communication (Smith, 2010).

1. *Be friendly.* We keep company with individuals who are pleasant and communicate in positive ways. Individuals who use a warm tone, smile, and positive words are people we want to be around.
2. *Think before you speak.* Have you ever interacted with someone who made you think, "He/she should really think before speaking!" Perhaps you have even thought to yourself, "I really should not have said that; if only I'd have thought about what I was going to say *before* saying it." Sometimes we find ourselves saying whatever comes to our minds without first thinking about how best to communicate. This can end in negative conversational outcomes and poor personal perceptions.
3. *Be clear.* In the chapter, we discussed the multiple meanings, content and relational, communication holds. Because our communication has so much value, it is important to think about what we are

going to say as well as to spend time carefully assessing the most efficient means to communicate. Efficient communication has a clear meaning. The receiver is able to decode what is being sent and does not have to ask him- or herself what is being said.

4. *Don't talk too much.* Have you ever interacted with someone who talked the entire time and barely let you speak? This can be very frustrating. Communication scholars have labeled this behavior **conversational narcissism** (Vangelisti, Knapp, & Daly, 1990), or extreme self-focus in a conversation.

5. *Be authentic.* Not only do we like surrounding ourselves with pleasant people, but we also enjoy sharing our time with individuals who are genuine in their communication behaviors. To be genuine means that we can be real and communicate in a way that is from the heart.

6. *Practice humility.* To have humility means that you have a modest view of your own importance. Have you ever interacted with someone who made him- or herself sound overly important or made you think that he or she was acting "too big for their britches?" We like sharing our time with someone who respects others and presents him- or herself in a genuine matter.

7. *Speak with confidence.* You needn't sacrifice self-confidence to practice humility. To be confident means you are self-assured, comfortable, and appreciate your own abilities. You can speak confidently by choosing and adjusting the words, vocal tones, body language, and eye contact you use.

8. *Focus on your body language.* Not only do our words matter, but our body language also serves as an indicator of how the other person should interpret those words. In paying attention to our body language, we are helping clarify the meaning and tone of our messages and making the receiver's job easier.

9. *Be concise.* Have you ever interacted with someone who just cannot get to the point? Perhaps you have felt frustrated while listening to someone ramble? We want to avoid these behaviors. When planning your words, ask yourself, "How can I say what needs to be said using the fewest number of words possible while still being courteous and respectful?"

10. *Listen first.* By listening before speaking, we can be sure to incorporate language the other person is using, ask follow-up questions, and avoid interrupting the other person.

11. *Check yourself.* While communicating with others, perform a brief, mental check-in concerning your behaviors. Ask yourself, "Am I using language that others would find offensive? Am I asking the other person questions? Am I contributing positively to the conversation?"**

LANGUAGE MISCOMMUNICATION AND BARRIERS

In order to communicate, we need language. When people can't communicate, we have a barrier to communication. This might happen due to impairments such as vocal or hearing difficulties, but even those without such issues may find themselves in situations where they misunderstand or misinterpret meanings of a message being sent. In this section, we will cover several different types of language miscommunications and barriers.

Speaking another language makes it difficult to use language with others who do not share the same understanding of the language. There is a story in the Bible, Genesis Chapter Eleven, that illustrates the difficulty of trying to communicate with people who speak other languages. During that time, all of the people spoke one language. Together, the people decided to build a giant tower tall enough to reach God in the heavens. According to the story, God looked down upon these people and decided that their efforts were not healthy for them. He decided to divide the people into different linguistic groups with many different languages so that they could not understand and communicate with each other. The building ceased as the communication barrier caused such trouble that orders were not followed and the plans could not be shared. The streets were in chaos as one would try to speak to the other, but the language coming from his mouth was not understood. People would go from one to another trying to communicate with no success. Needless to say, the building project stopped and never went further.

Language miscommunication and *barriers* also create conflict between genders, cultures, and political and religious views. Accents and dialects differ between people who have the same language but come from different parts of the country. Although their base language may be the same and is easily recognized and communicated, there will be times when the different accents or meanings may create misinterpretations and that of course leads to barriers.

Recently, I was visiting London, England, and asked for a biscuit only to find out that they thought I meant a cookie. I'm from Georgia in the United States, so I was really asking for a soft buttery baked piece of bread and definitely did not mean that I wanted a cookie. Of course, I took the cookie and said, "Thank you" with a smile because I did learn that good manners are good no matter the language or the meanings of language.

Have you seen the movie, *Pitch Perfect*? In the movie there is a girl in the singing group that never speaks above a whisper throughout most of the movie. The others could never hear her enough to understand what she was trying to communicate and that is another excellent example of a language barrier; although it may be a bit different from other language barriers. If the people to whom you are speaking are not able to hear your message, then you have a *communication barrier*.

Slang words are often used in certain cultural situations and are effective within the group; however, using the same slang words outside of your cultural group will result in strange stares and looks of confusion. Leave the jargons and slang language at home when out in public so that your message can be understood by others. Barriers are also evident when people use a poor word choice or sarcasm to convey meanings. Often a poor word choice will send a negative message that may be miscommunicated. This also is a type of language barrier that may send a completely different message than the one you intend to send.

My dear husband is quite the dinosaur and he was texting, believe it or not, to one of his friends. The friend responded LOL (Laugh Out Loud) and my husband was laughing because he thought his friend was having trouble spelling a word on his phone. Yes, even texting can cause language barriers.

Now that you know the many different types of language miscommunication and barriers, try to consider how you are communicating so that you are not guilty of saying one thing and meaning another.

What verbal cues are important for communicating?

Paralanguage is the vocal part of speech and involves volume, rate, pitch, pace, and color. To have vocal variance, you will want to incorporate varying degrees of all these aspects. To create more emphasis or effects for your speech topic, you might choose to say some words louder or softer, some faster and others slower, and some words with more emphasis showing energy for the topic, anger, or any other emotion.

Volume is the level at which a sound is heard. While it is important for the audience to hear your voice, your volume does not need to be so loud that it appears you are shouting. Speak at a volume that will allow everyone in the room to hear your message. You control this by the volume of air you project using your **larynx** or voice box. More air = louder volume. Less air = softer volume. If you normally have a softer voice, you might require a microphone to be heard comfortably by your audience. If this is the case, be sure to rehearse using the microphone prior to your speech so that you understand how to use it correctly.

Rate is the method we use to determine how fast or slow someone is speaking. Many speakers tend to speed up because their nerves often push them into overdrive. This is a normal result of adrenaline pumping through your body and causing your heart rate to rev up; resulting in faster speech. While this is not always a problem, it can cause your audience to have trouble following your message because they will not have time to comprehend everything that you say. What can you do to make sure your speech is presented at a comfortable rate? Rehearse your speech, video or audio record your rehearsal, and evaluate the rate at which you speak. Try to take notes of your speech as you listen to the recording. Do you have time to make notes? If not, then your speech rate may be too fast. Consciously make an effort to slow down your rate of speech. Is your rate too slow? Plan to speed up the speech to keep your audience sitting on the edge of their seats!

Pitch is determined by sounds produced by vocal cord vibrations. Faster vibrations result in higher pitches. Slower vibrations result in lower pitches. Typically, women and children have a higher pitch. Men normally have a lower pitch. While this is typical, it is not absolute. Women and children can slow the vocal cord vibrations to achieve a lower pitch and men can speed vocal cord vibrations to achieve a higher pitch when needed. Varying pitch is important to having good vocal variance. A constant pitch results in a monotone voice and this is truly one sure way to lose your audience. A monotone voice lacks interest, variety, and energy like the monotone teacher in Charlie Brown cartoons, "Mwa, mwa, mwa, mwa, mwa, mwa!"

Pace is the rate at which you say syllables in a word. For example, people from the southern states in America usually add a couple of extra syllables in words that folks from the northern states do not. Southerners tend to say the word, well, in two syllables. Here is an example of a typical slower pace to say, "Well, I don't think so!":

Pause and Rhythm

A skillfully inserted *pause* in the speech can be a powerful public speaking tool. Dr. Martin Luther King, Jr. was a master with inserting pauses and using rhythm to impact the message of his speech. Listen again to the "I Have a Dream" speech and pay close attention to the long and powerful pause inserted directly following his initial opening statement and following each time he says, "I have a dream." Notice also, the *rhythm* in his speech that carries the audience's attention along with his poetic placement of words. Pauses strategically used provide audiences the opportunity to stop and focus on the last word said. This dramatic use of pauses must be timed and used in such a way that it creates more impact for the message.

Color involves the energy, enthusiasm, feelings, and attitudes that are included in our message. It may have negative or positive implications and can extend to what we see as much as what we hear. Our voice can show color when we tell a story that describes our exhilaration about a new game or fear of the unknown.

Color can also be added as we discuss our customs, habits, or describe a place or a person. We love to hear color in a speech. It is how a speaker can add a little spark to the speech!

Dialects often surface as we discuss paralanguage. Dialects are a form of language heard from people living in a particular region, but this term can also be used as we discuss language indigenous to people from specific social or cultural groups. You will hear dialects referred to as local speech, regional speech patterns, languages, linguistics, vernacular, or accents. Dialects may include variations of grammar, vocabulary, and pronunciations. For example, if someone described the man at the store as having a French accent, they would be describing the man's regional speech patterns that would lead the listener to think the man was from a French-speaking part of our world. A phonetic and/or cultural analysis can result in identifying the continent or region where the dialect is most often spoken.

Effective language skills also surface as we discuss paralanguage. It is not enough to have a great topic with research and stories to support the topic, speakers also need to use effective language skills to be a good communicator. In other words, make sure your language skills are clear, concise, and constructive! Here are some tips for using effective language skills:

- ► Use standard English grammar, mechanics, and language.
- ► Use concrete and specific language and avoid using vague or abstract language.
- ► Avoid using acronyms or descriptions that only select audience members will grasp. If you need to use an acronym, identify the full meaning of the acronym before going into detail.
- ► Create images using adjectives to describe situations or people.
- ► Eliminate filler words that do not serve a purpose.
- ► Use vocabulary and grammar that is easily understood by your audience to establish a sense of commonality with the audience.
- ► Use language that is on the educational level of audience members. Do not talk "above" or "below" your audience's level of understanding.

Pronunciation and Articulation

How do you pronounce pecan? Do you pronounce it as pe-kan or pekahn? Do you pronounce tomato as tu-may-toe or tu-mah-toe? How do you pronounce aunt? Is she an "ant" or an "ahnt"? Although it is the very same word and the same meaning, we find that our pronunciations of these words can be quite different. Often, our *pronunciation* of words will stem from how the word was pronounced as we were growing up and is a product of our culture.

When giving a speech, you might stumble upon words that cause you to be unsure of the pronunciation. If this is the case, always consult with a dictionary which will show the phonetic pronunciations of a word. It is also important to pronounce people's names or the names of cities and states correctly. Incorrect pronunciations of words can distract an audience from hearing the message because they will dwell on incorrectly pronounced words.

Last week, I was coaching a student for an upcoming speech competition and noticed that every time she said the word "asked," she would say "axed." I asked her about this and she said that she didn't know why she pronounced the word that way when she clearly knew how the word was spelled and should be pronounced as written. We talked about it a few minutes and decided that the pronunciation of this one word stemmed from the dialect that was used in her culture. From this example you can tell that pronunciations and articulation of words can be determined from habit, from getting lazy with our speaking skills, or from learned behaviors. I'm happy to report that the student worked very hard to change the way she pronounced the word and during her speech competition, she pronounced it correctly and won 1st place in the state! Now, that's a CommunicationShark!

Articulation is the process by which the speaker sounds out words so that the audience can understand what is being said. Speaking too fast will cause words to become slurred or will mean that the end of one word is omitted as the next word begins. Most speakers find that by slowing their speech, they are better able to articulate the content to the audience.

Since this is the case, we should identify words or phrases that we have a habit of saying incorrectly and then work to correct them. Bad habits in pronunciations and articulation can distract audiences from hearing our message, but it can also tarnish our speaker credibility.

For the purpose of a basic speech class, please make sure you are always using Standard English. In other words, slang or off-color words are not acceptable. Also avoid using contractions during a speech as these can often become slurred or chopped to the point that they are hard to comprehend.

Vocal Self-Assessment

Now that we've spent time learning about volume, rate, pitch, pace, pauses and rhythm, color, dialects and effective language skills, let's explore your personal vocal skills. Are you concerned with the quality of your own voice? Did you know that your voice reflects your personality and intelligence? If you want to improve your vocal skills, it can be done, but it takes effort. Practicing vocal skills is much the same as practicing a physical skill. Set your goals, determine the best method for achieving the results, and get to work! Consistently working toward creating stronger vocal skills will help you to gain results you would like to see.

What are the vocal aspects of speaking that you would like to improve? Are you concerned about your vocal quality? Is your voice nasal or monotone? Do you run out of breath as you are speaking? Do people constantly ask you to repeat what you just said?

Using your phone, record yourself speaking or reading a paragraph from a book and play it back to critically listen to your voice. Take your time during the recording, but try to speak as you normally speak in order to create a more accurate evaluation. After you've completed the recording, play it back and complete the following worksheet to get a good idea of your strengths and weaknesses:

EVALUATE YOUR VOICE

Rate your voice using this self-evaluation. Check characteristics that apply to you.

Voice Description—Desirable Traits	Voice Description—Undesirable Traits
My voice sounds pleasant.	My voice sounds nasal.
My voice has pitch variations.	My voice sounds monotone.
My voice is light.	My voice sounds throaty or raspy.
My voice has a pleasant rhythm.	My pitch is too high or too low.
My pitch is appealing.	My voice is too soft or too loud.
I articulate words clearly as I speak.	I do not articulate words clearly.
I sound like I am smiling.	I sound bored with myself.
My vocal quality is clear.	My voice squeaks or cracks when I talk.
My voice sounds confident.	My voice sounds weak.
My accent is not distinguishable.	My accent is heavy and hard to understand.
I like hearing my voice.	I do not like hearing my voice.
I control my breathing well.	I sound like I am gasping for breath.

What would you like to change?

How can you plan to change it?

How do I avoid using "Filler Words"?

Well, you know, it is uhm, like, well, like totally the most annoying thing you can hear, you know, in somebody's well, uh, you know, their speech presentation. It's uhm, the words that people, uhm, well, you know, they add them to what they are uhm, trying to say, when well, you know what I mean, they are so darn aggravating, and you like, well you hear them literally all of the time. You know?

You are in good company because about six million other people have asked this question. *Filler words* are the types of phrases, sounds, or words that speakers use to fill in an awkward pause when trying to communicate a thought or make a speech presentation. Filler words are contagious and socio-linguistically, can be a tribal form of bonding. Filler words are heard in formal speeches and in social conversations. They are "like" everywhere and add no value to the sentence or thought being communicated.

Do you use filler words? Many people use these words without ever realizing how often they use them and how distracting they might be. Once you realize you are using them, you might discover that sometimes you use them more than other times. Often people use them as a filler when they can't think of the word or thought they are trying to share. We feel that the sound helps to soften the pause while we search for the right word. Truthfully, the sound distracts the listener from hearing the full meaning we are attempting to communicate.

Speakers use filler words when:

1. Searching for the right words
2. Filling an awkward pause
3. Making a sentence sound more passive
4. Making a sentence sound more active
5. Sharing what you are thinking
6. Bonding with a friend that speaks with fillers
7. Expanding the sentence to take more time
8. Sharing the idea/experience with the listener

While it is acceptable to use an occasional filler word, it is important that you do not overuse them. Pausing to think of an answer or to remember your next point is a much better option than uhm, well, you know, throwing in a word or two that well uhm, like basically stretches out the moment but not the meaning.

Here are the filler words that you hear most often: Like, ya know, okay, uhm, uh, er, hmmm, so, well, literally, totally, clearly, actually, basically, seriously, really, like, I mean, just, whatever, I guess or I suppose, very, right, but, sorry, anyway, and, uh huh, uh uh, and any combinations of the above. Whew, I'll bet you thought that sentence would never end!

So, well, like, what can do you do to like, totally, get rid of all the well, you know what I mean, those annoying filler words?

Become aware of your filler word habit! Prepare and practice before speaking opportunities. Video or audio-record your speech rehearsals. Count the number of filler words you have in your presentation, speech, audition, pitch, toast, and so forth, and keep working until you eliminate as many filler words as possible.

My friend, Audrey Mann Cronin, is an acknowledged and long-time communication expert in the technology industry. She is on a mission to help us all become better speakers and created *LikeSo: Your Personal Speech Coach,* a mobile app that helps you to talk your way to success. Using voice recognition technology, *LikeSo* is a fun and effective way to practice being a more confident and articulate speaker. Speak into the microphone of your smartphone and LikeSo captures your words and helps you train and remove all of those filler words that undermine your speech, weaken your meaning, and distract your listeners. *LikeSo* also measures pacing (150 wpm considered optimal) and allows you to set goals, reminders, and track your progress over time (day/week/month/year). It is like a "Fitbit for your speech." Just search the app store: http://Apple.co/1QBuByY or the Web site: https//sayitlikeso.com and for only 99 cents you can get your own personal speech coach that will help you to be a more powerful, persuasive, and articulate speaker.

I have the app and enjoy using it with students and speakers that I coach. It is so easy! Just choose "Free-Style," your open mic for any upcoming speaking opportunity, or "TalkAbout" a conversation game to practice speaking on the fly with topics including "The Job Interview," "Debate Team," and "Small Talk." Choose your talk time, the filler words you want to train against, and receive a Speech Fitness Report. You can also follow her on Facebook, Twitter, and Instagram at @LikeSoApp. Here is a picture so that you will recognize it in the Apple Store:

Source: Dr. Penny Joyner Waddell

Now that we know how to avoid distracting fillers, let's take a look at other important nonverbal cues.

KEY TERMS

- ▶ Albert Mehrabian
- ▶ Articulation
- ▶ Barriers
- ▶ Bias
- ▶ Certainty Message
- ▶ Cognitive Function
- ▶ Communication Accommodation Theory
- ▶ Communication Barriers
- ▶ Connotative Language
- ▶ Context
- ▶ Converge
- ▶ Defensive Message
- ▶ Denotative Language
- ▶ Dialect
- ▶ Diverge
- ▶ Ethical Communication
- ▶ Filler Words
- ▶ Group Identity Function
- ▶ Language

- ▶ Linguistics
- ▶ Nonverbal
- ▶ Pace
- ▶ Paralanguage
- ▶ Pause
- ▶ Pitch
- ▶ Pronunciation
- ▶ Rate
- ▶ Rhythm
- ▶ Color
- ▶ Self-disclosure
- ▶ Semantics
- ▶ Slang
- ▶ Solid Reality Function
- ▶ Supportive Communication
- ▶ Verbal
- ▶ Verbal Modeling
- ▶ Volume

REFERENCES

Afifi, W. A., & Caughlin, J. P. (2006). A close look at revealing secrets and some consequences that follow. *Communication Research, 33*, 467–488.

Department of Education, Employment and Workplace Relations. (n.d.). *Workplace communication.* Retrieved from www.regionalskillstraining.com/sites/default/files/content/WC%20Book%201.pdf.

Derlega, V. J., & Chaikin, A. L. (1977). Privacy and self-disclosure in social relationships. *Journal of Social Issues, 33*, 102–115.

Gibb, J. (1961). Defensive communication. *Journal of Communication, 11*, 141–148.

Giles, H., Coupland, J., & Coupland, N. (1991). Accommodation theory: Communication, context, and consequence. In H. Giles, J. Coupland, & N. Coupland (Eds.), *Contexts of accommodation*, (pp. 1-68). New York, New York: Cambridge University Press.

Giles, H., & Ogay, T. (2007). Communication accommodation theory. In B. Whaley & W. Samter (Eds.), *Explaining communication: Contemporary theories and exemplars*, (pp. 293-310). Mahwah, NJ: Erlbaum.

Giles, H., & Smith, P. (1979). Accommodation theory: Optimal levels of convergence In H. Giles & R. N. St. Clair (Eds.), *Language and social psychology*, (pp.45-65). Baltimore: Basil Blackwell.

Greenberg, M. A., & Stone, A. A. (1992). Emotional disclosure about traumas and its relation to health: Effects of previous disclosure and trauma severity. *Journal of Personality and Social Psychology, 63*, 75–84.

Johnson, R. (n.d.). *What are the benefits of effective communication in the workplace?* Retrieved from http://smallbusiness.chron.com/benefits-effective-communication-workplace-20198.html.

Kelly, A. E., Klusas, J. A., von Weiss, R. T., & Kenny, C. (2001). What is it about revealing secrets that is beneficial? *Personality and Social Psychology Bulletin, 27*, 651–665.

Knapp, M. L., Stohl, C., & Reardon, K. K. (1981). "Memorable" messages. *Journal of Communication, 31*, 27–41.

Prince. (2012, December 21). Dick Clark. *Entertainment Weekly, 1238*, 43.

Smith, T. (2010). *10 verbal communication skills worth mastering.* Retrieved from www.littlethingsmatter.com/blog/2010/11/30/10-verbal-communication-skills-worth-mastering/.

Toomey, M. (1999). *The power of language.* Retrieved from www.mtoomey.com/poweroflanguage.html.

Top words, phrases, names of 2012: Apocalypse, Gangnam Style, Newton. (2012, December 31). *Wisconsin Gazette.* Retrieved from www.wisconsingazette.com/breaking-news/top-words-phrases-names-of-2012-apocalypse-gangnam-style-newtown.html.

Vangelisti, A. L., Knapp, M. L. & Daly, J. A. (1990). Conversational narcissism. *Communication Monographs, 57*, 251–274.

Chapter Five

Nonverbal Communication

© Sharaf Maksumov/Shutterstock.com

CHARACTERISTICS OF NONVERBAL COMMUNICATION

Have you ever made an assumption based upon what you saw without ever hearing the full story? If your answer is yes, then you are in good company. Most of us will believe what we see before we believe what we hear. Communication that does not involve sound is *nonverbal communication* and makes up for the largest majority of all we communicate.

We send nonverbal messages and cues all day long every day. It can be the way you give someone a side-look when you question their motives, a wink or a smile, even the type clothing you wear sends a very clear and unspoken message. To have a good understanding of nonverbal communication, we realize that many different channels are used, but they all boil down to three simple languages: sign language, action language, and object language.

Sign language is used as we gesture to replace words. We often use this type of language to further explain things when words do not seem to be enough. When describing a fish to his sister, John said, "You wouldn't *believe* how *big* this fish was!" As he was talking to his sister, his hands were showing the size of the huge fish that he saw. The sister heard his words, but she was able to envision the actual size of the fish by watching her brother's hands. We use this type of nonverbal communication on a regular basis and some people will tell you that they can't talk if their hands are tied.

Action language involves movements that we use to supplement words and to share emotion. Someone who is walking confidently with head and chin up, shoulders straight, and a look of purpose in their step is using action language to show confidence. In the reverse, if someone walks in with shoulders hunched over, head drooped, and head nodding from left to right slowly, we get the cue that this person is not very happy about something. Further communication will tell us why the person is unhappy, but we get a clear message from the beginning that something is not right!

Object language is the intentional or unintentional use of objects to communicate. This may include types of clothing, shoes, jewelry, hair styles, or even the type car you drive. All of these objects communicate loudly something about YOU. Several years ago, my grown daughters were going wedding dress shopping with a friend. As they were leaving to go, I commented how they were all so beautifully dressed and how I usually went shopping in my blue jeans and t-shirt. The girls told me that when they go shopping dressed up, they get better service from the people working in the shops than if they are wearing their knock-around clothes. Being a curious person, I tried it out during my last shopping trip and the girls are right! I received much better service when my object language met with my budget. So, what does this say about the young man walking down the street with his pants sagging below his pants line? I'll let you answer that question!

One aspect of object language is called *artifactual communication*. This is the way we use our own appearance as a way to communicate nonverbally who we are. Clothing styles, the type of materials, the color of garments, and how we wear the clothing speaks volumes about us.

My daughter just graduated from the University of Georgia and was more than happy during the winter months to wear her UGA hoody to classes. Wearing the sweatshirt showed her pride in the college and a non-verbal cue that she was a proud student. Last week as our new semester began on the campus where I teach college, a young man came to class wearing all bright green articles of clothing: pants, shirt, shoes, bookbag, and jacket. As we were getting to know each other on the first day, he was sending a very clear nonverbal cue that his favorite color was green. Even his sunglasses had green frames. Artifactual communication goes further than clothing choice and colors, but also in the way we decorate our homes and the color of our cars!

Regardless of whether we are using sign language, action language, or object language, we all need to channel these cues through one direction or another using our bodies. We do this in two basic ways. The first is with movements we make with our bodies and the second involves the appearance our bodies communicate to others.

INFLUENCES OF NONVERBAL COMMUNICATION

Using our hands, face, and body gestures, we send communication cues. Consider how we lift a hand to wave hello to a friend. While this accompanied with a great big smile is a universal signal in the United States, it can also send a completely different message without the smile and may be read as saying no or stop.

A "thumbs-up" will mean you did a great job to one culture but means something entirely different in other cultures. Posture, poise, and gestures are also ways we use our body to send nonverbal cues.

Posture sends a nonverbal cue about how you feel about yourself. Not only will good posture show self-confidence, but it has a positive effect on your breathing patterns and the way you project as you speak. Good posture also lends itself to effective movements and gesturing during the speech. Have you ever heard someone tell you to "Stand tall"? Hold your chin up, keep your eyes focused and take your place among great leaders who know what it takes to deliver a strong message. As you go into a room, walk with a positive purpose to let others know that you are ready and prepared.

Poise is displayed with how you carry your body. Are you comfortable in your own skin? Shoulders should be up and eyes looking at your audience to display positive self-confidence. People who walk in looking at the floor and with shoulders drooping will send a negative nonverbal cue about themselves and their speech topic. Instead, walk confidently smiling at others and letting them know you are happy to see them. Avoid leaning against furniture or walls, shifting from one foot to the other, adjusting your clothing or hair, handling notes, or putting your hands in your pocket. All of these negative behaviors will send negative nonverbal cues to your audience and will be evidence of a poor self-image and lack of confidence in yourself. When all eyes are on you, make sure you are communicating through nonverbal cues that will increase your credibility.

Gestures are the ways you use your hands, body, and facial expressions to communicate. I've often had students ask, "What should I do with my hands when speaking?" My advice is to get immersed in your topic so that you do not think about your hands and body. When you do this, you will have more natural and meaningful gestures. Don't put your hands in your pockets, clench them in front of you, or hold them behind you. These movements send a negative nonverbal cue. Gestures should not seem rehearsed but should enhance

your delivery and make visual points about things you are describing. They should be natural movements. The important thing is to make sure your gestures mirror the message you are sending.

The study of gestures using face and body movements is called *kinesics* and through this study we have learned there are six ways we use our bodies to send cues: adaptors, affect displays, emblems, illustrators, regulators, and appearance. Some of these are intentional and others are unintentional, some are positive and others are negative, yet all send a message.

Adaptors are unusually unintentional forms of nonverbal communication. These gestures are used when we straighten our collars, adjust a skirt, or move the hair from our eyes. You'll also notice this when people take off their glasses to think before responding to a question. Folding arms in front of your chest or holding clasped hands in front of your body are adaptors and send a nonverbal cue.

Affect Displays are the easiest to spot because this is where we use our faces for smiling and frowning. The smile could be a genuine smile or a sarcastic smile, but they both send a message. *Smiling* is a nonverbal cue that says, "I am happy to be here!" A genuine smile will send a positive message. As you smile, you will be pleased to notice that others will also smile at you. This reciprocal smile will help you not be as nervous as you might be without positive nonverbal cues.

General body movements showing stress or extreme happiness are also affect displays. Have you ever seen someone who is completely relaxed? The look on his face along with the positioning of arms and legs can show complete relaxation. The same is true when you see someone under a great deal of stress. The stress is seen in furrowed eyebrows, pursed lips, but also in the manner in which they hold their hands and use general body movements of tight or jerky motions.

Emblems are movements or gestures that take the place of words. The waving "hello," making the thumbs-up sign, the distinct head nod to indicate a yes or no response, the thumb and forefinger in a circle to indicate you are OK with something, and folding hands for prayer are all good examples. I'm sure you can think of others to add to this list.

Illustrators are the way we use our bodies to gesture and indicate directions: right, left, up, down, over, under, close, or distant. We might use our head, eyes, or one of our limbs (legs, arms, or hands).

Regulators are used during communication with others to show interest or to motivate the speaker to continue speaking or to give room for you to speak. These are usually unintentional movements but can also be intentional. For example, when listening to their young teenager explaining a situation, the parents may use a regulator (smile, head nod, leaning forward) to show that they are listening and encouraging the teenager to continue with the story. *Head Tilting* and *Head Nodding* is a nonverbal cue which lets you know if the person to whom you are speaking comprehends your point or if they still might have questions.

Appearance tells a great deal about us. Are you young, old, female, male, fit, or unfit? Do you take care to make sure clothes fit properly, are pressed, and clean? What type clothing do you wear? What type bag do you carry? Your **General Appearance** is a large part of your communication. Even when you are not speaking, you are communicating to others around you. **Physical Appearance** during a speech presentation sends a positive or negative message about the speaker's credibility. For most speaking occasions, it is important to dress as if you are going to a job interview. Business or business casual dressing for a speech is always preferred. Occasionally, speakers may dress according to the topic they are presenting. For example, if you are giving a speech about cooking, you might wear a chef's hat and apron. But for the most part, your audience will appreciate the fact that you took time to dress professionally for the speech. Blue jeans and a t-shirt that says, "BITE ME," may not be the best choice if you want your audience to take you seriously. Overly bright outfits or unusual styles or garments that do not fit properly can be distracting. While it may be appropriate to show tattoos or piercings, if your speech topic is about tattoos or piercings, it is a better idea to avoid clothing that flaunt these. Have you ever heard "You only get one chance to make a first impression"? What message are you trying to send? Dress the part, Communication Shark! These same tips work whether you are speaking one-on-one with a friend, business acquaintance, or to a group of people at work. Be aware of your appearance because your appearance is speaking volumes about you!

We can't complete this section without also discussing eye contact. Speakers are always told to have strong eye contact because it allows the speaker to connect with whom they are speaking. While this is true for speakers with large audiences, it is also true when we are speaking one-on-one or in small groups. Notice eye contact the next time you are speaking with someone. Did they have strong eye contact or weak eye contact? Did their pupils dilate while you were speaking to them?

Eye contact promotes goodwill and a connection with the others. It also helps you appear more credible and knowledgeable about the topic you discuss. This is how you connect with others and have them invest in your topic. Avoid gazing at any one person or group of people for too long at a time. Share your eye contact and your attention with everyone in your group as you speak.

FUNCTIONS OF NONVERBAL COMMUNICATION

The functions of nonverbal communication involve the way we combine verbal and nonverbal cues to send messages and communicate with others. In the section about verbal communication, we shared the research conducted by Albert Mehrabian that shows only 7% of communication involves words, 55% involves body language, and 38% involves how we say the words. While this continues to be a point of contention for some, and many people have tried to say the percentages could not be true, subsequent research has revealed much of the very same data. It is the intonation of the voice that includes tone, volume, pitch, pace, rate, and color that influences the 38% Mehrabian detailed. If you were to add the 7% and the 38% together that involves language—the words and how the words are said—the figure is still smaller than the communication we see from body language. Integrating the two forms of communication, verbal and nonverbal, helps us to receive messages or cues by what we hear and also by what we see. In other words, nonverbal cues are used to enhance, alter, complement, contradict, or accent verbal messages that are delivered.

UNDERSTANDING SPACE, PLACE, TIME, TOUCH, AND SMELL

Now, it is finally time to talk about one of the nonverbal communication cues that I find most fascinating and that is *proxemics*. This is the study of spatial distances and reveals so much about your feelings of the people with whom you are around. We send spatial cues to show whether we are comfortable or uncomfortable with the space placed between us and the person speaking. Have you ever noticed a person back up when you move in to speak to them? If they do this, you might be moving into their personal space.

There are four distances that we will explore: *public, social, personal,* and *intimate distances*. Without going further, you already know that there are certain people that you will allow to be closer to you than others. My students can stand a bit closer to me than a stranger, but my children and husband can be even closer.

Whether you know it or not, you have an invisible wall that surrounds you. If someone stands a bit too close to that wall, you will find yourself backing up to position your wall for a comfortable distance. This diagram will help you to understand this better:

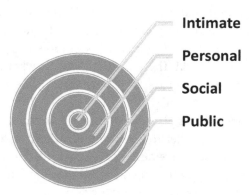

Source Waddell and Obis

Distance	Size of Space	When Used
Intimate	0–18 inches	Reserved for family and spouse
Personal	18 inches to 4 feet	Within arm's reach . . . Can touch only if you extend arms
Social	4–12 feet	Conducting business or visiting at a gathering
Public	12–25 feet	Shopping or public area Close enough to see, but can take defensive action if threatened

Source Waddell and Obis

Public Space is the space 12 to 25 feet away from others. It is appropriate to move closer to others when visiting or making a particular point, but advisable not to stay too close to any person for too long of a period. If you do, you will notice that it will make the other person nervous. If there is a table in front and you move closer to the table, the audience member may move their personal items closer to them and away from you. If you see this, take the cue that you are too close and back away.

Social Space allows you to get just a little closer. This is the space that others are most comfortable with when working with a co-worker or customer and is usually about 4 to 12 feet.

Personal Space allows someone to get closer, but not closer than 18 inches to 4 feet. This area is usually reserved for friends or family members.

Intimate Space is the closest and is usually 18 inches or less away and usually involves touching the person next to you. This area is reserved for very close family members and also a romantic partner. With intimate space, we usually allow someone there for a short period of time but will expect that same person to move to the personal space area at a certain point. We often will allow someone in the intimate space for a quick hug or to bid farewell, but also expect them to move back to the personal or social space once the hug is over.

As we conclude this section about proxemics, remember these designated spaces are the standards we recognize most often in the United States; however, they can change due to diverse cultures and circumstances. In all cases, whether speaking to an audience or speaking one-on-one to another person, be sure to read carefully the nonverbal cues being sent. Space distances with one person or a group of people may be altered according to that person or group's comfort level.

While we are talking about space, we should also cover *territoriality* which is the way we view our own space and/or objects. These can be broken down into three general areas: primary, secondary, and public.

Primary Territories are things or spaces we own or possess. This can be any number of objects such as your shoes, purse, hair, or your bank account, but can also extend to your apartment, family, and friends. *Secondary Territories* are spaces that you occupy or to which you are assigned, but do not necessarily belong to you. For example, your home town, school, or church are primary territories. If you sit in the second row—piano side—at church every Sunday morning, you may consider the seat as your territory and you might not appreciate someone else sitting in what you consider to be *your seat*. *Public Territories* are spaces that can be used and are open to everyone. An example of this would be a zoo, theme park, or beach. While the beach may be your very favorite beach in the world, it is still considered public territory because any number of people may visit the area and it is not designated for any one group of people.

The *Expectancy Violation Theory*, proposed by Judee K. Burgoon almost fifty years ago, covers how we perceive our territory and how we respond when someone violates our own expectations. According to Burgoon, we all have expectations of other's behaviors. When someone violates our own social norms or expectations, it can cause us to perceive that person in a positive or negative light. Any number of nonverbal communication factors come into play through this theory and involve space, time, objects, and behaviors. Would you like to hear a couple of examples?

Consider a situation where you and about a thousand other people are standing in line to purchase tickets for a P!nk concert. People are standing within 4–6 inches of each other and no one thinks this is odd. However, if you are at a grocery store at 11:00 a.m. on a Tuesday morning and there are only about six customers in the store, you would think it quite odd if one of the other customers comes to the produce aisle and stands less than one foot away from you without speaking. That is because of social norms. In a crowded line, you would expect someone to stand closer to you than is normally expected, but in an empty grocery store, you may become nervous or uneasy if another customer intruded upon your personal space.

© blvdone/Shutterstock.com

Another situation may involve nonverbal cues sent through clothing choices. For example, if you are on the basketball court with your friends shooting free throws, you would expect all of your friends to be wearing casual or athletic clothing. What would you think if someone walked on to the court wearing a tuxedo and decided to join in? Would you think that was odd? It actually depends on the situation. If it happened that the person in a tuxedo was your coach and on his way to his wedding, you would probably throw the ball to him and stand back to watch him perform a jump stop after receiving the pass, pivot around to square up to the basket, and then score points from the shot and from your friends watching! I'm sure that shot would be met with lots of high fives and handshakes! On the other hand, if the person in a tuxedo was a complete stranger, you and your friends might give him the once-over and then look at each other to question his motives. Try conducting your own Expectancy Violation Theory experiments. You might have fun with this but be careful so that you don't make someone mad! You might have fun with this but be careful so that you don't make someone mad!

Chronemics is the study of how we use time to communicate. If you arrive early or if you arrive late, you are sending a nonverbal cue about your time and the time of those who are expecting you.

I'm sure all of you have a friend who constantly arrives late for all functions. In fact, you might even find yourself telling this friend the event begins thirty minutes to an hour prior to the time it actually begins, just so they will arrive in time. If your friend constantly arrives late, they are sending you a message that their time is more valuable to them than your time. This is true for personal events and for professional events. They are being rude to you. Don't forget it!

If someone always arrives a few minutes early or on time, this means that they honor your time and they value you and the event. This is a nonverbal form of communication that many people dismiss, but the way you handle this will determine how others consider you in the long run.

Why are time restraints important when presenting a speech? When asked to present a speech, always ask the host about the time limit for your speech. Often other points of interest are included during the gathering and your speech will be just one portion of the event. Whether you are the keynote speaker or a support speaker, timing is extremely important so that the event planner can keep the event moving according to a planned schedule. If your speech is longer than needed, the entire event may run overtime.

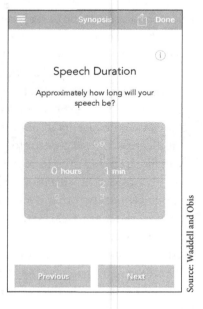

A good rule to follow is to meet the minimum time limit, but not go over the maximum time limit. A 4–6-minute speech should last five minutes. A 20–30-minute speech should last 25 minutes. It is always preferred to end your speech just short of the maximum time limit to keep your event host happy!

Your SpeechShark app has a built-in timer to help you stay on time! Just dial in the time that you have been asked to speak and the app will give you a visual reminder of the time left! The screenshot to the right will show what this looks like in your app. If a speech is designed to last 8–10 minutes, we suggest you dial in 9 minutes as your max time. This gives you a little cushion to make sure you do not go over the time limit.

Haptics is the study of communicating through touch. This happens when we shake hands with a colleague, share a friendly pat on the back, or hug a family member. We send nonverbal communication through touch.

When interviewing for a job position, it is almost always expected for the interviewee to shake the hand of the interviewer when thanking the person for the meeting and for the opportunity to speak about the job. The way you shake someone's hand sends a nonverbal cue about you and your credibility. Most of the time, people will use their right hands for a handshake. Just a word of caution, make sure you are sensitive to the way the other person shakes your hand so that you can match the touch. This is one way to make sure your handshake is not too weak or too strong so that you do not send the wrong message.

Complex emotions are obvious through our own use of touch during communication. For example, when speaking to a child, the mother may touch her child's shoulder or head to help calm the child. When communicating to strangers, it is doubtful we touch at all. Touching may enhance messages sent or emotions we feel during communication. Culture plays an important part with touch and we should always be mindful of cues the recipient sends to us to let us know if a touch is welcomed or not.

Olfactory Communication is another type of nonverbal cue that is quite interesting and involves taste and smell. We think of this type of communication primarily with animals, but it is also important to humans. This afternoon as my family came home for our weekly gathering, my daughters said they could smell the lovely meal cooking in the oven before they ever opened the front door. This smell triggers happy memories for my family and has them thinking not only about the smell of dinner cooking, but also the taste which never changes from one cooking to the next. Hopefully by using the scent and flavors, I was able to send a positive nonverbal cue that our family gathering would once again be a special time.

Smells can send positive or negative nonverbal cues. Have you ever been in the room with someone who wore too much cologne? If you have allergies the scent could have caused health as well as sensory reactions, but more often than not heavy scents are not pleasant. As with any form of nonverbal communication, use caution to make sure you are sending the right type of cue to others.

TYPES OF NONVERBAL COMMUNICATION

As we discussed the characteristics, influences, and functions of nonverbal communication, we also have covered most of the types of nonverbal communication. But just to make sure you understand the types, we will list them again: kinesics, *paralinguistics*, *haptics*, *proxemics*, *chronemics*, *territoriality*, *artifactual*, and *olfactory*.

Types of Nonverbal Communication	Area	Definition
Kinesics	Body	The use of facial and body language to communicate.
Paralinguistics	Vocal	The nonverbal aspect of speech that involves sound but not words.
Haptics	Touch	The use of touch to communicate feelings, intentions, behaviors, and attitudes.
Proxemics	Space	The use of space and distance to communicate relationships between people.
Chronemics	Time	The use of time and how you communicate to others by the way you organize and react to time.
Territoriality	Territory	The use of ownership to a space, objects, or persons to communicate.
Artifactual	Object	The use of objects (color, clothing, cars, homes, decorations, etc.) to communicate.
Olfactory	Smell	The use of scent and taste to communicate a wide variety of messages.

Source: Waddell and Obis

TYPES OF NONVERBAL COMMUNICATION
WORKSHEET

Name:_____ Date:_____

Complete the missing areas:

Types of Nonverbal Communication	Area	Definition
Kinesics		The use of facial and body language to communicate.
Paralinguistics	Vocal	
		The use of touch to communicate feelings, intentions, behaviors, and attitudes.
Proxemics	Space	
Chronemics		The use of _____ and how you communicate to others by the way you _____ _____.
		The use of ownership to a space, objects, or persons to communicate.
Artifactual	Object	
Olfactory		The use of _____ and _____ to communicate a wide variety of messages.

IMPROVING NONVERBAL COMPETENCE

We've probably shared just enough information here about nonverbal communication that you are nervous and now wondering what you should do to improve your own nonverbal communication skills. You may also be wondering if you are correctly reading other people's nonverbal communication cues. Here are some simple tips:

1. **Watch and Learn:** Pay attention to everything you see. Consider eye contact, body movements, posture, gestures, and object usage. As you watch others and recognize nonverbal communication cues, you will also become more aware of your own nonverbal communication cues. Increase your awareness of messages YOU send and also remember the connotation in which messages are sent or received. Look for multiple cues and avoid evaluating harshly based upon one cue.

2. **Listen and Learn:** Vocal tones can paint a clear picture. Whether happy or sad, the tone in your voice will affect the message you communicate or the message you hear. Listen carefully and as you do, you will notice that you also begin to have stronger eye contact with others. Consequently, you will hear and see nonverbal cues that might go unnoticed by others.

3. **Use Eye Contact:** The best way to connect with others is through good eye contact. Avoiding eye contact sends a message that you are not telling the truth or that you are trying to hide something. If your eye contact is too piercing, that also sends an intimidating and negative cue. Good eye contact is a happy mix of direct eye contact and sharing eye contact with others, but is comfortable when you spend only four to five seconds of direct eye contact with each person.

4. **Match Cues to Meanings:** We believe what we see before we believe what we hear. Are the cues matching the message being sent? Subtle nonverbal cues will tell the true story. Make sure your story is true before you tell it. If you don't, your nonverbal cues will tell it all.

5. **Consider the Message:** Consider the situation in which the message is being delivered. Match the nonverbal cues to the message and remember that there are often situations around that can alter the intended meaning. Avoid misreading signals or over-reading into things. The more aware you are of nonverbal communication, the better you will become reading the signals, understanding the cues, and getting to the true message.

6. **ASK Questions:** A friend once told me that ASK stands for Actively Seeking Knowledge. I liked that acronym and wanted to share it with you. If you see something but feel like you might be getting mixed signals due to nonverbal communication cues, then speak up! ASK! You can rephrase the message or ask if you have the correct understanding.

The more experience you get with identifying nonverbal messages, the better you will become at picking up on cues being sent. You will improve your own competence with sending nonverbal messages and also with interpreting nonverbal messages. Here is the secret: people who are good listeners are also very good with understanding and interpreting nonverbal messages. Good listeners have better eye contact than poor listeners. Along with the good eye contact, you will be seeing signals that others may miss.

CONTEXT AND SETTING

In this chapter, we have covered many aspects of nonverbal communication as it pertains to relational, professional, cultural, and gendered contexts.

Relational: As we take time to learn more about nonverbal communication, we find that it can help improve the relationships we have with others, whether family, friends, or co-workers. This occurs because we are able to encode and decode messages appropriately reading the nonverbal cues sent and received. We learn to read others' cues and, consequently, we develop a better understanding of when it is appropriate to express emotions or share thoughts and when it is not appropriate. As a result, our social networks expand and the relationships we have become stronger.

Professional: It is no secret that employers are seeking employees with effective communication skills. Employers want to know that their employees can communicate with customers, co-workers, and the administration. Contradictory or mixed messages in the workplace can lead to lack of job satisfaction and may affect performance evaluations. More than ever, it is important that we have a clear understanding of verbal and nonverbal communication cues so that we are able to be more effective in the workplace. Being able to encode and decode messages is the point that may make or break a career.

Cultural: Being sensitive to cultures different from our own and working to communicate effectively to everyone we meet will help us become better communicators and better people. Understanding nonverbal behaviors of people from other cultures can only be positive as we will be working with all types of people in our future. Being aware of eye contact, space, and touch may be the very thing that helps us to get along with people that may have a culture different from our own. Knowing whether to shake hands, bow, or nod, could be the difference between closing a deal or closing a door. Before meeting with others from a different culture, be sure to spend a little time understanding their nonverbal cues.

Gender: Men and women are more similar than you may think when it comes to nonverbal communication, but there are differences to note. Women tend to use more gestures, but men use larger gestures. Since women tend to orient their bodies directly toward the body of the person with whom they are speaking, they tend to send and receive nonverbal messages better than men. That is because women tend to have better eye contact than men. The biological difference between men and women account for the differences involved with vocal pitch and with volume. Spatially, men tend to take up more room than women and ironically enough, women are more comfortable in crowded rooms than men. Both genders want to socialize and present themselves in a positive manner. Generally speaking, nonverbal cues from men and women tend to be somewhat similar. Understanding the differences between the way that men and women use nonverbal communication is important and should be evaluated carefully.

KEY TERMS

- Action Language
- Adaptors
- Affect Displays
- Appearance
- Artifactual Communication
- Chronemics
- Cultural
- Emblems
- Expectancy Violation Theory
- Eye Contact
- Gender
- Gestures
- Haptics
- Head Tilting or Nodding
- Illustrators
- Intimate Distances
- Kinesics
- Nonverbal Communication

- Object Language
- Olfactory Communication
- Paralinguistics
- Personal Distances
- Poise
- Posture
- Primary Territories
- Professional
- Proxemics
- Public Distances
- Public Territories
- Regulators
- Relational
- Secondary Territories
- Sign Language
- Smiling
- Social Distances
- Territoriality

Chapter Six

Intrapersonal Communication

© pathdoc/Shutterstock.com

In this chapter:

As we consider communication, we often think about how *we* communicate with *others* or how others communicate with us. We think about listening skills, verbal and nonverbal communication, and various methods of communicating. But, have you ever considered the way that you communicate with *yourself*? This type of communication is called ***intrapersonal communication*** and is one of the most basic forms of communication that we know.

Not too long ago, I was walking through a grocery store and noticed the shopper in front of me was talking, but no one was around. For a few seconds, I thought perhaps she was talking on a telephone using a Bluetooth device. As I tried to go around her to get items on the shelf that I needed, I realized that she was talking to herself. Aloud. Most of the time when we talk to ourselves, we don't actually verbalize the conversations. This woman was having a full-on verbal conversation with herself about which brand of vegetable she should buy. She was asking questions and answering her own questions. Clearly, this type of behavior concerned me for a moment and I decided to move quickly to another aisle. But, it caused me to stop and think about intrapersonal communication because this is something that we do every day. The only difference is that most of the self-talk happens without verbalizing the conversation.

Have you ever rehearsed a phone conversation in your mind before you even picked up the phone to dial the number? If so, you have engaged in **intrapersonal communication. Intrapersonal communication occurs when we envision or have a conversation with ourselves. Because it involves only you, this is the most basic type of communication. You may have been faced with making a decision about something and had an internal dialogue weighing the pros and cons of your options. Or perhaps you have given yourself a pep talk before an interview or oral presentation. Each of these situations is an instance of intrapersonal communication in which we first talked to ourselves before adding others to our interaction.**

SELF-PERCEPTION

Now that you have a better understanding of communicating with yourself, let's look at the ways that you interpret things in order to make sense of it. After all, how will you ever communicate something unless you first understand how you perceive it? We call this *self-perception*. Have you ever been somewhere with a friend and find that as you are describing the situation, you both have different interpretations of the event?

This is seen quite often with the students I take on travel and study abroad programs. For example, we were all in Florence, Italy, visiting the Accademia Gallery Museum and looking forward to seeing Michelangelo's *David* sculpture. For days we talked about the art gallery and everyone had a different idea of what they would actually see. Of course, everyone had seen the pictures online, but there is nothing like the moment when you take your first glimpse of the seventeen-foot marble structure of the Biblical hero, David, and consider the magnitude of Michelangelo's project which he created in the early 1500s. Later in the day as students were comparing their photos, I thought it was particularly interesting to see the different angles and views they captured on film. One student took very detailed pictures showing the enormous hands and feet while another student stood back to capture the full sculpture. Both students' pictures were wonderful, but quite different according to their perception of the magnificent statue. Perhaps this next section will help you to understand the process of perception and may also help you to better understand the way you communicate with yourself.

**Perception* is a process consisting of three parts that we use to make sense of messages we encounter. We select, organize, and interpret stimuli so that they make sense to us. This happens constantly in our personal, professional, and public lives. For example, a friend asks you if you would like to go to a concert together.

You eagerly confirm that you would like to go, as long as the tickets are not too expensive. Your friend buys the tickets and sends you a text message informing you how much you owe. When you learn the price of the ticket, you are shocked because your perception of "not too expensive" is clearly much different than your friend's perception. Differences in perception may cause minor misunderstandings or even major communication breakdowns.

Since perception is a cognitive process that helps us to understand our experiences, how we receive, filter, and interpret behaviors and conversations may not be the same as how someone else will complete the process. In essence, perception is the key to how we assign meaning in our interactions with others and thus, it has a significant impact on how we communicate and how we understand the communication of others. Understanding the perception process will enable you to consider the potential misunderstandings that may occur and help you communicate more effectively.

THE PERCEPTION PROCESS

Selection

The *perception process* has three phases: selection, organization, and interpretation. The first phase is *selection*. Needless to say, at any given moment in our lives, there are many stimuli in our environment that may compete for our attention. We simply cannot focus on everything, so we select those stimuli that we feel are significant. That is why two people may see the same thing but "see" things differently. For example, when two fans watch the same football game, they may have very different perspectives about a controversial play. One fan may have

focused on watching one player while the other fan focused on a different player. Because the two fans selected different things to attend to in the game, they may have a difference of opinion about the outcome of the play. Although they have seen the same play per se, they each focused on something different. As a result, the selection portion of the perception process will affect how each of them moves through the next phases of the process. As we discuss later in the chapter, what you select may be influenced by who you are, your relationship with another person, your culture, your expectations or prior experiences, or even your mood at any given time.

Organization

Organization is the second phase of the perception process. Once we select or focus our attention on some particular aspect or characteristic of the stimuli we selected, we need to organize it in a way that makes sense to us. We may relate what we receive to something we have already experienced. For example, when you hear someone with a great laugh, you may be interested in getting to know that person because his or her laugh reminds you of one of your friends who also has a great laugh. In our quest to organize what we receive, we use a categorization process. We may categorize people based on the roles we view them as fulfilling or by our assumptions about their personalities. Is this person a student, a teacher, or a parent? Is this person funny, serious, or responsible? Using this organizational process to make sense of others is natural in our interactions; however, we need to be careful of our assumptions and conclusions, and be cautious of overgeneralizing others. Doing so may prevent us from being accurate in our overall perceptions. In addition, as your experiences change throughout your life, you may alter the way in which you categorize stimuli. Thus, the way you once categorized romantic relationships in middle school is probably very different from the way in which you currently look at romantic relationships. Once we have organized what we have received, we move to the interpretation phase.

Interpretation

The final step of the perception process is *interpretation*. This is where we attach meaning to what we have selected and organized. We may interpret what one person says to us differently than if someone else said it based on our relationship with the other individual. For example, if a friend says, "You are crazy!" you would likely assume the friend is joking; whereas, if someone you don't know or barely know said the same thing, you might interpret the same message as an insult. In addition, your personal experiences may also influence how you interpret a message. For example, you had a great relationship with your previous supervisor. It was very relaxed and you would even play jokes on each other. When your new supervisor was hired, you assumed you could approach tasks and the relationship in general in the same lighthearted and humorous way. The new supervisor, however, did not share the same view and told you to "take your work more seriously." The relationship you have with another person, the experiences you have had in your life, as well as other factors may cause you to interpret what you have received and organized in different ways.

Overall, the process of selecting something from the many stimuli received through our senses, and organizing and interpreting them in a way that makes sense, is the cognitive process known as perception. In the next section, we focus on the factors that influence how we go through the perception process.

THE INFLUENCES ON PERCEPTION

There are many factors that affect our perceptions. These may include characteristics such as our age, gender, physical characteristics, cultural background, past experiences, and even our present mood. Your awareness of these factors will help you understand the perception process more clearly.

Age

Your age may influence how you perceive something. When you were younger, you may have thought the stories your grandparents told you were repetitive and boring. As you grew older, you realized the importance of these stories and their significance for your family. Things that don't seem important to us when we are one age could become very important at another age. The reverse may also be true. Perhaps when you were younger, you couldn't imagine ever being able to sleep without your favorite stuffed animal. Now, you remember your stuffed animal fondly, but you can sleep well without it. Consider the fact that when you were younger you may have felt uneasy discussing your romantic interests with your parents, but as an adult, you may be much more comfortable sharing information and even asking them for their perspective on your romantic relationships.

Gender

Gender may also influence our perceptions. How we view things may be related to whether we are male or female. While this isn't always the case, males and females may perceive the same thing differently. For example, both males and females in the workplace want to achieve their goals; however, it has been said that females may be more interested in nurturing and enhancing their relationships, while males, on the other hand, may be more interested in simply getting the task completed without as much concern for the interpersonal relationships in the workplace (Wood, 2003). It may be the case that you are a male who is very concerned about your relationship with those in your department or you are a female who is not particularly concerned about these interpersonal relationships. However, in certain situations, your gender may influence your perception.

In addition to their different views and expectations, we may also have different perceptions of males and females. For example, Brann and Himes (2010) examined differences in how male and female newscasters were perceived when delivering the same message. While the information that both newscasters shared was identical, the perceptions of the newscasters were different. Male newscasters were rated as being more competent, more composed, and more extroverted than female newscasters. Thus, gender may cause us to perceive things differently or to be perceived by others in different ways.

Physical Characteristics

Another factor that has the potential to influence our perception is size or physical ability. For example, one of your authors had a pink stuffed bear as a child. She remembered the bear as being life-sized! Many years later when she found the bear in her parents' attic, she asked her mother if she had washed the bear and put it in the dryer, thus shrinking it. Her mother indicated she had not done that. Clearly, when she was very small, the bear appeared to be much larger than it actually was. While she had grown over the years, her perception of one of her favorite childhood toys had remained

© R.Gino Santa Maria/Shutterstock.com

unchanged. When we are small, things seem much bigger to us. Imagine what it is like for a child to walk in a crowded store holding a parent's hand. The much larger parent probably doesn't realize that the world looks much different from the small child's vantage point. The same thing might be true for those of you who exercise on a regular basis. Weights that may be considered "light" for someone who has lifted for some time may seem extremely "heavy" for someone new to strength training. As you reflect on these examples, imagine the miscommunication that might occur when your interpretation of something is different from someone else's interpretation.

Culture

Our culture also influences how we perceive the behaviors and messages of others. If you have ever traveled to another country, you have probably experienced firsthand how different things may be. Not only may the language be new to you, but also the types of food, styles of dress, and even smells may be unique. As a result, you probably perceived things differently from someone who was a native of that country. If you are from a culture that values direct eye contact, you would most likely perceive someone looking directly at you as being respectful. If, however, the other person is from a culture where it is disrespectful to look someone in the eyes when talking, you may perceive their lack of eye contact as being rude and misinterpret the situation if you don't understand the differences in cultural expectations. Suppose you are from a culture that values punctuality, and you are meeting a business client from a culture that views time as being flexible. She arrives to your scheduled meeting 25 minutes late, and you misinterpret her late arrival as being unprofessional even though it is acceptable to show up 25–30 minutes after a scheduled starting time in her culture. Examples like these occur more often than we realize and can cause individuals to misread a communication situation.

Personal Experiences

As we alluded to earlier, your own personal experiences may affect your perceptions. For example, suppose you hire a contractor to do some work in your home. Upon her arrival, the contractor thanks you multiple times and expresses her appreciation for the work. She explains that the recent economy has resulted in fewer jobs and more competition from other contractors. Her personal experience in struggling to find work has caused her to perceive the opportunity to work on your home differently than she would have if job options were readily available. Her personal experience of the shift in availability of work opportunities has changed the perceptions she had about her livelihood and the customers who pay for her services.

Moods

Our moods also influence our perceptions. Something that you would not usually find upsetting may bother or annoy you because of your present mood. Suppose you typically enjoy having a coworker or neighbor drop by your office unexpectedly to chat. On one particular day, however, you are trying to complete a project by a deadline and don't have time to talk. Due to your stress level, you may perceive that person to be bothersome or annoying on this particular day, whereas on other days, you would welcome the casual conversation. You may try to cut off the conversation, simply stop listening, or say something you might regret later.

If our mood is positive, it may also influence our perception of a situation. Suppose you have just received an "A" on a paper or a promotion at work. If you are in a great mood, something that might bother you on any other day simply does not seem to alter your positive outlook. Thus, whether your mood is positive or negative may influence your communication with others or their communication with you.

Stereotypes

The *stereotypes* or generalizations we hold about a group or a category of people may also affect our perceptions. When we stereotype someone, we apply our general perceptions of a particular group to an individual. This helps us simplify the process of perception and form a quick impression of the person. Reflect on some of your own perceptions of groups of people based on their economic status, cultural background, religious beliefs, education level, or other factors. Perhaps you perceive wealthy people as being self-absorbed and self-ish, while someone else may perceive them as being generous and hard-working. Being aware of our stereotypes is important to ensuring effective communication. When we only use our own stereotypes to guide our communication with others, we increase our risk of miscommunication. After all, our stereotypes are not always entirely accurate.

As you can see, there are many factors that potentially alter how you perceive something. Understanding that you may perceive something in a totally different way from others is key to becoming a more effective communicator. Unfortunately, many of us incorrectly believe that the way in which we perceive something is exactly how others perceive it. It is important to realize that others may not share your perception of the same thing and learn to engage in the practice of checking your perceptions.

PERCEPTION CHECKING

How do we make sure that our perceptions are accurate? While you may have heard the advice "Go with your instinct!" checking our perceptions for accuracy is an important step to ensure effective communication. *Perception checking* is the process whereby we validate the accuracy of our perceptions. There are several different strategies you can use to check your perceptions. The following suggestions are often used to help us ensure our perceptions are correct.

Use Our Senses

Your senses include what you see, hear, touch, taste, and/or smell. We often rely on our senses to help us determine the accuracy of what we perceive and how we process that information. For example, if you open the refrigerator and notice that the expiration date on a container of milk has passed, you probably assume the milk has spoiled. If you're brave enough, you might check your perception that the milk is sour by opening the container and smelling the milk. If it smells strange, our perceptions are confirmed. Perhaps you decide to further check your perceptions by pouring the milk into a glass. If you notice that it is curdled, your perceptions are confirmed again. You may even decide to go one step further and taste the milk to determine if your perception is correct. In this example, you used a variety of your senses (i.e., sight, smell, and taste) to ensure that you perceived something accurately. While it is easy to judge whether or not our perception of spoiled milk is accurate, it is not always quite as easy to check to confirm that our perceptions in communication situations are accurate. Our ability to check the accuracy of our perceptions to ensure we are on the "same page" as others is vital in our personal, professional, and public lives.

Ask

One way to determine if your perception of something is accurate is to simply ask the other person if your interpretation of the situation is correct. Suppose you are at a party and one of your friends has barely spoken to you all evening. In addition, the last few times you've seen one another, the friend has seemed quiet and standoffish. If you perceive that your friend is angry with you, perceptions might be checked by asking, "I feel like you are upset with me, is that true?" While your friend may respond, "No, I'm okay…," your friend's verbal response may not reveal her true feelings. Thus, it is important to listen to *how* the response is said to help you determine whether your perceptions are correct. Depending on the tone of voice or the facial expressions that accompany the response of "I'm okay…" a variety of meanings could be perceived. It could be that your friend has been preoccupied with a project or a personal issue. If, on the other hand, your friend's response isn't convincing, your perception of the situation may be accurate and you may need to discuss this further. Even if it is difficult to address the situation directly, asking about your interpretation of the situation is a good option to check the accuracy of your perception.

In some situations, we are unable or unwilling to directly ask the other person if our perceptions are accurate. In these situations, consider asking others who have observed the situation or people you trust to give you an honest assessment of the situation. For example, in the example above, you might ask another friend to confirm or reject your perception of the situation. This "third party" may indicate to you that he also has noticed the friend's cool and aloof behavior toward you. In fact, he may be able to share information about why your friend is angry with you, may indicate that the friend has responded in a similar way with other people, or may inform you that the friend has had some personal issues lately. Soliciting feedback from someone you trust can assist you in checking the accuracy of your perceptions, and perhaps provide you with insight regarding how to address the situation.

Replicate

When scientists want to test a finding to confirm their conclusions, they repeat the study. Each time they receive the same results, it helps them know their results were not simply due to chance. In much the same way, you may be able to confirm your perceptions by repeating the behavior. Suppose a supervisor asks an employee to take an additional shift on several occasions, and each time the worker replies "No." The supervisor may perceive the worker as someone who is unmotivated and not a team player. Each time the worker refuses to take on additional responsibility, a negative perception of this worker is reinforced. Furthermore, each time the supervisor asks and receives a negative response, it confirms the supervisor's perception. Of course, there could be other reasons why the worker is unable to accept additional responsibilities. In this example, to further check his perceptions, the supervisor could also implement the strategy mentioned in the previous section and directly ask the employee why he never accepts an additional shift.

Observe

In order to clarify our perception of a situation, we may need to simply observe. Words may provide us with information about how others are feeling or thinking, but nonverbal communication (i.e., tone of voice, facial expressions, gestures, eye contact, etc.) provides valuable cues to assist in perception checking. In the public arena, we may not ever have the opportunity to speak firsthand to a candidate who is running for political office. Instead, we check our initial perceptions of the candidate by observing them. Do they seem genuinely concerned about the issues with which we are concerned? What does the candidate's nonverbal communication say about his or her beliefs? Our observations help confirm or disconfirm our perceptions. It is important to remember that our own actions sometimes speak louder than words. Just as we use our observations to confirm our perceptions of others, they do the same when checking their perceptions of us.

Consider Your Relationship

Your relationship with someone can also help you to check your perceptions. If you have a close relationship, you might understand a behavior more readily than if this person was simply an acquaintance or someone you just met. For example, if you have worked closely with someone in your organization for several years and that person exhibits uncharacteristic behavior, your relationship with the person and knowledge of their typical behavior will assist you in checking your perception of their current behavior.

Overall, there are several strategies that can be used to check our perceptions and to enhance our ability to avoid misunderstandings. It is important to remember that there may be several interpretations of the same behavior, so checking your perceptions will help you interpret a situation more accurately. Think about being in a restaurant and receiving what you consider to be "poor service" from a server. Is your immediate conclusion that the server is terrible? Could it be that the person is just having a bad day? Is this person new at the job? Could the server be stressed because the restaurant has had a sudden influx of customers? Could the kitchen be to blame for not getting all of the orders from one party out at the same time? Might this person be stressed about an issue not related to waiting on tables at the restaurant? Checking your perceptions of a situation will help you correctly interpret a situation and will help you respond appropriately.

Our perceptions of others are only one part of the interaction equation. Another key element is our self-perceptions. Understanding how we see ourselves and the image that we want to portray to others is essential to ensuring effective communication.

PERCEIVING THE SELF

In the previous section, we discussed what perception is, what factors influence our perceptions, and some strategies we may use to check our perceptions. In the next section, we turn our attention to the way in which we perceive our "self" and how this influences the way in which we communicate with others and how they perceive and communicate with us.

Self-Concept

Our *self-concept* consists of the perceptions and beliefs we have about ourselves. It is relatively stable yet it can change and evolve as we grow and gain new life experiences. Self-concept is multidimensional and thus we describe ourselves in a variety of ways. Stop for a moment and consider how you would define yourself. Our gender, race, and ethnicity are some of the more common ways by which we define ourselves. We may also define ourselves by our occupation, roles, education, physical attributes, or personality traits. Each description of yourself contributes to your self-concept. Elements of your self-concept may change over time. For example, at one point in your life, you may define yourself through roles such as sibling, son or daughter, or student. Although some of these roles would not change, you may add new roles throughout your life such as spouse or partner, parent, aunt or uncle, employee, or supervisor to your list.

Some aspects of our self-concept are based on objective facts while other dimensions may be more subjective. For example, the color of your eyes and your height in inches are facts about you. You may say that you are "tall;" however, that is subjective because what may be perceived as being "tall" to one person may not seem very tall to another. Thus, if you are the tallest of your friends and family at 5 feet 7 inches, you may consider yourself tall until you become friends with someone who is 6 feet. If, on the other hand, you say, "I am 5 feet 7 inches," then you are communicating what is factual.

You may perceive yourself as a strong student, a great athlete, or a talented artist. Since we don't always judge ourselves exactly as others see us, others may not see us in this same way. For example, some contestants on *American Idol* auditions explain to the judges that they perceive themselves to be excellent singers. When they actually audition for the show, the judges may disagree with these perceptions.

The Development of the Self-Concept

From the time we are born, our self-concept begins to develop. Our experiences and interactions play an important role in the development of our self-concept. Sullivan (1953) noted that our view of self is created and shaped by how we think others view us. It is our perception of how we imagine others see us. This is known as *reflected appraisal.* Through our interactions with others, our self-perception may be confirmed or changed.

Significant others in our lives play an important role in the development of our self-concept. For most of us, our parents or primary caregivers provide the first messages that create our self-concept. When babies cry and their needs are met, a sense of security and love is communicated. As children grow older, they may receive positive or negative messages about behaviors ranging from manners, to athletic ability, to academic performance and these shape their sense of self. Your self-concept continues to evolve as you encounter new relationships and experiences. If we receive positive affir-

mation, we are more likely to embrace the feedback and enjoy something, thus adding to our self-concept regarding that element of our lives. Generally speaking, if we are told we are good at something, we are more likely to continue to do it and, as a result, often become better at it. For example, when you are learning to dance, if you receive positive feedback, you are much more likely to continue to practice. Because you continue to practice, you become better at dancing. In this sense, we may engage in what is known as the *self-fulfilling prophecy*. In other words, when we believe something is true, we respond in ways to ensure that the prediction is fulfilled. Naturally, there are many things that don't respond to the "think method." It is important to note that just because we "think" something is true, it will become a reality. Recall our earlier example of the *American Idol* candidates. Just because they believe they have talent and perhaps their friends or family members even tell them they sing beautifully, it does not necessarily make it true. We don't become a great singer just because others say we're good and we believe them.

Needless to say, the reverse is also true. If you believe you are not good at something, you may fear or avoid it and then the self-fulfilling prophecy is fulfilled. For example, perhaps you had a bad experience when you were asked to present the results of a team project to another department. From that time on, you avoided speaking in public because you believed you were not good at it. Naturally, avoiding all public speaking situations will perpetuate your belief in your inability to speak in public and hence, this becomes a self-fulfilling prophecy.

As we enter school, our teachers and our peers influence our self-concept as well. For example, if your teacher told you that you were good in science or if you received good grades on your assignments when you were in elementary school, this becomes part of your self-concept. If you receive positive feedback on your science homework and tests, it reinforces this element of your self-concept. In addition, you will most likely feel positive about doing your science homework, which, in turn, will help you maintain this portion of your self-concept. Unfortunately, teachers may also have a negative influence on the self-concept of their students by saying something negative about their work instead of offering constructive criticism. Hopefully, you have not had this experience but there is a vast difference between someone telling you that you did very poorly versus pointing out the areas that were not strong and indicating how you could have improved upon the assignment.

Likewise, our peers influence the development of our self-concept. Think back to elementary school again. If you were the one that other children invited for play dates in elementary school, you probably viewed yourself as friendly and likeable. Similarly, if you did something funny and your peers laughed, you most likely began to believe you are funny. On the other hand, if you did something you thought was funny and nobody laughed, you also received a clear message from your peers.

In your professional life, your self-concept may also evolve. For example, suppose you are sitting in a meeting with senior management and you make a suggestion that your boss confirms as being valuable and worthwhile. At the next meeting, another suggestion you offer is received with enthusiasm. With each instance, you begin to view yourself as someone who could pursue a higher management position in the organization. When you receive this type of feedback and are praised for certain traits, they are more likely to become part of your self-concept.

Overall, early in our lives, parents and caregivers, teachers and peers send messages that influence our self-concept. As we go through life, our friends, family, supervisors, and colleagues continue to influence our self-concept. In turn, this influences how we communicate with others. In the next section, we discuss some of the barriers that prevent us from having an accurate self-concept.

Barriers Preventing an Accurate Self-Concept

There are several issues that may prevent us from forming a clear and accurate self-concept. As previously mentioned, your self-concept is created and developed through your interactions with others. You tend to construct a sense of who you are based on how others see you and communicate with you. Unfortunately, their perceptions of you may be inaccurate and this can cause you to see yourself inaccurately. For example, what if you are told you are the *best* artist or the *smartest* child by your parents, but when you begin school, you do not receive the same messages? On the other hand, what if you are told you are *worthless* or that you were a *mistake*? Consider the impact these types of messages would have on a person's self-concept. For better or worse, the messages we receive from significant others have an impact on our self-concepts; but these messages may or may not be accurate, and this may cause inaccuracy in our self-concepts.

As we previously indicated, the self-concept consists of perceptions we have about ourselves that are relatively stable. Unfortunately, these relatively enduring perceptions may pose a barrier that prevents us from developing an accurate self-concept since they cause us to be resistant to information that could alter our perceptions. Certainly, having a strong sense of self is a good thing, but if it prevents us from accepting valid messages about who we truly are, it can be problematic. Suppose you have always considered yourself to be poor at expressing yourself when writing. Perhaps you earned good grades in your English courses, but struggled to complete essays and received very little positive feedback from your teachers about your writing. When you entered college, you took the writing course required for all first-year students and was placed in a course with a teacher who inspired a passion for writing. When your first paper was returned with a grade of "A," you thought it was a mistake or a fluke. When you received the next paper back with the same grade, you thought, "This can't be right." On the third paper, your teacher wrote that you had a strong talent for writing and that she hoped you would continue taking writing courses in the future. Despite the positive feedback, it was difficult for you to change your belief that you were only an average writer. The challenge is, once we have a relatively stable sense of self, we find it difficult to change our perceptions. This may prevent us from having an accurate self-concept at times.

Another type of inaccurate perception we have of ourselves is that we may judge ourselves more critically in some instances than others may. For example, a recent college graduate may perceive herself as unmarketable because her final grade point average was lower than many others in her major. She doubts she will get the job she wants due to this. During her interview, the interviewer is impressed with her enthusiasm and sense of responsibility and offers her the job. In this example, she judged herself more harshly than the interviewer judged her.

As mentioned earlier in the chapter, the self-fulfilling prophecy may also prevent us from possessing an accurate self-concept. What if you majored in accounting and took a job at a large public accounting firm that required all employees to pass the CPA examination within the first year of employment? If you believe you will do poorly on the exam because you simply "don't do well on standardized tests of any kind," you may wind up behaving in ways that ensure the fulfillment of your prophecy. For example, you may talk yourself out of going to the review course you signed up to take, preparing for the class, or studying on your own. You rationalize to yourself, "Why bother if I won't do well on this type of test anyway?" If you employ any of these tactics, you are on the path to confirming your own prophecy of poor performance. Having this type of perception can create a barrier to developing an accurate self-concept.

A final barrier is the *self-serving bias*. This involves a tendency for taking personal credit for the positive outcomes for our actions, and directing the blame toward others for the negative outcomes. Thus, if you do well on an exam, it is because you studied. If you do poorly on the test, however, you may attribute the negative outcome to the difficulty of the test, to the instructor's poor teaching style, or to the teacher's unfair grading. In a 1982 study of job-seekers in Britain, Furnham found that individuals tend to take credit for their own abilities and skills when they are successful in securing a job, while they blame their lack of success in securing a job on factors that are beyond their control. This self-serving bias, or our tendency to judge ourselves less harshly than we judge others, may again cause us to have an inaccurate self-concept.

Overall, there are several barriers that may prevent us from having an accurate self-concept. Additionally, there may even be elements of our self-concept about which even we aren't aware at a given point in time. Many years ago, one of the authors had a student whose young child was killed by a drunk driver. She became a tireless advocate for stronger laws to help prevent drunk driving. In her work with Mothers Against Drunk Driving, she did a great deal of public speaking. On one occasion she said to the class, "If anyone had ever told me I would be speaking in public and involved with trying to change public policy, I would never have believed it. I have always viewed myself as just a mom." Keeping this information in mind is important as we discuss self-esteem and its influence on perception and communication.

Self-Esteem

Closely related to self-concept is *self-esteem*, the subjective evaluation of our worth. How we feel about ourselves, or the value we place on our abilities and behaviors, is our self-esteem. Whereas self-concept deals with our identity or a description of ourselves, our self-esteem gauges the value or extent to which we are happy or unhappy with the various dimensions of our self-concept. For example, when you feel really good about your ability as an actor, you have high self-esteem about acting. As you audition for various roles, you do so with confidence. When you communicate about your ability to act, you do so in a positive manner. On the other hand, if you have low self-esteem regarding your acting ability, you may shy away from auditions and communicate in a negative manner about your acting ability.

Just as your self-concept is not always objective, neither is your self-esteem. For example, you may have low self-esteem because you do not have accurate information or feedback from others. You may be doing fine in your new job, but you may not be listening accurately to the feedback you receive from your supervisor or colleagues. Your misinterpretation of their messages may lead you to believe you are not good at what you do. On the other hand, even when some people aren't doing particularly well at something, they may ignore negative feedback they receive, and their self-esteem will remain intact despite the contradictory information. When a manager conducts an annual evaluation, an employee may perceive that he has been doing an outstanding job. If you were to ask the manager, she may view the employee as "unmotivated" because he is simply doing what is required based on his job description and "clocking out" at the end of the day. The employee will likely maintain the perception that he is great at what he does because he is completing the tasks that are required without taking into account the quality of his work performance. Overall, the set of perceptions we have about ourselves, our self-concept, and our self-esteem (i.e., the value we place on our abilities and behaviors) influence how we communicate with others. This, in turn, impacts the perceptions that others form of us. How we present ourselves and how we perceive others is the focus of the next section.

Self-Presentation

Have you ever behaved in a particular way to impress someone? Do you communicate differently with friends than you would with someone you are just meeting for the first time? If so, you are like most people. We tend to present ourselves differently based on the situation. *Self-presentation* influences how we want others to perceive us. Goffman (1959) spoke of the "face," which is the view you want others to have of you. We present ourselves differently as a situation changes, and we change our communication depending on our relationship with the other person. For example, you may present yourself one way as a student speaking with

your professor and in another way as a student speaking with a classmate. In the first scenario, you may be polite and positive about the course, commenting to the professor on the relevance of a recent lecture to your future career goals. When speaking with a friend about the course, you may use slang and indicate you are taking the course simply because it fulfills a requirement for your major.

While we willingly present one view of our "self" to the world, we simultaneously hide aspects of our private self by masking certain behaviors (Goffman, 1959). For example, have you ever put on a brave face when you are actually nervous about something? Have you ever been upset about a breakup but smiled and minimized the hurt you felt inside? If so, you have worn a mask to conceal how you truly feel about that part of your "self."

Self-presentation may influence how we present ourselves in personal situations versus professional ones. According to Guadagno, Okdie, and Kruse (2012), "People tend to present and sometimes exaggerate or fabricate their characteristics in an attempt to create their desired impression" (p. 642). In today's world, the notion of self-presentation naturally brings up how individuals present themselves online. If you have ever "met" anyone online, you may have presented yourself in a particular way. In a survey of 80 individuals who had submitted online profiles to a variety of online dating websites, Toma, Hancock, and Ellison (2007) found 81% of those surveyed lied about one or more of their physical attributes including their height, weight, or age. Similarly, individuals who are shy may be more confident when communicating online and present themselves in a much more self-assured manner because the interaction is not face-to-face. In fact, some of our students reported feeling more confident communicating online because they felt they were not being judged on how they look, dress, or sound. Presenting yourself online may not reveal your true self to another and others may wonder if the self you have revealed is accurate.

Is it possible to improve our sense of "self?" Absolutely! Becoming aware of who we are and who we would like to become may help us enhance our self-concept and self-esteem. Through careful reflection, we may be able to focus on the areas of our "self" that we would like to strengthen. Since our sense of self evolves and is always "in process," we have the ability to find ways in which we may improve. This can be accomplished a number of ways: through the courses we take, the relationships we nurture, or the help we seek from professionals.

Thus far, we have focused on perceiving the self. In the next section, we discuss how we perceive others. Our perceptions of others have an impact on how we interpret their communication and how we communicate with them.

PERCEIVING OTHERS

How We Perceive Others

At the beginning of the chapter, we talked about some of the factors that influence our perceptions such as gender, culture, age, and our past experiences. It is important to keep these in mind as we discuss how we perceive others.

Not only do the words that others say cause you to form impressions, but a person's nonverbal communication may also cause you to perceive that individual in a particular way. Seiter, Weger, Kinzer, and Jensen (2009) studied "whether a debater's background nonverbal behavior affected audience perceptions of her and her opponent's likeability" (p. 1). Four versions of a televised debate were created with the nonspeaking opponent shown on a sub-screen while listening to the speaker shown on the main screen. In one version, the nonspeaking opponent had a "neutral expression." In another, the nonspeaking opponent showed "occasional disagreement." In the third version, the nonspeaking opponent showed almost "constant disagreement" while in the fourth version, both "agreement and disagreement" were displayed by the nonspeaking opponent.

After viewing the debates, the participants rated the debaters' likeability. Analysis indicated that the "background behavior had no effect on perceptions of the speaking debater's likeability ratings. This suggests that, when judging a candidate's likeability, audiences rely on the candidate's own behavior, perhaps not trusting the opinion of the nonspeaking opponent, who may be seen as biased. On the other hand, such behavior was associated with lower likeability ratings for the debater who was communicating nonverbally" (Seiter et al., 2009, pp. 7–8).

Our perception shapes the impressions, or mental images, we form of others. Have you ever met a person for the first time and after only a few minutes of speaking with that individual thought to yourself, "What a friendly person?" You may also have met someone for the first time and not been impressed at all. Perhaps you've heard the phrase, "You never get a second chance to make a first impression." If so, you begin to realize the importance of first impressions. While first impressions are powerful, we need to keep an open mind and build on our initial perceptions in order to develop an accurate perception of that person.

When we perceive someone to be similar to us, we may decide to develop and maintain a relationship with that person (Wright, 2004). Consider the importance of similarity when initiating and developing relationships with others. If you start a new job and meet a colleague at employee orientation who attended the same college and shares a passion for the same professional baseball team, your apparent similarity with this person may cause you to perceive that you both view things in the same way.

Earlier in the chapter we discussed the impact of stereotyping. At times, we form impressions of others based on the stereotypes we hold. Our stereotypes may be positive or negative; however, we always need to be mindful of the fact that just because someone belongs to a certain group, it does not mean that person possesses all of the qualities you have come to expect about that group or that your stereotypes are accurate. Unfortunately, many of us hold on to our first impressions even when we receive information that contradicts those impressions. If you believe someone is insincere, you may maintain that impression even in the face of contrary evidence. Certainly, we need to keep an open mind about others and allow ourselves to move beyond first impressions when we receive new information that helps us obtain more accurate perceptions of others.

Another problem with our perceptions of others is that we may focus on the negative as opposed to the positive. Clearly, if the negative aspects overshadow the positive ones, we have a right to take that into consideration. However, if the individual has several positive qualities and we focus exclusively on one negative aspect, this distorts our perception of that person and influences our relationship.

Finally, when we are forming our impressions of others, we need to keep in mind that not everyone acts or thinks like us. Often, we assume that others hold similar beliefs, values, and attitudes. Have you ever pulled a prank on someone that you thought was funny, but the person became upset by your actions? While you may view your prank as humorous, the person pranked may consider it childish. The differing perceptions of your behavior may negatively impact your interaction with one another.

Improving How We Perceive Others

People may not always form accurate perceptions of others. How can we avoid the potential pitfalls of impression formation and improve our perceptions of others? First, we need to keep an open mind. Although we may form first impressions, we need to make sure we continue to gather more information and be willing to modify our impressions. Being open to receiving new information about the other person, even if it goes against our first impression, is important.

Another way to improve how we perceive others is through empathy. *Empathy* is the ability to understand how someone else is feeling or thinking. Seeing something from another person's perspective can help us understand what that individual is experiencing and how it may impact their communication. For example, if a parent and a teenager have a disagreement about a curfew, if they each stop for a minute and consider the perspective of the other, they may better understand one another's concerns and this may help to reduce the potential for conflict. Perhaps the parent could ask herself, "How would I feel if I were a 16-year-old?" in an attempt to see things from the teen's point of view. The teenager could reflect, "I guess if I was the parent, I would probably be nervous that something bad was going to happen to my child." The process of perspective-taking enhances our ability to see things from the other person's point of view and enables us to communicate more effectively.

Finally, as we mentioned earlier in the chapter, it is wise to check your perceptions. This will help ensure that the way in which you have interpreted something is actually how the other person intended to convey it. The same strategies you use to make sure your perceptions of situations are correct can be used to gain more accurate perceptions of others. Overall, increasing the accuracy of our perceptions helps reduce the potential for miscommunication. This approach can help us gain clarification, withhold judgment, and limit defensiveness.

KEY TERMS

- Empathy
- Interpretation
- Organization
- Perception
- Perception checking
- Perception process
- Reflected appraisal

- Selection
- Self-concept
- Self-esteem
- Self-fulfilling prophecy
- Self-presentation
- Self-serving bias
- Stereotypes

REFERENCES

Brann, M., & Himes, K. L. (2010). Perceived credibility of male versus female television newscasters. *Communication Research Reports, 27*(3), 243–252.

Furnham, A. (1982). Explanations for unemployment in Britain. *Journal of European Social Psychology, 12,* 335–352.

Goffman, E. (1959). *The presentation of self in everyday life.* Garden City, NY: Doubleday/Anchor Books.

Guadagno, R. E., Okdie, B. M., & Kruse, S. A. (2012). Dating deception: Gender, online dating, and exaggerated self-presentation. *Computers in Human Behavior, 28,* 642–647.

Seiter, J. S., Weger, Jr., H., Kinzer, H. J., & Jensen, A. S. (2009). Impression management in televised debates: The effect of background nonverbal behavior on audience perceptions of debaters' likeability. *Communication Research Reports, 26*(1), 1–10.

Sullivan, H. S. (1953). *The interpersonal theory of psychiatry.* New York: Norton.

Toma, C., Hancock, J., & Ellison, N. (2007). *Separating fact from fiction: An examination of deceptive self-presentation in online dating profiles.* Paper presented at the annual meeting of the International Communication Association.

Wood, J. T. (2007). *Gendered lives: Communication, gender, and culture* (7th ed.). Belmont, CA: Thomson Wadsworth.

Wright, K. B. (2004). On-line relational maintenance strategies and perceptions of partners within exclusively Internet-based and primarily Internet-based relationships. *Communication Studies, 55,* 418–432.

Chapter Seven

Interpersonal Communication

© Sharaf Maksumov/Shutterstock.com

In this chapter:

**If you were asked the question, "Are you currently involved in a relationship?" how would you respond? When we've presented this question to our own classes, more than half of the students are typically reluctant to raise their hand. However, after some encouragement we are able to persuade all students to raise their hand. A narrow perception of what constitutes a "relationship" causes them to refrain from responding. Usually students indicate that they perceive a relationship to be romantic in nature. The reality is that you are involved in a variety of relationships. In this chapter we examine how we use communication to initiate relationships and explore the progression of relationships from that first "hello." We also analyze the challenges of maintaining relationships over time and the strategies used to manage tensions we experience in relationships and provide suggestions for creating a satisfying communication climate.

INTERPERSONAL COMMUNICATION DEFINED

Interpersonal communication is defined as communication between two people in which one person stimulates meaning in the mind of the other. Whether you engage in conversation to reduce ambiguity about a biology class or share experiences as first-year college students, search the Internet for information to help build effective relationships or engage in conversation with others who share similar attitudes and beliefs, you have used communication to accomplish your goals. Chances are that you have engaged in interpersonal communication with a variety of individuals. When we engage in interpersonal communication with others, relationships may be formed.

TYPES OF INTERPERSONAL RELATIONSHIPS

When we asked you to indicate if you were currently involved in a relationship, your initial reaction may have been one of hesitation. As mentioned earlier, our initial perception of what constitutes a relationship typically focuses on romantic ties. By expanding our definition to include the wide variety of relationships we form, the impact of interpersonal communication on relationship formation is obvious. Relationships are created and defined by the mutual exchange of information and feelings over time. Within the various contexts of our lives, we form countless relationships with others as we exchange messages and communicate.

Some examples of relationships that have been examined by communication scholars include friendships, workplace relationships, physician–patient relationships, family relationships, educational relationships, and, of course, romantic relationships. Within each context, several relationships may exist simultaneously. For example, workplace relationships may include a variety of connections, including those between coworkers, supervisors, and subordinates as well as organizational members and their customers or clients. Similarly, our family interactions may consist of parent–child relationships, sibling relationships, and other connections with relatives. Researchers have also devoted

© Monkey Business Images/Shutterstock.com

attention to the study of educational relationships that are formed between teachers and students, or among students themselves. Each of these relationship contexts is unique, and we are strategic in our approaches to communication in each of them. After all, our relationships with our parents are managed much differently than those with our boss or coworkers. For example, while you may feel comfortable openly disagreeing with your sibling or parent, restraint may be in order if you don't see eye to eye with your boss.

Have you ever stopped to think about "why" or "how" each of your relationships began? In some instances, relationship formation is involuntary. We are born into our family and have no choice in selecting our parents, siblings, grandparents, and other family relationships. Similarly, it's rare that we get to pick and choose who we want to work with when hired for a new job. Other relationships are voluntary. Romantic partners choose one another based on looks or compatibility, patients have a choice of doctors to see when seeking medical treatment, and friendships may be formed for a variety of reasons. Regardless of whether our relationships are voluntary or involuntary, communication is the foundation for initiating, maintaining, and strengthening our connections with others. Likewise, poor communication may cause an interpersonal relationship to break down and even terminate.

RELATIONSHIP STAGES

Can you recall how you first met your best friend? What did you say to one another? Berger and Calabrese (1975) examined communication that takes place when we first initiate a relationship. Through their research they identified three primary stages of interaction that are experienced when speaking with someone for the first time: entry, personal, and exit (Figure 7.1).

The *entry stage* of relationship development relies heavily on cultural or societal expectations for behavioral norms. During this stage, individuals engage in "small talk," which is characterized by the sharing of basic demo-

Interactions during relationship stages.

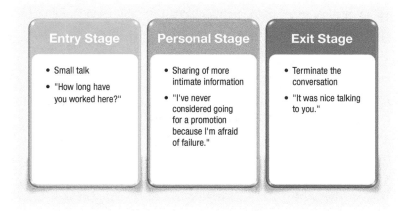

graphic information. Conversations are filled with back-and-forth questions such as "Where are you originally from?" or "What's your major?" Questions that are asked during this stage often follow societal norms for the initial stages of a relationship. Consider how you would respond to the question, "How are you?" Social norms would predict that you would say, "Fine! How are you?" During this stage it would be considered inappropriate to ask questions of a more personal nature or provide a detailed in-depth response about your day. Typically our communication focuses on demographic or superficial information.

Once the decision has been made to continue the relationship past the initial stage, we progress to the second stage of relationship development. The *personal stage* is characterized by the exchange of more personal or emotional information such as one's attitudes, beliefs, and values. There is no specified timeline for progressing from the entry stage to the personal stage. As you reflect on your initial conversations with your close friends, you may have discovered that you had an immediate connection and began to disclose personal issues fairly soon. Others may find that they need to spend more time in the "getting to know you" phase before moving on to share more personal information. While you may be willing to tell someone what your major is when asked, revealing the reasons for choosing your major or sharing why you're passionate about your field of study is often reserved for the personal stage.

The *exit stage* of relationship development involves making the decision to terminate or end the pursuit of a relationship. During this phase we decide if there is sufficient liking or similarity to continue our relationship. Can you recall a time when you met someone, but your communication focused solely on demographic questions and eventually you determined that you had nothing in common? It's important to note that we do not necessarily progress through all three of these stages. After all, you're probably able to recall a time when you met someone, exchanged some basic information about yourself, and quickly came to the conclusion that you didn't have enough in common to continue the conversation. Both verbal and nonverbal messages are used to indicate a lack of interest in pursuing a relationship. Avoiding eye contact or crossing one's arms and taking a step backward may signal disinterest, or a polite and vague statement such as "See you around sometime!" may signal that the relationship will not continue.

While it's important to understand "how" we use communication to start or initiate new relationships, we also need to explore the primary reasons why we decide to interact with others in the first place.

ATTRACTION THEORY

Byrne (1997) proposed that we are initially drawn to others on the basis of attraction. The reasons why we are attracted to others vary depending on our needs or goals. Suppose you were to create three lists that address the following questions:

► What are the characteristics that you consider physically attractive about another person?
► What are the characteristics that you look for when deciding with whom you would enjoy "hanging out" or spending free time together?
► What characteristics are important to you when deciding who you want to collaborate with on a group project?

If you were to compare the things included on each of the three lists, chances are that they would be different. McCroskey and McCain (1974) identified three different types of attraction that come into play when deciding to initiate a relationship (Figure 7.2). When we hear the word *attractive*, our initial instinct is to identify physical characteristics. *Physical attraction* refers to those aspects that cause us to be physically drawn toward another. Perhaps you've heard the phrase "Beauty is in the eye of the beholder." This reinforces the notion that each person has a unique perspective regarding what they view to be physically attractive. Some may be drawn to a particular hair or eye color, and others may focus on muscular physique or height. Earlier in this chapter we identified different types of relationships that we form. Romantic relationships are most often initiated as a result of physical attraction between two people.

FIGURE 7.2

Types of relational attraction.

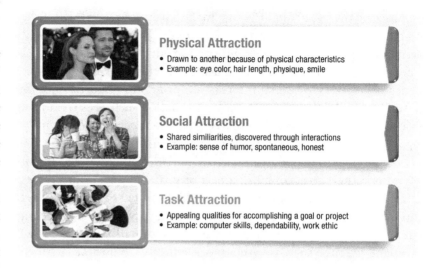

While physical attraction plays an influential role in our initial decisions to communicate and attempt to form relationships with others, it is only one type of attraction. As we talk to one another and exchange personal information, we may discover that not only are we physically attracted to the person, but there are social aspects that we are drawn to as well.

A second set of characteristics that influence decisions to form relationships is *social attraction*. While physical attraction focuses on physical characteristics, social attraction is defined as those characteristics that we seek in forming relationships with those whom we enjoy spending time and socializing. What qualities would you use to describe your best friend? Instead of focusing on their eye color or physique, chances are

---

FRIENDSHIPS IN THE WORKPLACE: BLENDING THE PERSONAL AND PROFESSIONAL

Should we be friends with our coworkers? A *Forbes* article (Habelow, 2010) reported that 67% of U.S. Americans feel that their workplace friendships make their jobs more enjoyable. Consider the fact that we sometimes spend more waking hours with our coworkers than those outside of the office. *Forbes* indicated that employees classify their workplace in three ways:

- 38% report that they are "personal friends" with a coworker and they communicate with one another "after hours" in addition to during work

- 32% described workplace friendships as "work friends" and indicated that they view the relationship as strictly limited to the office

- 17% viewed their relationship as created in an attempt to fulfill a workplace goal—to form associations or partnerships in order to accomplish work-related tasks

But before you rush out to form new friendships with your coworkers, consider the 12% of employees who said that they felt these workplace relationships were "risky," and the 37% who thought that it was best to separate the personal from the professional. While managers report that workplace friendships seem to build strong, cohesive teams, others emphasize the challenges of boundary issues and the potential for socializing to interfere with productivity. While we may be linked by our task attraction, elements of social attraction begin to emerge as we spend time together and begin to share details of our personal lives.

that you would use descriptors such as "honest," "spontaneous," or "funny" to explain why you enjoy spending time together. Friendships are the type of relationships that are most often described by referencing one's social attractiveness. However, it is not unusual for romantic partners to also explain their relationship by emphasizing the social qualities that make a partner special. This is because self-disclosure, or sharing private and intimate information with others, is often considered the foundation of social attraction. It's not until we begin talking with one another and sharing our preferences and attitudes that we discover shared similarities or compatibility. While social media sites provide a forum for posting photos for evaluating physical attractiveness, sharing of personal information promotes opportunities for forming relationships based on social attraction. Facebook profiles include information such as current place of employment, schools attended, and favorite quotes. Our "likes" are shared with the Facebook community. Others are able to see if we like Reese's Cups, Brad Paisley, or the Pittsburgh Steelers, and this information enables us to identify shared interests.

Task attraction focuses on characteristics that we seek in forming working relationships where we depend on others to accomplish a task or goal. Suppose your professor or boss instructed you to form your "ideal" project team. What qualities would draw you to invite others to work in your group? Dependability, a solid work ethic, and strong attention to detail may be some of the important aspects you would seek in your team. After all, their dazzling smile, dimples, shared interest in the *Twilight* book series, or sense of humor may make the time spent together more enjoyable, but these factors may not necessarily facilitate your progress toward your work goal. Instead, skills, attitudes, and work ethics are the primary qualities that we focus on in evaluating another as one with whom we would like to work on a project.

Depending on our needs or goals, we use one of the three types of attraction as the basis for initiating and forming relationships. Once we've identified our goal and evaluated someone as being attractive, the next step involves sharing information so we know what to expect.

UNCERTAINTY REDUCTION THEORY

How would you feel if your professor distributed a course syllabus that included the following list of assignments that would be used to assign your grade:

- ► Tests
- ► Term paper
- ► Discussion/participation

Suppose that no additional information is provided. How would you respond? Chances are that you would ask questions in order to clarify the expectations for the class. Some questions that may immediately come to mind may include:

- ► How many tests?
- ► What is the format for the exams: multiple choice, short answer, or essay?
- ► How many points is each exam worth?
- ► What chapters will be covered on each test?
- ► When will the tests be given?

Humans are generally uncomfortable with uncertainty. Just as there would be questions that need to be answered to reduce ambiguity about a class syllabus, there is also a need for information to decrease our uncertainty when forming relationships. Communication is the tool that we use to reduce our uncertainty, and question-asking is the most common strategy to reduce our initial discomfort or ambiguity.

In 1975, Berger and Calabrese established *Uncertainty Reduction Theory* to explain how we use communication in the initial stages of a relationship to decrease our uncertainty about the other person. This theory describes how we use verbal and nonverbal communication in order to decrease our level of ambiguity. It proposes that in situations where we are uncertain, we increase our communication to help us understand others and better predict how they may respond. While we may be physically attracted to someone, it is difficult to determine if we want to pursue a relationship until we actually talk with them. Eye contact and smiling are nonverbal cues that may indicate that the person is open to initiating a conversation and then verbal communication takes over. Job interviews are one way that potential employers and candidates reduce their uncertainty about one another. Even after a new employee is hired, the uncertainty reduction continues. Employee orientation programs provide valuable information about benefits and expectations, and during casual conversations in the break room or at lunch you may discover that your new boss is not a "morning person" and thus you should avoid approaching her with questions until after she's had her third cup of coffee.

COLLEGE STUDENTS AND DATING: WHAT'S YOUR GOAL?

Mongeau, Serewicz, and Therrien (2004) surveyed college students and asked them to identify their primary reason or "goal" for going on their most recent first date. Three "first-date goals" were identified:

1. **Reduce uncertainty** – the first date provides an opportunity to gain more information about the other person's attitudes, interests, and goals to determine if a relationship could be pursued

2. **Enjoyment** – views the date as an opportunity to simply have fun

3. **Relational escalation** – attempts to explore the potential for the relationship to progress into "something more" and leads to additional dates; explores romantic feelings

---

Most people use one of three tactics to reduce uncertainty: active, passive, and interactive strategies (Figure 7.3 on the following page). *Active strategies* involve soliciting information by asking third parties about another person. For example, if you are attracted to your friend's sibling, you may casually ask your friend if he or she is currently seeing anyone. At times, more discreet or indirect strategies are preferred to decrease our ambiguity. *Passive strategies* are implicit or unintended means to gather information during the initial stages of a relationship. Scanning someone's Facebook page, glancing at their hand to see if they're wearing a wedding ring, or observing them as they interact with others in the campus cafeteria are all passive strategies to reduce uncertainty. *Interactive strategies*, or direct communication, are an additional tactic for uncovering information about others. Directly asking a coworker what he thinks about a new reality show on television, seeking clarification from your instructor about concepts that will be included on an exam, or posting a question to a political candidate's blog to solicit additional information on an economics project are all interactive strategies to reduce ambiguity.

FIGURE 7.3
FIGURE 7.3
Uncertainty reduction strategies.

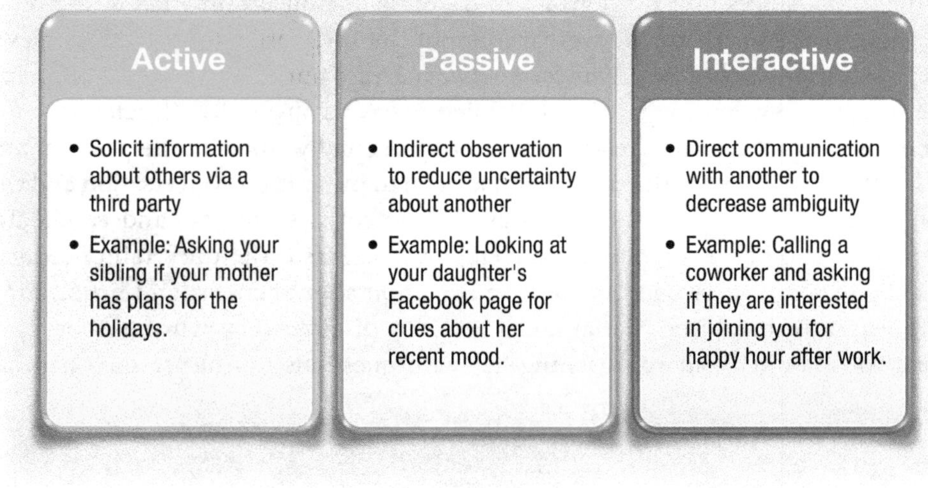

Active	Passive	Interactive
• Solicit information about others via a third party	• Indirect observation to reduce uncertainty about another	• Direct communication with another to decrease ambiguity
• Example: Asking your sibling if your mother has plans for the holidays.	• Example: Looking at your daughter's Facebook page for clues about her recent mood.	• Example: Calling a coworker and asking if they are interested in joining you for happy hour after work.

SELF-DISCLOSURE

Answering questions and exchanging information is an important part of the uncertainty reduction process. *Self-disclosure* refers to the sharing of personal information with others in an attempt to build or maintain a relationship. Our decision about what types of information to reveal and how much to share is often determined by the status of our relationship.

Breadth refers to the variety of topics we are willing to discuss with others. In the initial stages of a relationship, we tend to "play it safe" and discuss a wide array of demographic or superficial information as we attempt to reduce our level of uncertainty and get to know someone. During this time, we may focus on sharing only a little bit of information about a wide variety of topics. Speed dating offers a glimpse into just how quickly a variety of topics can be discussed. In this process, couples are given approximately 10 minutes to find out if they are potentially compatible. The goal is to meet several different people at a dating event rather than spending 2–3 hours on a date only to discover later that they had nothing in common with one another. A rapid exchange of information occurs, and the speed-daters quickly share information on topics ranging from occupation, life goals, hobbies, favorite foods, musical interests, and more. Given the time constraints, the opportunity to engage in an in-depth discussion about topics isn't possible.

WHO'S MORE APPREHENSIVE ABOUT EXPRESSIONS OF COMMITMENT?

While men are often stereotyped as being more apprehensive to express their commitment in a relationship, a 2013 article published in the United Kingdom's *Daily Mail* newspaper actually reports the opposite. On average men say those three little words (AKA: "I love you") 88 days after engaging in a serious relationship, compared to the 134 days that women wait before saying them. Men are also more likely to disclose their intimate feelings during the first month of dating, with 39% of men saying "I love you" compared with 23% of women.

Source: When WILL he say "I love you"? (n.d.).

The level of intimacy or details that you share about a given topic is referred to as the *depth* dimension of disclosure. Cultural and social norms often dictate what information is appropriate to share depending on the length of the relationship and the context or setting. During an interview, a candidate may answer questions about a variety of topics. At that time, there isn't an opportunity to discuss long-term goals for professional development or specific attitudes about a work team's compatibility. Sharing of personal attitudes and opinions is often reserved until after you've been employed with the organization for a while and are asked to share your thoughts during an annual employee review. Similarly, would it be appropriate to say "I love you" on a first date? Probably not. Disclosures of this depth would be reserved until partners have spent some time getting to know one another.

While the majority of research on self-disclosure has focused on face-to-face interactions, scholars are now exploring the ways in which information exchange has evolved on social media sites. Consider the types of information that are shared on sites such as eHarmony, Match.com, Facebook, LinkedIn, Twitter, and Instagram. Before social media, several conversations or dates may have been needed before reaching a point where we comfortably share personal information that is publicly displayed in online profiles and status updates. Now we openly reveal information that was previously reserved for possibly a third or fourth conversation with another person. By the time we meet one another face-to-face, our conversations focus on more intimate or personal sharing about topics already identified by scanning a Facebook page or online dating profile. In the professional context, interviewers may find they no longer need to ask a potential employee to disclose the reasons for leaving a previous job if the information was posted on a LinkedIn profile or Facebook page. Even university presidents and elected officials have turned to social media to disclose their attitudes and thoughts with public audiences. At Butler County Community College, President Nicholas Neupauer, Ed.D., created a President's Blog to share his attitudes about a variety of topics, ranging from "Superbowl XVII: 10 Reasons Not to Watch" to revealing details about his own experiences as a student (*www.bc3.edu/president*). Social media outlets provide celebrities with the opportunity to connect with their fans through personal disclosures. From Hillary Duff's sharing of her baby's first photos on Instagram to Mariah Carey's tweet to disclose the title of her next album, celebrities use these channels to create relationships with their fans and to enhance perceptions of closeness.

The option of sharing information openly and freely online comes with some cautions and responsibilities. Keep in mind that anything that is disclosed on Internet sites has the potential to be viewed by the public. As a rule of thumb, if you wouldn't be comfortable having your parents or employers read the information you share, think twice before disclosing it. Fortunately, sites provide users with the opportunity to manage

---

Facebook Disclosures: What Are We Sharing?

A 2010 study by Nosko, Wood, and Molema identified three types of information that Facebook users disclose on their profiles:

- Standard/identifying information – demographic information that enables others to locate you online (e.g., gender, email address, profile photo, city/state of residence)
- Sensitive/personal information – detailed information that could be used to locate a person (e.g., current status, tagged photos, employer, and relationship status)
- Potentially stigmatizing information – information that could be viewed as socially stigmatizing by others (e.g., sexual orientation, birth year, religious or political views)

Who is more likely to "play it safe" when posting information to their Facebook page? The study found that as we get older, we refrain from disclosing as much personal information on social media sites. How does relationship status impact the type of information that we publicly disclose to others? Those who are single and interested in pursuing a romantic relationship tend to disclose more information than those who are already involved in a committed relationship.

who they allow to see the breadth and depth of their disclosures through the use of privacy settings. While you may share a breadth of information—ranging from your anticipation for the upcoming weekend, frustration with a midterm exam, or exhaustion from a long shift at work—privacy settings enable you to limit who is able to read the depth of your disclosures. You can create a closed Facebook group with your friends to discuss a professor's class assignments in more detail, or private messages can be sent to coworkers to vent about a slacker on a recent project that you completed at the office.

Disclosure and liking often go hand-in-hand. Kowalski (1999) found that the more we like someone, the more likely we are to share personal information. As we exchange more disclosures with one another, our liking for one another tends to increase. The challenge lies in determining what information is "safe" to share and at what point in our relationship should we disclose it. Recall our earlier discussion of Uncertainty Reduction Theory. Employers attempt to reduce their level of ambiguity about potential employees by asking them to disclose or share personal information about themselves that is directly relevant to the job. However, due to the fact that you may have only briefly met the interviewer, you may be uncomfortable disclosing your answers to questions such as "What is your biggest weakness?" or "What are your salary expectations?" The awkwardness experienced may be explained by the lack of reciprocal disclosures that are exchanged in an interview setting. Interviewees are expected to share a lot of information, whereas interviewers reveal very little about themselves. *Reciprocal self-disclosure* refers to the notion that individuals will engage in a similar exchange in terms of the types of information shared and the amount of information disclosed when communicating with one another. Consider how awkward it would be for an instructor to ask students to disclose their most embarrassing moments during an icebreaker activity on the first day of class. Even though everyone would be expected to share a similar story, the disclosures would be perceived as inappropriate given the fact that individuals have just met one another. The following exchange illustrates our expectations for reciprocal disclosures in our interpersonal relationships.

KYLA: Wow! I'm overwhelmed! There has been so much information shared during today's new employee orientation that my head is spinning!

ANDRE: I know what you mean, but don't worry. We're in this together. My cousin got me this job, and he said that the first few days are overwhelming. By the way, my name is Andre.

KYLA: I'm so sorry for venting! I'm Kyla. It's nice to meet you.

ANDRE: No worries! To be honest, I'm feeling overwhelmed, too! I don't think I took as many notes in my entire college career as I've taken today. Where did you work before joining Avicon?

KYLA: Actually, this is my first job. I just graduated from West Virginia University in May.

ANDRE: No way! I'm a WVU alum, too! Communication studies major from the Class of 2010. What was your major?

KYLA: Corporate communication! Did you ever have Dr. Simpson for COMS 2040?

ANDRE: She was the best! I learned so much from her final case study project. What a small world! By the way, I'm meeting my cousin for coffee in the cafeteria after orientation. He's going to try to give me some "inside scoop" on what to expect on my first day on the job here. Would you like to join us?

KYLA: That's so nice of you to invite me. I'd love to!

Both new employees engage in reciprocal disclosures by sharing their mutual feelings of being overwhelmed, and as a result of their conversation they discover that they both attended the same school and studied with the same professors. As one person shares new and significant information that is revealed because of his or her increased trust and comfort with the other, the other discloses as well.

As you consider what information to share and when to share it, consider the following guidelines to ensure that you practice effective and appropriate self-disclosure:

- ► How well do I know the other person? Can I trust him or her with the information I'm about to share?
- ► If I share this information, do I risk embarrassing myself or the other person?
- ► Is our relationship at a point where sharing this information is appropriate? Will I seem pushy or do I feel pressured to disclose?
- ► How relevant is the information that I'm sharing?

Asking yourself these four simple questions may be the key to ensuring that your disclosures are appropriate and effective in reducing uncertainty and initiating relationships with others. As the level of intimacy and the nature of our relationships change, so do our disclosures.

SOCIAL PENETRATION THEORY

Altman and Taylor (1973) created *Social Penetration Theory* to explain how individuals share information with one another as relationships develop and move from one stage to another. Essentially, social penetration theory focuses on building and maintaining relational closeness. More specifically, the theory illustrates how we transition from discussing superficial topics in the beginning stages of a relationship to exchanging more private and personal information as the relationship becomes more intimate. Altman and Taylor used the analogy of an onion to describe the layers of information that are revealed as relationships become more intimate. Fans of the movie *Shrek* may recall how Shrek uses the onion analogy to disclose his feelings and emotions to Donkey:

SHREK: For your information, there's a lot more to ogres than people think.
DONKEY: Example?
SHREK: (*holds up an onion, which Donkey sniffs*) Example . . . uh . . . ogres are like onions!
DONKEY: They stink?
SHREK: Yes... No!
DONKEY: Oh, they make you cry?
SHREK: No!
DONKEY: Oh, you leave 'em out in the sun, they get all brown, start sproutin' little white hairs . . .
SHREK: (*peels an onion*) No! Layers. Onions have layers. Ogres have layers. Onions have layers. You get it? We both have layers. (*walks off*)
DONKEY: Oh, you both have *layers*. Oh. You know, not everybody likes onions. What about cake? Everybody loves cake! **

© Maridav/Shutterstock.com

MODELS OF SELF-DISCLOSURE

Social Penetration Model by Irwin Altman and Dalmas Taylor

The Social Penetration Model is a model of relationship bonding in which self-disclosure represents two interconnected components:

▶ **Depth:** a shift from non-revealing messages to more personal messages.
▶ **Breadth** which includes the range of topics.

When describing how this might look, Altman and Taylor used an onion to show the different layers of personality and even called it the "onion theory." Here is a diagram of how this might look as time passes and the layers of our personality begin to reveal the center or the core of a person.

#6: This illustrates the very core of our being and is the area where we honestly reveal the concept of ourselves and our self-worth.

#5: The arrow is pointing one level above the core—also, the center of the onion. This is the point where we reveal our deepest secrets and most intimate information regarding our deeply held fears and fantasies.

#4: This area illustrates our religious convictions.

#3: This arrow shows where we reveal our goals and aspirations for life.

#2: This area—almost to the surface—is where we share our preference for clothes, music, food, and other areas which are not completely private.

#1: This outside area illustrates information we provide to the world that is not private at all and includes our name, age, and gender.

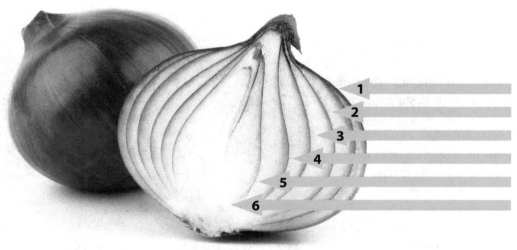

© Amero/Shutterstock.com. Adapted by Kendall Hunt Publishing Company

**The onion analogy helps illustrate the various levels of information that we reveal as our relationships progress from initiation to more intimate stages. Altman and Taylor identified four levels of information that we're willing to disclose depending on the nature of our relationships. These include superficial, personal, intimate and private information.

During our initial meeting with others, we tend to focus on more *superficial* or demographic information. Topics such as your college major and hometown are considered "safe" topics to disclose when we first meet someone. As our relationship progresses, we tend to reveal more *personal information* such as our favorite foods, hobbies, and pet peeves. Once we feel comfortable with the other person and have established a level of trust in our relationship, more *intimate information* is shared. Our experiences, occupational goals, and values are examples of topics that are disclosed at this level. *Private information* is often reserved for only our closest relationships. At this level, secrets such as our fears, hopes, and personal challenges are only shared with those with whom we've established a high level of trust.

Keep in mind that our disclosures progress from being superficial to private. Our decision to peel away layers of the onion and reveal the next layer of information depends on three factors:

▶ The costs versus the rewards of sharing the information (e.g., benefits vs. risks)
▶ Our satisfaction with the relationship
▶ The level of trust or security we feel with the other

We make decisions associated with social penetration in each of our interpersonal relationships. Depending on their level of closeness, a child may decide to reveal more intimate details with one parent as opposed to the other. For example, Janelle may find that she feels more comfortable sharing her fears about the upcoming birth of her baby with her mother rather than her stepfather. Employees share different information with coworkers and supervisors depending on the level of trust. Alaina may disclose to her coworkers that she has been calling in sick so that she can take care of her elderly mother who has been having health issues. She is not willing to share the same information with her supervisor because she's afraid that he will perceive her as being distracted by her mother's health concerns and not capable of leading her team of coworkers. She perceives the risks of telling her boss about the health issues as outweighing the benefits, so she keeps that information hidden from him.

FROM INITIATION TO INTIMACY: THE RELATIONSHIP DEVELOPMENT MODEL AND COMING TOGETHER

Now that we've examined the role that communication plays in our relationships, let's explore the ways in which our relationships progress from the beginning stages to the most intimate levels. Knapp (1978; Knapp & Vangelisti, 2003) expanded the model initially proposed by Berger and Calabrese (1975) and created the relationship development model to explain how individuals engage in initial conversations and build on their communication as they progress from one stage to the next in relationships.

Initiating

Have you ever struggled with finding the "right" words to say when you meet someone for the first time? *Initiating* a relationship focuses on the initial communication that occurs when we first meet someone. Communication during this stage typically focuses on demographic information that is superficial and descriptive. Often the most challenging part of this stage is figuring out how to "break the ice" and start the conversation. Polite questions such as "Is this seat taken?" or "Hi, how are you?" are considered "safe" conversation-starters to determine if the other person is interested in continuing the conversation. Earlier in this chapter we discussed the role that attractiveness plays in our decisions to form relationships. Physical attractiveness is often one of the most influential factors when we're deciding to initiate a conversation. Nervous anticipation and anxiety are typical during this stage, and we feel pressure to find the perfect opening line. Unfortunately, this nervousness may cause some to resort to the use of "cheesy" pickup lines that are uncharacteristic of their normal behavior. Here are examples of ineffective conversation-starters.

SAMPLE PICKUP LINES

► Are you an interior decorator? Because when I saw you, the room became beautiful!
► If I was a stoplight, I'd turn red every time you passed by just so I could stare at you a little bit longer.
► Are you from Tennessee? Because you're the only 10 I see!
► I must be a snowflake because I've fallen for you!
► On a scale of 1 to 10, you're a 9. I'm the 1 you need.

In the initiation phase, portraying a good first impression is important. While you may be tempted to use a witty pickup line to start the conversation, the best advice is to just be yourself. Sincerity and confidence go a long way in making a good first impression.

Experimenting

Once you have survived the challenging (and sometimes awkward) task of initiating a conversation, the next stage of relationship development involves reducing your uncertainty about the other person. *Experimenting* involves the exchange of multiple questions and answers in an attempt to gain more information and identify areas of commonality. The focus of disclosure in this phase is on covering a breadth of topics. Safe topics of conversation that are often discussed during this stage include one's major, hobbies, or other demographic questions. Social attraction is often uncovered during this phase as partners exchange information to identify commonalities. Recall our earlier discussion of uncertainty reduction. This is the goal during the experimenting stage, and reciprocal disclosures are expected. You'll know that you're in the experimenting stage when

---

RELATIONSHIP INITIATION IN ACTION: *THE BIG BANG THEORY*

On the television sitcom The Big Bang Theory, the character Sheldon exhibits a clear lack of social skills that is showcased in his attempts to build and maintain interpersonal relationships. In the season 3 "The Maternal Congruence" episode, Sheldon's struggle is evidenced in his efforts to start a conversation with his roommate Leonard:

SHELDON: I made tea.

LEONARD: I don't want tea.

SHELDON: I didn't make tea for you. This is my tea.

LEONARD: Then why are you telling me?

SHELDON: It's a conversation-starter.

LEONARD: That's a lousy conversation-starter.

SHELDON: Oh, is it? We're conversing. Checkmate.

you experience a rapid exchange of questions and answers. Questions such as "So is this your first job since graduating from college?" may be followed with "Yes, but I interned with a similar company for my last semester so I'm familiar with this organization. Was this your first job after college?" While the majority of our relationships stop at this stage and we are satisfied with being merely acquaintances, there may be times when we decide to proceed even further. As a result of the information gathered during this phase, we may decide to continue to the next stage.

Intensifying

If we decide that our goal is to pursue a long-term relationship with another, chances are that we will proceed to the intensifying phase of the relational development model. *Intensifying* is characterized by more intimate expressions of commitment and by testing the impressions that others may have formed about the relationship. During this stage, the depth of disclosures become more intimate as we share personal information with one another. Knapp and Vangelisti (2003) identified three verbal clues that are characteristic of intensifying. These include:

- ► First-person plural references ("We need to decide what we're going to do next weekend so I can submit my work schedule.")
- ► Direct references to the relationship and commitment to one another ("I can't wait for you to meet my family at my cousin's wedding this summer!")
- ► Creation of nicknames for one another ("Pumpkin," "Sweetie")

While the initiating and experimenting phases are encountered at the start of almost all types of interpersonal relationships, intensifying is typically reserved for romantic relationships and close friendships. When we're uncertain about the other person's commitment to the relationship, this stage may incorporate secret tests to reduce our uncertainty. Examples of tests may include physical separation for a period of time or making public verbal references to the other as your "boyfriend" or "girlfriend" to gauge the reaction.

RELATIONSHIP INITIATION IN ACTION: *THE BIG BANG THEORY*

In "The Desperation Emancipation" episode in season 4, Sheldon's uncertainty about the status of his relationship with Amy is evidenced in the following conversation with his roommate Leonard:

(Sheldon yelling Leonard's name all the way down the stairs until he finds him)

LEONARD: Yeah, what?

SHELDON: Amy Farrah Fowler has asked me to meet her mother.

LEONARD: Yeah, so.

SHELDON: What does that mean?

LEONARD: Well, you know how you're always saying Amy is a girl who is your friend but not your girlfriend.

SHELDON: Uh huh.

LEONARD: Well, you can't say that anymore.

Integrating

During the *integrating* stage of relationship development, the lives of both partners begin to merge and their status as a couple is acknowledged both personally and publicly. Their identities begin to merge as their social circles come together and they begin to share a network of friends who also view them as a couple. For example, signs that a romantic relationship has reached the integrating stage may include the exchange of personal items such as clothing and pictures that can be used to indicate the status of their relationship to others.

Bonding

Bonding is the final stage of coming together. Formalized or legalized declarations of commitment mark this phase as couples publicly acknowledge their dedication to one another.

Perhaps the most common indicators of personal bonding are engagements and weddings. At this stage of the relationship, couples want to declare their goal to pursue a long-term, exclusive relationship. In our professional lives, we may engage in formal bonding as we enter into formal business partnerships with other companies or organizations.

Movement from one stage of relationship development to the next isn't necessarily as clear and concise as it may seem. Knapp and Vangelisti (2003) proposed the following things to consider as you evaluate your own relationships and determine which stage you may be currently experiencing:

1. While we typically progress through the stages in the order presented in the model, we may need to revisit prior stages in order to strengthen the relationship before continuing on to future stages.
2. As we decide whether to proceed to the next stage, each partner engages in an analysis of the potential rewards of continuing the relationship. Questions that we may ask ourselves include "Do I feel the same way the other person does?" and "Am I ready to move to the next stage of this relationship?"
3. Each relationship is unique in terms of the amount of time spent at each phase of the relationship development process. While some relationships may go through all five stages in a matter of a few months, other couples may need a few years before reaching the point of being ready to publicly declare their commitment.

Throughout this chapter we have answered some of the questions about how we use communication to form interpersonal relationships and described various stages that we experience as relationships progress from the beginning stages to more intimate levels. While most of the research on these stages has focused on romantic relationships, we encourage you to consider the role that communication plays in your own relationships as you transition from the initial stages of a relationship to the later stages. Each relationship that you experience is unique, from initiating a conversation with a new coworker or sharing information with a group of classmates via an online discussion board. It is important to consider the appropriateness of the information you self-disclose to others depending on the nature of the relationship. While the process of initiating relationships may be filled with anxiety, communication is the key to reducing your uncertainty and building connections that can last a lifetime. **

By now, you have learned that interpersonal communication skills are important for the workplace and in your personal lives. While you have a better understanding of how to initiate relationships, a savvy Communication Shark will want to take this a step further and explore ways to maintain and grow relationships. Remember that sharks never swim or move backward. They constantly move forward and toward their goals. With solid relationships as the goal, let's move forward and take your relationships to the next level.

**EXPECTATIONS IN RELATIONSHIPS

Have you ever stopped to consider the expectations you hold for yourself? Because you're enrolled in college, chances are you anticipate that you will earn a degree that will assist you in your career goals. What expectations do you have for your performance in classes? Do you expect to do well in your science courses? Now reflect on the expectations that you have for those with whom you have a relationship. You may anticipate that your parents will call you on your birthday, your best friend will keep a secret that you shared, or your coworkers will keep you informed of the latest "office gossip." But what happens when those expectations are not met? How do you react? If you're like most people, you probably experience feelings of disappointment, hurt, or even anger.

As humans, we all form expectations for ourselves and for others. If someone greets you with "Hi! How are you?" the expectation is that you will respond with, "Fine! And you?" Consider how you would react if the person responded with, "I've had a horrible week! I lost my student ID card, failed my history exam, and now my car won't start." Chances are you would abruptly end the conversation and wonder why they responded that way. *Relational expectations* are the explicit and implicit anticipations for ideal verbal and nonverbal responses. They consist of our forecasts or predictions for how others should behave or reply in a given situation.

Unspoken or unrealistic expectations are often cited as a problematic area in relationships. Ironically, at times we may find that we are unaware of the expectations we hold for others. It should come as no surprise that relationship problems arise when we don't clearly communicate or don't realize that we anticipate others to behave in particular ways. Consider the following example of Jayme, who was a newlywed. She anticipated that her new husband would prepare breakfast, have a fresh pot of coffee ready when she woke, and greet her by commenting on how beautiful she looked. She was frustrated and disappointed to find that her husband liked to sleep late and didn't enjoy breakfast or coffee. As Jayme complained to her mother, she was shocked when her mom responded by laughing. Her mother commented, "What did you expect, Jayme? After all, you didn't marry your father!" That's when Jayme realized that she expected her new husband to follow the same routine that her own father had practiced each morning with her mother. We all have preconceived notions about how others should behave or respond, but we may not always be aware of them ourselves.

Burgoon (1978) examined the role of communication in situations where our anticipations are not met. *Expectancy Violation Theory* examines our communication responses when our anticipations are not met. When a person does not meet our expectations, we call it a violation. While initially we may perceive violations as being negative, it's important to note that at times they may be positive. Consider our earlier example where you anticipate that your parents will acknowledge your birthday with a phone call. Imagine your surprise if a positive violation occurs when your parents arrive at your workplace at the end of your shift to take you out to dinner at your favorite restaurant where they present you with front-row tickets to your favorite band's sold-out concert. You expected a phone call but instead were pleasantly surprised by their visit, dinner, and tickets. The same scenario could also have resulted in a negative violation if you expected a phone call from your parents and they forgot your birthday. This would be upsetting because you assume that parents would always acknowledge their child's birthday. Afifi and Metts (1998) surveyed people about their expectations for friends and romantic partners and asked them to recall the last time they said or did something unexpected. Nine categories of relational expectancy violations were identified. Figure 7.4 summarizes these categories.

The nine categories include both positive and negative expectancy violations. Criticism, relationship de-escalation, transgressions, and acts of disregard tend to be perceived as violations that have negative implications in the relationship. Relationship escalation, acts of devotion, and gestures of inclusion are categories of violations that are typically viewed in positive ways. Uncharacteristic relational behavior and uncharacteristic social behavior may be perceived positively or negatively depending on the nature of the violation. Consider the example from Figure 7.4 in which a coworker flirts with you and then asks you on a date. If you are interested in the coworker, this could be perceived as a positive uncharacteristic relational behavior. However, if you are already involved in a romantic relationship and are not interested in the coworker, the flirting may cause you to feel uncomfortable and would be perceived negatively.

FIGURE 7.4

Afifi and Metts's (1998) categories of expectancy violations in relationships.

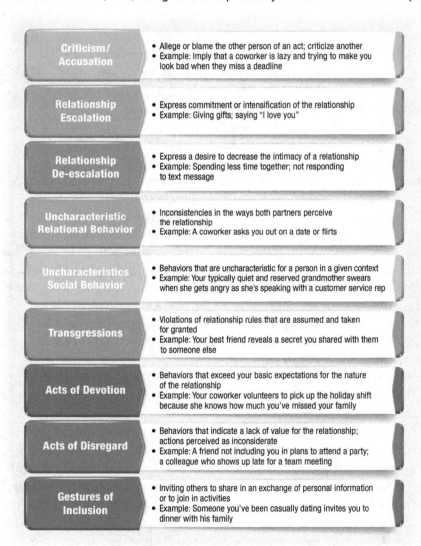

Criticism/ Accusation	• Allege or blame the other person of an act; criticize another • Example: Imply that a coworker is lazy and trying to make you look bad when they miss a deadline
Relationship Escalation	• Express commitment or intensification of the relationship • Example: Giving gifts; saying "I love you"
Relationship De-escalation	• Express a desire to decrease the intimacy of a relationship • Example: Spending less time together; not responding to text message
Uncharacteristic Relational Behavior	• Inconsistencies in the ways both partners perceive the relationship • Example: A coworker asks you out on a date or flirts
Uncharacteristics Social Behavior	• Behaviors that are uncharacteristic for a person in a given context • Example: Your typically quiet and reserved grandmother swears when she gets angry as she's speaking with a customer service rep
Transgressions	• Violations of relationship rules that are assumed and taken for granted • Example: Your best friend reveals a secret you shared with them to someone else
Acts of Devotion	• Behaviors that exceed your basic expectations for the nature of the relationship • Example: Your coworker volunteers to pick up the holiday shift because she knows how much you've missed your family
Acts of Disregard	• Behaviors that indicate a lack of value for the relationship; actions perceived as inconsiderate • Example: A friend not including you in plans to attend a party; a colleague who shows up late for a team meeting
Gestures of Inclusion	• Inviting others to share in an exchange of personal information or to join in activities • Example: Someone you've been casually dating invites you to dinner with his family

As you reflect on the list of expectations, consider how expectations permeate every relationship you encounter. From anticipated behavior during a job interview to perceptions of what's considered appropriate disclosures on one's Facebook page, we expect certain responses and behaviors. In order to avoid miscommunication, the best advice for healthy relationships is to clearly, explicitly communicate expectations. When others violate our expectations, pause and consider potential reasons why the violations occurred as opposed to rushing to judgment or jumping to conclusions. Doing so may help preserve the relationship. Sometimes our differing expectations for communication and behaviors in relationships may result in dialectical tensions.

DIALECTICAL TENSIONS

Can you recall a time when you were frustrated because you have an extremely close relationship with your best friend, yet you felt somewhat isolated from others? Maybe you've wondered why you've always enjoyed and looked forward to your family's annual summer vacations together at the Outer Banks, yet you yearn to go someplace different and exciting? Can you imagine the frustration you might experience if a professor didn't provide a syllabus outlining the schedule for the semester? While spontaneous class discussions and assignments may be a refreshing change from the traditional class format, the lack of structure and clarity about course grading and expectations may be frustrating. Expectations in our relationships create needs that motivate us to make choices about our communication. Sometimes we experience conflicting expectations, and there is a struggle between two opposing needs that we want to fulfill.

Baxter (1988) described *dialectical tensions* as contradictory pulls between opposing goals or desires in a relationship. She identified three primary dialectical tensions in her initial research.

Autonomy versus connectedness focuses on our desires to maintain our independence yet still be close to others. Consider the athlete who is dedicated to his team, yet also enjoys his individual time in the spotlight when he performs well during games. *Openness versus closedness* reflects our need to share information with others while keeping some aspects of our lives private. Teachers may allow students a glimpse into their personal lives by accepting friend requests from students and making some areas of their Facebook profile visible to the public, yet keeping some content private to cautiously refrain from sharing information that is too personal. *Novelty versus predictability* addresses our need to experience things that are new and different while simultaneously wanting routine and consistency. If your organization acquires a new company, you may look forward to the changes in your workplace and working with new colleagues, yet you worry about how you'll get along with one another and the impact the merger will have on your work responsibilities and routine.

How do these tensions influence our communication? In order to negotiate the tensions we experience in our relationships, we need to communicate with others. Consider the situation where you are comfortable and enjoy being part of a connected, committed relationship. However, from time to time you may experience a desire for a "night out" with your friends to maintain those relationships. Simply explaining your desire to spend time with others may help alleviate the chance of any inaccurate perceptions your partner may form. Reassurances about the relationship help confirm that you wish to remain connected while maintaining your own identity and friends.

Researchers have examined dialectical tensions across a variety of relationship contexts. It should come as no surprise that in long-distance relationships the tension most frequently experienced by romantic partners is the novelty versus predictability dialectic (Sahlstein, 2006). Couples plan times when they would communicate to ensure a level of certainty in their relationship, but also realize that the time spent apart produced uncertainty. In the professional context, employees indicate that openness and closedness is a tension often experienced with coworkers who are also considered to be close friends. Conflicting desires to be open in communicating with one another compete with workplace rules and guidelines for confidentiality of information (Baxter & Bridge, 1992).

Reflect on the tensions you have experienced in your own relationships with friends, family members, coworkers, or even classmates. Chances are you'll discover that you experience these struggles in virtually every relationship. The key is to communicate about the tensions when they arise in order to work through them instead of denying their existence. Doing so will enhance your ability to maintain your relationships with others.

RELATIONSHIP MAINTENANCE

As Ben Affleck pointed out in his Academy Awards speech, relationships take work. Not surprising, Duck (1988) pointed out that we spend more time maintaining and sustaining our relationships than in the initiation or termination phases of the relationship life cycle.

Maintaining the Existence of the Relationship

It is easier to keep in touch and maintain relationships now more than ever before. Social media sites such as Instagram and Facebook have made it easy for individuals to stay in contact with high school and college friends after graduation, and they enable families to share photos and keep up-to-date on activities from a distance. Before electronic media, family and friends often kept in touch with one another by sending cards at holidays and birthdays, or by making periodic phone calls to one another. By engaging in periodic communication with our friends, coworkers, and loved ones, we are at least able to keep the relationship alive.

Maintaining a Desired State in the Relationship

A second component of relational maintenance involves communicating to ensure that the status of the relationship "fits" with your goals and desires. Perhaps your goal is to maintain your current friendship with a coworker. This could be accomplished by extending invitations to go to lunch or out for drinks after work.

However, the goal may be to maintain the current state of the relationship and keep it from escalating and becoming more intimate. Suppose a coworker who you've been friends with for the past couple of years asks you out on a date. The notion of a romantic relationship with a coworker makes you uncomfortable, but you don't want to jeopardize your friendship. Once you identify your level of comfort with the relationship, you communicate in a way that will help you accomplish your relational goals.

Maintaining a Satisfactory State

Ensuring that both parties perceive the relationship as thriving and satisfactory is the goal of the third component of relationship maintenance. Friends from college may plan a weekend beach getaway in order to spend time together. While the sharing of text messages and Facebook posts keeps them connected in the interim, the annual trip and time spent together communicates how much they value the relationship. It is important to note that both individuals in a relationship should experience satisfaction with the current relationship state.

FIGURE 7.5

Communication strategies used to maintain relationships (Canary et al., 1993).

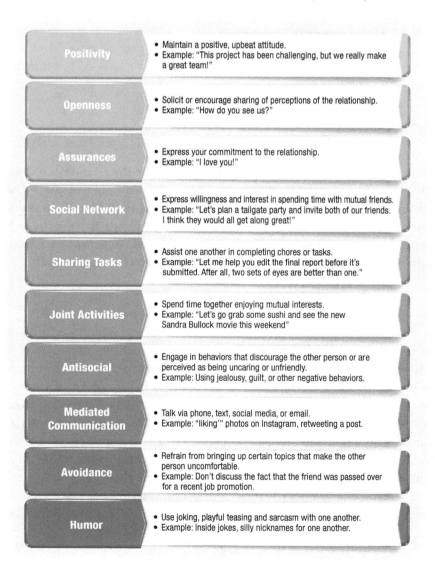

Positivity
- Maintain a positive, upbeat attitude.
- Example: "This project has been challenging, but we really make a great team!"

Openness
- Solicit or encourage sharing of perceptions of the relationship.
- Example: "How do you see us?"

Assurances
- Express your commitment to the relationship.
- Example: "I love you!"

Social Network
- Express willingness and interest in spending time with mutual friends.
- Example: "Let's plan a tailgate party and invite both of our friends. I think they would all get along great!"

Sharing Tasks
- Assist one another in completing chores or tasks.
- Example: "Let me help you edit the final report before it's submitted. After all, two sets of eyes are better than one."

Joint Activities
- Spend time together enjoying mutual interests.
- Example: "Let's go grab some sushi and see the new Sandra Bullock movie this weekend"

Antisocial
- Engage in behaviors that discourage the other person or are perceived as being uncaring or unfriendly.
- Example: Using jealousy, guilt, or other negative behaviors.

Mediated Communication
- Talk via phone, text, social media, or email.
- Example: "liking'" photos on Instagram, retweeting a post.

Avoidance
- Refrain from bringing up certain topics that make the other person uncomfortable.
- Example: Don't discuss the fact that the friend was passed over for a recent job promotion.

Humor
- Use joking, playful teasing and sarcasm with one another.
- Example: Inside jokes, silly nicknames for one another.

Repairing a Relationship

As we stated earlier, relationships require work. Maintaining relationships is a continual task that requires time and effort. Perhaps the recent birth of a new child has kept friends from enjoying weekly dinners together, and they begin to feel disconnected. Scheduling time to meet once a month for a meal or a movie communicates the value of the relationship and restores the level of closeness previously experienced. Because relationships take work, they will likely hit "rough spots" where the relationship isn't functioning as it has in the past. When this occurs, we have to repair the relationship.

What strategies do we use to maintain our relationships with others? A study by Canary, Stafford, Hause, and Wallace (1993) examined the communication strategies that we use to sustain our connections. These strategies are summarized in Figure 7.5 on the following page. As you review the list, notice that some of the tactics include negative behaviors such as avoidance and antisocial messages. Keep in mind that these may be effective in situations where we want to maintain a desired status in our relationship with another person. For example, if Xander only perceives Sierra as a friend when it becomes apparent that she is interested in pursuing a romantic relationship, he may flirt with other women in her presence to send a message that he's not interested in being more than friends. It's important to note that these behaviors have been studied across a variety of relationships, and researchers have found that friends, coworkers, romantic partners, and married couples report using many of the same strategies.

While we spend the vast majority of time invested in maintaining our relationships, there may come a time when it becomes apparent that the connection is beyond salvage or repair. In those instances, it may actually be healthier and ultimately more satisfactory for both partners to terminate the relationship as opposed to continue working on it.

RELATIONSHIP DISSOLUTION

Relationship dissolution occurs when one or both partners perceive the relationship as being dissatisfactory and make the decision to end their connection. Knapp (1978) also identified five stages that provide clues that a relationship may be in trouble and prompt partners to consider whether it is worth saving. It's important to keep in mind that partners may not necessarily perceive that they are experiencing the same stage at the same time. In fact, one person may "skip" a stage while the other follows them in sequence. Figure 7.6 summarizes Knapp's five stages that indicate that the quality of a relationship may be deteriorating.

Differentiating

In the initial stages of a relationship, partners spend considerable time communicating and getting to know one another better. In the *differentiating* stage, couples may find that they spend more time disagreeing or emphasizing their differences as opposed to focusing on the things they have in common. In fact, this stage may signal that two people involved in a relationship are heading in different directions. For example, Sasha states that she enjoys eating out; Kyla might comment that she is tired of going to restaurants and actually prefers cooking at home. Cory may talk about how much she looks forward to spending time with her friends, and Renea may comment on how annoying and obnoxious Cory's friends are. While on the surface it may appear as though this stage is solely negative, it can provide an opportunity for relational partners to reexamine their own individual identities and find ways in which to restore their independence. For example, Sasha might decide to go out to eat with friends a few times a week and Cory may go out with friends without Renea. Doing so can be beneficial when trying to manage the autonomy-versus-connectedness tensions that occur in relationships.

FIGURE 7.6

Knapp's and Vangelisti's (2003) stages of coming apart in relationships.

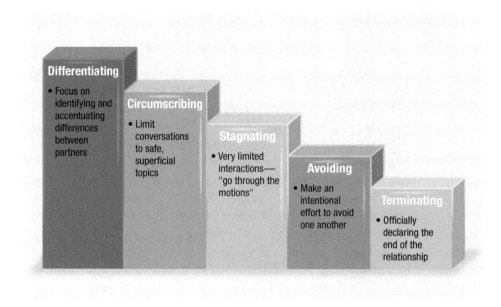

Circumscribing

The second stage of relationship dissolution, *circumscribing*, is indicated when couples begin to drift apart in the quality and quantity of their communication. Intimate conversations where thoughts, feelings, and dreams were shared are replaced with interactions that focus on safe, superficial topics. Questions such as "How was the traffic on your commute from work?" may be met with short responses such as "Lousy!" Partners find that they no longer feel comfortable engaging in discussions about intimate or personal topics.

Stagnating

Have you ever been near a stagnant pond? If so, you would probably describe the water as smelling "stale." It's quite appropriate that Knapp (1978) referred to his third stage of coming apart as *stagnating* since during this phase communication is at a standstill. Partners in this stage simply "go through the motions." They may attend events together, but once they return home they retreat into their own worlds with very little interaction between them. Conversations about the state of the relationship are ignored in an attempt to avoid a conflict. Preserving the relationship is no longer a priority, and it's almost as if they're playing a "waiting game." Eventually, the prospect of saving the relationship becomes difficult and partners may resort to physically avoiding one another.

Avoiding

Avoiding, the fourth stage of coming apart, is illustrated when relational partners make a conscious effort to avoid one another. Roommates may plan class schedules on opposite days to avoid being around one another, or married couples may spend time with friends or family members in an attempt to minimize the time they spend with one another. In essence, partners are exhausted at the prospect of acting like the relationship is worth saving, and they use avoidance to escape potential opportunities that might require them to discuss it.

Terminating

While counselors and self-help books often encourage relational partners to communicate with one another and try to "work it out," the reality is that some relationships are beyond repair. Let's face it, some relationships are toxic and are potentially damaging to one's identity, self-esteem, or physical or mental well-being. Rather than continue to live with a roommate when you dread being in your apartment, or working with colleagues who continually put you down and cause you to feel inferior, it may be in your best interest to *terminate* the relationship. As a result of the end of the relationship, partners are faced with the task of rediscovering their sense of self and reexamining their identity as individuals. It's important to note that just because a relationship experiences one or more of the stages of coming apart, it may still be repaired. A couple may decide that they want to try and work things out by seeing a counselor. As a result, the termination stage is avoided and the relationship is salvaged.

What communication behaviors contribute to the eventual demise of relationships? It's impossible to pinpoint specific ones. However, three factors that are frequently reported as causing issues in a variety of relationships include deception, jealousy and conflict.

BARRIERS TO EFFECTIVE INTERPERSONAL RELATIONSHIPS

Increasing awareness of some of the core communication issues that can create problems in our relationships is often a crucial element in maintaining or restoring our connections to a healthy and satisfactory state. While research has identified a variety of communication behaviors that often create relational challenges, three of the most common issues include the use of deception, the presence of jealousy, and the management of conflict. Why would we include a discussion of communication behaviors that have the potential to damage relationships in a chapter focused on improving them? An increased awareness and understanding of the messages that have the potential to destroy relationships may be the very key to repairing and maintaining them.

Deception

Can you recall a time when you have told a lie to avoid hurting someone's feelings? Perhaps you claimed that you needed to study instead of joining your parents or in-laws for dinner.

Maybe you told your boss that you already had plans for the weekend when she asked you if you were available to cover a coworker's shift. If you've ever been deceptive in your communication with others, you're not alone. Serota, Levine, and Boster (2010) found that on average people report telling approximately two lies per day (see Figure 7.7). While this may seem exaggerated, consider the various ways we deceive others. A salesperson may deceive a customer who asks "How do I look in this outfit?" in order to avoid hurting the customer's feelings or losing a potential sale. Perhaps you have lied to a server in a restaurant who asks, "How is your dinner?" and you respond "Great!" even though your dinner is cold. Simple responses to avoid hurting someone's feelings or to avoid an unpleasant situation can be considered deceptive communication. It's important to consider both the short- and long-term effects of deception on our relationships.

FIGURE 7.7

Statistics on the Number of Lies Told in the United States

Percentage of adults who admit to telling lies "sometimes" or "often"	12%
Percentage of women who admit to occasionally telling harmless half-truths	80%
Percentage of patients who lied about following a doctor's treatment plan	40%
Average number of lies per day told by men to their partner, boss, or colleague	6
Average number of lies per day told by women to their partner, boss, or colleague	3

Source: Database Records.com – Newsweek. (2012).

Deception has been defined as intentionally sharing a message with the goal of causing the other to adopt a false conclusion or belief. Recall our earlier discussion of relationship expectations. When a friend, coworker, or family member knowingly deceives us, we may experience hurt and disappointment. After all, our expectation is that relationships are based on honesty and trust.

Scholars have identified five types of deception that are often used in relationships: lies, concealment, equivocations, exaggerations, and minimizations. *Lies* involve fabricating or falsifying information. Suppose a coworker asks if you'd like to join her at a symphony performance on Saturday evening. If you don't enjoy classical music, you may lie and tell her that you already have other plans, even if you don't. *Concealment* involves withholding some important or relevant information. If your boss asks if you've received any updates from a vendor regarding a shipment date for software that is crucial to completing a project, you might reply, "He just sent an email this morning!" What you don't say is that the email indicated that the software would be delayed. *Equivocation* is often used in situations where we attempt to spare someone's feelings. This strategy involves using vague or ambiguous language to avoid speaking the truth. Suppose your best friend gets a new haircut. When she asks you what you think, you respond with, "Wow! It's so different!" In reality, you don't like the haircut, but you don't want to risk hurting your friend's feelings. *Exaggeration* involves stretching the truth, adding details or information to enhance a story, or repeating oneself in an attempt to be convincing. Job interviews or online dating profiles may be situations in which individuals attempt to make themselves look better by embellishing details about their lives. A final type of deception involves *minimizing* or downplaying the truth. Suppose you fall on the steps at work while carrying a pile of papers. A coworker asks if you're hurt and to avoid further embarrassment you state, "No, I'm okay" when you're really in pain.

Since statistics seem to indicate that 12% of people admit to telling lies "sometimes" or "often," how can you identify whether someone is telling you the truth or not? While some claim that it's as simple as looking for avoidance of eye contact, wringing hands, or fidgeting, it's not always that easy. The *truth bias* often interferes with our ability to see deception with close friends, romantic partners, or family members. Essentially, this bias involves our expectation that people with whom we are in a close relationship will be honest with us. Because we trust and expect them to be honest with us, deception may be ignored or overlooked. Perhaps you can recall a situation when your friend was deceived by his or her romantic partner. While the deception may have been blatantly evident to others, it may not have been as apparent to the person being deceived. *Behavioral familiarity* is one strategy that we can use to help identify dishonesty. Because we become so familiar with the typical behaviors of those with whom we have close relationships, we are better equipped to identify when their actions are uncharacteristic of their normal behaviors. For example, if your partner comes home from work and immediately launches into a detailed description about her day, yet she rarely shares any information about work, you may become suspicious or question why her behavior is atypical or uncharacteristic.

Park, Levine, McCornack, Morrison, and Ferrara (2002) studied 202 college students and identified three primary means through which deception is typically revealed. These include physical evidence, third-party information, and confessions. In 2009, professional golfer Tiger Woods's deception was revealed when his then wife Elin Nordegren discovered text messages to other women on his cell phone. Physical evidence can range from text messages that romantic partners discover on a cell phone to an incomplete report that an employee told his boss was finished. Third-party information involves others sharing or revealing information about the deception. A sibling who tells his parents about his sister coming home after curfew after she claimed that she was in bed by midnight serves as a third-party informant. Confessions may occur when guilt or direct confrontation occurs. A coworker may admit that she lied about not being able to cover her own shift last weekend as a result of the guilt she experiences after hearing how you had to miss your brother's birthday celebration because you were working in her place.

Deception can be detrimental to our relationship in that it has the potential to diminish our level of trust and respect for the other person. Another communication behavior that has also been found to impact our level of satisfaction in relationships is jealousy.

Jealousy

Fans of the Disney *Toy Story* series of films are familiar with the ways in which jealousy can impact relationships. The movie showcases the adventures of Woody, a toy cowboy who has always been Andy's favorite, as he becomes consumed with jealousy when he discovers that Andy prefers Buzz, a gift he received for his eighth birthday. Eventually the pair works through their mutual jealousy and discovers that their friendship is more important than vying for Andy's attention.

Jealousy is defined as a negative or destructive communicative response to a perceived threat to a relationship. Competition for the other person's time, attention, or affection may result in negative or damaging communication behaviors. One example of jealousy that can occur between siblings is often referred to as *sibling rivalry*. Competition for parents' attention may cause brothers and sisters to react in hurtful ways toward one another. Jealousy also occurs in our friendships and in our relationships with coworkers. Consider how you might feel if your boss promotes a coworker you worked with on a recent project instead of offering you the promotion. Jealousy can also be experienced in our public lives. Reviewing Facebook posts and Instagram photos from a friend's recent vacation in Hawaii can cause you to be envious.

Six types of jealousy were identified by Bevan and Samter (2004). These include family, friend, romantic, power, intimacy, and activity jealousy. The first three types (*friend, family*, and *romantic jealousy*) occur when we fear that our relationships with a friend, family member, or romantic partner will be altered by the presence of others. *Power jealousy* evolves in situations where other tasks or obligations are perceived as being more important than your relationship. Workplace friendships may become strained when status differentials or job responsibilities cause work to take precedence over the relationship. Status differentials, job titles, and social position can all result in power jealousy. *Intimacy jealousy* occurs in situations where partners choose to disclose intimate or private information with others outside the relationship. Suppose Mia decides to tell her friend about her recent financial strains instead of confiding with her sister. This decision to share intimate information with another person may cause a strain in the sister relationship. Finally, *activity jealousy* results from the amount of attention that a relational partner dedicates to an interest or hobby. Consider the frustration experienced if it's perceived that your friend would rather spend time playing Xbox or working as opposed to devoting time to your relationship.

Are you guilty of attempting to make a partner jealous? How do we try to invoke these negative reactions in others? Cayanus and Booth-Butterfield (2004) examined tactics that romantic partners use in an attempt to make one another jealous. The results of this study found that the longer we're involved in a relationship, our use of these jealousy-evoking behaviors decreases. Perhaps this is because we become more secure in our connection with the other person and no longer feel the need to test his or her commitment or loyalty.

Jealousy is communicated in a variety of ways. Giving others the silent treatment, flirting, expressing anger, and a variety of other emotional responses all offer clues that we perceive competition in our relationship.

Conflict

Evoking jealousy and deceiving others has the potential to evolve into conflict. While some partners may paint a beautiful picture of their relationship and insist that they never disagree or fight with one another, the reality is that all relationships encounter challenges from time to time. Why deny that conflict occurs in our relationships? Perhaps it's because of the negative perception typically associated with conflict. But not all conflict is bad—in fact, some conflicts may be productive for the health of a relationship. Differences of opinion are expressed and negotiated, diverse perspectives are shared, and frustrations are expressed openly with the goal of resolving them.

©Andresr/Shutterstock.com

Conflict is defined as "an expressed struggle between at least two interdependent parties who perceive incompatible goals, scarce resources, and interference from the other party in achieving their goals" (Hocker & Wilmot, 1991, p. 12). This definition proposes five key components of conflict, which are highlighted in Figure 7.8. By examining each of these components more closely, we are better equipped to understand and explain possible causes that contributed to the conflict in the first place.

FIGURE 7.8
Key components of conflict.

Expressed Struggle

Interdependence

Perceived Incompatible Goals

Perceived Competition for Scarce Resources

Perceived Interference in Achieving One's Goals

FACEBOOK JEALOUSY

Muise, Christofides, and Desmarais (2009) surveyed 308 undergraduate students to examine the impact that Facebook use had on their relationships. Researchers were interested in examining if viewing Facebook posts increased the perceived jealousy experienced in relationships. Participants in the study reported that they spent an average of nearly 40 minutes each day scanning Facebook posts. Time spent on Facebook resulted in significant increases in jealousy, with women indicating higher levels of jealousy compared to men.

Why does viewing posts on our relational partner's Facebook page cause us to experience increased jealousy? Scholars offer four potential explanations:

- Facebook makes it easier for people to reestablish relationships with former romantic partners.

- Partners may post information on Facebook that they haven't directly shared with one another, thus resulting in a perception of deceit.

- An individual's identity that is portrayed on Facebook may be different from the "real-life" identity that a partner experiences. Thus, they may feel as though they don't really know the person.

- The time that a person spends on Facebook may limit the amount of time available to spend with his or her partner.

One element that all conflicts have in common is that there is an *expressed struggle* between at least two partners. Expressed struggle emphasizes the importance of the open expression of conflict. If one partner is unaware of the problem, issues are not likely to be resolved. In order for conflict to occur, both partners in the relationship must be *interdependent*. We're more likely to experience frustration when issues arise with those to whom we feel connected. For example, you will likely experience conflict with romantic partners, family members, or coworkers but not the stranger sharing an elevator ride. *Perceived incompatible goals* contribute to the frustration experienced in conflict, and often impede the progress of accomplishing our objectives. Suppose Olivia is the leader of a team who must achieve a sales goal in order for team members to earn a bonus. She may become frustrated when she perceives Tyler as contributing very little to the team's efforts. The bonus depends on their success as a team, and Olivia perceives Tyler as being a slacker. Tyler feels that Olivia is trying to make herself look good so she can be considered for a promotion that he would also like to pursue. Olivia and Tyler are interdependent coworkers with *perceived incompatible goals*. In this example, we also see the presence of the fourth component of conflict, *perceived competition for scarce resources*. Suppose there is only one promotion planned in the company in the near future, and Tyler and Olivia both want to be the candidate selected. Another example of this can be witnessed in sibling conflict, where brothers and sisters may compete for their parents' time or attention. Resources that create conflict can include anything that we consider to be of value—time, money, relationships, material possessions, attention, or even status. A final component of conflict is *perceived interference in achieving one's goals*. Recall the conflict between Olivia and Tyler. Each of them perceives the other to be interfering in their ability to achieve the goal of a promotion. Conflict is likely to occur when others create barriers to our goal attainment. Learning how to use communication to effectively manage conflicts is important in our personal, professional, and public lives.

© conrado/Shutterstock.com

CONFLICT MANAGEMENT

Individuals choose to approach conflict in different ways. When we're faced with a conflict, there are typically two routes that we can pursue. Either we can communicate and address the conflict, or we can "bury our head in the sand" and avoid it. Understanding the implications of our selection of conflict management strategies is important in determining the best option for maintaining or preserving our relationship. Figure 7.9 summarizes the four approaches to conflict management and highlights the strengths and weaknesses of each.

FIGURE 7.9

Conflict Management Strategies

Conflict Management Strategy	Example	Advantage	Disadvantage
Avoidance	"Everything's fine—there's not a problem."	Protects feelings of others and gives time to reflect on the issues and analyze your perspective	Problem is not resolved
Competition	"You have no clue what you're talking about! I was selected as team leader and I know what's best for all of us."	Helps bring issues out in the open when time is of the essence and action needs to be taken.	May damage the relationship if one perceives that the other doesn't respect his or her feelings.
Accommodation	"You're right. I don't know what I was thinking" or "I don't care—you decide."	Quick resolution of the issue and preservation of the relationship.	May result in one partner often being "taken advantage of" in the relationship.
Collaboration	"I understand why you don't agree with me. Let's talk about this and see if we can find an answer together."	Preserves the relationship and both parties feel as though their voices were valued.	May take considerable time and effort.

Avoidance is probably the most frequently used strategy and it also happens to be the most ineffective approach for managing conflict. Denying the presence of a conflict means that the issue is unresolved. When this occurs, the frustration or anxiety remains and we may continue to harbor negative emotions and feelings. Taking time to "cool off" does not necessarily indicate that someone is avoiding conflict. In fact, reflecting on the issues and carefully considering the various perspectives of the situation may be beneficial to the discussion and resolution.

Often when both partners have strong opinions, a *competition* approach to managing the conflict emerges. Struggles for power or control are often present with this strategy, and relationships could potentially be damaged if the competition escalates to a point where aggressive communication behaviors are exchanged. Classmates working on a group project may experience high levels of stress as the deadline looms. Two team members both want to "take charge" of the project to ensure it is completed according to their standards. The stress and struggle for leadership may cause them to criticize one another's contributions, with neither team member willing to give in to the other's suggestions. While competition is effective at openly discussing issues when situations must be addressed quickly, continual debate and ongoing opposition may be frustrating and further escalate the conflict.

Accommodation differs from the avoidance approach in that this strategy recognizes the presence of a conflict, but one party concedes or gives in to the other in an attempt to resolve things. While this may be a "quick-fix" solution, one person runs the risk of being viewed as a pushover or a "doormat" for others. Consider our earlier example of the classmates who are working on a project that is due soon. Rather than struggling for control of the project, one member always "goes along to get along" with the rest of the team, even when he does not agree with their ideas.

Scholars agree that the most effective approach to conflict management is *collaboration*. This strategy requires both parties to communicate their concerns while proposing solutions that would be acceptable. The ultimate goal is to determine an option that is mutually agreeable to all parties involved. It's important to note that while this is the most desirable strategy for effective conflict management, it's also the most time-consuming.

Throughout this chapter we've explained some of the communication challenges encountered in relationships and identified opportunities for addressing these issues. Being able to recognize the warning signs of challenges or difficulties is important if the relationship is to be saved. In this chapter we have presented the final five stages of coming apart. It is important to note that simply because a relationship encounters one of these stages, it is not predestined for failure. Relationships are not always easy. We often hurt the ones we love the most because we have a vested interest in one another. Recognizing the warning signs and identifying potential communication behaviors that got us to that point in the first place are important steps in ensuring our potential to maintain healthy relationships.

KEY TERMS

- Accommodation
- Active Strategies
- Attraction Theory
- Autonomy vs. Connectedness
- Avoiding
- Behavioral Familiarity
- Bonding
- Circumscribing
- Collaboration
- Competition
- Concealment
- Conflict
- Dialectical tensions
- Differentiating
- Entry Stage
- Equivocation
- Exaggeration
- Exit Stage
- Experimenting
- Expectancy Violation Theory
- Expressed Struggle
- Integrating
- Intensifying
- Interdependent
- Initiating
- Interactive Strategies
- Interpersonal Communication

- Intimate Information
- Jealousy
- Lies
- Minimizing
- Novelty vs. Predictability
- Openness vs. Closedness
- Passive Strategies
- Perceived Incompatible Goals
- Personal Information
- Personal Stage
- Physical Attraction
- Private Information
- Reciprocal Self-Disclosure
- Relational Expectations
- Relationship Dissolution:
- Self-Disclosure
- Social Attraction
- Social Penetration Theory
- Stagnating
- Superficial
- Task Attraction
- Terminating
- Truth Bias
- Uncertainty Reduction Theory

REFERENCES

Afifi, W. A., & Metts, S. (1998). Characteristics and consequences of expectation violation in close relationships. *Journal of Social and Personal Relationships, 15,* 365–392.

Altman, I., & Taylor, D. (1973). *Social penetration: The development of interpersonal relationships.* New York, NY: Holt, Rinehart & Winston.

Are Friendships Key To Workplace Happiness? (n.d.). *Forbes.* Retrieved March 20, 2014, from http://www.forbes.com/2010/04/21/workplace-happiness-friendship-forbes-woman-well-being-relationship.html.

Baxter, L.A. (1988). A dialectical perspective on communication strategies in relationship development. In S. Duck (Ed.), *Handbook of personal relationships: Theory, research, and interventions* (pp. 257–273). Chichester, UK: Wiley.

Baxter, L. A., & Bridge, K. (1992). Blended relationships: Friends as work associates. *Western Journal of Communication, 56,* 200–225.

Berger, C. R., & Calabrese, R. J. (1975). Some exploration in initial interaction and beyond: Toward a developmental theory of communication. *Human Communication Research, 1,* 99–112.

Bevan, J. L., & Samter, W. (2004). Toward a broader conceptualization of jealousy in close relationships: Two exploratory studies. *Communication Studies, 55,* 14–28.

Burgoon, J. K. (1978). A communication model of personal space violation: Explication and an initial test. *Human Communication Research, 4,* 129–142.

Byrne, D. (1997). An overview (and underview) of research and theory within the attraction paradigm. *Journal of Social and Personal Relationships, 14,* 417–431.

Canary, D. J., Stafford, L., Hause, K. S., & Wallace, L. A. (1993). An inductive analysis of relational maintenance strategies: Comparisons among lovers, relatives, friends, and other. *Communication Research Reports, 10,* 5–14.

Cayanus, J. L., & Booth-Butterfield, M. (2004). Relationship orientation, jealousy, and equity: An examination of jealousy evoking and positive communicative responses. *Communication Quarterly, 52,* 237–250.

Database Records.com – *Newsweek.* (2012). *Little white lies: The truth about why women lie.* Retrieved from www.statisticbrain.com/lying-statistics/.

Dindia, K., & Canary, D.J. (1993). Definitions and theoretical perspectives on relational maintenance. *Journal of Social and Personal Relationships, 10,* 163–173.

Duck, S. (1988). *Relating to others.* Monterey, CA: Brooks/Cole.

Graham, E. E. (2003). Dialectic contradictions in postmarital relationships. *Journal of Family Communication, 3*(4), 193–214.

Habelow, E. (2010, April 21). Are friendships key to workplace happiness? *Forbes.com.* Retrieved from www.forbes.com/2010/04/21/workplace-happiness-friendship-forbes-woman-well-being-relationship.html.

Hocker, J. L., & Wilmot, W. W. (1991). *Interpersonal conflict.* Dubuque, IA: William C. Brown.

Knapp, M. L. (1978). *Social intercourse: From greeting to goodbye.* Boston, MA: Allyn & Bacon.

Knapp, M., & Vangelisti, A. (2003). Relationship stages: A communication perspective. In K. M. Galvin & P. J. Cooper (Eds.), *Making connections: Readings in interpersonal communication* (3rd ed., pp. 158–165). Los Angeles, CA: Roxbury.

Kowalski, R. M. (1999). Speaking the unspeakable: Self-disclosure and mental health. In B. R. Kowalski & M. R. Leary (Eds.), *The social psychology of emotional and behavioral problems* (pp. 225–248). Washington, DC: American Psychological Association.

McCroskey, J. C., & McCain, T.A. (1974). The measurement of interpersonal attraction. *Speech Monographs, 41,* 261–266.

Mongeau, P., Serewicz, M., & Therrien, L. (2004). Goals for cross-sex first dates: Identification, measurement and contextual factors. *Communication Monographs, 71,* 121–147.

Muise, A., Christofides, E., & Desmarais, S. (2009). More information than you ever wanted: Does Facebook bring out the green-eyed monster of jealousy? *CyberPsychology and Behavior, 12*(4), 441–444.

Nosko, A., Wood, E., & Molema S. (2010). All about me: Disclosure in online social networking profiles. The case of Facebook. *Computers in Human Behavior, 26,* 406–418.

Park, H. S., Levine, T. R., McCornack, S. A., Morrison, K., & Ferrara, M. (2002). How people really detect lies. *Communication Monographs, 69,* 144–157.

Sahlstein, E. M. (2006). Making plans: Praxis strategies for negotiating uncertainty–certainty in long-distance relationships. *Western Journal of Communication, 70,* 147–165.

Serota, K. B., Levine, T. R., & Boster, F. J. (2010). The prevalence of lying in America: Three studies of self-reported lies. *Human Communication Research, 36,* 2–25.

When WILL he say "I love you"? Men take 88 days to say those three words - but girls make their man wait a lot longer... (n.d.). *Mail Online.* Retrieved March 20, 2014, from http://www.dailymail.co.uk/femail/article-2289562/I-love-Men-88-days-say-girlfriend-women-134-days-say-boyfriend.html.**

Chapter Eight

Intercultural Communication

oneinchpunch/Shutterstock.com

In this chapter:

**As you look around campus on the first day of class, you notice the diversity that exists among students at your school. On the surface, you seem so different. But after a while the distinctions seem to blur. Sound idealistic? Probably. After all, one only needs to glance at the daily news headlines for stories of the challenges faced when cultures clash. Our goal in addressing the topic of culture as it relates to communication is simple—if by the end of this chapter you have an increased understanding for *how* cultures differ and *why* these differences influence our interactions, we will have accomplished our objective. Have you ever heard yourself describe another culture's behaviors or norms as "weird," "strange," or "gross"? How would you respond to the question, "On which side of the road do the British drive?" If you said, "The wrong side of the road!" this demonstrates our tendency to judge cultures based on our own cultural practices. Rather than label differences as "wrong," our goal is for you to view them as merely "different."

While we might think that we know how our cultural differences influence our own communication style and how we interpret the messages sent by others, the reality is that we do not. If we become comfortable with the knowledge that it is not possible to understand the nuances of every culture, we may reduce our frustration with miscommunication and become more effective in our personal, professional, and public communication. In this chapter, we explore the many facets of culture and diversity and their relationship to communication. In addition, we discuss various reactions to diversity in an attempt to enhance our interactions with others.

DIVERSITY AND CULTURE DEFINED

Diversity can be defined as that which is different. While this definition is simple, it serves as the conceptual foundation that influences our interactions with others. Consider the diversity encountered on a daily basis as you travel from home to school and work. If you were to create a list of the differences you see, items included might identify racial, ethnic, and gender differences. However, diversity runs much deeper than what we are able to see on the surface. In fact, the most important aspects of culture are often those that we never talk about in our interactions with others. If we took the time to communicate and truly get to know the other person, we would uncover an excess of differences that would be mind-boggling. Additional characteristics such as religious beliefs, value of education, and attitudes toward work would likely be revealed as you begin to interact with others. We typically draw conclusions about how similar we are to others by focusing our attention on specific characteristics we decide to use when evaluating the ways in which we are alike or different. For example, we might choose to focus on age or political affiliation to assess how similar we are to someone while ignoring other characteristics such as gender or religious beliefs. In order to understand the most influential aspects of our differences, we need to add culture to the equation. *Culture* is a term that refers to the common characteristics and shared perceptions that unify a group of people and shape their communication expectations. These commonalities create a sense of unity and identity for a group. Anthropologists have broadly defined culture as being comprised of perceptions, behaviors, and evaluations. Others have adopted a more descriptive approach to explaining culture. These definitions include components such as knowledge, morals, beliefs, values, customs, art, music, and laws.

Scholars have examined the creation of cultures in a variety of contexts ranging from organizational culture to family culture to fan culture. From Disney employees who adopt a common language of words such as "guests" instead of "tourists" and "cast members" instead of "employees" to the Japanese students who are committed to doing what is best for their project team and who avoid eye contact with their instructor as a sign of respect, we are bombarded with cultural differences on a daily basis.

Most cultures take pride in accentuating their distinctions from others. The more distinct we are, the more defined our culture becomes. While we take pride in our differences from other cultures, we expect the members of our own culture to conform. Values, beliefs, and attitudes serve as core principles, and members of an organization often reward those members who adhere to the cultural norms and form negative perceptions of those who do not.

Have you ever researched the Internet for information about another country before traveling abroad or downloaded an iPhone app to provide you with insights on a city that you are visiting on vacation? A lot of time is devoted to researching and understanding the customs and highlights of a new city or country when we are traveling, but we often fail to devote the same amount of time to considering the cultural differences that we might encounter in our daily interactions with others.

THE RELATIONSHIP BETWEEN CULTURE AND COMMUNICATION

Explaining the relationship between culture and communication is simple. Communication and culture are inseparable. Communication is the primary means for teaching the core characteristics of a culture. We share stories about our heroes and legends in an attempt to instill commonly held values. However, our culture also teaches us "how" to communicate. We begin learning the preferred language of our culture at a very young age. Family members teach us appropriate words and gestures for expressing ourselves, and they reprimand us for deviations that are considered to be unacceptable. This learning continues as we attend school.

As you pursue your personal and professional goals in the 21st century, you will encounter a society and workforce that are much more diverse than in previous decades. This chapter builds on that foundation by exploring theories and concepts relevant to enhancing your understanding of and appreciation for diversity and its impact on communication.

THE REASONS FOR STUDYING INTERCULTURAL COMMUNICATION

The phrase "shrinking world" has been used to describe the increased potential for interactions between diverse people. With the introduction of Facebook and other new media, students now can interact and build relationships with others from cultures that would never have been possible before the Internet. We no longer depend on letters or library research to inform us of cultural nuances. Instead, if we have a desire to build relationships with diverse others we can simply "friend" them and begin exchanging messages. In the following section, three specific reasons for the importance of exploring culture and communication are discussed.

Understanding the Self

Perhaps the most fundamental reason for studying culture and communication is the opportunity it provides us for understanding our own cultural background and identity. Have you ever stopped to consider *why* you communicate the way you do? While language and history classes provide insight into the "big picture" of cultural influences that have shaped our identity, a closer look at distinctions that shape our perceptions and responses is invaluable. One of the authors was raised in a rural community with a population of approximately 350 people that could best be described as extremely homogeneous. The entire community was Caucasian, with most having a connection to the occupations of farming or coal mining. Imagine the challenges encountered when she moved from a small town to a large metropolitan city following high school graduation. Initial descriptions of her encounters with others focused on their "strange" behaviors and "odd" styles of dress. New words and phrases such as "market" in reference to the "grocery store" and "gum bands" instead of "rubber bands" were confusing. Enrolling in an intercultural communication class proved to be "eye-opening." Learning the unique words, phrases, and gestures was simple. On the other hand, examining core components of the culture of origin provided insight into *why* she reacted the way she did to the deviations from expected behaviors. Our culture becomes part of our core identity and we become comfortable being around those who are like us. When we step out of this comfort zone, we may experience culture shock. There is truth in the phrase, "In order to truly understand others, you must first understand yourself."

Technological Responsibility

When Marshall McLuhan first coined the term "global village" in the 1960s, many thought his predictions were so far into the future that we would never be affected by the changes he proposed. Little did we know then that when Atari introduced its first game console in 1972 that only 30 years later Xbox would launch a technology that would enable game play with people from around the world. McLuhan was a visionary who anticipated widespread opportunities for people to interact and travel with ease. Coworkers utilize Skype to communicate with colleagues from halfway around the world, and travelers can encounter new cultures first-hand through enhanced modes of transportation. Technology has exponentially increased our opportunities for intercultural contact. Elementary schools collaborate with other schools to create international email "pen pal" programs to enhance students' cultural awareness and language skills, while colleges encourage students

FIGURE 8.1

Estimated demographic composition of the U.S. labor force in 2020. Source: Workforce 2020, Hudson Institute, www.diversitycentral.com/business/diversity_statistics. html#labor_force.

to broaden their cultural horizons through study-abroad programs. Because of these increased opportunities for interactions, understanding the factors that influence culture and communication is essential to appreciating these learning opportunities.

Demographic Influence

The demographic composition of the United States has changed dramatically over the past two decades. Predictions for the 2020 census highlight the significant demographic shifts that will continue to occur in the workplace as a result of immigration and changes in educational achievement (Figure 8.1). With these changing demographics come increased opportunities for confusion and misunderstanding. No longer will we be interacting solely with those who "look like us." Instead, we will encounter a workforce that is more diverse in terms of age, sex, and racial and ethnic composition.

CHARACTERISTICS OF CULTURE

Culture Is Learned

As indicated earlier in the chapter, we begin learning about our culture as children. Language learning begins at a young age and continues through college. Standardized exams such as state achievement tests, the SAT, and the ACT ensure that we are correctly using the words and phrases preferred by our culture. Foods are

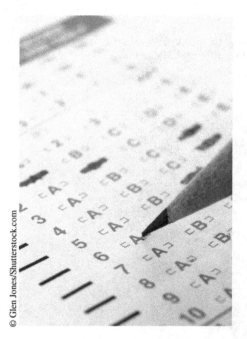

© Glen Jones/Shutterstock.com

connected to a culture's identity, and radio stations promote the musical styles that are representative of a culture's preferences in music. Everywhere we turn, messages are being conveyed that inform us of the norms of behavior in order to be viewed as a member of our culture.

How do we learn about culture? Learning occurs at two levels. *Explicit learning* involves more formalized instruction. In the United States, schools teach students about the history of our country in U.S. history courses, and many states promote their identities through classes such as "Ohio History" or "West Virginia History." As we prepare for our professional careers, business dining etiquette classes provide instruction on which fork should be used to eat salad and how to determine which bread plate is yours. We may ask friends and family members for insight or information about cultural differences we encounter. Programs such as Rosetta Stone and Berlitz promise rapid learning of a second language; however, this explicit instruction of language provides us with only a small portion of information about a culture.

In order to truly understand a culture, implicit learning must take place. Colleges recognize this when they provide students with experiences for language immersion. *Implicit learning*, or acquiring information by observing, often provides valuable insight into what is considered acceptable and unacceptable by a culture. One implicitly learns what a culture values, how its members view various communicative behaviors, and its approach to forming relationships by using this information. Reading about cultural differences provides us with only a snapshot of a culture. Spending time with diverse others gives us the opportunity to experience the details of cultural distinctions from differences in styles of humor to varied perceptions of gender roles. For example, someone from the United States may use self-deprecating humor to "break the ice" at the start of a business meeting only to discover that other cultures view this as diminishing one's credibility. Both explicit and implicit learning can enhance our understanding of cultural differences.

Culture Is Dynamic

While cultures take great pride in their history, most are unable to resist the pressure to change. Events occur, innovations are revealed, and members learn about "new" ways of doing and being. Sometimes change is forced upon a culture in order to adapt to its social and physical environment, or cultures may choose to adjust their norms and expectations. Consider the change that has occurred as a result of the widespread introduction of the Internet in the mid-1990s. Many organizations have forced employees to adopt this technology in order to gain access to company information. Paper memos and even faxes are things of the past. Now documents are shared electronically, and rather than wait for a signature to be delivered via the U.S. mail we simply scan a document into PDF format and send it. What cultural

FIGURE 8.2

Characteristics of culture.

changes have you witnessed during the past five years? Changes in clothing styles, the introduction of new words and gestures, and an evolution in the view of women's roles in the workplace are only a few of the cultural adjustments that we have encountered in the United States.

Later in this chapter we discuss uncertainty avoidance as a factor that distinguishes cultures from one another. Some cultures are eager to introduce change, and thus can be described as embracing uncertainty. Others are more comfortable in promoting tradition and history, and often view change with hesitation or suspicion. How do you know if your culture is one that promotes uncertainty and embraces change? Create a list of the changes you have noticed. However, labeling a culture as "innovative" or "traditional" may not be as easy as simply looking at one aspect of change. Japan is known for its technological innovation, yet it is a culture that encourages its members to value tradition. For example, elders are viewed as the wisest members of society and are often consulted on important decisions.

Klopf (1995) identifies two primary factors that influence a culture's approach to innovation and change. *Cultural borrowing* occurs when one culture sees the benefits of aspects of other cultures. In the United

States, comparisons are made to the business practices and educational systems of other cultures in order to ensure that we maintain our corporate and academic competitive edge. *Disasters and crises* often force cultures to change. The 2011 earthquake and tsunami in Japan have prompted proposed changes in architectural styles and building codes to ensure the safety of its residents. Post-9/11, the United States adapted its attitudes toward safety and security and new procedures for screening guests to our country were implemented. While some members of a culture may be resistant, our interactions with others often result in inevitable change.

Culture Is Pervasive

Take a look around you and identify anything that is representative of your culture. From the Apple icon on your computer or cell phone to your classmates' style of clothing, examples of cultural influences are visible everywhere we turn. However, it is important to note that culture also influences us in invisible ways. Artifacts may be used to communicate outwardly what a culture values. Culture is represented not only in our material possessions, but also in the values, beliefs, and attitudes that comprise our personal orientation system. It shapes virtually every aspect of our lives and influences our thoughts and actions.

CO-CULTURES WITHIN THE UNITED STATES

Within the broader cultural context, multiple co-cultures exist. *Co-culture* refers to the smaller cultures that comprise the larger culture. These smaller cultures may create names or labels to refer to themselves in order to establish their identity within the larger culture. The term "co" is used to refer to these smaller cultures because they must coexist through interactions with other smaller cultures within the communication environment of the larger culture. Membership is not restricted to only one or even a few co-cultures. Rather, an individual may associate or identify with multiple co-cultures. It is important to understand how these groups have shaped your identity to begin to appreciate the impact that these co-cultures have on our communication. Create a list of the co-cultures of which you are a member. Did you include political or religious affiliations, college or university, gender, hobbies and interests, or ethnic heritage on your list? A student whose list includes teenage, male, Caucasian, Texas, Methodist, athlete, and Republican readily claims membership in at least seven co-cultures. Negotiating the differing expectations by multiple co-cultures can prove to be challenging. At election time, we may question our political affiliation when candidates express beliefs and attitudes that differ from our own. Combining the conflicting elements of various co-cultures highlights the complexity faced in our personal, professional, and public lives. In this chapter, we examine three of the many co-cultures that have been identified as contributing to our distinct preferences for communication (Figure 8.3). The three co-cultures we examine here are race, age, and gender.

FIGURE 8.3
Examples of U.S. co-cultures.

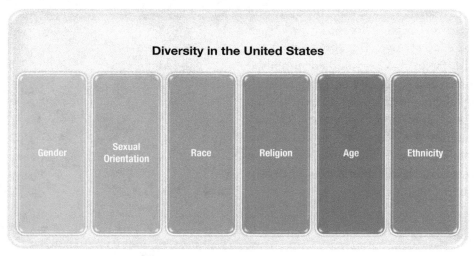

Diversity in the United States

Gender · Sexual Orientation · Race · Religion · Age · Ethnicity

Race

Race is a term often used to refer to inherited biological characteristics such as hair texture and color, eye shape, skin color, and facial structure. Categories used to describe these racial differences include Caucasian, African American, and Asian. Similar categorizations occur in other cultures around the world although the names assigned to racial groups may be different. While the terms race and ethnicity have often been used synonymously, these two categories are distinct from one another. *Ethnicity* refers to the common heritage,

© Rawpixel/Shutterstock.com

nationality, ancestry, or background shared by a group of people. Categories may be established to identify the culture from which one's ancestors came. These include Irish American, Polish American, or Mexican American. While there has been some debate over the connotations associated with the labeling of some of these groups, the intention of naming is simply for identification purposes.

Age

Chances are that you have probably heard your parents reference the generation gap that presents us with unique communication challenges. Many colleges and universities are experiencing a growth in their nontraditional-age student population (e.g., 23+ years of age), and the diverse age span of the employees within a single organization highlights the importance of understanding the impact of age as a factor that contributes to cultural misunderstandings. From musical preferences to political views, members from different generations sometimes clash in the differences among their values and beliefs. Websites such as "When Parents Text" (*www.whenparentstext.com*) highlights the challenges faced by the older generation as it attempts to adapt to the preferred communication channels of today's younger generations. Samples of texts exchanged between parents and their children showcase the humorous misunderstandings or annoyances that occur when different generations try to interact via innovative modes of communication. Consider the following example:

MOM: Your great aunt just passed away. LOL
ME: Why is that funny?
MOM: It's not funny, David! What do you mean?
ME: Mom. LOL means laughing out loud!
MOM: Oh my goodness!! I sent that to everyone. I thought it meant lots of love.
         I have to call everyone back!

FIGURE 8.4

Distinctions among generations in the workplace. Source: www.generationsatwork.com.

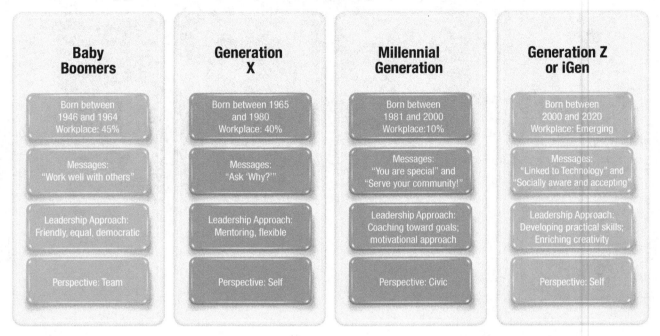

Not only do generational differences result in misunderstandings when it comes to technology use, but this age diversity also influences our interactions in the workplace. Economic, social, and personal reasons have resulted in some employees deferring retirement to later in life. At one point we equated the age of 65 with that ideal milestone that employees dreamed of achieving. Today, according to Social Security Online (*http://ssa.gov/pubs/ageincrease.htm*), the "full retirement age" of 65 has increased to 67 for those individuals born in 1938 or later. What does this mean for our workplace interactions? The increasing diversity in generational differences results in unique preferences for leadership approaches, work ethic, philosophies of work–life balance, and attitudes and preferences for the workplace environment. Figure 8.4 highlights a few of these differences that you may encounter as you begin your professional career and work with colleagues of different ages.

While categorizing the general preferences for each generation in the workplace is important, we need to be cautious about assuming that employees of similar ages are the same. Stereotyping all Millennials as having an "attitude of entitlement" can be inaccurate and unfair. Rather than using the labels and descriptors to stereotype employees, organizations should use this information to promote effective workplace relationships and enhance the promotion of products and services to a more diverse audience. For example, knowledge that a Millennial would rely on the feedback and reviews posted by strangers on product websites is important. This information could be invaluable in shaping how messages about the product are distributed. Equally important is the knowledge that Baby Boomers place more value on the recommendations of friends and family members in making purchasing decisions.

PERSONAL ORIENTATION SYSTEM AND COMMUNICATION

At the core of any culture is the personal orientation system that guides the communication of its members. Our *personal orientation system* is composed of our needs, values, attitudes, and beliefs that guide our behaviors and responses toward others. Personal identity influences our interactions with others. Recall that our identity is composed of needs, beliefs, values, and attitudes. These predispositions are often instilled through our interactions with others in our culture. These same components also guide our decisions when communicating with others.

Our personal orientation system reinforces our sense of self. As we increase our self-awareness, we better understand the choices we make in our reactions to and interactions with others. Consider the fact that each of us has a unique set of experiences that shapes our perceptions of events, people, and cultural differences. Sometimes these experiences are the result of your own encounters, and other times they stem from the experiences of others. What are your initial thoughts about being assigned to work with a student from Germany on a class project? How easy will it be to work together? If you have never encountered someone from Germany, you may rely on the portrayal of Germans in news stories and other media to provide you with a foundation for understanding your classmate. If you draw upon stories about Hitler from your world history classes, negative perceptions may occupy your thoughts. Alternatively, perhaps you recall a story that was shared by a work colleague who described a business trip to Germany and recounted how much fun she had during Oktoberfest. Even if you lack any direct experience with individuals from Germany, you create impressions about them based on the information shared by others.

At the core of both verbal and nonverbal behaviors are the rules and norms that guide their use. In addition to the words being spoken, our personal orientation system guides us in understanding the amount of verbal expressiveness preferred by a culture or the guidelines for communication based on the roles of the interactants. For example, some cultures encourage younger members to speak up, whereas others promote silence by listening and learning from elders. Reactions to differences in clothing and hairstyles may result in overt nonverbal responses that may lead to verbal conflict. Each culture's time consciousness creates misunderstandings in our interactions. Cultures that are very *monochronic* view time as a commodity that must be carefully scheduled and not wasted. The United States is an example of a monochronic culture. *Polychronic* cultures approach time as flexible and secondary in importance to the relationships. Many Latin American cultures are considered to be polychronic, and rather than interrupt lunch with a friend to head back to a business meeting, their focus is on the relationship, which they view as being most important. They believe business can wait for a few minutes.

Every individual has a set of predispositions that serves as a guide for our thoughts, actions, and behaviors. These predispositions are composed of one's needs, beliefs, values, and attitudes. Communication plans are developed and organized by these characteristics. Many of these components of the personal orientation system are learned within the cultural context. When faced with decisions regarding the proper way to respond in situations, our needs, beliefs, values, and attitudes assist us in guiding our perception of the situation.

Needs

Most of us recall studying *Maslow's Hierarchy of Needs* (Figure 8.5) at some point in our academic careers. The needs can be categorized as ranging from basic physiological needs such as food, clothing, and shelter to the higher-level need of self-actualization, which encompasses elements such as our morality and reaching our full potential. Our needs prompt us to experience desires that in turn motivate us to communicate with others in an attempt to fulfill these wants. A community member who perceives cultural diversity as a threat to his need for safety may communicate in negative ways in public settings. Employees who perceive their self-actualization needs as being threatened may express prejudice against affirmative action hiring practices. A student whose desire is to fulfill social needs may seek out opportunities to interact with other students.

Some cultures are limited in their ability to provide the resources necessary to meet some of even the most basic needs of their members. Communication is the key to understanding individual needs and in comprehending the value placed on need fulfillment.

FIGURE 8.5
Maslow's Hierarchy of Needs.

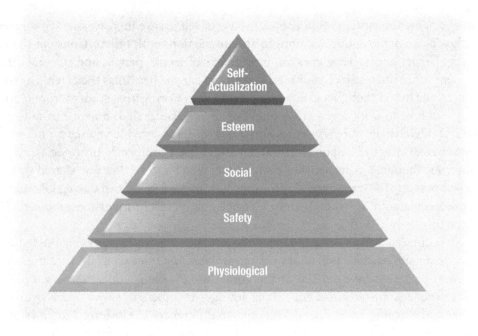

Beliefs

A second component of our personal orientation system is the beliefs that guide our thoughts and behaviors. Beliefs play a key role in shaping our decisions to approach relationships with others or to avoid communication. They guide the words that we use to let others know what we believe to be true. *Beliefs* are defined as personal convictions regarding truth or existence. Miscommunication may be attributed to our inability to take into consideration the role that our differing beliefs plays in shaping our impressions of others. Consider the beliefs that you possess as a student in the United States. Based on information you receive from the *U.S. News and World Report* or the Princeton Review, you may believe that some colleges provide a better education than others, and perhaps these beliefs include judgments about the best "value" for your tuition dollar, best social climate, and best faculty. These beliefs shape our messages. During a job interview, you may find yourself saying, "I probably don't have a chance because there were Harvard graduates who applied." Each culture's method of reasoning influences the development of beliefs in its members, and it is important to consider how these judgments influence our interactions. Beliefs about religion, morality, and even superstitions may cause us to view others as irrational. However, it is important to respect differences of beliefs. Simply appreciating that these different beliefs exist may be the first step in understanding how difficult it is to change someone's beliefs. Respecting these differences may help us avoid confrontations or offensive interactions.

Values

Values refer to our personal philosophy that guides our actions or our behaviors. They assist us in evaluating what we should and should not do in an ethical situation. Kluckhohn and Strodbeck (1961) describe values as being either explicitly or implicitly expressed. This definition highlights the relationship between values and communication. Most of our communicative behaviors reflect the values that are firmly established in our personal orientation system.

Cultures explicitly communicate those values they deem as being important through the use of proverbs. Statements such as "A bird in the hand is worth two in the bush" indicate our culture's emphasis on practicality, while the Japanese proverb of "The nail that sticks out gets hammered down" emphasizes the cultural values of conformity and group harmony. Organizations communicate their values through mission statements to identify the principles that guide their approach to doing business. Wendy's mission statement includes the phrase "Quality is our recipe." This communicates the value of providing customers with the best product possible. Understanding the values that are being communicated explicitly and implicitly is essential to avoiding misunderstandings. Consider the communicative messages associated with the practice of gift-giving in many Asian cultures. It is common practice in Asian cultures for students to give their college teachers a small gift or token of appreciation to indicate the value of the knowledge shared and the lessons learned. To many in the United States, this custom would be viewed as a form of bribery that conflicts with the U.S. values of ensuring equality and fairness in education. Understanding the values held by a culture's members as well as the ways in which values are communicated might assist us in avoiding misunderstandings.

© PhotoProfndonesia/Shutterstock.com

CULTURAL VALUE ORIENTATIONS

In order to understand the values shared by a culture's members, many scholars have developed models for studying these value orientations (e.g., Figure 8.6). Scholars such as Hall (1976) and Hofstede (1980) proposed models of cultural values that assist us in identifying and understanding the differences that often result in frustration and miscommunication. Differences are characterized along a continuum representing the broad range of communicative responses that reflect what a culture views as being important.

Cues that provide the context for our interactions are used to describe the value that a culture places on the spoken word versus nonverbal cues. Cultures classified as *low context* value the spoken word and encourage members to be direct in their verbal expressiveness. A philosophy of "say what you mean" is embraced. The United States is considered to be a low-context culture. *High-context* cultures prefer a more indirect style of communication in which cues about the messages intended by others are inferred through nonverbal channels. Silence is highly valued in a high-context culture, and a greater variety of meaning is attributed to what we do not say as opposed to what we do say. Many Asian cultures are considered to be high context. Meanings are perceived through unspoken, nonverbal behaviors. For example, someone from a high-context culture may be able to accurately perceive that you were having a bad day by paying attention to nonverbal cues, such as your late arrival to lunch, lack of facial expressiveness, or negative posture. However, consider the communication challenges encountered when a person from a low-context culture conducts business with a colleague from a high-context culture. Low-context cultures expect direct messages in response to inquiries about the feasibility of suggestions for organizational improvement, while high-context cultures will remain silent and assume their silence is interpreted as disapproval as opposed to directly communicating their lack of agreement.

Individualism and *collectivism* are used to depict the relative value of an individual versus the value of a group's members. In general, U.S. culture promotes and values individualism. Group members are encouraged to compete against one another and to assert their individual needs and goals, which is reflected in

FIGURE 8.6
Cultural values.

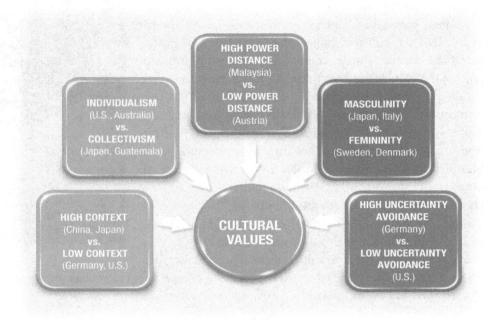

messages such as "You need to take care of yourself first!" Collectivism is the primary value held by many Asian cultures. Group harmony and support are paramount and take precedence over individual needs.

Cultures have also been classified in reference to the value they place upon power, status, and distance. Power distance refers to the distribution of power in personal relationships as well as within organizations. *Low power-distance* cultures value equality among members. Tendencies to communicate favoritism based on characteristics such as age, status, or gender are minimized. *High power-distance* cultures value status and emphasize power differentials in their communication.

Masculinity and *femininity* are also categories that can be used to classify and understand distinctions among cultural values. Masculine cultures demonstrate a preference for assertiveness, ambition, and achievement. While not always true, expectations for distinct gender roles may also be found in masculine cultures. At the other end of the continuum are cultures that promote the feminine values of nurturance, cooperation, and support. Gender roles in these cultures are perceived to be more blurred or equal. Why is it important to understand if a culture tends to value achievement over nurturance? Would you respond differently to one team member who feels that the entire team should be recognized and rewarded upon completion of a project and another team member who constantly reminds everyone of his individual contributions to the project's success? Knowing how to respond to these team members could mean the difference between a positive team experience and a negative one.

A final dimension used to classify value distinctions among cultures refers to the willingness of a culture to be innovative and embrace change or its preference to adhere to tradition and avoid change. Earlier in this chapter we discussed the fact that cultures are dynamic and encounter opportunities for change. Cultures that are *high in uncertainty avoidance* are often steeped in tradition. They place high value on customs, rituals, and ceremonies and prefer to avoid change unless absolutely necessary. Cultures that score *low in uncertainty avoidance* are excited and intrigued by innovation and are eager to take risks and alter their routines.

Understanding these dimensions provides valuable insight into the values promoted within a culture. By equipping ourselves with this information, we will be more effective in determining the appropriate methods to approach our interactions with others. In addition, an increased awareness of our culture's values provides insight into our own approach to communication.

Attitudes

Attitudes are learned predispositions that result from our decision to respond in a favorable or unfavorable way toward a particular object or person. At the beginning of this chapter, we stated that our primary goal is to help you identify your tendency to respond in positive and negative ways to cultural differences. Understanding our own attitudes and how our culture has influenced their formation is an essential component of effective interactions in our personal, professional, and public lives. Consider the attitudes described in the following story that have influenced a student's college experience.

Stereotyping

Stereotyping refers to our tendency to view individuals as possessing the characteristics we have assigned to a group to which they belong. Rather than exploring unique aspects of an individual, we rush to make generalizations in order to make decisions about "how" to communicate. Three steps are involved in the process of stereotyping. The first involves categorizing a group of people based on observable characteristics they have in common. Next, we associate observable characteristics as being typical across a group of people. Finally, we apply those characteristics to any person who is a member of that group. A teacher who stereotypes student-athletes as lazy and not focused on their academic goals is one example of how these conclusions impact our interactions.

SELF-SEGREGATION ON COLLEGE CAMPUSES

Qiannan Chen—or "Nancy," which she has adopted as her English name—is one of thousands of international students studying at U.S. colleges and universities. In her role as president of the Ohio University Chinese Student Scholar Association, Chen gained valuable insight into the frustrations both she and her fellow students experience when studying in a different country. She stated that many international students indicate a desire to "self-segregate," or communicate with members of their own culture rather than interacting with other students on campus. Students from similar racial and ethnic backgrounds can be found sitting together in classes or at the library on many college campuses. Why does this occur? Chen attributes it to the language and cultural barriers that exist. She reports that classmates stereotype her based on English-speaking difficulties, and they assume that her quiet demeanor indicates that she does not wish to contribute to class projects and discussions or engage in social conversations.

Source: Li (2012).

Prejudice

Prejudice is one type of attitude. It refers to the outward and visible expression of our negative reactions based on inflexible assumptions. Examples of how these attitudes and preconceptions have created problems for interactions among members of co-cultures within the United States can be seen in the expression of racism, ageism, and sexism in our society. Assumptions that senior citizens are incapable of making rational decisions or valuable contributions to society are promoted and reinforced through media portrayals. Sexist attitudes have traditionally been directed toward females in the United States, and females have experienced discrimination in the workplace and other walks of life.

Scholars have identified two primary forms of prejudice. *Verbal abuse* refers to the process of engaging in verbal comments, name-calling, or jokes that are insulting or demeaning to members of a culture or co-culture. Recently, ESPN reprimanded two of its employees for racist comments made in reference to New York Knicks player Jeremy Lin. Just making others aware of the negative impact of these comments may sometimes be a deterrent, as this awareness often leads to embarrassment about this type of behavior.

Discrimination refers to the practice of denying others their equal rights. Perhaps this attitude is rationalized by the belief that if the group experiences frustration as a result of the denied access, they will go away and we can avoid communication. Title VII of the 1964 Civil Rights Act bans organizations from discriminating against employees on the basis of sex, race, religion, color, and national origin. Affirmative action laws are designed to protect members from inequitable treatment. In 2014, the U.S. Supreme Court reviewed a case filed by a Muslim woman who asserted that she was discriminated against by Abercrombie & Fitch due to her religious beliefs. During her job interview with the retailer, she wore a head scarf and received an acceptable evaluation for her fashion style from the hiring manager. However, she was later informed that she was not hired for the job.

In addition to the forms that prejudice takes, there are also several functions that are fulfilled by communicating prejudice to others (Figure 8.7). The *acceptance function* is reflected when we make prejudiced statements about a group that we do not actually believe in an attempt to gain the approval or acceptance of others. An example of this function is when a fraternity member expresses his hatred for a rival fraternity's members. Upon closer examination, he admits that he does not really know "why" he makes such strong statements, other than to fit in with his own fraternity members.

FIGURE 8.7
Functions of prejudice.

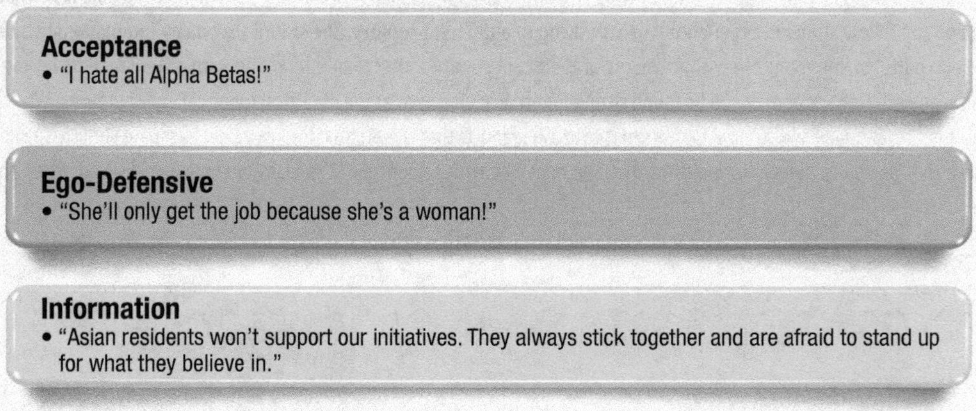

Acceptance
- "I hate all Alpha Betas!"

Ego-Defensive
- "She'll only get the job because she's a woman!"

Information
- "Asian residents won't support our initiatives. They always stick together and are afraid to stand up for what they believe in."

Sometimes we express prejudices against others in an attempt to protect our ego. This *ego-defensive function* provides us with a scapegoat to blame others for our misfortunes. Not receiving a job offer may result in comments such as, "I was the best candidate for the position. I'm sure they hired a woman or a minority because of the affirmative action laws." This outward expression of prejudice enables us to save face by hinting at unfair treatment.

The *information function* of prejudice is simply to provide us with information to use in guiding our communication with others. Humans are uncomfortable with uncertainty. Unfortunately, we use prejudice as a way to build a knowledge base about diverse people with whom we have had little or no previous interaction. We jump to conclusions and assume we understand the other person's values and beliefs without ever getting to know him or her. Often the source of information is the media's portrayals of diverse groups.

EFFECTIVE COMMUNICATION WITH DIVERSE OTHERS

Since we know that our attitudes can impact our ability to communicate effectively across cultural differences, how do we manage our tendencies to respond and react? Fortunately, you are already engaging in the first step to enhancing your interactions with diverse others. Examining and understanding the impact of your culture's value system will help us explain the different approaches to communication. While it is sometimes easy to simply believe news stories or media portrayals about diverse groups, avoid the tendency to assume that you have accurate knowledge about a culture and its members based solely on secondhand information. Three strategies that you can incorporate into your communication plan to enhance interactions with diverse others include:

1. *Be open-minded.* While stereotyping is a typical behavior that enables us to form expectations for our interacting with others, be flexible and willing to alter your preconceived notions. Talk to others to gain a full understanding of what they are like as an individual. You may discover you have more in common than you initially anticipated.

2. *Seek opportunities for interacting with diverse others.* Talking with people from other cultures can be intimidating. Approaching someone who is different and starting a conversation requires you to step outside your comfort zone. However, consider the impact these interactions can have on your professional and personal success. The more you seek out opportunities to interact with diverse others, the more comfortable you will be with intercultural encounters in your professional career or your personal relationships.

3. *Speak up for those whose voices are not being heard.* If you believe that prejudice and discrimination are wrong, speak up on behalf of others. This often requires careful thought and consideration, but the benefits of speaking up are important to ensure that others are treated with respect.

Throughout this chapter, we have discussed the impact of cultural differences on our interactions with others. Rather than focus on viewing our diversity as "strange," our goal is to promote an approach that views differences as only that—differences. Understanding the ways in which our culture has shaped our personal orientation system is essential to managing our responses to differences. While our initial instinct may be to identify diversity based solely on observable characteristics such as race, ethnicity, or sex, the core elements that are most influential in our interactions with and reactions to others are our needs, beliefs, values, and attitudes. Understanding yourself and the cultural influences on your perceptions and communication style is an important first step in enhancing your interactions in your personal, professional, and public lives.

KEY TERMS

- Attitudes
- Beliefs
- Co-culture
- Collectivism
- Culture
- Culture Borrowing
- Discrimination
- Diversity
- Ego Defensive Function
- Ethnicity
- Explicit Learning
- Femininity
- High-context
- High Power-Distance

- Implicit Learning
- Individualism
- Information Function
- Low-context
- Low Power-Distance
- Masculinity
- Maslow's Hierarchy of Needs
- Monochromatic
- Prejudice
- Polychronic
- Race
- Stereotyping
- Values
- Verbal Abuse

REFERENCES

Hall, E. T. (1976). *Beyond culture.* Garden City, NY: Anchor.

Hofstede, G. (1980, Summer). Motivation, leadership, and organizations: Do American theories apply abroad? *Organizational Dynamics*, pp. 42–63.

Klopf, D. (1995). *Intercultural encounters: The fundamentals of intercultural communication.* Englewood, CO: Morton Publishing.

Kluckhohn, C., & Strodbeck, F. (1961). *Variations in value orientations.* Evanston, IL: Row, Peterson.

Li, A. (2012, February 12). Self-segregation alive and well on the OU campus. *Athens News.* Retrieved April 6, 2014, from www.athensnews.com/ohio/article-36073-self-segregation-alive-and-well-on-the-ou-campus.html.

Mandell, N., & Deutsch, K. (2012, February 21). Racist headline about Jeremy Lin and the Knicks prompts quick apology from ESPN. *New York Daily News.* Retrieved from www.nydailynews.com.

Communication SH🦈RK™

Unit #3

Individual and Group Communication

Individual Communication through Public Speaking

Group Communication

Communication SH▲RK™

NOTES

Chapter Nine

Individual Communication through Public Speaking

© garetsworkshop/Shutterstock.com

HAVE YOU EVER FELT LIKE A GUPPY IN A SHARK TANK?

© Minerva Studio/Shutterstock.com

One day, I approached a client who was scheduled to present his first informative speech and he looked terrified! He was sweating, had almost no color in his cheeks, and his hands were shaking. I sat with him in the corner of the room for a few minutes and tried to help calm his fears. Following my instincts, I told the client that I was confident he would do a great job! For weeks, I watched this same man present impromptu speeches and he clearly had no trouble communicating his ideas to others. Yet, here he was looking quite frazzled. After a few minutes of "pep talk," I asked him to take a deep breath and then tell me exactly how he felt. He looked directly at me and said with a shiver, "Have you ever felt like a guppy in a shark tank?"

Truthfully, we can all say that we have felt like a guppy in a shark tank when faced with presenting a speech! We feel like ALL eyes are on us and that we are the tender morsel of the day. We believe the audience members are staring at every part of our bodies, evaluating every piece of clothing, shoes, even judging the fact that we brought note cards to the lectern. They are listening to every word and hearing every unplanned pause, every stutter or stumble, and are critically judging us and finding fault with the information we are trying to share. Yes, we know what it feels like to be the guppy in a shark tank!

You don't have to feel like a guppy any longer—YOU are the Shark! Using the information in this book, along with the SpeechShark app, you can maneuver your way through murky waters and move confidently and fearlessly toward your goal! So, grab your device, click over to your speech notes, and walk to the stage area prepared to knock your audience out of the water! Make your points clearly because you wrote the speech with the end purpose and your audience in mind! No longer are you a guppy, you are a Communication Shark!

SPEAK WITH CONFIDENCE: TAKING A "BITE" OUT OF THE FEAR OF PUBLIC SPEAKING

Just as a shark swims boldly forward to pursue his goal, you can also walk toward the stage with confidence and deliver your speech without hesitation! The first thing that you will want to do is to examine your own confidence level when speaking to an audience.

© bazzier/Shutterstock.com

Unsure of whether your speaking anxiety level is low or high? Take this self-evaluation from **George L. Grice and John F. Skinner's** *Mastering Public Speaking.*

Directions: This instrument is composed of thirty-four statements concerning feelings about communicating with other people. Indicate the degree to which the statements apply to you by marking whether you **(1) strongly agree, (2) agree, (3) undecided, (4) disagree,** or **(5) strongly disagree** with each statement. Work quickly and record your first impression.

PERSONAL REPORT OF PUBLIC SPEAKING ANXIETY

1	2	3	4	5	Statements Concerning Feelings about Communicating with Other People
					1. While preparing for giving a speech, I feel tense and nervous.
					2. I feel tense when I see the words Speech and Public Speaking on a course outline when studying or on a job description.
					3. My thoughts become confused and jumbled when I am giving a speech.
					4. Right after giving a speech, I feel that I have had a pleasant experience.
					5. I get anxious when I think about a speech coming up.
					6. I have no fear of giving a speech.
					7. Although I am nervous just before starting a speech, I soon settle down after starting and feel calm and comfortable.
					8. I look forward to giving a speech.
					9. When the instructor announces a speaking assignment in class, I can feel myself getting tense.
					10. My hands tremble when I am giving a speech.
					11. I feel relaxed when I am giving a speech.
					12. I enjoy preparing for a speech.
					13. I am in constant fear of forgetting what I prepared to say.
					14. I get anxious if someone asks me something about my topic that I do not know.
					15. I face the prospect of giving a speech with confidence.
					16. I feel that I am in complete possession of myself while giving a speech.
					17. My mind is clear when giving a speech.
					18. I do not dread giving a speech.
					19. I perspire just before starting a speech.

1	2	3	4	5	Statements Concerning Feelings about Communicating with Other People
					20. My heart beats very fast just as I start a speech.
					21. I experience considerable anxiety while sitting in the room just before my speech starts.
					22. Certain parts of my body feel very tense and rigid while giving a speech.
					23. Realizing that only a little time remains before a speech makes me very anxious.
					24. While giving a speech, I know I can control my feelings of tension and stress.
					25. I breathe faster just before starting a speech.
					26. I feel comfortable and relaxed in the hour or so just before giving a speech.
					27. I do poorer on speeches because I am anxious.
					28. I feel anxious when I hear an announcement of a speaking assignment.
					29. When I make a mistake while giving a speech, I find it hard to concentrate on the parts that follow.
					30. During an important speech, I experience a feeling of helplessness building up inside me.
					31. I have trouble falling asleep the night before a speech.
					32. My heart beats very fast while I present a speech.
					33. I feel anxious while waiting to give my speech.
					34. While giving a speech, I get so nervous I forget facts I really know.
					TOTAL Points

To determine Your Score on the PRPSA, Complete the Following Steps:

1. Add the scores for items in purple (1,2,3,5,9,10,13,14,19,20,21,22,23,25,27,28,28,30,31,32,33,34).
2. Add the scores for items in peach (4,6,7,8,11,12,15,16,17,18,24,26).
3. Complete the following formula: PRPSA = 132 – (total points from step #1) + (total points from step #2).
4. What is your score? _____

NOTE: Your score can range between 34 and 170. There is no right or wrong answer because this report just helps you to understand if you do have speaker anxiety and the level of speaker anxiety that you may have. Understanding Your Score:

- ► 34–84—Very low anxiety about public speaking
- ► 85–92—Moderately low level of anxiety about public speaking
- ► 93–110—Moderate anxiety in most public speaking situations, but not too severe that the individual cannot cope and be a successful speaker
- ► 111–119—Moderately high anxiety about public speaking. People with this score usually tend to avoid public speaking situations.
- ► 120–170—Very high anxiety about public speaking. People with these scores will go to considerable lengths to avoid all types of public speaking situations.

Whether your level is low or high, it is good to realize that we ALL get nervous when speaking in public; even sharks get nervous, especially when they are swimming in waters teaming with other sharks! So, that means you are normal! Yes, I said it—you are NORMAL!

Some people like to use *breathing exercises* before the speech to help channel the adrenaline running through their bodies. Slowing down their heart beat will also slow down the flow of adrenaline and will help calm nerves. Here are some breathing exercises to try before your next speech.

BREATHING EXERCISES

Before the Speech—Meditate:

- Sit straight with both feet on the floor.
- Close your eyes.
- Focus your attention on this thought, "I am a good speaker", "I am confident", "I will do a good job", and "My audience wants me to succeed."
- Place one hand on your stomach.
- Take a deep breath and recite the positive thought as you exhale.
- Dismiss any distracting or negative thoughts.
- Repeat this exercise for ten minutes prior to going into the room to speak.

While Waiting for the Speech:

- Sit with shoulders touching the back of the chair.
- Make sure your legs are not crossed and your feet are flat on the floor.
- Hang hands loosely to the side.
- Close your eyes and inhale slowly and deeply.
- Fill your chest with air and count four seconds to yourself.
- Hold your breath for another four seconds.
- Exhale air slowly through your mouth for four seconds.
- Imagine the tension flowing out of you and dropping from fingertips onto the floor.
- Feel yourself relaxing as you exhale.
- Continue this until called to present the speech.

After the Speech—Decompress:

- Place a warm heat wrap around your neck and shoulders for ten minutes.
- Close your eyes and relax your face, neck, upper chest, and back muscles.
- Breath deeply and exhale slowly as you relax.
- Remind yourself of the good things you did during your speech.
- Dismiss any distracting or negative thoughts.

Learning to deal with stress associated with public speaking will be your key to speaking with confidence. We all get nervous, so the best thing to know right now is that you are normal! See, doesn't that make you feel better? As you speak, you will experience good stress and bad stress.

Audiences WANT speakers to succeed. Audiences WANT speakers to be amazing and to wow us with their presentations! Why? Because the audience is investing their time to hear your speech. They don't want to waste time, but want to hear a message that is relevant and riveting! You can be the SpeechShark that provides what the audience WANTS!

Using the SpeechShark app will help you to do just that! The app is designed to create a speech that is geared toward your audience and is designed to satisfy the purpose for which you have been asked to speak! SpeechShark provides you with prompts that will help you maneuver through murky waters so that you, too, can swim easily and confidently toward your goal and deliver a crowd-pleasing presentation without hesitation or FEAR!

Dealing with Speech Anxiety

How do you cope with speech anxiety? What is stage fright? Stage fright is different for everyone and speakers compensate for stage fright by using techniques that work for them.

The feeling of stress is produced as adrenaline rushes through your body. *Adrenaline* is physiological and involves increased heart and respiration rate as a result of a situation perceived to be frightening or exciting. With this adrenaline rush, you may feel more energetic, excited, sometimes stronger and happier. This is good stress and will help you to rise to the challenge. Bad stress will cause you to feel fear and anxiety. Fear is a negative emotion which truly does not help the situation at all. With this in mind, I want to show you ways to focus on the good stress and alleviate the bad stress. Try all of these different strategies and you will soon discover the strategy that works best for you.

I've discovered that the people who have stage fright the most are the people who enter the stage unprepared. The best remedy for stage fright is again—**Plan, Prepare, and Persevere!** Know what you are going to say and most of the stage fright will disappear.

We've heard from lots of speakers who say that using the SpeechShark app (www.speechshark.com) helps them to be less anxious because it helps them to know what they should say during the speech. The app also provides note cards for presenting the speech.

PLAN

KNOW your audience, understand your purpose, and know what you need to say. If you can do that, you will have less stage fright and will be a more effective communicator! The **SECRET** is to do everything and anything that will help you be more confident. It is a confidence factor, not a personality or knowledge factor.

Here is what SpeechSharks do BEFORE the speech:

- ▸ **Walk around the room before the speech.**
- ▸ **Stand by the lectern and rehearse in the room where you will be giving the speech.**
- ▸ **Rehearse with people listening to you instead of rehearsing to an empty room.**
- ▸ **Rehearse by audio or video taping yourself.**
- ▸ **Rehearse in front of a mirror.**
- ▸ **Exercise positive self-talk.**

Rehearse, rehearse, rehearse—and rehearse some more. Change wording to make sure the words are coming to you comfortably. Believe in yourself! Feel comfortable with yourself, your location, and your content. As a result, you will be more confident and you will be happier with your presentation.

PREPARE

How do you cope with speech anxiety? Here is what SpeechSharks do BEFORE the speech:

- **Walk around the room before the speech**, instead of sitting in a chair and waiting to be called up front. It will help you to work off some of the nervous energy, and you can greet audience members as you move around the room waiting for the event to begin.
- **Stand by the lectern and rehearse in the room where you will be giving the speech.** This is difficult when the room is full, so arrive early and spend time rehearsing in the SAME PLACE where you will be giving the speech.
- **Rehearse with people listening to you** instead of rehearsing to an empty room. Having a rehearsal audience will give you a similar experience as having the presentation audience. That will help you to feel more confident because you can see how the audience will react to certain points that you make.
- **Rehearse by audio or video taping yourself.** Be AWARE of words that you tend to "chew" up. It may mean changing the wording so that your message will have a smoother delivery.
- **Rehearse in front of a mirror.** This is awkward, but it will help you see your gestures and facial expressions as you make the presentation. It will also give you a chance to check your appearance before you meet your audience.
- **Exercise positive self-talk.** Don't let anything negative come into your brain—tell yourself, "I am going to do a GREAT job!" "This will be my BEST speech!" "The audience is really going to LOVE my topic!" "Nobody in this room KNOWS this topic like I do!" "I am an EXPERT!"

PERSEVERE

Ultimately, the main thing you can do is rehearse, rehearse, rehearse—and rehearse some more. Don't quit. Move forward. Keep your goal in mind. Change wording to make sure the words are coming to you comfortably. Believe in yourself! Feel comfortable with yourself, your location, and your content. As a result, you will be more confident and happier with your presentation.

Look forward to your next speech!

Knock out stress using the **BAM** Approach:

B = *Breathing exercises* can help affect your state of mind, lower heart rate, and bring stress under control. The trick to this is to use controlled breathing exercises. As you follow the breathing exercises, you will notice that your muscle tension will relax when providing your body with much needed oxygen. The result will have a positive effect on your thoughts and feelings. The Internet is packed with breathing exercises to use before your next speech!

© GraphicsRF/Shutterstock.com

A = *Aromatherapy* involves the sense of smell and uses scents to overcome stress and improve overall mental health. Certain scents may help you to feel more calm than others, so it is important to find the scent that helps you to feel "ahhhh!" Some popular scents used to calm stress are lavender, chamomile, lemongrass, and peppermint. Diffusers are readily available online and in department stores along with vials of essential oils. There are also mixtures of various essential oils designed to bring a sense of calmness to the user. Experiment to find the oil/scent which works best for you. Diffuse the oil as you sit in your home or desk prior to giving the speech. Dab a tiny bit of oil on the inside of your wrists before a speech. There are even diffusers available that plug in to your car so that you can experience the calming scents while driving to your speech location.

M = *Meditation* enhanced with music will calm stress. Use imagery and positive visualization to think your way to success! Positive self-talk and imagining a successful speech are achieved as you concentrate on feeling successful while communicating to others. First, imagine yourself walking confidently to the stage, delivering the best speech of your life, and then hearing the welcomed applause of audience members! Tell yourself, "I can do this! I know my topic. I am prepared for this speech. I have a message my audience needs to hear. I am the best person to share this topic to my audience. I will do a great job and my audience will be glad they heard this speech." Do not allow negative thoughts or feelings to enter this moment. Only concentrate on positive thoughts and visualize your success. Using calm music or sounds of nature while meditating can intensify this effect and will help you feel composed and ready to meet the challenge.

There are many strategies available, but as with anything, it is important to do what works for you and to understand your personal stress triggers and indicators.

DO YOU NEED HELP FINDING YOUR VOICE?

Have you ever been asked what you think about an issue? Were you able to answer immediately? Did you feel confident with your answer? Did you feel like your answer was delivered effectively? Since before the time of Aristotle, it was evident that speaking and sharing opinions and facts are important to our society.

We all have opinions and the right to voice those opinions. Becoming a competent speaker is a goal that most of us have, but many of us are not entirely sure how to find our own voice, to exercise the freedom of speech, and to use our voices to bring about societal change.

Quite often, you will be asked to participate in group presentations or to make solo presentations. The higher you proceed in a college education and the more you advance in your company or organization, the more often you are going to be challenged with the prospect of public speaking. Since this is going to be an ongoing reality in your life, why not take time now to find your voice and learn to speak professionally and eloquently?

Communication Sharks understand that *public speaking* is a process in which speakers and listeners participate together. This involves the speaker and the audience accepting their own responsibility toward the positive outcome of messages shared and received.

SPEAKER RESPONSIBILITIES

© Sergey Nivens/Shutterstock.com

Speakers have a responsibility to the audience. It is your job to know who will be in your audience and to plan your speech for them! Just because it is your opportunity to deliver the speech does not mean that you can stand on your soap box and use the time with a captured audience to share just exactly what you think about anything and everything. No, you will need to provide content that the audience needs and it is your responsibility to present it in a way that is effective, clear, and to the point. Prove you are a competent speaker by the content that you provide and the manner in which you provide the content.

Speak to your audience using a conversational tone. Your speech should not sound canned or rehearsed. It should sound as if you are sitting with one person in your audience at your kitchen table and discussing the topic over a nice cup of hot tea! Audiences do not want to be talked at. They want a conversation between you and them. This is the type of interaction you want on a small scale between you and another person. This is also the type of interaction an audience desires with a speaker. Talking "with" someone, sharing information, feelings, convictions are so much more enjoyable than having someone talk "at" you! It is a more intimate transaction. Just remember, the same type of interpersonal communication skills that work on a one-on-one or in a small group setting will also work beautifully between a speaker and an audience.

Show the audience that you care about them with the content you provide. Mention their names or the town where you are speaking. Say something positive about their local sports team, mayor, or director of the business where you are speaking. This will help your audience to feel like you wanted to be there with them enough to know what is important to them. It will help you to get the audience in your corner and will also make your speech so much more effective! Consider yourself as a host or hostess at a gathering. Your job is to make your audience comfortable and to supply their every need. To do this, the speaker is responsible for conducting an *audience analysis*, defining the purpose of the speech, choosing a topic that will interest the audience, conducting research to support the topic, and constructing an outline to organize the content.

WILL YOU SINK OR SWIM?

© Sergey Nivens/Shutterstock.com

Preparation is the key to success! It is the difference between success and failure and will make the difference in whether you will sink or swim! Never forget that the buck stops with YOU! When facing the task of making a speech presentation, it is your job to plan, prepare, and present the speech. These simple steps to SUCCESS will help you to swim with the sharks!

Even with a great tool, like the SpeechShark app, you still have to make time to work through the plan. The first thing that a speaker should do before planning a speech is to conduct an audience analysis and gain an understanding about the speaking environment.

Once you understand **WHO** is in your audience and **WHERE** you will be speaking, you will be able to make a better decision regarding **WHAT** content to include in the speech.

Toward the end of this chapter you will find an **Audience Analysis Worksheet** that provides several key questions to ask yourself as you begin the planning process. Take time to answer each of the questions every time you plan for a speech. The questions will help you to know which topic is suitable for the audience and the speaking environment you will have.

Once you answer these questions, you have entered the planning stage. All that you have to do at this point is to take a deep breath and dive in. There will be no sinking here—you will swim and you will swim with ease!

All of these steps may seem time-consuming, but if you want to SWIM and not sink, these are details that cannot be overlooked or ignored.

CONDUCT AN AUDIENCE ANALYSIS

Questions to Consider:	Answers to Help Plan:
What is the purpose of the speech?	
When will the speech be presented? (Date/Time of Day)	
Do you have a time limit for the speech?	
Is this speech being directed to a particular type of audience? (Example: Senior Citizens, High School Glee Club, Community Volunteers, etc.)	
What is the occasion for this speech?	
Is there a stage?	
Will you have a lectern for notes?	
Will you need visual aids?	
Will you require a Tech Team for sound, lights, setup, breakdown?	
Will you need a microphone?	
Will someone introduce you or will you introduce yourself?	
How many people will attend the speech?	
How many women will attend?	
How many men will attend?	
Is there a large gender gap?	
What is the average age of audience members?	
Is there a large age gap?	
What is the cultural background of the audience?	
Is there a large cultural gap?	
Are there political and religious differences to consider? If so, explain.	
What is the educational status of the audience?	
Are there restrictions which might limit your topic?	
Will the audience enjoy your topic?	
Will the audience be receptive to you as the speaker?	
What does your audience expect from you?	
What kind of information should you share with your audience?	
What type of clothing should you wear for this audience? Are there certain types of clothing and/or jewelry items that would distract your audience?	
Is this audience formal or casual?	
Are there other factors to consider?	

Here is a diagram to help you understand the planning process better:

PLANNING THE SPEECH

1. Conduct an Audience Analysis

2. Determine the Purpose

3. Select and Narrow the Topic

4. Research and Gather Materials

5. Develop Three Main Points

6. Develop the Introduction Step

7. Develop the Conclusion

8. Rehearse and Deliver the speech

Source: Dr. Penny Joyner Waddell

RESPECT DIVERSITY

Since all of us are unique in our own way, it is important that your presentation should be designed to respect everyone in your audience. Most likely, there will be diversity in religious and political beliefs, cultures, genders, age, educational levels, and a multitude of other pre-conceived notions held by each audience member. The larger your audience, the more diversity plays into the way you plan a speech.

Make no assumptions about the beliefs of your audience members and remain ethical by keeping this in mind as you plan presentations. Ethical issues should be considered as you speak and as you listen to the speeches of others. Establish positive ethos by being the kind of person the audience thinks you are based upon what you say and how you project yourself as a speaker.

You've heard the terms ethos, pathos, and logos. These are defined as follows:

Ethos is an appeal to ethics. This is answered as you establish credibility in the introduction section of your speech.

Pathos is an appeal to emotion. This happens as you appeal to the audience's passions or emotions and as you create an emotional response through story telling or argument.

Logos is an appeal to logic. We do this as we reason with our audience and provide logical uses of examples and research to support points we are making in the speech.

The combination of all three (ethos, pathos, and logos) are incorporated as we show respect to our diverse audience members. Know your audience so that you are sure to accomplish these appeals and exhibit respect. Avoid stereotyping and consider situations which might surface. As a speaker, seek to maintain the highest standards of ethics because you are responsible for the content you share with others. As you do this, you will show respect for your audience and they in turn will respect you.

Be aware of the nonverbal cues that are being sent your way during the speech and be flexible enough to change your plan if you notice that audience members are uncomfortable with your topic. A good speaker should never push his/her own agenda on the audience. Show respect for your audience by considering their views and incorporate them into your speech. This will show your audience that you are striving to meet them where they are.

Every person in your audience will have different perspectives, backgrounds, and experiences. We each see, hear, and respond to the world in our own way. It is because of this that we need to learn ways to embrace differences that we have and find common ground to connect with each person in our audience. Your primary responsibility as a speaker is to understand that differences between your audience members will exist. Therefore, you will need to consider every aspect in planning the speech so that your speech will be well received by the majority of people in your audience. In other words, for speaking situations you may need to adapt to others who are different than you and overcome barriers which tend to spotlight our differences.

Before I end this section about diversity, I would like to ask you to go to the Internet and in your search engine bar, type in: TED Talks: Chimamanda Ngozi Adichie: *The Danger of a Single Story*. For your convenience, I will post the URL Address and a link:

https://www.ted.com/talks/chimamanda_adichie_the_danger_of_a_single_story

You've all heard of TED Talks and I'm sure you have spent time watching great speeches through this venue. All of the topics offered in TED Talks are fascinating to me, but this one struck a different chord because of the honesty shared. In less than twenty minutes, this amazing young woman tells a story of the dangers of knowing only one story and not seeing the whole picture.

As I watched this speech, I realized just how guilty **all** of us are. For the most part, we understand our own cultures and we think we understand the cultures of others, but often we do not. It is our own assumptions and perceptions that dictate our innermost thoughts about others from different cultures. Whether we are talking about a culture of gender, age, race, ethnicities, locations, political or religious beliefs, or any number of other categories that we seem to box ourselves and others into, we need to be aware that we may only view that culture as a single story. And, that is wrong. To reach a diverse audience population means that we must look further than the box or category that we perceive as the only story to realize there are always more stories to uncover and more perceptions to understand. Please watch this video and let me know if it also helps you to think in a broader term when planning for your diverse audience members!

DEFINING THE PURPOSE

Strategic planning is needed for speeches. Once you understand who will be in your audience, your next step is to define the purpose of the speech. Size up the situation and use this information to make choices to help you reach your goal. Strategic planning includes knowing when to speak, what topics to cover, how to phrase your points, how to explain, how to demonstrate a process or procedure, how to defend a point or motivate your audience to solve a problem, how to organize the message and relate the message to the audience. Making choices are important for strategic planning!

Your speech will have two purposes: a general purpose and a specific purpose. The *general purpose* is the type speech you will present. Are you speaking to inform, entertain, motivate, or perhaps all three? This is your general purpose. The *specific purpose* is more detailed. As you determine the purpose for a speech presentation, you are actually creating a plan to achieve a particular goal. Determining the purpose helps the speaker know what information to share in the body of the speech, how to introduce the topic, and how to conclude the speech.

Here is an example of how this might look on your speech outline:

General Purpose: Inform
Specific Purpose: The purpose of this speech is to inform my audience about the dangers of texting while driving.

General Purpose: Motivate
Specific Purpose: The purpose of this speech is to motivate my audience to give blood at the Red Cross Blood Drive at City Hall next week.

General Purpose: Entertain
Specific Purpose: The purpose of this speech is to entertain my audience as I Roast and Toast our volunteers at the annual end of the year celebration.

GOALS

Having a clear understanding of the purpose of your speech presentation will help you to achieve your speaking goals, develop strategies for a successful presentation, and stay within the time frame that has been offered.

Some use the SWOT strategy to define speaking goals: **S**trengths, **W**eaknesses, **O**pportunities, and **T**hreats. Work through each area analyzing the area and recording your responses. Consider each area as they pertain to the specific speech type that you will be presenting. Each speech is different. Each audience is different. With this in mind, you will want to revisit the SWOT strategy each time you plan a speech.

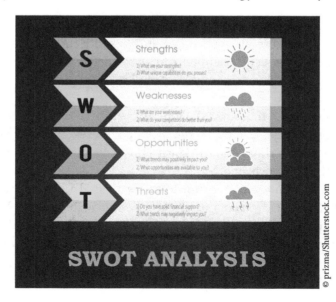

© prizma/Shutterstock.com

This table will help you understand the goal to achieve a general and specific purpose for each type of speech. Plan to use these suggestions for your general and specific purpose.

Type of Speech	General Purpose	Specific Purpose
Introduction Speech	Inform	The purpose of an Introduction Speech is to introduce yourself or someone else to the audience.
Informative Speech	Inform	The purpose of an Informative Speech is to inform the audience about a topic.
Demonstration Speech	Inform and Entertain	The purpose of a Demonstration Speech is to demonstrate a process or a product.
Persuasion Speech	Motivate	The purpose of a Persuasion Speech is to motivate the audience to solve a problem.
Special Occasion Speech	Inform and/or Entertain	The purpose of a Special Occasion Speech is to inform or entertain an audience through work-related, social, and ceremonial occasions.
Group Presentation	Inform, Entertain, Motivate	The purpose of a group presentation is to present a topic as a group effort with each member taking equal responsibility to inform, entertain, or motivate the audience according to the topic.
Sales Presentation	Motivate	The purpose of the sales presentation is to motivate a buyer to purchase a product or service.

STRATEGIES

Develop a timeline for creating and presenting the speech. Start with the date for the speech and work backward from there. Allow time to conduct the audience analysis, determine the purpose, and select the topic. Critical thinking skills are used during this stage as you plan the topic with the audience and purpose in mind.

Once your topic has been selected, narrow the topic and begin conducting research to develop and support your points. Add personal stories and experiences along with research to appear more credible to your audience. Create the presentation outline by starting with the three main points of the body, build the introduction step, and finally, draft the conclusion.

Once the outline has been completed, it is time to create a visual aid and handout to support the speech and make presentation notes. The final part of the task is to Rehearse, Rehearse, Rehearse to prepare for a successful presentation. Don't forget to pack supplies for your speech and meet with your Tech Team to make sure all is ready for your presentation! This is the easiest part, Sharks! This is where you are confident because you have taken the time to plan and prepare!

TIME

When asked to speak, make sure you meet with the organizer of the event and find out exactly how much time the organizer needs for you to speak. Plan your speech according to the time frame allotted. Many times, your speech will not be the only point of interest for the event. The organizer will appreciate knowing that you will stay on time because that will mean that her event will also end on time.

Time each rehearsal and take an average of each rehearsal time to get a good idea of the length of time for your speech. If you find that you are going "over time" you will need to cut some of your sub-points. If you find that you are going "under time" you will need to add sub-points. Now, you are almost ready! These details will not "just happen" and it is up to you to make sure that they do happen and at the time that you choose.

The SpeechShark app has a handy timer built in. Simply choose the amount of time you will need to complete your speech and the app will remind you when you need to move from one point to the next. Just another way that you can swim with ease through murky waters!

© Jahthanyapat/Shutterstock.com

SEARCHING FOR A TOPIC?

Now that you have conducted an audience analysis and determined the purpose of your upcoming presentation, you can begin to think of a topic that will interest your audience and a topic for which you have experience and prior knowledge! This can be an overwhelming task and you might feel like you are a shark circling the waters for just the right target. Truthfully, that is not too far from reality.

When asked to speak for a particular event, you may not have the luxury of choosing a topic because it may be assigned to you; however, you still have the freedom to plan, develop, and add your own personal touch to the topic. For this type situation, it is a good idea to meet with the organizer of the event and ask about their expectations. Some speakers have been known to make phone calls to random audience members to ask what topic they would like to hear and to pinpoint information that is relevant for their personal or professional situations.

If you are still having trouble settling on the topic for your presentation, look through books or magazines for inspiration. Meet with friends and colleagues to brainstorm possible topic choices. Listen to news stations or read news articles to pick up on trending topics. Dive into the Internet and search "Speech Topics" to see what you find. There are billions of topics. Choose the one that is right for your audience and the one that is right for you! Once you have your topic, you will be able to choose three main points, sub-points in the form of research, personal stories or examples, and create the message to make it memorable for your audience

NARROWING THE TOPIC

Narrowing the topic is one part of the process involved with choosing a topic. In a short ten-minute speech, you will not be able to cover everything there is to say about the topic. With this in mind, it becomes necessary to narrow the topic to a manageable size.

Here is an example: You LOVE sports, so you are thinking about giving a speech about sports. But, sports is a huge topic and can't be covered in less than ten minutes. Choose one type of sport. Do you want to talk about baseball, basketball, tennis, soccer, racquetball, swimming, skydiving, biking, golf, running, boating, parasailing, skydiving, zip lining, or—Oh My Goodness! Do you see the problem with this? There are so many sports and I love them, ALL! How do I choose? Well, it is obvious you can't speak about all of them in less than ten minutes.

Settle on one **type** of sport and then from that category, narrow the large topic down to a smaller manageable **category**. You are still not finished. Break that down again into a **point** about that sport that is interesting. Almost done . . . Narrow that point into three clear **points**! Aha, now you are swimming and thinking like a Communication Shark!

Here is a way to narrow a topic:

TOPIC
- Topic - **SPORTS**

TYPE
- Narrow this broad topic to a type of sport that is interesting for the audience and for you.
- **Tennis**

Category
- Narrow the topic of tennis to one category.
- **Professional Tennis**

Point
- Narrow the category to a more specific point
- **Types of Tennis Courts**

Points
- Narrow the point into three support points
- **(1) Clay , (2) Hard, (3) Grass**

Source: Dr. Penny Joyner Waddell

Does this help you understand the process? Often people try to make speeches without really thinking about the points they will cover. It's time to get to the point. Think of specific and clear points that will add information to your audience's existing knowledge.

Why not give this a try with your own topic for the next speech? Write your answers here:

Topic
- Topic

Type
- Narrow the broad topic to a type

Category
- Narrow the type to a category

Point
- Narrow the category to a point

Points
- Narrow this into three points
- 1.
- 2.
- 3.

Source: Dr. Penny Joyner Waddell

If you are using the SpeechShark app (www.SpeechShark.com), there is a section early in the development stage where you will be prompted to share the topic of your speech. Before you begin that process, make sure you know the answer!

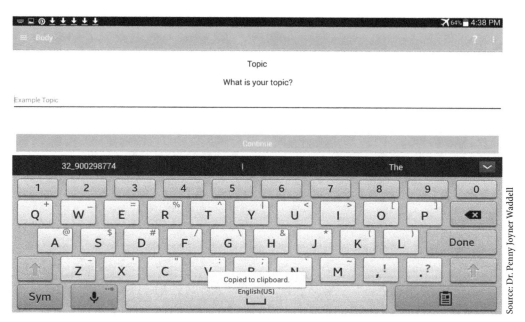

Whether you have been given a topic or if you can choose a topic, you will want to answer important questions to create a strategic plan.

Here is a guide to help choose the topic for your next speech.

General Topic Proposal

Write Your Topic Choice Here: _____ **Answer These Questions:**	YES	NO
Does your topic satisfy the general purpose for the presentation?		
Is your topic narrow enough to be completed within your allotted time?		
Will your audience relate to the topic?		
Will this topic be meaningful to the audience?		
Can you add information about the topic that your audience may not already know?		
Is this topic appropriate for your audience? Consult your audience analysis again and examine the topic as it will appeal to diverse audiences.		
Is the topic you have chosen controversial?		
Will your audience be receptive to a controversial topic?		
Are you passionate about this topic?		
Are you excited about sharing this topic with others? Remember, enthusiasm is contagious. If you are excited and enthusiastic about the topic, there is a good chance that your audience will "catch" your enthusiasm.		
Can you choose three points to develop for this topic? List the three points here: 1. 2. 3.		
Do you need to conduct research to support your topic?		
What type of research do you need?		
Do you have personal stories and experience about this topic to share?		
Can you provide simple examples of your main points that are clear and easily understood?		
Will you need to supply your audience with a handout after the speech?		
Will you need to create a PowerPoint or Prezi Presentation as a visual aid?		
Will you have a Tech Team to handle your visual aids?		
Can you think of a creative way to introduce this topic to your audience?		
Is the setting for the speech conducive to this topic?		

Complete the topic proposal for the next speech you are planning and present it to your instructor for approval.

Informative Speech Topic Proposal:
Student's Name:
Speech Date:
Topic:
Title of Speech:
Three Main Points: 1.   2.   3.

Persuasion Speech Topic Proposal:
Student's Name:
Speech Date:
Topic:
Title of Speech:
Three Main Points: 1.   2.   3.

Special Occasion Speech Topic Proposal:

Student's Name:

Speech Date:

Topic:

Title of Speech:

Three Main Points:

1.

2.

3.

Group Presentation Topic Proposal:

Student's Name:

Speech Date:

Topic:

Title of Speech:

Three Main Points:

1.

2.

3.

Topic Suggestions to Get You Thinking

Informative Speech Topics:	
Bargain Shopping	Learning Disabilities
Body Piercings	Learning How to Knit
Carpooling Tips	Meditation
Cloning	Privacy Rights
College Requirements	Recycling
Coping with Online Courses	Rescuing Pets
Dressing for Success	Smoking Policies
Facebook Security	Television Viewing Habits
Finding Balance	To Tweet or Not to Tweet?
Going Green	Volunteering in Homeless Shelters
Home-schooling	Wikis are Wonderful
Healthcare Options	Working from Home
Kid-Friendly Activities	Would you like to go Skydiving?
Labor Unions	Zip-Lining in Costa Rica
Learning a Foreign Language	Zoo Animals at Risk

Persuasion Speech Topics – Notice the Topics All Begin with an Action Word	
Adopt a Grandparent	Go Back to School
Avoid Artificial Sweeteners	Grow a Vegetable Garden
Apply for Scholarships	Invest in Your Future
Ban Beauty Pageants	Join a Club
Be a Mentor	Join a Community Theater
Become a Vegetarian	Learn to Cook
Buy Organic	Learn to Play
Care for Your Elders	Lose Weight
Donate Blood	Lower the Drinking Age
Don't Text and Drive	Make a "Bucket" List
Dress for Success	Practice Safe Sex
Eat Healthy	Prayer in Schools
Exercise	Register to Vote
Keep Prayer in Schools	Save Money
Search Your Family History	Support the Arts
Make a Bucket List	Teach Children to Save Money
Freedom of Speech	Train Your Dog

Group Presentation Topics:
Choosing a College (Report on different aspects: history, courses, sports, campus life, cost)
Creating a Bucket List (travel, adventure, learning a new skill, volunteering)
Health Benefits of Exercising (heart, lungs, muscles, mental)
Making Money (time involved, benefits, getting started, mentor/mentee)
Movies to Remember (categories, story lines, themes, genres)
Plan a Meal (include recipes: appetizers, soup, salad, main course, desserts, beverages)
Plan a Trip (who, when, where, how)
Report on a Country (culture, foods, government, sports, traditions)
Sales Presentation (product, demonstration, costs, benefits)
Volunteer Opportunities (time, money, benefits, getting started)

CONDUCTING RESEARCH

Now that you have chosen a topic for your speech, it is time to develop your understanding of the topic by conducting research. During the research process, speakers will often refine three main points or use research they have gathered to craft sub-points. Information found during research can be used as the attention step, the conclusion, or as support for main points within your speech.

Research can come in the form of data, statistics, opinions, or ideas, but can also be as simple as someone's experience or a story that supports your topic. It is up to you to decide what type of research will be most effective for your particular topic. Speakers also use videos, music, art, photography, and other mediums to support points or create visual aids to support the speech topic. In all cases, if it does not belong to you, it is necessary to cite the source.

Research is defined as the process for finding support materials and credible information. This information will be added to your already vast knowledge of the topic you have chosen to cover. One mistake people often make is to use a base search engine on the Internet to find support material. While this is a simple way to conduct research, it does not always promise credible results.

Read the research guidelines and methods in this chapter to learn the best way to use online resources to support your topic. Credible research will help you appear more credible as a speaker. On the other hand, weak research choices can undermine your speaker credibility and may create confusion, especially if sources are not vetted and reviewed.

As you begin to conduct research, please follow these simple checkpoints:

- ◯ Use research that is current: preferably less than five years old.
- ◯ Use research that is credible. Avoid using Wikis, blogs, advertisements, or Web pages.
- ◯ Use research that will support the topic and your view of the topic.
- ◯ Use research that will clarify the topic.
- ◯ Use research that will expand your knowledge of the topic.
- ◯ Use research that has been written or published by recognizable credible sources.

In years past, the only way that someone could conduct research was to visit a brick-and-mortar library and spend hours looking through books and reference materials. Once the desired article or data was found, the research would need to be photocopied or typed into a document. Thankfully, finding credible research now is simply a click away as most of us conduct research using the Internet. If you do choose to visit a library to conduct research, you will be pleasantly surprised by the amount of online materials available through the library and also by the helpfulness of local librarians to help narrow down sources to find the most useful and productive sources for your topic.

Whether you conduct research online or at the library, you may find it helpful to create a speech materials file to store articles which may prove helpful as you plan your speech. Online articles can be e-mailed to yourself and digital files can be created to store quotes, data, brainstorming ideas, anecdotes, or stories to support your topic. This will be helpful as you sift through possible sources searching for the two or three best sources to serve your needs.

Plagiarism

We can't talk about research without including tips to avoid plagiarism. The interesting thing about plagiarism is that it can occur verbally as well as in writing, so make sure you cite everything you use that is not your own. *Plagiarism* is the act of using someone else's ideas or work as if they are your own. In essence, this is stealing and in the educational and professional arena, plagiarism is an act which may lead to immediate dismissal. Copyright laws are in place to protect authors of written works.

The best way to avoid plagiarism charges is to verbally or in writing cite everything that belongs to someone else. Turnitin.com is a Web site that checks for plagiarism. Many colleges and universities use this site regularly to check students' work for plagiarism. In the corporate world, a plagiarism charge can harm your reputation and career. Just to be safe, always verbally and in writing cite the source of research and give proper credit. Citation guidelines are noted toward the end of this chapter.

Guidelines

How do you know if a source of research is credible? Blogs on the Internet can appear to be quite credible. They can be written and posted by someone with a Ph.D., but even that will not determine if the source is credible. Often blogs or Wikis will provide interesting or amusing information, but that also does not determine if the source is credible. Interesting or amusing does not equal credible. With this in mind, I always warn the speech students that I coach to never use a blog, Wiki, or advertisement link—no matter how legitimate it may sound. The point is to evaluate the research and make decisions regarding whether or not the source is credible and offers information you can use to support your speech.

Use credible research owned, reviewed, and monitored by reputable organizations, government sources, newspapers, journals, books, and magazine sources. Stay away from blogs, Wikis, and advertisements which might link to credible sources, but are not credible in their own rights.

Use the following checklist to determine if the source is credible:

- ☐ Would my audience recognize the source?
- ☐ Does the source list an author?
- ☐ Does the author have credentials to verify his/her credibility?
- ☐ Does the source list copyright information?
- ☐ Was this source published within the past five years?
- ☐ Is the content clear and helpful? Is the content accurate and unbiased?
- ☐ Does the content offer opposing viewpoints?
- ☐ Does the content support my topic?

Research Methods

Gathering materials online has never been easier than it is right now. Through the Internet, online research has become the primary source for gathering information for college students and professionals. The Internet can be an incredible source for locating great information, but it is also a source for spreading misinformation! Take care to choose sources of research from credible sources and con-

firm that the information you share with your audiences is something that will clarify the topic and not confuse your audience.

The **Internet** is one of the most popular go-to sources for people who want to conduct research for any topic in the world. Online search engines like Google, Bing, Yahoo, and Google Scholar have become quite popular. Do not rely solely upon Google; however, if you search Google Scholar, it is possible to find credible research for your speech. Print materials from periodicals, newspapers, encyclopedias, dictionaries, journals, and books are also available through the Internet in digital formats.

Many states offer credible online search engines for a small fee. A student in any of the state of Georgia high schools, technical colleges, community colleges, and university systems are able to use the well-known virtual library called GALILEO (Georgia, Library of Learning Online). Everything in GALILEO is credible. Students are able to search, save, e-mail sources, and get citation help through this easy to navigate system. Many of the sites found in GALILEO offer audio versions of articles, as well as translations into many other languages. Other states have programs similar to GALILEO to help with student research.

Through various search engines, we are able to use key words in a search window to limit the search and to make the research process simpler. The downside is that search engines usually provide a broad expanse of materials, all of which are not credible or relevant for the topic you have chosen. Directories, on the other hand, allow people to link with key words or matches regarding the topic and are manned by a librarian who chooses the prospective sites based upon the quality of that site.

Here are other options:

- ▶ **Government and survey sites** such as the Gallup Polls offer reliable information that can be used as support materials.
- ▶ **Libraries** often have resources that cannot be found online; therefore, you may want to visit your local library as you conduct research for your speech.
- ▶ **Magazines and journals** are the most common forms of research and are readily available in hard copy and online.
- ▶ **Television and radio programs** provide transcripts of trending stories that can be used as support for speeches.
- ▶ **Newspapers**, available in hard copy and online, offer current and trending information about topics of interest.
- ▶ **Books** are an excellent source of information, but readers should understand that it takes months for books to be published and the information contained in a book may not be the very latest information released to the public. Be sure to check the copyright date before using a book.
- ▶ **Interviews** are a perfect way to get stories and personal experience about your topic. Just make sure your interviewee is a credible source for your topic.

When using **key words** to initiate a search, take care to spell the key words correctly, use nouns and avoid using more than six words per search. If your search is not successful, try using different key words. As you type in key words into the search box, you will notice that other popular searches will pop up. Sometimes following the pop-up trails will lead to sources that are useful, but other times they will not.

Research is a way to find the answers you need to support points and explore facts that will make you appear more credible to your audience.

Just remember that conducting research is a process. It's like fishing. You have to bait a lot of hooks before you catch the prize fish. With research, you have to review a lot of sources before you find the right data, anecdote, or information to support the point you want to make!

Interviews

Interviews are often used as a source of experiential research to support speech topics. For example, you may choose to integrate an interview with credible print or electronic research to support your topic. We often associate interviews as part of a job-search process and that is true; however, interviews can provide information to help further your knowledge about a subject. An *interview* is defined as the asking of specific questions with the intent to gather information from the person being interviewed. All interview types follow the same basic formula. Prepared questions are chosen depending upon the purpose. Questions are asked and answers are provided. Here are the different types of interviews:

► **Information gathering interviews** are often conducted with many people responding to a question asked.

► **Job interviews** are structured conversations with a goal to discover if a person is suitable for an open position within a company.

► **Problem-solving interviews** are designed to bring peace or solve grievances between two parties. A mediator is usually present in the event of a problem-solving interview.

► **Performance reviews** are considered interviews and are initiated by management authorities in a company to review the performance of employees.

There are three parts to every interview: opening, body, and closing.

The **opening** sets the stage for the type of interview and is usually a time where the interviewer creates a rapport with the interviewee to establish open communication lines in the hope of having a positive interaction between the two.

The **body** of the interview includes questions that are asked. There are different types of questions used for interviews. The most appropriate question to use during the interview is the **open question**. These are broad questions that cannot be answered with a simple "yes" or "no" answer. These questions open the interviewee to answer in-depth thereby adding knowledge for your topic.

Probing questions are good questions to use during an interview because these questions encourage the interviewee to elaborate about the topic.

Avoid asking *closed questions*, as this limits the responses you might receive and will also limit the amount of information you are able to gather about the topic. Closed questions are usually answered by a "yes" or "no."

The **closing** of the interview is an opportunity to summarize the interview and to close on a positive note. Each person, the interviewer and the interviewee, has a responsibility to the other.

Audio or video recording an interview is a good idea, especially when you will be writing and presenting a transcript of the interview. After the introductions and before beginning the interview, ask your interviewee if he/she would mind if you record the interview. You can decide if you want to audio or video record the session. Most electronic devices, whether it is your phone, tablet, or iPad, have the audio and video recording feature, making this an easier task. If the interviewee agrees to the interview, place your electronic device in full view of the interviewee and pointed toward the speaker so that it will pick up both of your voices. If by chance the interviewee does not allow the recording, then it will be your responsibility to repeat back the interviewee's answers to make sure that your note-taking skills are accurate and that you are able to fully understand the interviewee's response.

The purpose of this unit is to work through expectations so that your next interview will be successful. E-mail, telephone, and Skype interviews are sometimes appropriate; however, face-to-face interviews yield the most promising results.

There are advantages and disadvantages of both types of interviews:

Advantages:	Disadvantages:
E-mail, telephone, and Skype interviews take less time than a personal visit.	You cannot be sure who is replying to your e-mail or phone questions.
E-mail questions are efficient and provide a paper trail.	A breakdown in communication can happen with phone conversations.
E-mail questions allow the interviewee time to formulate a response.	Skype interactions rely on Internet connections and contact could be disrupted.
E-mail responses are useful if the interviewee lives in another time zone.	E-mail restricts your ability to question the response.
E-mail, telephone, and SKYPE are more convenient for both parties.	E-mail and telephone interviews cannot communicate nonverbal cues.

To include experiential research as support for your upcoming speech, here is a convenient checklist to make sure you are prepared:

BEFORE the Interview	DURING the Interview	AFTER the Interview
Decide WHO you will interview.	Behave professionally.	Thank the receptionist as you leave the office area.
Prepare interview questions.	Shake hands with the interviewee.	Write a thank you note or e-mail as soon as you return from the interview.
Craft open-ended questions.	Smile and make eye contact.	Include an invitation to hear the speech.
Contact the interviewee.	Wait to sit until you are invited by the interviewee.	Use the audio recording to write the transcript.
Request an appointment.	Ask permission to audio record the interview. Ask permission before taking a photo with the interviewee.	Include the entire conversation in the transcript.
Pack a recording device.	Ask questions clearly and one at a time.	Using the transcript, include the interview as a source of research in your outline and speech.
Arrive ten minutes early.	Wait patiently for answers.	Correctly cite the interview source in the outline.
Dress professionally.	Clarify answers.	Include the interview on the Works Cited page.
Have note-taking materials.	When through, stand and extend your hand for a handshake.	If the interviewee attends the speech, be sure to acknowledge this during the speech.
Introduce yourself to the receptionist.	Thank the interviewee for his time.	Correctly cite the interview verbally during your speech.
Wait to enter until you are invited into the office.	Invite him to hear your speech. Provide the day/time/location.	During the speech, be sure to offer the interviewee's credentials for the audience.
Enter the room with a smile!	Do not overstay.	If using the audio or video, preface the content and then offer a recap during the speech.

A thank you note following the interview should follow standard letter-writing guidelines.

Example of Thank You Letter:

Name
Address, City, State, Zip Code
Phone Number
E-mail Address

Date of the Interview

Interviewee's Name
Interviewee's Address

Dear Mr./Ms./Dr. Last Name:

Thank you for taking time to meet with me and answer questions I had about (enter the topic of your speech). I appreciate your time. The information you supplied will be used as research to support my speech.

I would like to invite you to attend the speech that will be given at (time) on (date) and held at (location). It would be an honor to have you as a guest.

Thank you again!

Sincerely,
(Add your signature)
Type Your Full Name

Type the interview transcript using this template:

Interview Transcript Template

Interviewer:
Name
Address, City, State, Zip Code
Phone Number
E-mail Address

Interviewee:
Name
Address, City, State, Zip Code
Phone Number
E-mail Address

Interviewee's Credentials: Provide details regarding why you chose to interview this person as a source of research for your speech topic. What experience have they had with this topic that would prove credibility for the topic?

Interview Date/Time:
Interview Location:

Question #1:

Interviewee's Response:

_____

Question #2:

Interviewee's Response:

_____

Question #3:

Interviewee's Response:

_____

Question #4:

Interviewee's Response:

_____

Question #5:

Interviewee's Response:

_____

WRITTEN CITATIONS OF RESEARCH

Let's talk about citation of sources, since this is a big responsibility for the speaker! First, you should know that there are different ways to cite research. The most frequently used citation styles are APA, MLA, CSE, and CMS. With each style, you will notice a specific set of rules and guidelines established to indicate the author, title, publishing source, date of publication, and page numbers of the source.

Additionally, you will notice there are different ways to cite each type of source, whether it is a book, e-book, dissertations, Web sites, radio or television episodes, videos or film clips, magazines, journals, or newspaper articles, music, art, or pictures.

How do you know which style to use and what makes each style unique? Each style is formulated for a particular discipline. If you are not tasked with using one specific guideline, then please follow the notations below to make sure you are using the style most suited for the topic you are covering. We have also included the links to their Web sites so that you can go directly to the source to see clear instructions regarding how to cite the source of research in your outline or document.

Here is a breakdown of styles, a notation of when they should be used, and the link to their Web sites:

APA is known as the American Psychological Association style of citing research. Disciplines that cover psychology, sociology, social work, criminology, education, business, and economics may use the APA style of citing research. For APA Guidelines, please visit their website at http://www.apastyle.org/.

MLA is known as the Modern Language Association style of citing research. Documents using research for literature and language will use this style of citing research. Since you are learning about public speaking and crafting speeches to inform, persuade, and entertain, you will need to cite your sources of research using the MLA Guidelines for source citations. We'll provide examples of MLA citations in this book. For MLA Guidelines, please visit their website at https://www.mla.org/MLA-Style.

CSE citations follow the guidelines established by the Council of Science Editors and are used primarily when the writer or speaker is citing research in the applied sciences areas. These will include biology, chemistry, physics, astronomy, and earth science. For CSE Guidelines, please visit their website at https://www.councilscienceeditors.org/publications/scientific-style-and-format/.

CMS is known as the Chicago Manual of Style. These guidelines are used to cite research that involve the arts and humanities. For CMS Guidelines, please visit their website at http://www.chicagomanualofstyle.org/home.html.

Example of a written citation for a book following MLA Guidelines:

Waddell, Penny. SpeechShark: A Public Speaking Guide. Kendall Hunt, 2019.

Example of a written citation for an electronic source following MLA Guidelines:

Cox, Lindsey. "Six Secrets to Urban Gardening with No Yard." *OffTheGridNews: Better Ideas for Off the Grid Living,* Off the Grid News. 2019. https://www.offthegridnews.com/survival-gardening. Accessed 15 April 2019.

The example shown above is demonstrating the documentation of two different types of sources using MLA Guidelines for a Works Cited page. When creating a Works Cited page, center the words—Works Cited. This should be introduced as a completely separate page from the outline and should only include sources used for the speech. The Works Cited page should follow MLA Guidelines for citations. Entries should be double- spaced and shown in alphabetical order according to the authors' last names. If no author is listed, the writer should alphabetize the articles. Titles beginning with A, An, or The should be alphabetized by the title's second word and the A, An, or The is moved to be the final word of the title.

A simple formula to follow for MLA citations is as follows:

1. Author (Last name, First Name).
2. Title of source.
3. Title of container,
4. Other contributors (editors),
5. Version,
6. Number,
7. Publisher,
8. Publication date.
9. Location.
10. Accessed day month year.

Notice that each of the ten areas above include punctuation following the notation. Many of the notations end with a period, but others end with a comma. Also, if the source does not contain the notation listed, the writer can eliminate that part of the citation.

For example, for the book citation, there isn't a container, other contributors, version, or number. Therefore, those areas are eliminated.

For the electronic citation, there are no other contributors, version, or number. Therefore, those areas are eliminated.

Sources with more than three authors should be listed as showing the first author as last name, first name and any subsequent authors as first name then last name. If the source has three or more authors, the writer should name all of the others or simply use the first author's name and add the term et al., which is a Latin term for "and others."

If the full written citation takes up more than one typed line, the writer should use *hanging indentions* for additional lines. Notice how the electronic citation in the example uses hanging indentions. The first line goes to the far left of the margin while the additional lines are indented.

In-text citations are required for the speech outline. Writers will need to place the primary source information in parenthesis within the area where the source will be used. We call this a *parenthetical citation* and it involves having the author's last name and the page number of the work surrounded by parenthesis.

If citing the title of the book mentioned above, the written citation would be shown as (Waddell 168). If the speaker mentioned the author's name in the preceding statement along with the title of the book, the writer could then simply include the page number as (168). Notice how there is no punctuation between the author's last name and the page number. Also, notice how the period goes outside of the parenthetical citation.

Quotes that are longer than four typed lines should be included in the written document and there should be a parenthetical citation following the *block indented margin*. It is obvious to see the block indented margins because they are one inch or ten spaces from the left margin. Quotation marks are not used for block indented quotes.

VERBAL CITATIONS OF RESEARCH

Whether in writing or verbally, any source of research used must be cited. To avoid plagiarism charges during your speech, cite every source you use. In recent news, we learned of a case where one prominent politician plagiarized the words and ideas of another. The words used were so identical that the news reporters and commentators had a field day reporting how this one person blatantly used the very same words as the other. It was quite embarrassing for the politician, who then made a formal statement apologizing for the error. Make sure that you do not find yourself in the same situation.

When you are speaking to an audience and you want to support your point with a credible source of research, it is important to give a verbal indication that you are using someone else's work, ideas, or opinions. The best way to do this is to lead into the research and then indicate whether you are offering a direct quote of the research or paraphrasing the information. Audience members cannot see when the research begins or ends as they do when reading your written document and having the benefit of a parenthetical citation. For this reason, it is the speaker's responsibility to clearly detail the research verbally.

Transition into the research using a signal word which offers a cue for your audience that you are going to cite a source. Vary the signal words you use as the transition and use words that move nicely into the information you are sharing. Here is a short list of signal words that you might use: said, claims, asserts, denies, disputes, expresses, generalizes, implies, lists, maintains, offers, states, suggests, responds, replies, reveals, acknowledges, advises, or believes. Here is an example of how you might use these words:

> **Example of a verbal citation of a direct quote:** In his 2013 New York Times Bestseller book titled *Cooked*, Michael Pollan said this about bread, and I quote, "One way to think about bread—and there are so many . . . is simply this: as an ingenious technology for improving the flavor, digestibility, and nutritional value of grass." End quote.

This process will involve indicating the author's name, the title of the article or the title of the book, and the publication date—not necessarily in that order. If it is a direct quote, you will add the words, ". . . and I quote." Following the direct quote, you will end with the words, ". . . end quote."

PARAPHRASING

If paraphrasing, you will indicate the author's name, the title of the article or the title of the book and the publication date, just as you would for a direct quote. Then you will announce that you are paraphrasing the content. This allows your listener to know where your research begins and where it ends. The listener will know which words belong to the author of the source and which words belong to you. This can be a bit tricky, but with a little practice, you will find that inserting this information as you use a source of research will also help you to appear more credible for your audience. It is easier to paraphrase thoughts, opinions, or ideas, such as the following:

Example of a verbal citation of a paraphrased quote: I would like to paraphrase a unique perception held by Michael Pollan in his 2013 New York Times Bestseller book titled *Cooked*. As the author was talking about bread, he explained how a great recipe can produce something extremely delicious, even though it is nothing more than grass.

Notice in the paraphrase example, the speaker still needed to transition to the research material, supply the author's name, the title of the book, and then paraphrase the idea of the information read in the book.

Some research can NOT be paraphrased. This would include information that includes numbers, dates, proper names, and places. For example, you cannot paraphrase the number 12,643,279. That number is too precise to be paraphrased. For the same reason, you cannot paraphrase June 30, 1935. To paraphrase these, you will need to generalize the information. You can do that by saying "over twelve million" or for the date you could say toward the middle of 1935. The same is true for a person's name or the name of a place. For example, you cannot paraphrase Savannah, Georgia. What do you think you would say, if you needed to paraphrase a person's name? How you would paraphrase the name of a city and state? When do you think paraphrasing would be appropriate?

CITING PRESENTATION AIDS

Citations also need to be included in your visual aids. The only time you will not need to cite visual aids will be if the visual aid belongs to you or if it is considered **public domain**. Merriam-Webster's Online Dictionary defines public domain as "the realm embracing property rights that belong to the community at large, are unprotected by copyright or patent, and are subject to appropriation by anyone" *("Public Domain")*. Here is an example of a PowerPoint slide with a picture that belongs to me and therefore does not need to be cited:

Source: Dr. Penny Joyner Waddell

Here is an example of using a picture that does not belong to me and is <u>not</u> public domain. In this case, I included a full citation on the PowerPoint slide where the picture is shown. It is not good to have a Works Cited slide at the end of your PowerPoint Presentation because the audience will not know which citation goes with which picture. Cite the picture in the footer area of the slide where the picture is shown.

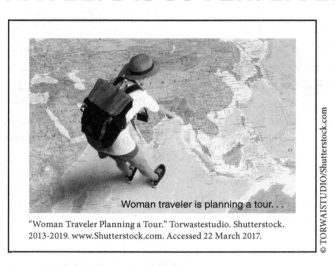

TRAVEL. DISCOVER. LIVE.

Woman traveler is planning a tour. . .

"Woman Traveler Planning a Tour." Torwastestudio. Shutterstock.
2013-2019. www.Shutterstock.com. Accessed 22 March 2017.

© TORWAISTUDIO/Shutterstock.com

ADDING PERSONAL STORIES

Storytelling, personal stories, anecdotes, even hypothetical examples are ways to add interest to your speeches. While it is good to have credible sources to support points, don't forget to always add the human element by including stories. Whether they are your own personal stories or stories from some of your friends or family, including this into your speech will make your topics so much more interesting for the audience.

This is a good time to use material discovered while conducting a personal interview with an interviewee who has experience with your topic. Asking questions and receiving personal stories and information from the interviewee will provide strong material to support points during your speech. Don't forget to also verbally cite the sources for your stories!

Example of a verbal citation of an interview: Last week I was able to interview Mr. Thaddeus Nifong, who is a public speaking instructor and advises a college Toastmasters International Club. During the personal interview, I asked Mr. Nifong what is one of the biggest challenges of advising a college club? Mr. Nifong revealed, and I quote, "The biggest challenge of advising a college Toastmasters International Club is to continually recruit officers and members. College members are going to graduate, transfer to other colleges, and sometimes life just gets in the way. It is because of this that our club officers and members are continuously recruiting and spreading the word about this great club on our campus! With that said, yes, there are challenges, but the rewards far outweigh the challenges when you can become involved as a college club advisor." End quote.

As you can see, when verbally citing a personal interview, it is important to use a transition to lead into the quote, include the interviewee's name, tell your audience why you chose to interview this person based upon his experience, and set the stage for the response. Here is another way to think about it:

1. Transition to citation
2. State the interviewee's full name
3. State the interviewee's credentials
4. Share the question asked
5. Share the response

If you are including a direct quote, preface the quote with . . . "and I quote" before sharing the quote. Following the quote, it is important to conclude with . . . "End quote." In doing this, the audience will clearly differentiate between the words said by the interviewee and your own words. When paraphrasing content within the interview, include all of the information shown above, but indicate that you are paraphrasing instead of using a direct quote.

UNDERSTANDING SPEECH OUTLINES

Have you ever planned a trip to a place you've never been before? I'll bet you began by dreaming of visiting the place before you decided how you were going to get there. Having the end goal in mind will give you the motivation to plan the trip.

It's the same type of thing Communication Sharks do when planning a speech. First, imagine yourself standing onstage, delivering a show-stopping speech, and hearing the thunderous applause affirming that you have done a great job. That is the end result, but you'll never get there without proper planning and that includes understanding why we use speech outlines. You've heard the saying, "If you don't aim for something, you'll hit nothing every time."

CREATE A STRATEGY

This means that you need to have a strategy to help achieve your goals. Think of the outline as a roadmap to help reach your desired destination. With a roadmap, you will pinpoint where you are now, the stops you need to make along the way, and then the location of where you want to be. From there, you can see several different ways of achieving your goal. There may be a way that would involve less traffic and better roads as compared to a way that may involve back roads, but with more beautiful scenery. At this point, think about your priorities, the amount of time you have, and how many stops you plan to make. Knowing this information is important for planning the route that suits you best.

The speech outline will help you sequence your information and include all main points to present a speech that is clear and coherent. Like a roadmap, the *outline is a tool that will help place related items together and will ensure that your ideas flow from one main point to another supported by sub-points.* As with a roadmap, the outline helps create a plan or structure for the speech. Just as you have to take time to plan a trip, you will also need to allow time to plan for a great speech presentation. It doesn't happen in just a few minutes, but the results are well worth your time.

In previous chapters, we explored the types of speeches, methods of delivery, the importance of conducting an audience analysis, defining the purpose of the speech, and narrowing the topic you plan to cover. We also looked at ways to add research to support your topic and to add to your audience's knowledge of the topic. Depending upon the amount of time given for the speech, the speaker will usually choose three carefully designed main points. Additional main points can be covered if additional time is provided. Now, it is time to learn about the speech outlines and what is involved with writing a great outline.

TWO TYPES OF SPEECH OUTLINES

There are two types of speech outlines to consider. First, we create a ***preparation outline*** and from that we create a ***presentation outline*** and useful notes for the presentation.

The Preparation Outline

Preparation outlines begin with a header, which includes your name, course name, and date of the speech. If using MLA Guidelines, show the last name and page number in the top right corner of your page. The date should be written as day month year without any commas. Double-space between the date and the next section as shown in the diagram below. Following this, you will complete the header by including the speech category, title, and general and specific purpose of the speech. The general purpose will state whether you plan to inform, entertain, demonstrate, or motivate your audience. It is the specific purpose that breaks down your speech plan in one sentence to show how you will achieve the primary focus of the speech. If you want to review this process, please go back to Chapter Six: Defining the Purpose.

Porter 1

Katie Porter

Public Speaking 1101

4 September 2019

Speech Category: Informative Speech

Title of Speech: How to Improve Time Management Skills

General Purpose: Inform

Specific Purpose: The specific purpose of this speech is to inform the audience how to improve time management skills in order to make time for priorities in life, use time effectively, and save time for themselves.

The next part of your preparation will include the **Introduction, Body, and Conclusion**. Each one of these three areas will include basic speechwriting details as follows:

The Introduction Step will include the Attention Step, Establish Need/Relevance, Establish Credibility, and Thesis. Also, the Introduction step will include a Transition/Link to the Body of the speech. For more information on how to plan the areas included in the Introduction Step, please see Chapter Ten of this workbook.

To follow the Standard Outline Format for the **Body** of the speech, you will need to be systematic and logically structure the speech by using a consistent pattern of symbols. We accomplish this purpose by using Roman Numerals for the three main points in your outline and follow that with capital **ABCs** for the sub-points and numbers **123s** for the sub-sub-points. Add a *Transition*/**Link** sentence between each of the three main points and one leading into the conclusion. The Body of the Outline should look like this:

Transition/Link to the Body and First Main Point:

Body

    I.   First Main Point

        A. First Sub-Point

            1.   First Sub-Sub Point

            2.   Second Sub-Sub Point

        B. Second Sub-Point

Transition/Link to the Second Main Point:

    II. Second Main Point

        A. First Sub-Point

        B. Second Sub-Point

Transition/Link to the Third Main Point:

    III. Third Main Point

        A. First Sub-Point

        B. Second Sub-Point

Transition/Link to the Conclusion:

Notice how the **Roman Numerals** are offset from the left margin and the sub-points are indented and line up directly under the main points. This type of outlining creates the structure needed to offset important main ideas from the supporting sub-points.

During a short 5–7-minute speech, you may not need to include sub-sub-points; however, during a longer speech, this second set of sub-points may become necessary as demonstrated above in the first main point. In the case that you use sub-sub-points, these should be noted with numbers.

The **Standard Outline Format** is used in speech writing and is expected as you plan the speech. If you have an A) Sub-Point, you must also include a B) Sub-Point. The Standard Outline Format can include as many sub-points as needed to cover the main points. The same type pattern is expected if you use sub-sub points. For example, if you have a 1) Sub-Sub-Point, you must also include a 2) Sub-Sub-Point. As with sub-points, you can use additional sub-sub-points as needed, but they do not have to match the sub-points used in other main points.

The **Conclusion** of the speech will include a Summary of main points and Closing Statements which are usually noted as an Appeal to Action.

Use the following Preparation Outline Checklist to make sure you have everything you need for your outline. More details of what to include in your outline will be found in Chapter Ten: Constructing the Outline.

PREPARATION OUTLINE CHECKLIST

Completed	Standard Preparation Outline, Works Cited Page, and Visual Aid Explanation
❑	Header includes Name, Course, and Date
❑	Speech Category (Introduction, Informative, Demonstration, Persuasion, Special Occasion, Group, Sales Presentation)
❑	Speech Title
❑	General Purpose (Inform, Demonstrate, Entertain, Motivate)
❑	Specific Purpose
❑	Introduction: • Attention Step • Establish Need/Relevance • Establish Credibility • Thesis (Preview of Three Main Points)
❑	Body: • Transition to the Body of the Speech • Roman Numerals to Indicate the Three Main Points • ABCs to Indicate Sub-Points • 123s to Indicate Sub-Sub-Points • Transition/Link between each Main Point and to the Conclusion
❑	Conclusion: • Summary • Appeal to Action
❑	Works Cited or Bibliography Page—*separate page from outline* • Did you check with your instructor to determine which citation style is expected? • Are you using MLA or APA? • Did you parenthetically cite all research in the outline (in-text citation)? • Did you include a full citation for each source of research used?
❑	Visual Aid Explanation Page—separate page from outline • List and describe all visual aids you plan to use during the speech

The Presentation Outline

Now that you have completed the **Preparation Outline**, it is time to begin work on the **Presentation** or **Speaking Outline** that is used during the delivery of the speech. This outline will look different from the preparation outline because it is designed to help the speaker remember what to say by providing a scaled down version of data or statistics, key words, phrases, quotes, or cues. Speakers should rehearse using the presentation outline so that when needed, they will remember where to look for the information.

If you are using the SpeechShark app, this has already been done for you. Just place your phone, iPad, or tablet on the lectern while speaking. A quick swipe of the screen will take you to the next on-screen note card.

Speakers who prefer notecards instead of using the notes feature in the app, can simply e-mail the speech to themselves and copy and paste the speech into a Word document. Doing this will automatically format the speech following MLA Guidelines and will provide a paper document for notes. Check out the SpeechShark app at www.SpeechShark.com and see how much easier speech writing and presenting can be.

CREATING USEFUL NOTES

For those not using the app, you will want to create a *very* brief outline to be used as notes during the delivery of your speech. The more streamlined your notes, the less chance you will read notes to the audience. Audiences do not want speakers reading to them and they will enjoy your speech so much more if you talk to them in a conversational tone instead of a reading cadence.

If not using the notes feature on your app, my tool of choice for transporting notes to the stage is a simple black folder. Attach only one or two note cards or attach a streamlined one-page outline inside the folder. Tuck the black folder under your arm on the side of your body that does not face the audience. This allows you to take notes to the stage without being obvious that you have notes. As you approach the lectern, place the folder on the lectern in an open position and begin your speech.

Avoid holding notes in your hand while speaking, as shown in the picture, because this will prevent you from gesturing and will also cause problems with eye contact. Speakers who hold notes are more inclined to read or fidget with their notes during the speech. As you might imagine, this will be distracting to the audience and will make the speaker look less confident.

© fizkes/Shutterstock.com

Create Presentation Notes

First, save the presentation notes as a separate file. Create presentation/speaker notes and a script for the tech team by a quick "copy and paste" of the preparation outline onto a blank document. Then, begin deleting information. Take out all of the header information, category, title, and purpose. Leave the Attention Step and keep the notation of Establish Need/Relevance and Establish Credibility, but it is not necessary to include the entire credibility content because this is information you know. For the thesis, just write your three main points.

In the body of the speech, keep all of the main points and sub-points using your Roman Numerals, ABCs, and 123s. Remove most of the words in the main points and sub-points so that you only have one key word or a short phrase for each one. Keep the summary and closing statements.

If you are using research to support the introduction, body, or conclusion, keep the parenthetical citations to remind you of the research and the source. The key information is all that is needed in order to jog your memory and to keep you on track. Often, speakers will not use presentation/speaker notes, but just knowing you have them nearby may be all that is needed to boost confidence. I said it before, but it stands to be repeated. Rehearse using your presentation/speaker notes. By doing this, you will have a good idea of where on the paper you can quickly find the point, sub-point, or research that you have forgotten. As you move to look at notes, make the movements smooth so that it is not obvious you are moving back to the lectern to peek at notes. If you use one-word or short phrase main points, a quick glance down will allow you to see the words and then your eye contact is back with the audience as you continue the speech.

Presentation notes should be typed with a larger font size than used for the preparation outline. Small type and handwriting are hard to read at a quick glance. Highlight key words in different colors to remind you of places where you need to slow down, pause, breathe, or speak louder. Use one color for key words, one color for research, and another color for directions. You can also include a smiley face at the top of the page to remind you to smile at your audience.

On the following page is an example of brief presentation notes. Notice how the key thoughts are highlighted in yellow, the research and support items are in green, and directions are in blue. Some people choose to circle or **bold** key words instead of using highlighters. If all of these colors distract you, use a system that works for YOU. After all, you are the speaker and the presentation notes should be designed to help you. All you have to do is put this in a black folder, rehearse, and you are ready for your presentation.

Attention Step: Play video clip from Alice in Wonderland's "I'm Late"
Scene: 23 seconds: https://www.youtube.com/watch?v=zpiB0COTM_M

How many of you can identify with the White Rabbit because you are continuously late? Pause and wait for the audience to respond.

Establish Need, Credibility, and Thesis:
I. Spend Time on Priorities
   A. Faith
   B. Family
   C. Fitness and Health
II. Use Time Wisely
   Stephen Covey's *Seven Habits of Highly Effective People*
   A. Budget Time
   B. Avoid Procrastination
   C. Learn to say NO
III. Save Time for Myself
   A. Focus on Personal Goals
   B. Focus on Relaxation

Summary: Three Points—Spend Time, Use Time, Save Time

Closing Statements: Play video clip from Alice in Wonderland's "Opening Three Doors"
Scene: 10 seconds: https://www.youtube.com/watch?v=di7dZwidXZU

Just as Alice opened three doors in a search to satisfy her curiosity, Pause and move toward the center of the stage. I hope that I've satisfied your curiosity about ways to manage time so that YOU are not continuously late. Pause and SMILE.

Manage your own time more effectively. Pause.

You'll find that you will enjoy the time you spend, use, and save!

WRITING STYLE

Style. You show it in the way you wear your hair, the clothes you choose, the car you drive, even the type of computer you use. Every one of us has style. You also show your style in the way you write and speak. Depending upon your audience, your writing style may vary. As you conducted the audience analysis, I'm sure you found out a great deal about your audience. What do they need to know about your topic? How will hearing this topic help your audience? Do you need to gather supporting materials to make your speech more credible? True, the public speaking class is a captive audience and they are asked to stay for your full speech even if the topic is not appealing to them. With this in mind, please try to consider what topics your audience may want to hear. Think of them as individuals and find out as much as you can about them prior to planning a presentation so the speech will be more appealing. Your ability to grasp and retain the attention of your audience will make you a more successful speaker. How do you do this?

1. Get organized
2. Get the audience's attention
3. Get to the point
4. Get the audience motivated.

Now that you have learned about the two different types of outlines that speechwriters use, I'm sure you are wondering about ways to find material for the outline and where to start.

FIRST THINGS FIRST

The first step in creating style with your writing is to begin at the beginning. Speechwriters begin with the body of the speech. Get organized and decide how to order the content. This step is not as hard as you might think when using a simple brainstorming technique known as *Clustering and Webbing*. There are as many ways to conduct clustering and webbing as there are sharks in the sea. It works for writing a speech, but also works for other projects where organization is important such as planning a party, a vacation, or a shopping trip. The best part about this strategy is that you can organize this to fit your own way of thinking and your own style.

Clustering and Webbing is a visual way of organizing and mapping a plan. Seeing the various options sometimes is the best way to determine the route you plan to take. When you finish, you can actually see potential ideas to use for your speech.

Begin with a blank sheet of paper. Somewhere near the center of the page, draw a circle and write the topic of your speech inside the circle. You might not know the title just yet, and that is OK. Just focus first on the topic.

Now, write any ideas that relate to the topic. You'll add lines and circles all around the topic that relate to the topic. As you brainstorm the ideas, you will begin to cluster or group ideas that seem to belong together.

Continue this planning session until you have no more ideas to add. Using several different colors to highlight clusters or groups that make sense together may help you to visualize the speech taking shape. Once completed, you can look at the paper and notice how the groups begin to take shape. Count the number of groups you have and those become main points. Extensions become sub-points. Draw lines through points you don't have time or don't want to cover. This process may look messy and that is fine because your outline will be neat and organized. The Clustering and Webbing page will highlight options as groups and clusters of ideas. It might also reveal if the topic is too broad or too narrow and needs to be adjusted.

Here is an example to show the possibilities when planning a speech using ecology as the topic. Notice there could be five possible main points to cover with this plan: climate change, water, soil, air, and energy. Also notice that you can easily see the sub-points developing.

If the speech will last for thirty to forty-five minutes, having five main points is not unreasonable, but if the speech will last only five to seven minutes, you could be in trouble with five hefty main points. In this case, it is a good idea to **get to the point** as you narrow the topic and shift to one of the main points that has ample sub-points. Notice how the Clustering and Webbing project will help visualize the direction needed for the speech topic.

Look at the three sub-points for Climate Change. Obviously, Climate Change has the potential to become the topic of a five- to seven-minute informative speech. Notice how one of the sub-points, sustainability, easily moves into three main points: Resource management, Environmental Management, and Green Building. Here is how my next speech plan may look:

Climate Change Sustainability

If I go with this plan, I'll still need to consider the sub-points that will support the three main points. My next task will be to conduct research on the topic of Climate Change: Sustainability. As I do this, the research will reveal sub-points that will be a perfect fit for the speech. It might also help as I decide which of the three main points should come first in the speech. This brings us to our next subject: how do we order our main points?

ORDERING MAIN POINTS

After the general and specific purpose of the speech has been targeted and the topic has been chosen, the biggest question I get is, "How do I know which point to put first, second, and third?" There are strategic ways to organize main points for a speech. As the speechwriter, it is up to you to determine which way is more effective for your topic and for your audience.

Examine the various ways for ordering main points, but keep in mind the amount of time you have for the speech. Use that information to decide if you can cover the topic's main points in the time allotted. If not, you may need to choose different main points or choose to develop only one of the main points you are considering.

The following table will help you to understand the different options for ordering speech points:

Order	Description
Topical	Consider the topic of your speech and divide that one topic into three sub-topics. If the order is not critical as long as points are covered, you will choose to use the *topical* order.
Chronological	If you are crafting a speech that involves time, you will want to use the *chronological* order. The first point will show what needs to happen first, then subsequent main points will follow. This order is most often used when discussing the history of something or when demonstrating a process or the use of a product. Chronological order is also used when introducing yourself or someone else and you cover that person's past experiences, present or current events, and future plans.
Cause-Effect	Often referred to as a causal order, this type of order is used when the speaker needs to show a relationship between a cause and effect. The first point will expose a problem (cause) and the next point will cover the consequences that arise (effect) due to the problem. For a third point, the speaker will usually tell a story to describe the *cause-effect* of the topic. This type of order is used to explain why something may be happening.
Problem-Solution	This order is used with persuasion speeches as we work to motivate someone to do something or think differently about something. The *problem-solution* order is referred to as Monroe's Motivated Sequence. During this type of speech, the speaker will first discuss a problem. Second, the speaker will offer realistic solution(s) to the problem. Third, the speaker will help the audience to visualize the results if the problem is solved and consequences if the problem is not solved.
Spatial	When the topic involves location or direction such as up or down, left or right, top or bottom, north or south, the speaker will use *spatial* ordering. Using this type of ordering will help the audience to visualize the place the speaker is describing and helps the audience to experience the information shared. Consider a high-rise office building as the topic. The speaker may give a virtual tour starting with the bottom floor and moving to the top floor. If the zoo is a topic, the speaker may give a tour starting at the first gate and work through the exhibits to the last gate.

USING WORDS THAT MATTER

When creating the outline and showing the main points, it is advisable to make sure you keep the main points separate and clear. Begin each main point or sub-point using the same type of pattern. For example, you might begin each main point with a question, a verb, or with a noun. Look carefully at each main point and think of ways to develop each point equally. Instead of spending too much time on any one point, try to approach each one equally so there is a balance. This will help your outline to be consistent and clear.

As mentioned earlier in this guidebook, each speech has three main parts: Introduction, Body, and Conclusion. With the body of the speech taking shape, it is time to focus on how to **get the audience's attention** with the **Introduction.**

Introduction

This part of the outline will include the **Attention Step, Establish Need/Relevance, Establish Credibility,** and will preview the body of the speech with a clear **Thesis.** Use full sentences as you craft this step because it will force you to think in complete thoughts, help as you learn the speech, and will help gauge its length. The full Introduction Step will usually last about a minute to a minute and a half and certainly not more than 10% of your speech time. Once you have the content for the Introduction Step, you will move seamlessly from one part to the next without citing the headings, even though they are shown in the preparation outline. Let's look at each one of these steps so that you have a better understanding of how to craft different areas with the finesse of an accomplished speechwriter.

It has been said that you have between three to five seconds to get an audience's attention and for them to decide if what you have to say is worth their time and attention. The key word here is attention. What will you say or do to get the audience's attention? How will you plan to keep their attention once you have it?

Your speech begins from the moment you stand up to enter the stage. The audience watches as you enter the stage and as you move to the lectern. Make a conscious effort to walk with a purpose and avoid lingering at the lectern looking at notes before you begin speaking. Never begin your speech by saying, "Hello! How is everyone today? My name is _____ and I want to speak to you about _____." Do this and you will notice how their first glance at you will lead to the second glance as they check their phones, look at the program, begin making a grocery list, or speak to the person sitting next to them. You've lost them already and there is a good chance that your message will never reach them.

Instead, walk confidently to the stage, smiling and nodding to your audience as you approach the lectern. Quickly place your notes on the lectern and step to the side as you begin the first words you planned for the speech—the **Attention Step.**

Attention Step

While there are many ways to get the audience's attention, you must relate the attention step back to the main idea or topic of your speech. It is not good enough to simply get the audience's attention; instead, you should provide a clear preview of the topic. Try using one of these strategies to get your audience's attention and keep it!

1. **Startling statement:** Winston Churchill, known for his powerful speeches, would often begin the speech with a powerful statement that would command the attention of his audience from the very first word. Some speakers choose a shocking statement that might have been featured as front-page news, and will

hold up the newspaper as the statement is spoken. Others start by boldly stating a problem that needs to be solved and then follows this with a question to ask "How can YOU help to solve this problem?"

2. **Refer to a historical event:** Gain the audience's attention by choosing a historical event that will introduce the topic of your speech and beginning by saying, "On this day in history, ___ years ago. . . ." The important thing to remember is that after you introduce the event, it is important to relate how that same type of event is prevalent today. Show the correlation between the historical and current events.

3. **Quote from a person:** Anyone can open a speech with a quote. They are a dime a dozen, but using a carefully chosen quote can be quite effective and will set the tone for the rest of your speech. Choose a quote that directly relates to the topic you are covering and be sure to tell your audience where you found the quote. Avoid using a quote by an unknown author because it packs less of a punch.

4. **Quote from recent research:** This can be an effective strategy as the speaker will begin the speech by quoting a recent research report or journal article. Be sure to lead into the quote with the source of the research by saying, "According to a story . . . recently published in . . ., I learned that . . ."

5. **Data or statistics:** Powerful or personalized data and statistics will speak clearly to your audience and will get to the point right away. Making data or statistics relevant to the audience by explaining how it impacts the audience will help the speaker to immediately grab attention in a show-stopping way.

6. **Question:** Whether you are asking a rhetorical or a literal question, this type of attention step will cause the audience to think of ways they would answer. If you want them to answer your question out loud, you will need to prompt the response. Also, let the audience know if you want them to respond by a show of hands. Be careful with this type of attention step and make sure your question is meaningful and leads to the main point of your topic. Correctly phrasing a question will determine whether it is rhetorical or literal.

7. **Refer to a recent conversation:** Start the speech by telling a story about a recent conversation with someone as it deals with your topic. This is a good place to use a personal interview. For example, you could say, "Two weeks ago, I was speaking to . . . about . . . and he told me that . . ."

8. **Imagery:** Invite the audience to be part of the attention step by using imagery to help the audience visualize or imagine an extraordinary thing. You might begin by saying, "Imagine you are . . ." Then follow up the imagery with a question. "How would this change your . . .?" Or "What would you think about . . .?"

9. **Scenario:** Ask the question, "What if . . .?" and your audience will immediately be drawn into the speech as it invites the audience to consider their own answer to the question. "What if" scenarios may also start with "What would happen if . . .?" or "How different would our lives be if . . .?"

10. **Story:** Everyone loves a good story, especially a personal story. For this to be effective, be sure to paint a picture using words so that the audience will feel as if they are part of the story. Just any story won't do. It needs to be a story that lends a dramatic effect to the topic of your speech using vocal variance and gestures to make the story come to life. Once, I heard a speaker begin a story by moving as close to the end of the stage as possible, leaned in toward his audience, and motioned to the audience as if he was pulling them closer to say, "Let me tell you a story." It was a powerful opening and he had us so involved with the story that we were sad when he didn't finish it during the attention step, but saved the ending of the story for the conclusion of his speech.

11. **Share information about a personal experience:** Allow the audience to identify with you as you share a personal experience as it relates to the topic of your speech. You might start by saying, "When I was eighteen years old, I never guessed that I would be standing here in front of you forty years later explaining . . ." Audience members will feel you are authentic and credible if you start with a personal experience.

12. **Begin with a music tag:** This could be music played as you enter the stage. The tag should last only until you reach the lectern and then should include a comment about the music. For example, if you are speaking to a group of students about a SkillsUSA competition, you could enter with the music from Queen playing, "We are the champions, my friends; and we'll keep on fighting 'til the end; we are the champions, we are the champions, no time for losers 'cause we are the champions—of the world." Your first words following this will need to refer back to the SkillsUSA champions that are being celebrated!

13. **Begin with a scene from a movie:** One of the best speeches I've heard this year was from a student who was giving an informative speech about professional sports management. The attention step from his speech was a brief ten-second clip from the Jerry Maguire movie starring Tom Cruise in which we heard Tom Cruise shouting, "Show me the money!" After the clip, and with the audience still smiling, the student began with a strong statement about sports management and the money players are paid.

14. **Humor:** Be careful with this one! Don't just tell a joke to get the audience's attention and don't tell just any joke! If you decide to use humor, make sure you are good with using humor and make sure what you are saying will be accepted by your audience. Avoid off-color humor or humor that may be offensive to a diverse population. Remember that your goal is to get the audience's attention in a positive way so that you can keep their attention throughout the speech. You'll also want to make sure the humor you use will point directly to the topic of your speech. If you get a good laugh from your audience, please wait until the laughter begins to settle down before adding your next lines that lead to your core idea of the speech.

Establish Need/Relevance

Now that you have the audience's attention and they have an idea of the topic you will be covering, it is your job to establish why the audience needs to hear your speech. In one or two brief sentences, explain the relevance of the topic to their lives.

During this step, you might say, "It is important that you are here today because I'm going to speak to you about (the topic). This affects everyone in this audience because . . ." You could also say, "The topic of ___ should be particularly interesting to you because . . ." The primary goal is to keep the audience's attention by letting them know the next few minutes will provide valuable information and the time they take to hear your speech will not be wasted.

Establish Credibility

What experience do you have with the topic? Why are you the person to speak to this audience and provide information about the topic? These are questions you need to answer as you establish your own credibility as the speaker. A brief statement regarding your personal experiences which led to your understanding of the topic is necessary. If possible, add the number of years you have had experience with the topic or if you have conducted research regarding the topic. The audience needs to know you are up for the task and that you are speaking from experience.

Thesis

The thesis is the point in the Introduction Step where the speaker can preview the topic and the main points that will cover the topic. It needs to be brief and clear. Here is a good example: "Today, I will explain the topic of _____ by covering three areas of importance: (1) First Main Point, (2) Second Main Point, and (3) Third Main Point."

The thesis is the last step in the Introduction Step and now you will be ready to connect the Introduction to the Body of the speech.

Connectors

Moving from the Introduction to the Body of the speech, to each of the main points, and then to the conclusion can be awkward unless the speaker uses effective connectors to accomplish the task. These will be accomplished by using **transitions** *also known as links, internal previews, signposts or signals, and internal reviews.* Audiences respond well to speakers who do this, because it is clear where the speaker has been and where she is planning to go.

Internal Previews are statements which will let the audience know what will be covered next in the speech. These are excellent to use for the transition that links the Introduction Step to the body of the speech. The thesis is also considered a preview of the full speech as you detail which three main points you will plan to cover during the speech.

Internal Reviews are areas where you summarize what you have covered in a previous area of the speech. Often speakers will include this in the transitions between main points as you summarize the point just covered and before you lead into the transition to the next point. You'll also provide a complete summary of the three main points in the conclusion step.

If you are using the SpeechShark app, the transitions are automatically built in; however, if you are manually building your speech, you will need to carefully place transitions in four areas of the speech. Creating these transitions ahead of time and placing them in the correct area of your outline will help you to remember to use them and you won't be struggling to find the right words during the delivery of the speech. This is when some speakers have that awkward moment of silence as they consider how to get from one point to the next. Nonverbal cues can emphasize your links. Pausing, gesturing, changing locations on the stage area, facial expressions, smiling, and changing the pitch of your voice or the rate in which you speak can help to signal to the audience that you are moving from one point to another.

Here are examples of how you might craft the four transition/links that should be found in your speech outline.

> **Transition/Link #1:** This is placed after the Introduction Step and leads to the first point in the body of the speech. It can be as simple as saying, "Let's begin with the first point, (Add the point heading) . . ."
>
> **Transition/Link #2:** This follows Point #1 and leads to Point #2. It will provide an internal summary that leads smoothly to the next main point. Here is an example: "Now that we have covered the first point, (Add the point heading) . . ., let's move to the second point, (Add the point heading) . . ."
>
> **Transition/Link #3:** This follows Point #2 and leads to Point #3. Again, as an internal summary, it will lead to the final point. You might say, "Now that you understand Point #1 (Add the point heading) . . . and Point #2, (Add the point heading) . . ., allow me to share with you about Point #3, (Add the point heading) . . ."
>
> **Transition/Link #4:** This follows Point #3 and leads to the Conclusion Step of the speech. This internal summary shouldn't summarize the entire speech since that is done in the Conclusion step, but will wrap up Point #3 and lead seamlessly into the Conclusion Step. A Signpost in conjunction with a Transition/Link is effective for this point in the speech. An example of this is, "It's been a privilege to speak to you about (the topic) and to hopefully add additional knowledge of this topic to the information you already have. Above all, you need to know (Add something about the topic's relevance) . . ."

From these examples you can tell that transitions are ways of signaling movement from one point to another as well as how the points relate to each other. There are four separate types of transitions to consider. Below is a table that will help you find the words you need to craft each type of transition:

Transition Types	Definition	Example
Time	Demonstrates the passing of time	Now that we have . . . We are now ready to . . . First . . . Next . . . Later . . .
Viewpoint	Demonstrates a situation shift	On the other hand . . . However . . . Although . . .
Connective	Unites related thoughts	In addition to . . . Also . . . Another . . . Not only . . . but also . . .
Concluding	Signals the end of the section	To summarize . . . In conclusion . . . As a result . . . Finally . . .

Conclusion

This is the very last step that you will take when planning your speech. Audiences appreciate a speaker who will use a **signpost or signal** at the end of the speech. This can be easily done as the speaker says, "To conclude . . .," "To summarize . . .," "As I conclude . . .," or "Above all, remember. . . . This signal will lead smoothly to the conclusion of the speech which includes a *Summary* or internal review of the three main points and a final statement, also known as the **Appeal to Action**.

Summary

The purpose of the summary is to offer a review of all that was covered in the speech. This is a brief sentence or two in which the speaker will review the topic and the main points covered during the speech. The clearer, the better! Here is an example: "To summarize, it's been a pleasure to meet with you today to discuss (the topic) and I've been able to share three areas of importance as they deal with (the topic): Point #1 . . ., Point #2 . . ., and Point #3 . . ." After you finish the summary of the speech and before moving to the closing statement, slow down the pace of your speech to add impact to the final words you will say.

Closing Statements

This is the point where the speaker can **get the audience motivated**! The final words of a speech should be carefully crafted word-for-word in order to keep the audience thinking about the topic and the main points shared. Double the number of pauses you used during the speech or in normal conversation in order to emphasize what you are saying. The audience will be able to tell from this that you are about to share something they really need to hear. Use dramatic pauses at the end of a sentence to allow time for the audience to process what you have said.

SpeechSharks never end a speech with, "That's all" or "That's all I've got." That may be humorous for Porky Pig's *Looney Tunes Cartoons*, but a weak conclusion may mean that the audience will not retain the main points covered. They will only remember the last words you say and you don't want them to think that's all you've got. It is for this reason that speakers must spend time constructing a closing statement that will be remembered and acted upon. There are different strategies to end a speech, but the strategy you choose should leave the audience begging for more. The ultimate goal is to motivate your audience to action and end the speech with a BANG!

While you can use many of the same strategies that are used to introduce a speech topic, here are some strategies for ending a speech so that you get a standing ovation.

1. **Appeal to action:** A strong appeal should leave the audience with a positive lasting impression of the topic and a desire to act upon the speaker's challenge. Sometimes labeled as a "call to action," this part of the speech should make the audience want to get out of their seats and DO something about the topic covered. You'll want to carefully craft this and say it as if it has ten exclamation points after it!!!!!!!!!!

2. **Story:** Just as you might open a speech with a personal story, it is also effective to end the speech with a personal story. Better yet, finish the story you begin in the attention step so that the audience is hanging on throughout the speech just to hear the end of the story. As a child, I would listen to Paul Harvey, a noted radio celebrity who perfected this in his show entitled, "The Rest of the Story." Speakers can follow his lead by presenting little known or forgotten facts in the introduction of the speech only to complete the rest of the story during the closing statements. Paul Harvey's ending tag line was, "and now you know the rest of the story." As he would say this line, all of my family members who were gathered around to listen would all smile a knowing smile. Yes, we did know the rest of the story and it was worth listening to the full program just to learn the ending.

3. **Humor:** Again, be careful when using humor. It can be so effective, yet can fall flat if not delivered correctly. If choosing a joke, make sure it circles back to the topic and repeats the main points you are making with a story that will cause the audience to laugh. Smile or chuckle if the line you are saying is funny and be serious if the line is more thought-provoking. The audience will follow your lead. It is fun to end a speech with an audience full of people laughing at the last lines you say.

4. **Quote or inspirational poem:** There are many quotes and poems that contain messages which might summarize the main points of a speech. Selecting a quote or poem for the closing statement is effective, but will need to be moving or emotional. Leaving the audience with moving final lines will keep them thinking about your topic.

There are conflicting views of whether the speaker should end a speech with "thank you" or should simply leave the stage. As a member of Toastmasters International, our club members are taught to say the final words planned for their closing statements, pause, and then relinquish the stage back to the Toastmaster of the day by saying, "Mister or Madam Toastmaster," waiting until he comes to the lectern, shake his hand to signify giving the stage back to the Toastmaster, and then leave the stage area while members applaud.

While attending conferences, I notice that it is not unusual for conference speakers to thank the audience with a brief, "thank you" following the closing statements. Sometimes they end their speech with a closing "thank you" slide signaling that the speech has ended. I'm never offended by this because I believe they are being courteous and thanking the audience for their attention, just as the audience will show appreciation by applauding as the speaker leaves the stage.

In the classroom, I ask students to finish the prepared closing statements, pause and look at the audience, nod their heads, smile toward the audience, pick up notes from the lectern, and while the audience is applauding, confidently leave the stage area and move to a seat. Sometimes, it is difficult to know if a student has finished the speech or if he is still thinking about what he wants to say. This is especially true if he continues standing at the lectern for too long after saying the final words. That usually occurs because the closing statement is not effective.

For students who want to include a thank you following their speech, I suggest they add a thank you as part of the summary as it leads to the conclusion. Do this by saying, "It's been a privilege to speak to you about (the topic) and to cover (List all three points). Hopefully, this has added additional knowledge of this topic to the information you already have. Thank you for your time and for your attention. Above all, you need to know . . ." Then follow the sentence with the closing statement.

Bibliography or Works Cited Page

The outline is not complete until you've attached a separate page which includes a complete source citation of all research used during the speech presentation. This could be noted as a Bibliography or a Works Cited page depending upon whether you are following APA or MLA Guidelines for citing research. Be sure to ask your instructor which type of citation guidelines should be followed for your class.

For most public speaking situations, MLA Guidelines are used. On this page, the speaker will offer a full citation which will identify the author's name, the title of the source, title of the work, other contributors, version, volume number, publisher, publication date, page number, location, and accessed day month year. More information regarding the different types of guidelines and suggestions for citing research can be found in Chapter Eight: Conducting Research.

In Chapter Three of this textbook, as you read through the types of speeches, you will find that for each type of speech there is a brainstorming worksheet along with an outline template, and an example of a speech outline. Please use the brainstorming worksheet and the template when writing your next speech or use the SpeechShark app and you will be very pleased with the end results.

As this chapter comes to an end, remember that having a great preparation outline can be a confidence booster. Knowing your material is the best way to lower anxiety. The best way to learn material in your speech is to rehearse, rehearse, rehearse. Being meticulous, comprehensive, and systematic when creating the outline of your speech is just another form of rehearsal. Every semester, I realize that a great outline usually leads to a great student presentation and that, of course, leads to a higher end of course score. Spend extra time creating the outline and you will be pleased with the speech you present.

SERVING UP A "SHARK-O-LICIOUS" TREAT?

My daughter brought home a bag of gummy treats yesterday that were shaped like sharks! Isn't that fun? Sharks are everywhere! These fun shark treats made me think about great speeches and how they have a lot in common with a great meal. Since you might be presenting a speech soon, I wanted to share this with you so that you can serve a "Shark-o-licious" treat to YOUR audience.

Every memorable meal begins with an appetizer and then moves to a second dish before leading to the main course which usually includes a protein dish, starch, and vegetable before concluding with a delicious dessert.

Memorable speeches should follow the same type of menu as I will explain in the following table:

Memorable Meal	Memorable Speech	Similarities
Appetizer	Attention Step	Just as you arrive at a meal hungry and ready to eat, your audience will arrive anxious to hear your speech. This is where you set the stage, get the audience's attention, and provide your audience with a "taste" of what is to come.
Soup	Establish Relevance for the Topic Establish Credibility to Speak About the Topic Preview of Main Points (Thesis)	The soup prepares your palate for the main course of a meal, but it is this step in the speech that prepares your audience for the topic. First, explain why it is important that the audience hear about the upcoming topic. Then, tell your audience why YOU are credible to speak to them about the topic. The next thing that you will do during this phase is to clearly state the three main points that you will cover. This prepares your audience and allows them to anticipate the "main course"!
Bread	Transitions	Bread during a meal is often used to cleanse the palate and is enjoyed between courses. For the speech, transitions, also called *connectors*, are essential as they transition the content from one thing to the next. A great speaker will use clear transitions to move from the Introduction Step to the Body of the speech, to each Main Point, and then finally into the Conclusion.

Main Course:
  Protein
  Starch
  Vegetable
	Body	The main course is the purpose of the meal and the body is the purpose of your speech! The body of the speech contains three main points that support the topic. Often the main points include research, stories, and examples that further define the topic.

Dessert	Conclusion	All great meals culminate with a sweet treat! The dessert that concludes the memorable meal is my favorite part of the meal because it leaves a sweet taste in my mouth! A great speech conclusion should leave your audience wanting more! Signal that you are concluding the speech, re-state the three main points, and then provide closing statements or an appeal that will make your audience wish the speech could last just a little longer! Now, isn't that sweet?

It is time to start cooking, or should I say, writing the speech! How are you going to make sure your next speech is "Shark-o-licious"? Plan, Prepare, and Persevere! Keep these tips in mind and your next speech is sure to be a crowd pleaser with your audience having an appetite that will have them demanding an encore!

Plan

Even the simplest things need to be considered as you prepare for your presentation. And, yes, there are still more questions:

- ▶ What can you say or do to get your audience's attention from the very beginning?
- ▶ How can you get your audience to relate immediately to your topic?
- ▶ Why are YOU credible to talk to an audience about this topic?

▶ How can you conclude the speech so that your audience continues thinking about your speech topic even after your speech is over?

Answering these questions will help you prepare an Introduction Step that introduces the topic to your audience and will have them in the palm of your hand before you actually begin speaking about the topic. A strong Introduction Step (appetizer and soup) is important for an effective presentation, but this step cannot be written until AFTER you have planned the body (main course) of your speech (topic and three main points). This will also help you to prepare a Conclusion Step (dessert) that ends your speech with a BANG!

Prepare

The speaker has a responsibility to begin the speech with an Attention Step or Opener that will get their attention within the first few seconds of your presentation. Consider how you would feel if you were one of the audience members sitting and waiting to hear a great speech from YOU. Start strong with an engaging Attention Step. Here are some suggestions and why they work:

1. **Questions:** This works because a well-designed question is just begging to be answered. Be careful that your question leads directly to the topic you will be covering and remember that presentation is everything. A great question with a weak delivery will not make for a memorable Attention Step.

2. **Empathy:** This allows you to connect with your audience on a personal level. This starts the feeling of an intimate relationship between you and the audience in the first few seconds of your speech. Ask, "Have you ever thought about why. . .", "I'll never forget the moment when", or "Just like YOU, I was brought up to believe. . .".

3. **Announcement of a NEW Policy or Procedure:** While this might not always be met with full cooperation, it does get the attention of your audience and they will be very interested to see how this change will affect their own area or their lives.

4. **Secrets:** Everyone loves a secret! Start your speech by saying, "I want to let you in on a little secret—this is a secret that not even my husband knows. . ." Doing this provides you with the opportunity to promise something to your audience that they simply cannot refuse. They want to know the secret!

5. **Startling Statement:** Beginning your speech with a shocking statement that makes your audience feel like they may be making a huge mistake about something will certainly give them reason to sit up straight and listen to what you have to say!

6. **Warnings:** If you start your speech by saying, "There are three warning signs to look for when. . .", then your audience will want to hear you identify the three warning signs.

7. **Quotes:** This is always a good strategy, but can get a bit boring if every speaker that day begins with a quote. If you are going to use a quote, make sure that it is a quote that will make the audience want to sit up and take notice! Also, make sure you have the name of the person correct who is cited with the quote.

8. **Imagery:** You can start by saying, "Imagine, if you will. . ." People love imagery and they will enjoy an Attention Step that begins with imagery!

9. **Stories:** Everyone loves a good story. Start by saying, "Do you mind if I share a story with you? Last week when I was a XYZ, I heard about. . ." Now, they want to hear about it, too!

10. **Choices:** If I were to ask you to choose between this donut and an apple, which would you choose? Wait for the answer? Of course, you are hoping they will choose the apple, but you notice that more than half of your audience raised their hands saying they would choose the donut! Give them a choice! Then, allow that choice to help shape the direction of your speech topic.

Don't introduce yourself in the opening words of your speech. Save your introduction for the portion of your introduction step where you will establish your own credibility as a speaker for the topic. Here is an example:

Introduction to the Speech:

Attention Step:

Establish Need/Relevance for the Topic:

Establish Credibility: For the past twenty years, I have been a public speaking coach helping young people to prepare for interviews and competitions. Hello, my name is Dr. Penny Joyner Waddell and I am happy to be here with you today to discuss the importance of dressing for success when giving a speech presentation.

Thesis:

Persevere

Using the speech writing formula that we have presented in this book, we want you to begin thinking like a speech writer. You are on the right path—you are a Communication Shark swimming easily toward your target! Take a deep breath. It's almost time to meet your audience!

CREATING EFFECTIVE VISUAL AIDS FOR PRESENTATIONS

After the preparation and presentation outlines have been completed, it's time to complete the fun part of the speech—the visual aids. This isn't just one more assignment for you to do in a speech class. In fact, there is a very important reason behind the task. Why do speakers need visual aids during a speech? *A well-designed visual aid clarifies the topic, generates interest, and promotes retention of the material.*

Clarifies the Topic

Visual aids can be powerful tools to help bring your topic to life. Words and images seen as the speaker covers a point will add structure and power to the spoken words. Keeping visual aids simple is key, but will help your audience to see the topic unfold as they visualize key points covered. Technical terms, often lost by many in the audience, will be better understood if they are seen as the speaker is discussing them. Images shown will lend clarity and an understanding of points which might be new knowledge for audience members. Charts and diagrams answer questions which will support the credibility of the speaker and add credence to the subject content.

Generates Interest

Audiences come in all sizes, shapes, and each one has a diverse knowledge base. Using visual aids helps keep the audience's attention, because they help the audience to become involved visually. Visual aids serve as a memory aid or learning support. Since we have so many different types of learners in an audience, a visual aid can expose the audience to information in a way that will help improve interest in the topic. Showing key words will keep the audience's interest as you move from one point to another. Interactive technology used during a speech will not only jazz up the presentation, but will help gain and keep the interest of audience members. Including music sound-bites or video clips will add interest and variety to presentations.

Promotes Retention

Attention spans vary for individuals. It is for this reason that many people in an audience have a difficult time remembering information they hear during a speech. When speaking one-on-one, it is easier to keep someone's attention; however, when speaking to a large audience, it is more of a challenge to retain each individual's attention. The larger the audience, the more challenging this becomes. It's even difficult to read and remember the information in a textbook unless that information is illustrated for you.

Speakers should plan speeches so they reach the intended audience and so the audience will retain the message. Take into consideration the many different types of learners that may be in your audience. Some people react better to information presented visually, while others react through using the other senses: hear, smell, taste, and touch. Visual learners make up the largest majority of learners in our population; therefore, it is important for speakers to consider ways to present material that can be processed and understood by the majority of audience members.

While earning a degree in instructional design, I learned that three days after a speech or class, my audience will remember only about **10%** of what they hear. If I add a visual aid to my presentation, their ability to recall the information will increase to somewhere around **35%**. Adding a visual aid and having the students do something during the presentation with the information I present, will improve their recall to somewhere around **65%**. Adding a physical handout for the students to take with them following the speech will further add recall to somewhere around **85%**. Ultimately, this means that there is about **15%** of a presentation that will be lost completely. Hopefully, my experiences will help you to realize the importance of using visual aids to promote retention.

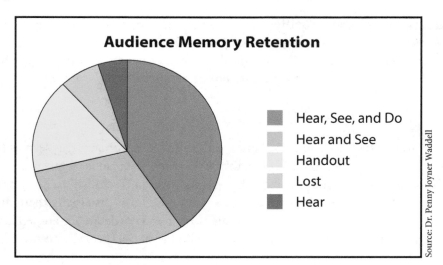

Source: Dr. Penny Joyner Waddell

Most of us can only retain a small percentage of what we read or hear. However, if we add a visual stimulus to the information read or heard, our brains are better able to interpret the information so the content is processed and understood. The more senses involved during the presentation, the longer your audience will remember the message delivered. A big part of this is because a good visual aid can make the information clearer and more appealing. It also helps to emphasize key ideas the speaker wants to share. The more data and statistics included in a speech, the more important it is for the visual aids to include charts, graphs, or tables. Pictures or diagrams will help audience members to visualize the items or processes that are discussed. Video clips and music add emotion to content and that will also aid in retention of content. We often use technology to deliver some of the different types of visual aids by creating PowerPoints or Prezi Presentations that can combine all types of visual aids making abstract ideas much more concrete and more retainable.

A visual aid can be any number of things that adds value to content presented. These may include yourself, objects, models, photos, maps, graphs, charts, diagrams, table displays, handouts, video clips, music, PowerPoint, Prezi, and technology. Here are some basic things to remember as you create your visual aids: Keep it Simple, Keep it LARGE, Keep it Interesting, Keep Visuals in the Background, and Keep It Going by following the basic DOs and DON'Ts.

BASIC DOS AND DON'TS	
Do	**Don't**
KISS: Keep It Simple Sweetie!	Don't clutter posters or slides with too much
Limit each visual to ONE main idea	Don't use more than six lines
Use sans serif fonts—large enough to be visible by all audience members	Don't change font styles
Be consistent with fonts and colors	Don't use dark fonts with dark backgrounds
Bullet points, key words	Don't use complete sentences unless it is a quote
Use very little text	Don't use too many visual aids
Illustrate with pictures, graphs, charts	Don't add more visual aids than you can handle
Rehearse using the visual aids	Don't wait until the last minute to get a Tech Team
Cue video clips and music sound-bites to desired screen	Don't use more than thirty seconds of video for a five-minute speech
Check audio for desired levels	Don't show things that can't be seen by the entire audience
Explain purpose of video or music before playing it or summarize purpose directly after showing it	Don't turn your speech into a dull slide show
Show interest in video or music while playing it	Don't write on a dry-erase board or flip chart unless you are an amazing artist
Make sure visual aids support content	Don't read from a slide
Cover tables with a table cloth	Don't break eye contact as you show visual aids
Position table displays so all items are visible	Don't turn OFF all audience area lights while showing a video or PowerPoint
Pick up items on display table and show them as you speak about them	Don't ignore items on a table display
Use a Tech Team to set up visual aids	Don't use equipment or props you don't understand
Have a back-up plan if visual aids fail	Don't have items saved in just one way
Pack visual aids the day before the speech (USB drives, memory sticks, items for table displays)	Don't wait until the last minute to organize or rehearse with visual aids
Ignore the visual aid during presentations and talk to the audience	Don't talk to the visual aid

Design Theories

Without taking you through a complete instructional design course, I'd like to share some of the highlights to help as you plan visual aids. There are three design theories that may be used separately or in conjunction with each other to create and manage visual aids for clearer understanding and retention. The three design theories are *Figure/Ground, Hierarchy, and Gestalt.*

Figure/Ground is a design theory that allows the audience to see information that is most or least important. Our brains will seek distinctions between the subject of the image and the background. The visual aid designer will demand attention for the figure (subject) by using fonts that are larger, smaller, bolder, brighter, or subdued on the screen. Spacing of fonts can be used in conjunction with size and color to achieve the desired effect.

As you design a visual aid using the Figure/Ground theory, you will be able to visually thrust the key information toward the audience or withdraw the information toward the background depending upon the purpose of your visual aid. As audiences see a larger, bolder presentation of material, they will perceive the information as being more important and worthy of consideration. Likewise, smaller, less obtrusive presentations of material (ground) will cause the audience to perceive the information as not as important. Since a picture is worth a thousand words, I'd like to show an example of how this might look:

<table>
<tr>
<td rowspan="2">

Figure/Ground

Brings

IMPORTANT

Information to the Front

</td>
<td>

Three Design Theories:

- Figure/Ground
- **Hierarchy**
- Gestalt

</td>
</tr>
<tr>
<td>

Figure/Ground

Can Take

Less Important Information

To the Background

</td>
</tr>
</table>

In the examples shown above, notice how the word, **I M P O R T A N T** jumps out from the slide? Simply using a bolder, larger font, and adding a space between each letter helps us to incorporate the Figure/Ground principle. In the same way we can make Less Important Information move into the background by using a smaller font and a lighter, less obtrusive color.

The Figure/Ground design is an arrangement of shapes, sizes, and space. Consider how proximity uses space to connect and separate the elements. Because of this, space also becomes a design element and performs visually by allowing design elements room to speak. I've heard it explained in relation to music. If every note on a piano was played at the same time, we would have *noise* instead of music. However, if you give space for the notes to be played with silence between keystrokes, then we get a pattern of sound which creates the rhythm that is beautiful music.

Hierarchy is an organizational tool which uses graphs, charts, tables, diagrams, directional arrows, outlines, lists, and maps to command the audience's attention. We use these types of visual aids often to show information in relation to other information. This design theory is based upon the way our brains organize and group things of importance together and can follow several different types of paths to accomplish the same type of thing.

Hierarchy can be demonstrated with our use of headings and bullet points in PowerPoint slides. The same slide is often duplicated and the separate bullet points are highlighted to show the information as it is discussed. Here is an example of a slide about the design theories and shows that we are focusing on Hierarchy.

Organizational schemas are another way of demonstrating the hierarchy design theory. Notice how the title of the theory is in the larger quadrant and the smaller quadrants detail support for the topic.

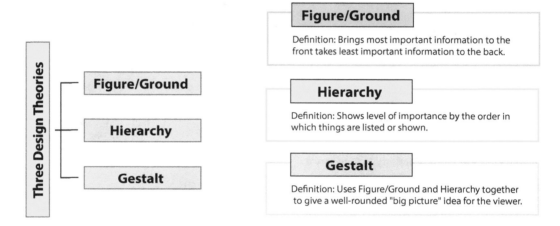

This type of hierarchy design is demonstrated as a list and is a good choice when you need to show several different areas and supply definitions.

This type of hierarchy design indicates a cycle and will demonstrate the order in which the cycle progresses.

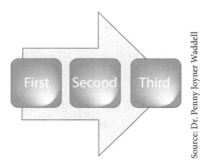

Source: Dr. Penny Joyner Waddell

This example uses directional arrows to show a process. Arrows can be used in conjunction with text boxes or separately to show direction.

This example can show relationships of one type thing to another. Identifying PROs and CONs are a good way to illustrate relationships.

As you make choices regarding which types of hierarchy designs to use, just remember to choose the type that will produce the results you hope to see.

Source: Dr. Penny Joyner Waddell

Line graphs, pie charts, bar charts, tree maps, tables, and combinations of these are other options that can be used to allow the audience a graphic which moves the eye from one bar of information to the next. This helps the instructional designer choose where the audience's eye will follow and that in turn leads to a point the speaker wants to make. Here are some examples:

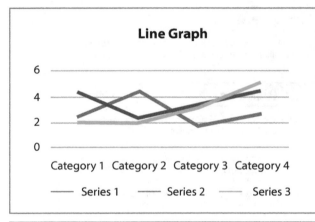

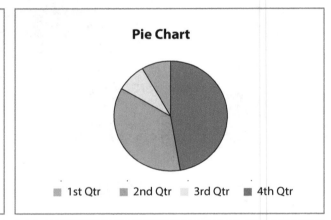

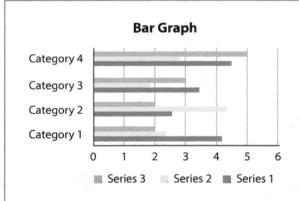

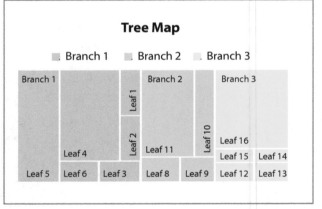

Source: Dr. Penny Joyner Waddell

All of these graphics are easy to design and insert into your PowerPoint or Prezi slide using the features in Microsoft Word. I created all of the charts and tables found in this textbook to illustrate various concepts. Go to the top of your computer screen in Microsoft Word and choose the "Insert" tab. From there, you can choose to add SmartArt, Charts, or Tables. From there, you can customize any of the templates to fit your needs. If I can do it, you can do it too!

Gestalt is the last design theory that I would like to share with you. This one is actually my favorite because it incorporates figure/ground AND hierarchy. This type of design theory is based upon the big picture. Gestalt is not the name of a person, as you might suspect. Instead, it is *a German word which means the whole is greater than the sum of many parts* and was developed by a group of German psychologists who were developing theories of visual perception. Using a combination of design elements will help your audience to view your visual arrangements as connected.

© Eric Broder Van Dyke/ Shutterstock.com

One area to note is that audiences will pay attention to designs where there is a similarity between elements of color, size, shape, texture, or value. The new Amazon logo uses Gestalt continuation in the logo where the arrow entices the observer to see a curve or path as a continuous figure rather than separation. Also, the arrow can be seen as a smile indicating the customer will be happy. As the logo was designed, it was done so with the underlying theme for the customer to perceive continuous and happy service from A to Z as merchandise moves from the organization to the customer. This makes sense, doesn't it?

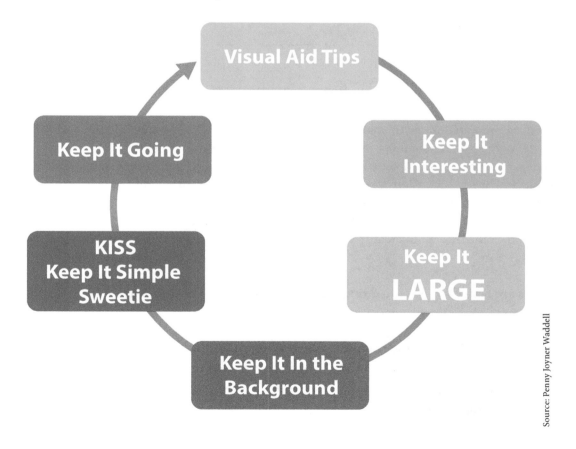

Source: Penny Joyner Waddell

When you use Gestalt to design a visual aid, you are going to use words, colors, shapes, textures, and pictures to produce one primary thought. For example, when creating a PowerPoint presentation, you might choose to use a heading at the top of the slide and the picture to illustrate a point.

We're not through, yet! Here is another example of Gestalt design which will remind you of all the visual aid design principles in one visual aid.

PRESENTATION TECHNOLOGY

Commonly used presentation technology, such as PowerPoint and Prezi, are excellent visual aid tools when used correctly. Both are excellent tools and create easy to see visual aids. Most speech instructors will require students to use presentation technology for the Informative and Persuasion Speeches. Some will also require this for Group and Special Occasion Speeches. Please check with your instructor to make sure you are following their assignment requirements for speech presentations.

When creating a PowerPoint or Prezi as a visual aid, there are several things to keep in mind. As with any presentation, you will want to create the presentation outline first and then create the visual aid to follow the presentation plan.

Most speeches are better served with a simple PowerPoint that only includes five slides:

- ▸ Slide #1: Title Slide (Title of the speech and a supporting picture)
- ▸ Slide #2: Point #1 (Name of the Point and a supporting picture or three bullet points)
- ▸ Slide #3: Point #2 (Name of the Point and a supporting picture or three bullet points)
- ▸ Slide #4: Point #3 (Name of the Point and a supporting picture or three bullet points)
- ▸ Slide #5: Conclusion Slide (Statement or Quote and supporting picture)

Guidelines for Creating and Using Presentation Technology

Guidelines	Explanation
Advance Planning	Consider the topic, audience, and room where speech will be presented. Rehearse with the Tech Team prior to the speech. Make sure the Tech Team understands the presentation technology. Give the Tech Team a script so they will know when to advance slides.
KISS	Keep It Simple Sweetie. Make visual aids simple, clear, and concise. Do not overcrowd slides with words and pictures. Avoid animations and background music.
Visibility	Make sure visual aids can be seen. Use fonts that are easily seen and read by everyone. Check all seats in the room to make sure the screen is visible. Use color effectively. Use dark fonts on light backgrounds. Use light fonts on dark backgrounds. When adding pictures, make sure pictures are not stretched. Choose high-resolution images that will not blur. Show slide while speaking about that point.
Design	Use sans serif font types. Use consistent font sizes, colors, and types. Titles and headings should be 36–44-point type. Sub-titles and text should be no less than 24-point type. Use consistent background colors with consistent headings. Limit the amount of text used on slides. Avoid using all CAPS on slides—even for headings. Line up pictures and graphics so they are balanced on the slides. Balance pictures and text on slides by limiting content. Leave whitespace when placing graphics and bullet points. Have one-line bullet points—keep lines to words and simple phrases. Check spelling before showing the slides. Keep charts and graphs simple. Add a title or heading for each chart or graph. Edit video or music sound-bites to be the length allowed. Limit charts to show no more than eight items.
Cite Sources	Cite research used in the footer of each slide. This includes photographs, graphs, diagrams, data, statistics, and quotes.
Rehearse	Rehearse with Tech Team prior to speech presentation. Provide a script for Tech Team members so they know what to do. Play videos and music sound-bites before speech to check volume. Look at PowerPoint or Prezi design in the room where it will be used. Make adjustments as needed to make sure slides are visible and clear. Rehearse to make sure visual aids are displayed properly. Discuss visual aids only as they are being used.

Table Displays

Let's talk about Table Displays! Often speakers will use a table display to show off objects or to create interest for their speech topic. They can be very effective when designed well and are used to enhance the speech topic. Here are some things to remember:

- ▶ Use a clean, ironed tablecloth placed so the table is evenly covered.
- ▶ Design the display so that it is eye appealing and useful.
- ▶ Coordinate colors, textures, shapes, and sizes.
- ▶ Include items that will be used during the speech. Show it and use it, or don't include it in the display.
- ▶ Make sure all items can be seen by every member of the audience.
- ▶ Use picture stands or easels to lift up items and show contents standing. Avoid laying items flat on the table.
- ▶ Rehearse using the items on the table display.

Notice how the tablecloth is placed on this table. It is important to have the tablecloth draped neatly. If you have one side longer than the other, your audience will have a hard time focusing on your speech because they will want to straighten the cloth.

This Communication Shark is using the notes feature on his phone while giving a demonstration speech. Using the red cooking pot as the centerpiece, he has the vegetables to the right and mixing bowls to the left. All of these colors are a good contrast to the white chef's coat and hat he is wearing for the speech. Of course, he is also demonstrating that he is using the SpeechShark app for speech notes and that is my favorite part!

Handouts

As discussed earlier in the chapter, the purpose of a handout is to help the audience to retain information shared during the speech. Many of the same rules for designing a PowerPoint or Prezi presentation will apply to creating a handout, so you will want to KISS and *Keep It Simple Sweetie* when planning the handout for your speech. Please check with your instructor prior to creating a handout to make sure you are following his or her assignments created for you.

Most instructors prefer for students to create their own handout rather than using a handout that is created by a company. The reason for this is because if created by a company, it will usually advertise that company or the company's product. For example, if you are giving a speech about spaying or neutering family pets, you could go to your local veterinarian's office and get one of their beautiful handouts that covers all of the areas pet owners need to know about spaying and neutering pets. This handout will be filled with useful information to support the speech, but the flyer will also contain the name, phone number, and address of the veterinarian who owns the office. Since we are giving speeches for a closed or captive audience, speakers need to make sure they are not endorsing any one company or product unless, of course, they are making a sales presentation. As examples of items you should not use, please know that a copy of your PowerPoint is NOT a handout. It's a note-taking device. A printed copy of an article found on the Internet is also NOT a handout.

Handouts come in all shapes and sizes. I've seen everything from personally crafted items to items purchased in a store and then personalized. Handouts should support the speech. Speakers who are demonstrating a cooking activity will create a beautiful recipe card for the audience members. If the speech is to motivate the audience to drink water, a water bottle with a personally printed label printed with "Drink More Water" is appropriate. Refrigerator magnets are great reminders for audience members to "Choose Healthy Snacks" and posters created to detail "Items to Recycle" can later be placed on home recycling bins as a reminder of what can or cannot be recycled. A bookmark is a great handout idea when the speech topic is motivating the audience to read hardcover books instead of e-books.

The key purpose of the handout is to provide your audience members with something that will further explain the topic or will help audience members remember the message of the speech.

Please keep the following tips in mind when designing the handout for your speech:

- Plan to tell your audience about the handout while presenting the speech. It is best to do this in the part of your speech where it makes the most sense. For example, if the handout is supporting a particular point in the speech, that is when it should be introduced.
- SHOW the handout to the audience as you speak about it and tell them what you want them to do with the handout they receive.
- Ask your Tech Team members to distribute the handout.
- Design an appealing handout using quality paper, color, and usable content.
  —Paper: Heavy cardstock is best for recipe cards, bookmarks, tri-fold brochures, and posters.
  —Color: Use color fonts and pictures when printing on a white background. Use color paper if using black-and-white ink with no pictures.
  —Content: Put the title of your speech on the handout along with any supporting information.
  —Use consistent font styles, font sizes, and colors.
- Use a tri-fold brochure, twin-brochure, or book format when applicable.
- Use diagrams, charts, pictures, or graphs to illustrate a point.
- Design the handout to complement the speech presentation.
- Make one handout for each person in the class including the instructor.
- Use technical writing skills when designing a handout.
- Laminate handouts when needed to protect the content. Not all handouts need to be laminated. Speakers should laminate items that could be damaged after repeated use such as recipe cards, instructions, and book marks.

Distributing the Handouts

Knowing when and how to distribute the handout is just as important as designing the handout. Work with your Tech Team members before the day of your speech so that they will know you expect them to distribute the handout you have worked so hard to create. Consider the following suggestions:

1. **Enlist Tech Team Members to distribute handouts.** The speaker should not distribute their handouts personally. Having a Tech Team member distribute handouts will make the presentation appear more professional and will help ease the speaker's stress because it is one less thing to think about.

2. **Avoid distributing handouts to the audience during the middle of a speech.** Doing this will require the Tech Team member to walk through the audience and distribute handouts while the speaker is still talking. Audience members may even be asked to pass handouts to those around them. This is disruptive and your audience will quit listening to the speaker to turn their attention to the person distributing the handouts.

3. **Distribute handouts BEFORE the speech** if the handout will be used as a note-taking aid, a fill-in-the-blank format, or if it is to be used as a visual during the speech. Be sure to relay any instructions from the speaker to the audience as you distribute the handout.

4. **Distribute the handout AFTER the speech** if the handout is offering additional information for your audience to read later.

ASSIGNING A TECH TEAM

As a speaker, you will notice there are many pieces to the speech puzzle and you will need help pulling it all together. To do this, you need a **tech team**. What is a tech team? This is a group of people qualified to help complete your speech presentation by setting up or breaking down, managing the PowerPoint/Prezi slides, managing lighting and sound requirements, and distributing handouts. Most speeches will require visual aids, handouts, lighting effects, sound, microphones, and backstage support. As with anything, the buck stops with you. The success of your speech depends upon you to cover every detail and that includes working with a tech team.

Never assume that your tech team will know what you want them to do. Consider yourself as a project manager and the speech is your project.

To accomplish the project, there are many strategies for getting the job done and according to expectations. Yet, these things do not just happen on their own. You have to plan for the success of your speech presentation.

First take a look at your speech plan. Answer the following questions:

1. What will you need to complete the speech project?

   _____

2. Who can help you reach your goals?

   _____

3. Is your tech team member qualified with the areas where you need help?

   _____

4. Did you supply a script for the tech team?

   _____

5. Can your tech team rehearse with you?

   _____

6. Do you have the materials and supplies needed for the tech team to do their jobs?

   _____

7. Can you count on your tech team member to be there and to be prepared?

   _____

Once you know what you need, you can begin assigning responsibilities for your tech team.

Ask questions! Make sure you KNOW that your tech team members understand how to run a simple PowerPoint or Prezi presentation. If they do not know, make plans to rehearse with them and show them how to do this. OR, fire that tech team member and appoint a new one!

Choose the number of tech team members you need for the speech. One or two tech team members may be enough, but if the presentation is complicated and involves multiple aspects, you will need to add tech team members.

Without a shadow of a doubt, you should be able to count on your tech team members to arrive on time and to be prepared. There is nothing in this world that can shake your speech-making resolve faster than to arrive for the speech and not see tech team members until five minutes before the speech begins! YIKES! That is when you will feel like a guppy navigating in murky waters and the results may not be pretty. Be a Speech-Shark and be prepared!

Use a Tech Team Checklist to make sure you are prepared. You'll find an example of one with the Checklist for a Great Speech on page 216.

REHEARSING WITH A TECH TEAM

© meviogra/Shutterstock.com

This part of your responsibility does not happen on its own. It is YOUR speech and it is YOUR responsibility to arrange the rehearsals with your tech team. Your speech will only be as good as your tech team! One slide out of place, one video that does not play as planned, one sound-bite or music segment that is not properly executed will affect your credibility as a speaker.

Now that you have identified tech team members, arrange at least two rehearsals with them prior to your speech. If possible, have the rehearsals in the place where you are going to make the presentation so that you can also become familiar with the stage, lights, and sound system.

As your tech team members arrive, shake their hands and tell them how much you appreciate their help with the presentation. Introduce the tech team members to each other and identify their responsibilities during the presentation. After the rehearsals and after your presentation, please make sure to thank each person who helped make your presentation spectacular! Even small details completed on your behalf add up to a big deal on speech day.

Distribute a script to each tech team member. Although you will have one basic script, it is a good idea to highlight and personalize each script so that it is clear what you want each tech team member to do during the presentation.

In the pages that follow, you will see a separate script for each of the three tech team members needed for the informative speech. Notice how each script is designed for the tech team member and highlights the job tasks needed for the speech.

EXAMPLE

SCRIPT: PowerPoint Presentation–Tech Team Member #1

Penny J. Waddell
Toastmasters International Meeting
30 June 2020

Speech Category: Informative Speech
Title: How to Dress for an Interview
Purpose: The purpose of this speech is to inform my audience how to dress for an interview.

Introduction: As speaker is introduced, please have Slide #1 up.

Attention Step: (Show pictures on a PowerPoint Slide of different people dressed in different ways. One person is dressed in jeans, flip-flops, and a T-shirt; another is dressed in a short minidress with tattoos showing on her arms and legs; another is dressed business casual.) Take a look at the pictures of these three candidates who are about to interview for a job position at a Fortune 500 Company. Which candidate do you think will get the job?

Establish Need/Relevance: The truth is that any one of these candidates MAY get the job. The secret is knowing with which company the candidate is interviewing? If interviewing for a position at GOOGLE, the jeans and T-shirt may be appropriate. If interviewing for a position with The Coca Cola Company in Atlanta, the candidate dressed business casual may get the job. Before interviewing for a job position, be sure to know what type of dress is expected.

Establish Speaker Credibility: I am credible to speak to you today about dressing for an interview because I have recently interviewed for a job position and got the job! For the position, I needed to dress in an upscale suit, very little jewelry, and I needed to project extreme professionalism.

Thesis: Today, I will cover three points to inform you how to dress for an interview. (1) Research the company, (2) Understand the culture of the company, and (3) Put your best foot forward.

Body: During the transition sentence, please go to Slide #2—Research the Company.
Transition/Link: Let's begin with the first point, research the company.

    I. Research the Company
        A. What type of business does this company do?
        B. What type of work responsibilities are expected?

Transition/Link: I've shared the importance of researching the company with you, now I'd like to tell you how to understand the culture of the company. During the transition sentence, please go to Slide #3—Understand the Culture of the Company.

    II. Understand the Culture of the Company
        A. Make a trip to the company prior to the Interview (Quast).
        B. Watch to see how other employees dress.

Transition/Link: You've heard how to research the company and how to understand its culture, now I want to show you how to put your best foot forward. During the transition sentence, please go to Slide #4—Put Your Best Foot Forward.

III. **Put Your Best Foot Forward**

    A. Choose clothing, shoes, and accessories that mirror how other employees in this company dress.

    B. Err on the conservative side, but don't forget to show your personality.

Transition/Link: Now you should understand a little more about how to dress for an interview.

Conclusion: During the transition sentence, please go to Slide #5—Quote.

Summary: Today, I shared with you three points: (1) Research the company, (2) Understand the culture of the company, and (3) Put your best foot forward.

Appeal to Action: As you interview for what might very well be the most important interview of your life, be sure to remember that "You never get a second chance to make a first impression" (Quast). With this quote, I want to challenge you to dress for success and make sure this interview is the one that will help you get your dream job!

Following the Appeal to Action, please go to slide #6—Blank Slide. After speaker leaves the stage, please take down the PowerPoint.

(Note: The Works Cited page should be added as a separate page following the Outline.)

Works Cited

Quast, Lisa. "8 Tips to Dress for Interview Success." *Forbes*. 2014. Accessed 12 March 2017.

(Note: The Visual Aids Explanation page is a separate page from the Outline and the Works Cited page.)

Visual Aids Explanation Page

PowerPoint Presentation:

Slide #1:   Title of Speech—**How to Dress for an Interview**
             Pictures of Three People Dressed Differently

Slide #2:   (Point #1): **Research the Company**
             Bullet Points:
- Type of Business
- Type of Work Responsibilities

Slide #3:   (Point #2): **Understand the Culture of the Company**
             Picture of Business with Employees Entering the Door

Slide #4:   (Point #3): **Put Your Best Foot Forward**
             Picture of Professionally Dressed Employee

Slide #5:   **"You Never Get a Second Chance to Make a First Impression" (Quast)**
             Picture of a Group of Professionally Dressed Employees

REHEARSING THE SPEECH

You have heard it said that practice makes perfect. This is true, but only if you practice properly. You will do little to improve your speech delivery unless you practice the right things in the right ways. **Here is a five-step method that works well for presenters:**

1. Go through your outline to see what you have written.
   - ▶ Are the main points clear?
   - ▶ Do you have supporting materials?
   - ▶ Does your introduction and conclusion come across well?
2. Prepare your speaking notes. In doing so, be sure to follow the guidelines. Use the same framework as in the preparation outline. Make sure your speaking notes are easy to read. Give yourself cues on the note cards for delivering the speech.
3. Practice the speech aloud several times using only the speaking outline. Be sure to "talk through" all examples and to recite quotations and statistics. If your speech includes visual aids, utilize those as you practice. The first couple of times, you will probably forget something or make a mistake, but don't worry. Keep going and complete the speech as best as you can. Concentrate on gaining control of the ideas; don't try to learn the speech word for word. After a few tries you should be able to get through the speech extemporaneously with surprising ease.
4. Polish and refine your delivery. Practice the speech in front of a mirror to check for eye contact and distracting mannerisms. Record the speech to gauge volume, pitch, rate, pauses, and vocal variety. Most important, try it out on friends, roommates, family members—anyone who will listen and give you honest feedback. Because your speech is designed for an audience you need to find out ahead of time how it goes over with people.
5. Finally, give your speech a dress rehearsal under conditions as close as possible to those you will face in class. Some students like to try the speech a couple times in an empty classroom the day before they actually present the speech. No matter where you hold your last practice session, you should leave it feeling confident and looking forward to speaking in your class.

If this or any practice method is to work, you must start early. Don't wait until the night before your speech to begin working on delivery. A single practice session—no matter how long—is rarely enough. Allow yourself at least a couple of days, preferably more, to gain command of the speech and its presentation.

PRACTICE WITH YOUR VISUAL AIDS

We have mentioned several times the need to rehearse using your visual aids, but the point bears repeating. No matter what kind of visual aid you choose, be sure to employ it when you rehearse. Go through the speech multiple times, rehearsing how you will show your aids, the gestures you will make, and the timing of each move. In using visual aids, as in other aspects of speechmaking, there is no substitute for preparation.

If you are using presentation technology, don't just click through casually or rush quickly over your words when you practice. Make sure you know exactly when you want each slide to appear and disappear, and what you will say while each is on-screen. Mark your speaking notes with cues that will remind you when to display each slide and when to remove it.

Rehearse with the mouse, remote, keyboard, or iPad until you can use them without looking down for more than an instant when advancing your slides. Also concentrate on presenting the speech without looking back at the screen to see what is being projected. Rehearse with your tech team, if you need one!

Given all the things you have to work on when practicing a speech with any kind of presentation technology, you need to allow extra time for rehearsal. So, get an early start and give yourself plenty of time to ensure that your delivery is as impressive as your slides.

Practicing Visual Aids Checklist	Yes	No
• Have I checked the speech room to decide where I can display my visual aids most effectively?		
• Have I practiced presenting my visual aids so they will be clearly visible to everyone in the audience?		
• Have I practiced presenting my visual aids so they are perfectly timed with my words and actions?		
• Have I practiced keeping eye contact with my audience while presenting my visual aids?		
• Have I practiced explaining my visual aids clearly and concisely in terms my audience will understand?		
• If I am using handouts, have I planned to distribute them after the speech rather than during?		
• Have I double-checked all equipment to make sure it works properly?		
• If I am using PowerPoint, do I have a backup of my slides that I can take to the speech with me?		

CHECK THE ROOM AND EQUIPMENT

For classroom speeches, you will already be familiar with the room and equipment. Even if you have used PowerPoint on previous occasions, you need to check the setup in the room where you will be presenting.

If you are using a computer that is installed in the room, bring your slides on a flash drive so you can see how they work with that computer. If your presentation includes audio or video, double-check them using the room's audiovisual system.

Sometimes, of course, it is not possible to visit the room before the day of your speech. Never assume that everything will be "just fine." Instead, assume that things will not be fine and that they need to be checked ahead of time.

Finally, always bring a backup of your slides on a flash drive. This may seem like a lot of fuss and bother, but anyone who has given speeches with PowerPoint—or any other kind of visual aid—will tell you that it is absolutely essential.

Have a Backup Plan

No matter how much time presenters invest in mastering the technology, they can still be undermined by technological glitches. This is why experts recommend that you always have a backup plan in case the technology fails. Because we have all encountered sabotage by technology at one time or another, audiences usually have sympathy for a presenter who encounters such problems. When in doubt, be prepared to present without technology.

SPEECH DAY CHECK LIST

- ▸ Plan, Prepare, Persevere! The more planning and preparation you do before the speech, the more confident you will be.
- ▸ Think positively—YOU can do this!
- ▸ Understand what is expected of you for the speech.
- ▸ Pack all materials you need the day before your speech. Have a checklist planned to keep you on target.
- ▸ Take care of you!
  - ▸ Get a good night's sleep before the speech.
  - ▸ Eat a healthy high protein meal.
  - ▸ Stay away from milk products which can coat your throat.
  - ▸ Drink plenty of fluids before your speech, but avoid caffeine and sugar which can make you feel jittery.
- ▸ Rehearse with your tech team so they know what you need.
- ▸ Arrive early to become familiar with the speaking area.
- ▸ Rehearse using a microphone, if you need to use one.
- ▸ Rehearse using a remote for your PowerPoint, if you choose to use one.
- ▸ Visit with people as they arrive for the speech. It helps to create a bond with the audience prior to your presentation.

Consider these areas carefully and pre-pack for your presentation. Begin to pack a bag of things you will need to carry for the speech. If you need visual aids, you will also need to work with a tech team and have them rehearse with you to make sure they understand all that you will require them to do for your presentation. This means providing a script so they will know when to set up your table display for props or so they will know when to advance the slides of your PowerPoint presentation. Preparation also includes rehearsal.

First, rehearse *without* your tech team to smooth out the rough edges and to make decisions regarding the point in your speech when visual aids, sound, light changes, or PowerPoint slides should be introduced. Once you have worked through these details, then bring in the tech team.

CHECKLIST FOR A GREAT SPEECH

Before each presentation, follow this checklist to make sure every detail is in shipshape!

The Outline:
- ☐ Typed
  - ○ Correct outline format
  - ○ Header (name, company name/class name/date)
  - ○ Headings for each item is in bold letters
- ☐ Speech Category
- ☐ Title
- ☐ General Purpose
- ☐ Specific Purpose

Introduction:
- ☐ Full sentence format
- ☐ Attention Step
- ☐ Establish Need/Relevance
- ☐ Establish Speaker Credibility
- ☐ Thesis/Preview Statement (clearly states main points)

Body:
- ☐ Roman numerals (I., II., III.) Capitalized letters for sub-points (A., B., C.) and numbers for sub-sub-points (1., 2., 3.)
- ☐ Three main points (using key words or phrases)
- ☐ Transition sentences between the introduction step to the main points, between each main point, and between the last main point and the conclusion
- ☐ Each main point is covered equally

Conclusion:
- ☐ Full sentence format
- ☐ Signal to let your audience know you are concluding the speech
- ☐ Summary restates all main points clearly
- ☐ Final appeal keeps the audience thinking about the speech

Visual Aids:
- ☐ Visual aid explanation page is included with the outline
- ☐ PowerPoint/Prezi slides follow outline
- ☐ PowerPoint follows design requirements
- ☐ Handout is usable, designed by the speaker, and supplies one for each person
- ☐ Rehearse using visual aids with tech team

Research:

- ☐ Follow citation guidelines for the topic
- ☐ Include credible research sources
- ☐ Include the minimum number of sources required
- ☐ Vary types of research used
- ☐ Parenthetically cite research in the document
- ☐ Include a separate page for the Works Cited

Presentation:

- ☐ Rehearse using presentation notes
- ☐ Rehearse with the tech team
- ☐ Place a water bottle on the lectern
- ☐ Check EVERYTHING—lights, sound, computer, PowerPoint, notes folder

TECH TEAM CHECKLIST

Complete this form as you plan the use of visual aids so you are prepared for the speech. Speakers who use visual aids will need to make use of a tech team. It is the speaker's responsibility to meet with tech team members ahead of time, provide a script, and rehearse with the tech team to make sure they understand what is needed. Visual aids are an important part of the speech and a direct reflection of your credibility as a speaker.

Speaker's Name: _____ **Date:** _____

Time of Speech: _____ **Type of Speech:** _____

Description of visual aids:

_____

_____

_____

_____

Note: In the area below, please list each tech team member's name and their assigned duties. Be sure to assign a member for the PowerPoint, sound, lights, setup, breakdown, and distribution of handouts. All duties may not be needed for all speeches.

Tech Team Member's Name: _____

Duties Assigned: _____

Tech Team Member's Name: _____

Duties Assigned: _____

Tech Team Member's Name: _____

Duties Assigned: _____

Tech Team Member's Name: _____

Duties Assigned: _____

_____

_____

METHODS OF DELIVERY

The most effective way for a speaker to reach his audience is to present the speech using elements of formal speaking skills combined with aspects of conversational delivery. In other words, speakers should combine skills along with personality. Audiences want the experience of hearing a great speaker, but they LOVE speakers that are authentic and immerse themselves into the presentation. A true SpeechShark knows that it is not simply the information delivered that impacts the delivery of the speech. Decide which of the methods of delivery are the most effective for your purpose: extemporaneous, impromptu, manuscript, or memorized. Then you can begin planning a speech that will deliver!

Extemporaneous Speaking

Most speeches required in a human communication course will use the extemporaneous speaking model. We use this type for Introduction, Informative, Persuasive, Group Presentations, and Special Occasion Speeches. You'll also notice that extemporaneous speaking models are used with all of the TED Talks you've heard. Extemporaneous speaking is audience-centered speaking and is presented using an outline instead of a fully written speech. It almost feels impromptu since it is not a manuscript or memorized speech, yet the speaker has had time to choose a topic, research the topic, write an outline, create visual aids and handouts, and rehearse the speech.

The benefit of presenting extemporaneously is that it gives the audience the impression that you are presenting the speech as it is created. In drama classes, we call this the "illusion of the first time." In other words, you have time to plan what you will do, but will make it sound as if it is the first time you have spoken about it. That's not to say that speakers can't memorize certain portions of their extemporaneous speeches. In fact, we suggest that speakers memorize their attention step and concluding statements so they are assured the beginning and ending of their speech presentations will go according to plan.

Extemporaneous speeches are conversational in nature and that is the key reason audiences prefer this type of speech over any others they hear. Speakers spend less time looking at notes and more time connecting directly with their audience members through direct eye contact and a more relaxed stage presence.

SpeechSharks are especially good with extemporaneous speeches when they use the SpeechShark notes feature in the app because it provides the brief notes needed, but allows the speaker the flexibility to speak conversationally without reading a speech.

Tips for Extemporaneous Speaking

1. Enthusiasm is contagious. Choose a topic you love and your audience will also enjoy the topic.
2. Use the SpeechShark app (www.SpeechShark.com) to plan the speech with your audience in mind. Think about areas of a topic the audience would like to know.
3. Include personal stories and research to support the topic. When using research, verbally cite the sources you use and explain how the research connects with the topic.
4. Create useful notes or use the app notes on your phone for the lectern. Keep them simple and easy to use. You might not need them, but it is always comforting to know they are there.
5. Rehearse the speech a minimum of three times so that you are familiar with the content. Time each rehearsal and get an average time for the three rehearsals in order to have a good idea of the amount of time your presentation will take. If your speech is too long, remove some of the sub-points. If it is too short, add sub-points. It is important to stay within the time frame expected.

6. Prepare effective visual aids. Choose a Tech Team member to help with the visual aids and rehearse with your Tech Team member using the visual aids.

7. Pack everything you need for your speech the day before the presentation.

8. Choose a professional outfit to wear the day of your speech and make sure it is comfortable. This is not the day to wear uncomfortable shoes!

9. Arrive early so that you can become familiar with the room, upload a copy of the PowerPoint, and set up a table display.

10. Greet others as they arrive so that you can establish a connection with audience members prior to giving the speech.

Impromptu Speaking

During the first day of class and several times throughout the semester, your instructor may ask you to present an impromptu speech. This type of speech is used in college-level courses, at work, and in social gatherings. You'll start to recognize this as speaking without prior preparation, otherwise known as thinking on your feet. It is an informal way of communicating without having time to think of a clever answer or rehearsing what you might plan to say. Impromptu speaking requires you to give a quick answer or response at a moment's notice.

In the public speaking course, we lovingly call impromptu speeches **ZAPs**. If you have ever been asked to give a speech without notice and discover that you feel like you've had a surge of electricity running through your body, then you will understand why we call these ZAPs. For the sake of understanding, we've created the ZAP acronym to explain how impromptu speaking works.

Z stands for zero time to prepare for a speech.

A represents the attention to detail required during an impromptu speech.

P reminds us that points need to be clear and complete.

Of all the speeches covered during a human communication course, students will say the impromptu speech is the most valuable because it has a practical application. People who learn this skill will find they are much more effective answering interview questions, responding to questions from customers and fellow employees, as well as being able to speak intelligently at any work or social function.

If you would like a guaranteed shark strategy for answering questions at a moment's notice and with no prior preparation, please be sure to use the P.R.E.P. model. This works for any opportunity in which an impromptu speech or answer needs to be presented.

Acronym	Stands for...	Description
P	Point	Restate the question asked and then clarify the point of the question.
R	Relevance	Thank the person who asked the question, explain why the question is relevant, and provide a brief answer to the question.
E	Example	Provide a clear example as a follow-up to your answer and to make sure the audience has an understanding of the answer.
P	Point	Summarize the impromptu speech by re-stating the point and affirm that you answered the speaker's question.

Tips for Impromptu Speaking

1. Anticipate impromptu speaking opportunities and be **PREP**ared.
2. Memorize the **PREP** model and be ready for anything.
3. Listen, so that you don't have to ask for the question to be repeated.
4. Don't rush! Take a moment to process the question before you begin to answer it. Restating the question before you answer the point of the question will help give you a little extra time to decide how to answer the question. Your audience members will just think you are establishing good eye contact with them, when in reality you are thinking of a clever answer. People who get in too big of a hurry are the very same people who forget the question and stumble over their answers. Take your time.
5. The **PREP** model calls for brevity. Answers that get directly to the point of the question, connect relevance of the question to the answer, and offer real-life examples will affirm your credibility as a speaker.

Manuscript Speaking

Manuscript speaking is a method that involves reading a speech word-for-word as it is written. Many politicians, executives, and broadcasters use this method of speech delivery when they have a message that must be delivered exactly the way it is planned. Speeches that include data, statistics, details, or critical information will need to be delivered from a written manuscript. This is not one of the best types of speech delivery simply because there is very little eye contact or connection with the audience; instead, it is simply an opportunity to present information.

Speechwriters understand the importance of opening and closing this type of speech with a personal note to break the monotony of having the entire speech read to the audience. Speakers who resort to manuscript speaking will often use teleprompters so that it does not fully appear the entire speech is being read.

Tips for Manuscript Speaking

1. Rehearse using a teleprompter prior to the speech.
2. Rehearse! Rehearse! Rehearse! While rehearsals are important for all types of speeches, it is especially important that the speaker be extremely familiar with the script. This allows more opportunity for eye contact and a connection with the audience. Pause often so that eye contact can be established.

3. Rehearse adding vocal variance to the speech. Avoid speaking using a reading cadence or a monotone quality. Adding variations to the pitch, volume, pace, and rate will create added interest in your voice.

4. Check pronunciations of names and places.

5. Use large gestures so they are evident as you stand behind a lectern. Gestures will add interest to a manuscript speech.

Memorized Speaking

A manuscript speech that has been committed to memory is memorized speaking. Like the manuscript speech, this presentation involves presenting a speech word-for-word; however, it is memorized. Speakers will choose to memorize a speech when accuracy is of great importance along with a warm rapport with the audience that is not achieved when reading a speech.

Often during extemporaneous speech planning, students will try to write their entire speech and memorize it thinking a written speech will result in a stronger speech presentation. This is not always true because when memory fails, it is hard for the speaker to pick up where she left off and move forward. This is one reason why memorized speeches are usually short and to the point. The shorter the speech, the less opportunity the speaker has for forgetting parts of the speech.

Speakers will *not* use notes for memorized speaking because it is too difficult to glance down at a full written page of paper and immediately find the lost thoughts.

Another problem associated with memorized speaking is that the speaker will not be able to respond quickly to the audience if something unplanned happens. Flexibility is almost impossible with a memorized speech.

Tips for Memorized Speaking

1. Memorize the speech. Now you know why they call it memorized speaking!

2. Try memorizing the speech in the three sections they occur: Introduction, Body, and Conclusion. This will help in the event that you forget a portion of the speech and will need to move to the next area.

3. Rehearse, rehearse, rehearse! This is the best advice for preparing for a memorized speech. Knowing the speech from one end to the other will help with your confidence level.

4. Use "the illusion of the first time" and keep the material sounding fresh even though you might have rehearsed it hundreds of times.

5. Since it is memorized, you should establish eye contact with audience members.

6. Connect with your audience, respond to their nonverbal cues, and watch how the audience will also respond to you.

TYPES OF SPEECHES

There are three basic purposes or types of speeches: informative, entertaining, and motivational. Some speeches will address just one purpose or type, but there are many speeches that will include all three.

Informative speeches are designed for the speaker to provide interesting and useful information and to add knowledge to the listener's existing understanding of the topic. For this type of speech, the speaker takes on the role of an instructor and will teach, instruct, explain, report, and/or describe.

Entertaining speeches are enjoyable speeches. Some organizations list this type of speech as a humorous speech. Although not all speeches are categorized as entertaining speeches, it is possible for all speeches to contain entertaining aspects. Audiences enjoy speeches that are light-hearted, incorporate humor, and provide entertaining factors within the speech. Storytelling is considered one strategy for delivering an entertaining speech. Special Occasion Speeches usually include entertaining aspects. Due to the nature of this type of speech, speakers are able to build relationships, bond with the audience, and enhance networking possibilities.

Motivational speeches are designed to inspire the audience to act on information. Most often, Persuasion and Special Occasion Speeches will incorporate motivational strategies. Speakers who have the purpose of motivating the audience will need to consider incorporating information, research, and stories which will influence the audience's values, beliefs, attitudes, or behaviors. More information about this is covered in the Persuasion Speech section of this book.

Unsure about how to write a speech? The SpeechShark app was created just for you! Select the type speech you need, answer the questions in full sentence format, and SpeechShark will do the rest of the work. For those who want to know more details about the types of speeches, here is a description and important facts about each type.

Whether you are speaking to inform, entertain, or motivate, the following content areas will provide a description of solo speeches that you will present in the Human Communication Course. These speechwriting tools include strategies for planning the speech and brainstorming worksheets, outline templates, and example outlines to help you as you prepare for your presentation. With the use of these tools along with the SpeechShark App, you'll be planning and presenting speeches like a pro!

Introduction Speech

In your personal and business life, you will have plenty of opportunities to introduce yourself or others. Whether your introduction is planned or unplanned, understanding the tips below will help you complete the introduction with ease. Introduction Speeches are informative in nature because the purpose of the speech is to provide your audience with information about you or the person you are introducing.

Usually, Introduction Speeches are not very lengthy and last between two and three minutes. This isn't much time, so you will need to consider specific points to include, but without too much detail.

©ESB Professional/Shutterstock.com

When introducing yourself, choose a theme and plan the introduction around the theme. If the setting is casual or informal, then you could introduce yourself with a theme about your hobbies, work, or family. Personal introductions on an informal scale will often include a handshake along with eye contact and a smile.

If the setting is business or formal, then you should introduce yourself by including information about your work, innovative ideas, experience in the field, and future goals. In both cases, consider the setting and provide information you think the audience would like to know. Avoid giving so much information that your introduction becomes tiresome! It should be light and positive.

One safe rule of thumb for an introduction speech is to follow a chronological or time-ordered sequence to introduce yourself or someone else. Begin your speech by briefly covering the **past**, then move to the **present**, and finally, share your hopes for the **future**.

If you are using the SpeechShark app to create this speech, then you can begin now to craft the speech. If you are not using the app, you may want to use the Introduction Speech Brainstorming Worksheet to get your thoughts together and prepare to write your presentation outline. Remember that all speech writers follow the **Standard Outline** procedure for creating a speech outline. We will only show you this type of outline in this book so that you will begin thinking like a professional speech writer!

Consider your audience and the speech making situation so that you know what type of information to include. **Answer the following questions:**

- ► What is your ultimate purpose for the introduction?

- ► Are you speaking to a room full of people or to one person?

- ► Is the introduction in a formal or informal setting?

- ► What information do you need to share?

- ► How much time do you have for the speech?

- ► What can you do to make the introduction relevant to the audience?

Brainstorming Worksheet

Speech Category: Introduction Speech

Speech Title: Give your speech a clever title. _____

Specific Purpose: Write a full sentence to show what you plan to accomplish by introducing yourself or introducing someone else.

Introduction:

Attention Step: Consider how you will get your audience's attention. Write all you plan to say using full sentences.

Establish Need/Relevance: Explain why this introduction should interest the listener. Write all you plan to say using full sentences.

Establish Credibility: Explain why YOU are credible to introduce yourself or another person. Write all you plan to say using full sentences.

Thesis (Preview) Statement: Write a complete sentence and clearly state the three points you will cover:

Point #1: Past _____

Point #2: Present _____

Point #3: Future _____

Body:

Transition Sentence: Write a full sentence to transition from the Introduction Step to the first main point.

    I. **First Main Point—Past:** (Share information about your past—stay with a theme.)
       A. **First Sub-Point**
         1. **First Sub-Sub-Point** (Not all points will require sub-sub-points.)
         2. **Second Sub-Sub-Point**

      B. **Second Sub-Point**
          1. **First Sub-Sub-Point**
          2. **Second Sub-Sub-Point**

Transition Sentence: Write a full sentence to transition from the past to the present.

  II. **Second Main Point—Present:** (Share information about your present—stay with the theme.)
      A. **First Sub-Point**
          1. **First Sub-Sub-Point** (Not all points will require sub-sub-points.)
          2. **Second Sub-Sub-Point**
      B. **Second Sub-Point**
          1. **First Sub-Sub-Point**
          2. **Second Sub-Sub-Point**

Transition Sentence: Write a full sentence to transition from the present to the future.

  III. **Third Main Point—Future:** (Share information about your goals for the future—stay with the theme.)
      A. **First Sub-Point**
          1. **First Sub-Sub-Point** (Not all points will require sub-sub-points.)
          2. **Second Sub-Sub-Point**
      B. **Second Sub-Point**
          1. **First Sub-Sub-Point**
          2. **Second Sub-Sub-Point**

Transition Sentence: Write a full sentence to transition from the third main point to the conclusion.

Conclusion:

Summary: Write in full sentence format a summary of your three main points.

Point #1: _____

Point #2: _____

Point #3: _____

Appeal to Action: Leave your audience thinking about your introduction. End with a **BANG!**

(NOTE: Place the Works Cited Page on a page separate from the outline).

Works Cited

*Note: If you use visual aids, please include a Visual Aid Explanation Page
as a separate page following the Works Cited page.*

Visual Aid Explanation Page

Outline Template

Last Name 1

First Name/Last Name
Introduction Speech
Day Month Year

Speech Category: Introduction Speech
Title:
Purpose:

Introduction:
Attention Step:
Establish Need/Relevance:
Establish Speaker Credibility:

Thesis: Today, I want to share three points about (Topic): (1) _____,

(2) _____, and (3) _____.

Body:

Transition/Link: First, I will start at the beginning by sharing a little about (Point #1).
   I. First Main Point
     A. Sub-point
     B. Sub-point

Transition/Link: I've shared (Point #1) with you, now I'd like to tell you about (Point #2).
   II. Second Main Point
     A. Sub-point
     B. Sub-point

Transition/Link: You've heard about (Point #1 and Point #2), now I'll cover (Point #3).
   III. Third Main Point
     A. Sub-point
     B. Sub-point

Transition/Link: My purpose today was to (insert purpose and add a statement about the topic).
Conclusion:

Summary: Today, I shared with you three points: (1) Point #1 _____, (2) Point #2 _____

_____, and (3) Point #3 _____.
Appeal to Action: As I conclude this speech, (End with a BANG).

(NOTE: Place the Works Cited Page on a page separate from the outline).

Works Cited

*Note: If you use visual aids, please include a Visual Aid Explanation Page
as a separate page following the Works Cited page.*

Visual Aid Explanation Page

Example Outline

Waddell 1

Penny J. Waddell
Introduction Speech
30 June 2020

Speech Category: Introduction Speech

Title: A Penny Saved Is a Penny Earned

Purpose: The purpose of this speech is to introduce myself to the readers of this book.

Introduction:

Attention Step: Benjamin Franklin, one of the most famous Americans in our history, once said, "A penny saved is a penny earned" (*Benjamin Franklin Quotes* 1).

Establish Need/Relevance: My father would say this quote every time he introduced me to someone because he loved my name. Since we will be spending time together this fall, it is important that you get to know a little about me. Through the years, my name, Penny, has become a way to start conversations with complete strangers and so I wanted to share this quote with you and a few tidbits of information to let you know how a person's name can help that person build a life.

Establish Speaker Credibility: Hello, my name is Penny and I am credible to introduce myself to you because I know myself better than anyone else in this room, unless of course, it is my father!

Thesis: Today, I want to share three points about my life as a speech coach: (1) Past Speaking Experiences, (2) Present Speaking Experiences, and (3) Future Speaking Experiences.

Body:

Transition/Link: First, I will start at the beginning by sharing a little about my past speaking experiences.

    I. **Past Speaking Experiences**
        A. Learning Public Speaking Tips
        B. Not a Penny to My Name
        C. College Experiences Worth Every Penny

Transition/Link: I've shared past speaking experiences with you, now I'd like to tell you what is going on presently.

    II. **Present Speaking Experiences**
        A. Not a Bad Penny, But a Good Penny
        B. Turning a Penny Postcard into a SpeechShark Postcard
        C. Developed a SpeechShark app for speechwriting and authored the *SpeechShark* and *Communication Sharks* textbooks

Transition/Link: You've heard about my past and present speaking experiences, but the best is yet to come!

    III. **Future Speaking Experiences**
        A. Throwing a Penny Over My Shoulder into a Wishing Well
        B. A Good Penny is Worth a Pound of Cure
        C. A Penny for your Thoughts

Transition/Link: My purpose today was to introduce myself to you and to help you know a little more about me. Do you think you might be able to remember my name, if we met again somewhere along the way?

Conclusion:

Summary: Today, I shared with you three sweet points—you might call them Penny Candy: (1) Past Speaking Experiences, (2) Present Speaking Experiences, and (3) Future Speaking Experiences of a new friend named Penny.

Appeal to Action: As I close this speech, the next time you see me at a meeting or in a crowd, I hope you will remember that I am not a "bad penny." I am a "good penny" and a speech coach that can help you "Save" face when asked to speak in public and "Earn" the respect of those in your audience. Remember, "A Penny Saved Is a Penny Earned" (*Benjamin Franklin Quotes* 1).

(NOTE: Place the Works Cited Page on a page separate from the outline).

Works Cited

Benjamin Franklin Quotes. Your Dictionary. Lovetoknow.com 2017. Accessed 12 March 2017.

Note: If you use visual aids, please include a Visual Aid Explanation Page as a separate page following the Works Cited page.

Visual Aid Explanation Page

Informative Speech

© Rawpixel.com/Shutterstock.com

What is an **Informative Speech?** It is an opportunity to share something of value with your audience. You may choose to provide information about a hobby, career, politics, religion, or something that is happening in your school, college, or community. The purpose of an informative speech is to share knowledge with your audience. Often, the audience may already have a good understanding of the topic, but you will then be able to expand their knowledge by providing credible research, data, and personal stories to support your main points.

Conducting research will allow the opportunity to provide a strong attention step and conclusion for the informative speech. You may choose to begin the speech with a great quote or startling statistics that will get your audience's attention and will also lead to the informative speech topic you will present. Research can also provide options for the conclusion to keep your audience thinking about the information you shared. Supplementing your informative speech with credible research and personal experiences will make the topic come alive for your audience and will help your audience to remain more attentive.

Once you know who will be in your audience, consider choosing a topic that will be interesting to those in your audience. Also, consider a topic that interests you. Remember, enthusiasm is contagious! If you are enthusiastic about your topic, then your audience will enjoy your speech so much more.

Don't be afraid to share a topic that may be personal in nature. Audiences truly enjoy hearing personal stories and your experience with the topic will help support the points in the speech. Let us see your personality and passion for the topic.

An **Informative Speech** is often called a **Key Idea Speech** or a **Central Idea Speech**. You will hear these titles interchangeably because you begin with one general topic idea, but find it necessary to narrow your topic down to one key or central idea. From that point, you will have a better chance of informing your audience about the topic you have chosen.

The best informative speeches have titles that lead to the information the speaker wishes to share. Most of these titles will begin with *"How to. . .", "Why You Should. . .", "Did You Know. . .", "Tips for. . .", "The Pros and Cons of . . .", "Examples of. . .",* and *"The Problems With. . .".*

Here are some examples of informative speech titles:

Informative Speech Topics	
How to Make Brownies	How to Choose a Church That Is Right for Your Family
How to Start a College Club on Your Campus	Where to Go on Your Next Vacation
Why You Should NOT Text and Drive	The Problem with an HOA (Home Owners Association)
Why Homeowners Should Have an HO3 Insurance Policy	Examples of GMOs (Genetically Modified Organisms)
How to Hang Glide	Time Management Skills
Tips for a Winning Interview	How to Name Your Child
The Pros and Cons of Being a Stay-At-Home Mom	The Problem with Sugar
What are the Symptoms of Alcohol Addiction?	How Do I Handle a Fire Alarm at My School
Is Vaping Safe?	What's So Wicked about WIKIs?
What Are the Pros and Cons of Artificial Insemination?	My Favorite Vacation
How I Learned about Attention Deficit Disorder	How to Change a Tire
How to Be GREAT at Bargain Shopping	How to Ask for a Date
Have You Considered Carpooling?	What is FERPA?
How to Feed Your Family for $100.00 a Week	How Do I Appeal a Grade?
Why You Should Recycle	Why Should I Register to Vote?
How Much Television Is Too Much?	What Is SkillsUSA?
Choosing a Child Care Facility for Your Family	How to Pack for a Trip Abroad

Visual aids are often used during informative speeches to help the audience visualize content being shared by the speaker. If you are not familiar with creating effective visual aids for a speech, please refer to Unit #4 of this textbook to learn more.

An important visual aid tip to remember for an informative speech is to keep it simple and show one slide per main idea. Too many slides and too much information will be distracting, but a visual aid that is effectively designed will help the audience to visualize the speaker's points. No murky waters here for Speech Sharks who know how to combine quality research, personal experience, and visual aids to paint a clear picture of the speech topic!

Whether you are informing your audience about people, places, careers, hobbies, objects, procedures, or events, you can be sure that the more time you spend crafting a speech FOR your audience, the more successful you will be communicating that information TO your audience. Use the Informative Speech Brainstorming Worksheet to help craft your next Informative Speech.

© BeautyLine/Shutterstock.com

Brainstorming Worksheet

Speech Category: Informative Speech
Speech Title: Give your speech a clever title. _____
Specific Purpose: Write a full sentence to show the purpose of your speech.

_____

Introduction:
Attention Step: Consider how you will get your audience's attention. Write all you plan to say using full sentences.

_____

Establish Need/Relevance: Explain why this informative speech topic should interest the listener. Write all you plan to say using full sentences.

_____

Establish Credibility: Explain why YOU are credible to speak about this topic. Write all you plan to say using full sentences.

_____

Thesis (Preview) Statement: Write a full sentence clearly stating the three points you will cover:

_____

Point #1: _____

Point #2: _____

Point #3: _____

Body:

Transition Sentence: Write a full sentence to transition from the Introduction Step to the first main point.

    I. **First Main Point:**
      A. **First Sub-Point**
         1. **First Sub-Sub-Point** (Not all points will require sub-sub-points.)
         2. **Second Sub-Sub-Point**
      B. **Second Sub-Point**
         1. **First Sub-Sub-Point**
         2. **Second Sub-Sub-Point**

Transition Sentence: Write a full sentence to transition from the first main point to the second.

    II. **Second Main Point:**
      A. **First Sub-Point**
         1. **First Sub-Sub-Point** (Not all points will require sub-sub-points.)
         2. **Second Sub-Sub-Point**
      B. **Second Sub-Point**
         1. **First Sub-Sub-Point**
         2. **Second Sub-Sub-Point**

Transition Sentence: Write a full sentence to transition from the second point to the third point.

    III. **Third Main Point**
      A. **First Sub-Point**
         1. **First Sub-Sub-Point (Not all points will require sub-sub-points.)**
         2. **Second Sub-Sub-Point**
      B. **Second Sub-Point**
         1. **First Sub-Sub-Point**
         2. **Second Sub-Sub-Point**

Transition Sentence: Write a full sentence to transition from the third main point to the conclusion.

Conclusion:

Summary: Write in full sentence format a summary of your three main points.

Point #1: _____

Point #2: _____

Point #3: _____

Appeal to Action: Leave your audience thinking about your speech. End with a **BANG**!

(NOTE: Place the Works Cited Page on a page separate from the outline).

Works Cited

*Note: If you use visual aids, please include a Visual Aid Explanation Page
as a separate page following the Works Cited page.*

Visual Aid Explanation Page

Outline Template

First Name/Last Name
Informative Speech
Day Month Year

Speech Category: Informative Speech
Title:
Purpose:

Introduction:
Attention Step:
Establish Need/Relevance:
Establish Speaker Credibility:

Thesis: Today, I want to share three points about (Topic): (1) _____,

(2) _____, and (3) _____.

Body:
Transition/Link: First, I will start at the beginning by sharing a little about (Point #1).
    I. First Main Point
        A. Sub-point
        B. Sub-point

Transition/Link: I've shared (Point #1) with you, now I'd like to tell you about (Point #2).
    II. Second Main Point
        A. Sub-point
        B. Sub-point

Transition/Link: You've heard about (Point #1 and Point #2), now I'll cover (Point #3).
    III. Third Main Point
        A. Sub-point
        B. Sub-point

Transition/Link: My purpose today was to (insert purpose and add a statement about the topic).
Conclusion:

Summary: Today, I shared with you three points: (1) Point #1 _____, (2) Point #2 _____

_____, and (3) Point #3 _____.

Appeal to Action: As I conclude this speech, (End with a BANG).

(NOTE: Place the Works Cited Page on a page separate from the outline).

Works Cited

*Note: If you use visual aids, please include a Visual Aid Explanation Page
as a separate page following the Works Cited page.*

Visual Aid Explanation Page

Example Outline

Penny J. Waddell
Toastmasters International Meeting
30 June 2020

Speech Category: Informative Speech
Title: How to Dress for An Interview
Purpose: The purpose of this speech is to inform my audience how to dress for an interview.

Introduction:

Attention Step: (Show pictures on a PowerPoint slide of different people dressed in different ways. One person is dressed in jeans, flip-flops, and a T-shirt; another is dressed in a short minidress with tattoos showing on her arms and legs; another is dressed business casual.) Take a look at the pictures of these three candidates who are about to interview for a job position at a Fortune 500 Company. Which candidate do you think will get the job?

Establish Need/Relevance: The truth is that any one of these candidates MAY get the job. The secret is knowing with which company the candidate is interviewing. If interviewing for a position at GOOGLE, the jeans and T-shirt may be appropriate. If interviewing for a position with The Coca Cola Company in Atlanta, the candidate dressed business casual may get the job. Before interviewing for a job position, be sure to know what type of dress is expected.

Establish Speaker Credibility: I am credible to speak to you today about dressing for an interview because I have recently interviewed for a job position and got the job! For the position, I needed to dress in an upscale suit, very little jewelry, and I needed to project extreme professionalism.

Thesis: Today, I will cover three points to inform you how to dress for an interview. (1) Research the company, (2) Understand the culture of the company, and (3) Put your best foot forward.

Body:

Transition/Link: Let's begin with the first point, research the company.

  I. **Research the Company**
   A. What type of business does this company do?
   B. For this position, what type of work responsibilities are expected?

Transition/Link: I've shared the importance of researching the company with you, now I'd like to tell you how to understand the culture of the company.

  II. **Understand the Culture of the Company**
   A. Make a trip to the company prior to the Interview (Quast).
   B. Watch to see how other employees dress.

Transition/Link: You've heard how to research the company and how to understand its culture, now I want to show you how to put your best foot forward.

  III. **Put Your Best Food Forward** (Smith).
   A. Choose clothing, shoes, and accessories that mirror how other employees in this company dress.
   B. Always err on the conservative side, but don't forget to show your personality.

Transition/Link: Now you should understand a little more about how to dress for an interview.

Conclusion:

Summary: Today, I shared with you three points: (1) Research the company, (2) Understand the culture of the company, and (3) Put your best foot forward.

Appeal to Action: As you interview for what might very well be the most important interview of your life, be sure to remember that "You never get a second chance to make a first impression" (Quast). With this quote, I want to challenge you to dress for success and make sure this interview is the one that will help you get your dream job!

> **(Note: The Works Cited page is a separate page from the Outline).**

Works Cited

Quast, Lisa. "8 Tips to Dress for Interview Success." *Forbes*. (2014). Accessed 12 March 2017.

Smith, Chris. "Dress to Impress: what to wear for a job interview." *The Guardian*. Guardian Careers. (2017). Accessed

12 March 2017.

> **(Note: The Visual Aids Explanation page is a separate page from the Outline and the Works Cited page).**

Visual Aids Explanation Page

PowerPoint Presentation:

Slide #1:   Title of Speech—How to Dress for an Interview

Pictures of Three People Dressed Differently

Slide #2:   (Point #1): Research the Company

Bullet Points:

- Type of Business
- Type of Work Responsibilities

Slide #3:   (Point #2): Understand the Culture of the Company

Picture of Business with Employees Entering the Door

Slide #4:   (Point #3): Put Your Best Foot Forward

Picture of Professionally Dressed Employee

Slide #5:   "You Never Get a Second Chance to Make a First Impression" (Quast)

Picture of a Group of Professionally Dressed Employees

Persuasion Speech

© Jacek Dudzinski/Shutterstock.com

We use persuasion strategies all day long as we inspire or motivate others to do something. It begins in the morning when you are persuading your child to get dressed for school; it continues as you go to work and try persuading your co-workers to embrace a new policy or procedure at the office. Then at night when you go home, you are still using your persuasion strategies to motivate your family to get outside for a little exercise after supper. Just face it, we will use this type of skill more often than any other. Not only are you attempting to persuade others to think of something in a different way, but they will also be attempting to persuade you to think another way.

Did you sit with friends or family members after the last presidential election and try to persuade them to think like you? Were they trying to change your mind about the way you think about politics? These types of interactions happen quite often. Sometimes we actually stop to consider another way of thinking. What strategy motivates you to think of things in a different way? What strategy motivates you to action?

The key word here is—motivate! That is because as we attempt to persuade someone to consider the view we present, we are actually motivating or influencing their values, beliefs, attitudes, or behaviors. Let's look at an explanation for each one of these areas.

Area to Influence (Motivate):	Explanation
Values	Do you think something is right or wrong? Do you consider something is good or bad?
Beliefs	Do you perceive the topic to be true or false?
Attitudes	Do you look at the topic in a favorable or unfavorable light? What is your attitude toward the topic?
Behaviors	Behaviors are a combination of your personal values, beliefs, and attitudes. We behave a certain way when we are reacting to these different areas.

The best strategy for being persuasive without sounding preachy or gimmicky is to follow *Monroe's Motivated Sequence*. Perhaps you would like to know a little more about Monroe's Motivated Sequence, especially if you have never heard of this term before. According to Frymier and Shulman, authors of the article, "What's in It for Me?" published by the *Communication Education Journal*, one way to truly motivate someone to do something or to think differently about something is to show the benefits or "What's in it for me?" This allows the speaker the opportunity to make the content relevant to the listener and to increase their motivation toward a solution.

The person who developed the Motivated Sequence Theory was Alan H. Monroe, a professor at Purdue University and well known for his theory of persuasion. **Monroe's theory involves five steps:** begin with a strong attention step, describe a problem showing a need for change, introduce a realistic solution which includes having the listener help solve the problem, help the listener visualize the results of solving the problem, and finish by challenging the listener to solve the problem.

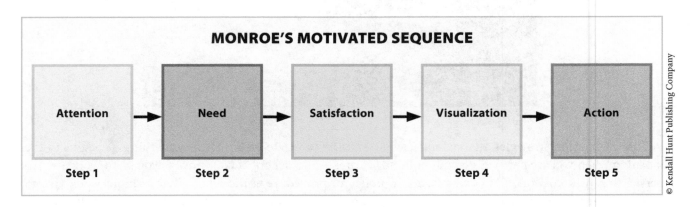

First, the speaker should describe the problem using examples that will get the attention of the audience and will cause the audience to agree that there is, indeed, a problem.

Second, credible research and/or experiential research should be used to support the problems listed. Explain the problem in detail and show how this problem affects listeners. It is important that the audience relate to problems described in order for them to be motivated to take part in the next step.

Third, the speaker should propose realistic solutions to solve the problem. The solutions should be something that every person in the audience can do to help solve the problem. If the solution is too difficult, the listener will not be motivated to help with the solution. It is imperative that the speaker present steps toward solving the problem and uses research to prove this solution is effective and doable. Using this strategy does not sound preachy because you are not blaming the audience for the problem, but enlisting their help to solve the problem. It is not gimmicky because the solutions are realistic and attainable.

Fourth, the speaker should help the audience visualize the results of solving the problem, whether it is the benefits of successfully solving the problem or consequences if the problem is NOT solved. This strategy involves connecting with the audience so they can see the vision of solving the problem as something that actually can happen.

Fifth, the speaker will need to challenge the audience to become an integral part of the solution. The Appeal to Action portion of the Persuasion Speech is the moment where the speaker challenges the audience with such passion and enthusiasm that the audience members are motivated to begin work that very moment to solve the problem that has been described. If the speaker has indeed influenced the values, beliefs, attitudes, and behaviors of the audience members, they will feel compelled to help the speaker solve the problem and they will want to begin immediately!

When choosing a topic for a persuasion speech, avoid choosing topics that are too controversial. Topics that are overly controversial can alienate your audience and you might find yourself in an unpleasant and hostile situation. In the few short minutes you have been given to present a Persuasion Speech, you will never be able to persuade an audience to completely change their way of thinking. Remember, people spend years deciding how they feel about things, whether it is religion, politics, personal rights, or simply things they like and dislike. Since people have very strong feelings about things, your topic will automatically be met with support or with opposition. Most speakers do not choose to cover a topic that would make most of the audience members angry. Even if your topic is not overly popular, you can motivate your audience to think about your topic in a different way. That is why following Monroe's Motivated Sequence is the best way to influence and motivate audience members to action!

What is a **Persuasion Speech**? This is a type of speech in which the speaker provides useful information and supporting research that will motivate the listener to action. When crafting a persuasion speech, the speaker will need to answer questions of fact, value, and policy. Let's take a moment to look at all three of these areas.

Questions of Fact: During the problem statement, it is important to answer questions of fact by using credible research for support. Choose one side or the other as your topic. This is not a good time to "sit on the fence." If your speech is titled, "Don't Text and Drive," then you will want to motivate your audience to never text and drive—ever! If you say it is allowed to text while you are at a traffic light, then you are defeating your point. Your audience needs to know you are 100% committed to the topic you are covering; otherwise, you will destroy your credibility as a speaker for the topic and will not be able to motivate the audience to help solve the problem you describe.

Questions of Value: The problem statement will also need to cover questions of value. For most of us, this involves whether something is moral or immoral, whether it is just or unjust, whether it is good or bad. Choose the moral argument to cover and then offer appeals that will tug at the hearts of your audience members. A good strategy for this is to use arguments that will strengthen the audience's attitudes or beliefs toward the topic.

Questions of Policy: The questions of policy are answered during the portion in the speech where you offer a realistic solution to solve the problem. Solutions often involve changing laws or enforcing existing laws or revising procedures that are not working effectively. The speaker should focus on offering solutions that are something that any person in the audience can do. Audience members will not be able to change a law and many of them are also not in the position to enforce an existing law. Many of us are not in the position to revise procedures that are no longer working. So, what can we do to solve a problem? We can talk to those in our circle of friends and family about the problem. We can volunteer to help in areas that will impact the problem. We can contact or write the mayor, Governor of our state, County Commissioner, or State Representative. We can let those people know that we want to see a solution to the problem, a change to laws, or the enforcing of existing laws. THAT is something we can do and this will answer questions of policy.

© ibreakstock/Shutterstock.com

Brainstorming Worksheet

Speech Category: Persuasion Speech
Speech Title: Give your speech a clever title. _____
Specific Purpose: Write a full sentence to show the purpose of your speech.

_____

Introduction:
Attention Step: Consider how you will get your audience's attention. Write all you plan to say using full sentences.

_____

Establish Need/Relevance: Explain why this persuasion speech topic should interest the listener. Write all you plan to say using full sentences.

_____

Establish Credibility: Explain why YOU are credible to speak about this topic. Write all you plan to say using full sentences.

_____

Thesis (Preview) Statement: Write a full sentence and clearly state the three points you will cover:

_____

Point #1: Description of the Problem: _____

Point #2: Proposed Solution to the Problem: _____

Point #3: Visualization of the Results of Solving the Problem or the Consequences if the Problem Is NOT

Solved: _____

Body:

Transition Sentence: Write a full sentence to transition from the Introduction Step to the first main point.

   I. **The Problem:**
      A. **Discuss the problem you are covering.**
         1. **Support the problem with research.**
         2. **Support the problem with a personal example.**
      B. **Why is there a need for change?**
         1. **Who or what is negatively affected by this problem?**
         2. **Use logical and emotional Appeals.**

Transition Sentence: Write a full sentence to transition from the first main point to the second.

   II. **Solution to the Problem:**
      A. **Offer a realistic, detailed solution which solves the problem.**
         1. **Explain how the audience can help to solve the problem.**
         2. **Provide personal examples and research to support your solution.**
      B. **Answer questions of policy.**
         1. **The solution affects values, beliefs, attitudes, and behaviors.**
         2. **Use logical and emotional appeals.**
         3. **Support points with credible research.**

Transition Sentence: Write a full sentence to transition from the second point to the third point.

   III. **Visualization of Results**
      A. **Benefits of Solving the Problem**
         1. **Does it answer questions of value?**
         2. **Use descriptions to help audience members visualize benefits.**
      B. **Consequences if the Problem is Not Solved**
         1. **Use imagery to show the consequences of not solving the problem.**
         2. **Use personal examples and vivid descriptions.**

Transition Sentence: Write a full sentence to transition from the third main point to the conclusion.

Conclusion:

Summary: Write a full sentence to summarize your three main points.

Point #1: The Problem _____

Point #2: The Solution to the Problem _____

Point #3: Visualization of Results _____

Appeal to Action: Leave your audience challenged to help solve the problem. End with a **BANG!**

(NOTE: Place the Works Cited Page on a page separate from the outline).

Works Cited

*Note: If you use visual aids, please include a Visual Aid Explanation Page
as a separate page following the Works Cited page.*

Visual Aid Explanation Page

Outline Template

Last Name 1

First Name/Last Name
Persuasion Speech
Day Month Year

Speech Category: Persuasion Speech
Title:
Purpose:

Introduction:
Attention Step:
Establish Need/Relevance:
Establish Speaker Credibility:

Thesis: Today, I want to share three points about (Topic): (1) The Problem with _____,

(2) Possible ways to solve the problem _____, and (3) a Visualization of the world if

this problem is solved _____.

Body:

Transition/Link: First, I will start at the beginning by sharing a little about (Point #1).
  I. **First Main Point—Problem**
    A. **Sub-point**
    B. **Sub-point**

Transition/Link: I've shared (Point #1) with you, now I'd like to tell you about (Point #2).
  II. **Second Main Point—Solutions**
    A. **Sub-point**
    B. **Sub-point**

Transition/Link: You've heard about (Point #1 and Point #2), now I'll cover (Point #3).
  III. **Third Main Point—Results**
    A. **Sub-point**
    B. **Sub-point**

Transition/Link: My purpose today was to (insert purpose and add a statement about the topic).

Conclusion:

Summary: Today, I shared with you three points: (1) Point #1 _____,

(2) Point #2 _____, and (3) Point #3 _____.

Appeal to Action: As I conclude this speech, (End with a BANG).

(NOTE: Place the Works Cited Page on a page separate from the outline).

Works Cited

*Note: If you use visual aids, please include a Visual Aid Explanation Page
as a separate page following the Works Cited page.*

Visual Aid Explanation Page

Example Outline

Penny J. Waddell
Political Rally
30 June 2020

Speech Category: Persuasion Speech
Title: Support America
Purpose: The Purpose of this speech is to persuade my audience to support America.

Introduction:
Attention Step: Arnold Whittaker, Tom Malcolm, Buck Brownlee. What do these three men have in common? They all are from Georgia and they all are World War II Veterans who defended our country's freedom and came back home to raise families and make an impact on their communities, their state, and their country! But, there are also differences.
Establish Need/Relevance: At a time in our country where the political parties are at odds with each other, it is important for us to realize that we are all members of one country. Regardless of our political beliefs, regardless of whether we are Democrat, Republican, or Independent, we are ALL Americans!
Establish Speaker Credibility: As an Independent American, I am credible to speak to you about how importance it is for our countrymen and women to stand together first as Americans. Also, the three men that I mentioned in the beginning of this speech were all very dear to me. I loved them, all.
Thesis: Today, I plan to share with you (1) the problem of a country divided, (2) solutions to this problem, and (3) help you visualize a future where we all stand together as one country.

Body:

Transition/Link: The first point that I'll share is about the problem we have with divided political parties.
    I. The Problem: Divided Political Parties in America (Pennock 203)
        A. Democrat Party
        B. Republican Party
        C. Independent Party

Transition/Link: I've shared with you the problem of divided political parties in our country, but there is a solution.
    II. The Solution:
        A. One Country: Bi-partisan Solutions (O'Neil 158)
        B. Working together as one country

Transition/Link: You've heard about the problem of divided political parties in our country, and you've heard about a solution where we all choose to work together to find bi-partisan solutions to a divided problem.
    III. Visualization of Results:
        A. Results: See other party's views and work together for a solution (Dalton 191)
        B. Consequences: Continue divided

Transition/Link: My purpose today was to motivate you to consider a world where we all work together to find the best solutions for America.
Conclusion:
Summary: Today, I shared three points: (1) the problem of a country divided, (2) solutions to this problem, and (3) a future where we all stand together as one country.
Appeal to Action: As I close this speech, the three WWII heroes that I mentioned to you did have ONE thing in common. They are all Americans. They also had differences. One was a Democrat. One was a Republican. One was an Independent. However, they did not let that stand in their way when they stormed the beaches of Normandy and fought to preserve the freedoms that so many of us hold dear. All three men have recently passed away. The last one, Mr. Brownlee, just passed away this year. They all three left behind families and friends who are enjoying the freedoms we have every day simply because they chose to overlook differences and worked together to make sure YOU are free. Free to worship, work, and live the way you choose. You can do the same. Will you stand with me today as an American? Not as a political party, but as an American? God Bless America!

(Note: The Works Cited page is a separate page from the Outline).

Works Cited

Dalton, Russell J. *Citizen Politics: Public Opinion and Political Parties in Advanced Industrial Democracies.* 6th ed.

 Washington DC: CQ Press, 2014.

O'Neil, Patrick H. *Essentials of Comparative Politics.* 5th ed. International Student. 2015.

Pennock, James, Roland. *Democratic Political Theory.* Princeton: Princeton University Press, 2016.

(Note: The Visual Aid Explanation page should be placed on a separate page from the Outline and Works Cited page).

Visual Aid Explanation Page

PowerPoint Presentation
Slide #1: Introduction—Title of Speech and pictures of the three men
Slide #2: The Problem—Pictures of each Political Party
Slide #3: The Solution—Picture of an American Flag
Slide #4: The Results—Picture of American Flag with Citizens
Slide #5: Conclusion—Picture of Soldiers and Their Families with American Flag

Handout
Tri-Fold Brochure—American Flag on the front
Inside Left—Definition of Republican Party
Inside Center—Definition of Democratic Party
Inside Right—Definition of Independent Pary
Back—Center—Research Citations for Further Reading

Special Occasion Speech

© Rawpixel.com/Shutterstock.com

EVERYBODY LOVES A PARTY!

See how happy they are! This group of students just finished toasting each other and you can tell how much fun they had! There is always an abundance of laughter and mouths frozen into happy smiles as friends come together to celebrate! This is why we have Special Occasion Speeches. Although there are many reasons and occasions for Special Occasion Speeches, not all of them are the happy celebration that you see above. Some are more formal and subdued. Others are informal and spontaneous. Whether formal or informal, it is always a great opportunity to share your expertise at presenting a Special Occasion Speech as long as you understand the occasion and make a presentation your audience will remember fondly!

Most Special Occasion Speeches are not very lengthy. They are usually short and to the point, so they need to pack a punch! The words used during this type of speech need to be carefully chosen and precisely delivered to achieve the results that you want. Tribute speeches are delivered with dignity, grace, and sincerity. Ceremonial speeches will involve pomp and circumstance. Roasts and toasts can be delivered with humor. All Special Occasion Speeches will take on the personality of the occasion. With this in mind, it is important that you understand the different types of Special Occasion Speeches so you can choose the right one for your special occasion.

The three basic types are (1) work-related speeches, (2) ceremonial speeches, and (3) social occasion speeches. Most of these speeches will last three to seven minutes. A Keynote Address, Eulogy, Commencement, or Commemoration could last between twenty to forty minutes. As with any speech, you should always check with the host who invites you to speak and ask for the time frame the host requires. A good rule to remember is that you should always end your speech before the final time that you are given. A three- to seven-minute speech should last five minutes. A twenty- to forty-minute speech should last no longer than thirty-five minutes.

Work-Related Speeches

- ▶ **Keynote Address:** Consider yourself a good speaker if you have been chosen to deliver the Keynote Address of a meeting or conference. This honor is usually reserved for established speakers with an impressive résumé. The first order of business is to establish a connection or bond with the audience and then welcome them to the event. Make sure that you thoroughly research the event, audience members, and organization sponsoring the event so that your speech will reflect the values, attitudes, beliefs, and behaviors of audience members. Choose a topic that will set the tone for the meeting or conference. Realizing the participants at this meeting or conference are already quite knowledgeable about the purpose for the gathering, your topic will need to be on-point to add to their existing knowledge and create value for each participant.

▶ **Announcement:** Regardless of the organization, you can bet there will be announcements delivered at each meeting. If asked to make the announcement, plan to deliver a brief explanation and address the announcement in a speech that is short and to the point. Having notes for this speech is a good idea so you do not leave out pertinent information which might lead to the need for a second announcement.

▶ **Public Relation:** This type of speech is made to inform the audience about aspects that are designed to improve a problem. It may deal with attendance, insurance changes, policy, procedure adjustments, or changes in protocol. This speaker will need to establish goodwill and a positive atmosphere prior to delivering the required information. It is important to set a stage that will encourage the audience to accept the information you are sharing. Public Relation Speeches are not always met with approval; therefore, it is important that you have the audience in your corner before giving the information needed.

▶ **Report:** The purpose of presenting a report is to communicate information to the audience. This information will not be entertaining and usually involves numbers, charts, and data as a vehicle for the information. Audience members will appreciate a visual aid to see a visual report in the form of charts or graphs as you provide the information. Keep your visual aids simple, but include all necessary material for a complete report. This report is short, to the point, and detail oriented.

▶ **Nomination:** Corporations and Clubs that follow Roberts' Rules of Order will allow formal nominations to nominate people for positions or to make a motion to consider a change or alteration of a policy or procedure. This is usually not considered a formal speech, but will need to be treated as such as the person making the nomination will need to offer verbiage that is concise, clear, and complete.

Ceremonial Speeches

▶ **Installation:** Installations usually take place during a ceremony, but are also delivered in workplace situations. The purpose of this type speech is to install a person into a particular office or position. Once installed, the person who is installed will usually offer a few, well-chosen words of thanks to those who might have made the decision for the installation. This speech usually lasts two to three minutes.

▶ **Presenting an Award:** The actual presentation of an award is an extremely short speech. This involves referring to the occasion, acknowledging the contributions of the recipient, and then presenting the award with dignity and grace. This is a solemn presentation and care must be made to correctly name the award and to pronounce the recipient's name correctly.

▶ **Accepting an Award:** Often, the recipients of the awards will not know ahead of time that they are receiving an award. In this impromptu type situation, it is important that the recipient understand the gravity of the honor and accept the award in such a manner that the presenter of the award feels they made a good choice. The recipient should show sincere appreciation for receiving the award, delivering the acceptance speech with dignity and grace and should acknowledge the organization presenting the award. If advance notice is given, the recipient could add personal stories that led to the award and could thank individuals who contributed to the presentation of the award.

▶ **Dedication:** Dedication ceremonies happen at the birth of new babies, and for the opening of new buildings, parks, or monuments. This type speech is short and to the point. The person or object being dedicated is the focal point of the speech and allows those gathering to honor the occasion. The person chosen to present the Dedication Speech is usually someone quite close to the child being dedicated or to the organization or person who initiated the building, park, or monument. The speaker will need to establish a connection with the audience in the beginning before completing the formal dedication service.

▶ **Eulogy:** A Eulogy is a ceremony delivered with the purpose of honoring or paying tribute to the deceased. Some people say they are *paying respects* to the person. Culture dictates how this speech presentation will be handled. The length of the speech will vary according to the culture of those attending and the circumstances for which the group has gathered. Often the speaker who has this task will recount personal experiences and stories of times spent with the person being honored.

▶ **Commemorative:** This type of ceremony is appropriate when a group wishes to celebrate a person or event and is most often delivered as a tribute speech. The speaker will need to emphasize people or history involved with the subject being commemorated. Accurate data and stories are necessary to present the information with dignity and honor. The speaker will need to correctly pronounce the person's name or the subject of the commemoration.

▶ **Commencement:** Everyone enjoys attending the graduation of a loved one, but no one enjoys a Commencement Speech that is long and boring! Therefore, it is important that the speech focuses on the actual event and those who are graduating, offers words of encouragement and motivational stories for the graduates, and keeps the speech short and to the point. It is a good idea to include research data and facts of positive employment trends that will give hope and encouragement to the graduates and their families.

I would like to propose a toast to all the Communication Sharks in our world!
To those of you who said you would never give a speech
and to those of you who are great at sharing your thoughts and feelings with others,
I invite ALL of you to raise your glasses high as I wish you **oceans of success**.
May you be as stealthy and goal driven as a shark
and may all of your speeches be delivered with ease and finesse.
Cheers!

Social Occasion Speeches

▶ **Toast:** While not everyone at your event may drink alcohol, a Toast is a wish that can be shared with everyone. Always make sure the glasses are filled prior to making the Toast. Raise your glass to eye level as you present the Toast. Plan your Toast ahead of time making sure to put a great deal of thought into the sentiment so that it truly means something to the person you are honoring. Memorize the Toast (it isn't cool to read notes at a Toast). Acknowledge those present in the room and those who are not there to share the moment. Show emotion and passion for the moment. Keep

© Heinrich Knoetze/Shutterstock.com

the Toast short, light, and meaningful. As you finish, raise the glass above your head as a symbol of extending the wish.

▶ **Welcome:** This is another speech that could easily move over to the Work-Related speeches; however, it is also appropriate to list it with the Social Occasion Speeches. The Welcome Speech is presented at the beginning of a social event. This should be used as a point to welcome those who are attending the event and should be short, light, and to the point. This also may be the time to introduce the agenda for the day and to introduce the next speaker or event on the agenda.

▶ **Farewell:** There are two different ways to offer a Farewell Speech. It can be presented by someone who is leaving or it can be presented by a person who is remaining and chooses this opportunity to honor the person who is leaving. It can be work-related or socially-related. Again, this is a speech that is offered in less than two minutes and offers regards with kindness, grace, and dignity. The Farewell can also be delivered as a Toast. There are lots of options here, but it is always important that it is brief and that every word is carefully chosen to say the things that need to be said.

▶ **Retirement:** There are distinct similarities with the Farewell and the Retirement Speech, in that the speech can be presented by the person who is retiring or by a person from the organization who would like to honor the person who is retiring. This should be a short presentation that highlights the accomplishments of the person retiring and is delivered with kindness, grace, and dignity.

▶ **Roast:** Full disclaimer about this type of speech . . . we saved this one for last because it truly is one of our favorites. Also, this type speech is BEST when combined with a Toast at the end of the Roast. This type of speech has become quite popular recently and creates a stand-alone event where people attend just to hear and participate in the Roast. Usually this type of gathering begins as a dinner and ends with the Roast as the after-dinner entertainment. A traditional Roast will involve several speakers and might focus on just one person or can focus on many people. Each speaker will take three to five minutes to Roast the guest of honor and the purpose is to have lots of laughter. Research is not always necessary for this type of speech, but if research is used, please make sure that you correctly cite the source in the outline and include a Works Cited page to show the complete citation. My speech class always ends the semester with a Roast followed by a Toast. During the assignment, the students are asked to Roast the people who are in their class. Often, they will Roast the three or four people in their Speech Groups providing one funny item about each person; however, they can also choose to Roast one person in the class and include three areas of humorous events about that one person. We tell the students that they have a full semester to gather material for the Roast that is held the last day of class. The result is three hours of non-stop laughter and an opportunity for the classmates to bid farewell to each other. They all conclude their speech by ending with a well-designed Toast to the person or persons that they just roasted.

Each Special Occasion Speech should be planned according to the occasion where the speech will be presented. Since the Roast and Toast is our favorite Special Occasion Speech, we will provide an example to help as you plan your next Roast and Toast! Use the Brainstorming Worksheet as you plan for your own Special Occasion Speech!

© Skovoroda/Shutterstock.com

Brainstorming Worksheet

Speech Category: Special Occasion Speech

Identify whether your speech will be Work-Related, Ceremonial, or Social: _____

Identify which category you will cover: _____

Speech Title: Give your speech a clever title: _____

Specific Purpose: Write a full sentence to show the purpose of your speech.

_____

Introduction:

Attention Step: Consider how you will get your audience's attention. Write all you plan to say using full sentences.

_____

Establish Need/Relevance: Explain why this topic should interest the listener. Write all you plan to say using full sentences.

_____

Establish Credibility: Explain why YOU are credible to speak about this topic. Write all you plan to say using full sentences.

_____

Thesis (Preview) Statement: Write a full sentence and clearly state the three points you will cover:

Point #1: _____

Point #2: _____

Point #3: _____

Body:

Transition Sentence: Write a full sentence to transition from the Introduction Step to the first main point.

_____

   I. **First Main Point:**
      A. **Sub-Point.**
      B. **Sub-Point.**

Transition Sentence: Write a full sentence to transition from the first main point to the second.

_____

   II. **Second Main Point**
      A. **Sub-Point.**
      B. **Sub-Point.**

Transition Sentence: Write a full sentence to transition from the second point to the third point.

_____

   III. **Second Main Point**
      A. **Sub-Point.**
      B. **Sub-Point.**

Transition Sentence: Write a full sentence to transition from the third main point to the conclusion.

_____

Conclusion:

Summary: Write a full sentence to summarize your three main points.

_____

Point #1: _____

Point #2: _____

Point #3: _____

Toast: Plan a Toast to leave with your audience as you conclude the speech. Toasts can be original or you may use one that has been passed down for years and years. If you use a Toast that has a copyright, be sure to cite the source and include a Works Cited page.

(NOTE: Place the Works Cited Page on a page separate from the outline).

Works Cited

*Note: If you use visual aids, please include a Visual Aid Explanation Page
as a separate page following the Works Cited page.*

Visual Aid Explanation Page

Outline Template

Last Name 1

First Name/Last Name
Special Occasion Speech
Day Month Year

Speech Category: Special Occasion Speech
Title:
Purpose:

Introduction:
Attention Step:
Establish Need/Relevance:
Establish Speaker Credibility:

Thesis: Today, I want to share three points about (Topic): (1) _____,

(2) _____, and (3) _____.

Body:
Transition/Link: First, I will start at the beginning by sharing a little about (Point #1).
    I. First Main Point
        A. Sub-point
        B. Sub-point

Transition/Link: I've shared (Point #1) with you, now I'd like to tell you about (Point #2).
    II. Second Main Point
        A. Sub-point
        B. Sub-point

Transition/Link: You've heard about (Point #1 and Point #2), now I'll cover (Point #3).
    III. Third Main Point
        A. Sub-point
        B. Sub-point

Transition/Link: My purpose today was to (insert purpose and add a statement about the topic).
Conclusion:

Summary: Today, I shared with you three points: (1) Point #1 _____,

(2) Point #2 _____, and (3) Point #3 _____.

Appeal to Action: As I conclude this speech, (End with a BANG).

(NOTE: Place the Works Cited Page on a page separate from the outline).

Works Cited

Note: If you use visual aids, please include a Visual Aid Explanation Page
as a separate page following the Works Cited page.

Visual Aid Explanation Page

Example Outline

Penny J. Waddell
Roast and Toast
15 May 2020

Speech Category: Special Occasion Speech

Title: Out of the Frying Pan and Into the Fire: An Opportunity to ROAST my Students!

Purpose: The purpose of this speech is to Roast and Toast my speech students on the last day of class.

Introduction:

Attention Step: Have you ever opened the oven while you have potatoes roasting and felt the heat that comes from the oven? Well, that is nothing compared to the heat all of you might feel today as I take you out of the frying pan and throw you into the fire of an authentic Speech Roast and Toast!

Establish Need/Relevance: We have spent 16 weeks together in the speech class and today will be our last class of the semester. This will be a perfect time for us to have fun with each other before we part ways.

Establish Speaker Credibility: Since I have had the pleasure of being your instructor this semester and I have graded every homework assignment, every speech, every outline, and every Chapter Quiz, I find myself completely qualified to Roast and Toast all of you today!

Thesis: There are three main points I would like to cover during this good-natured Roast, (1) E-mails and Frantic Phone Calls, (2) Outlines and Visual Aids, and (3) Speech Day Attire.

Body:

Transition/Link: Let's begin with the first point, E-mails and Frantic Phone Calls the morning of speech assignments.

    I. **E-mails and Frantic Phone Calls**
        A. Yes, Students, due dates are due dates!
        B. All assignments are given to students the first day of class.
        C. Heartburn and Antacids are in your future, if you don't work ahead!

Transition/Link: I've shared stories of e-mails and frantic phone calls the morning of speech assignments, now I'd like to tell you about the Outlines and Visual Aids

    II. **Outlines and Visual Aids**
        A. Outlines – Did you see the example I left for you in the textbook?
        B. Visual Aids – Are you going for "Hall of Fame" and "Hall of Shame"!

Transition/Link: You've heard about the e-mails and frantic phone calls the morning of speech assignments, the outlines and visual aids that I saw this semester, now, I would like to talk to you about the way you dressed for speeches.

    III. **Speech Day Attire**
        A. Yes, I would hire you, if you dress as if you are going to an interview.
        B. Oops, you are fired, if you show up in Blue Jeans, T-Shirt that says, "Bite Me," and Flip-Flops!

Transition/Link: My purpose today was to Roast all of my speech students who gave speeches this semester that can only be defined as, "The Good, The Bad, and The Ugly"—No, Really, I would call them, "The Best Speeches I've Ever Heard!"

Conclusion:

Summary: Today, I shared with you three points: (1) E-mails and Frantic Phone Calls, (2) Outlines and Visual Aids, and (3) Speech Day Attire.

Appeal to Action: I would like to propose a Toast to all the Communication Sharks in this class! To those of you who said you would never give a speech and to those of you who are great at sharing your thoughts and feelings with others, I invite ALL of you to raise your glasses high as I wish you oceans of success. May you be as stealthy and goal driven as a shark and may all of your speeches be delivered with ease and finesse. Cheers!

(Note: Research was not used for this speech, so a Works Cited page was not necessary. The Visual Aids Explanation page is a separate page from the Outline).

Visual Aids Explanation Page

PowerPoint Presentation:

Slide #1:   Title of Speech—Out of the Frying Pan and Into the Fire
Picture of the Class (Group)

Slide #2:   (Point #1): E-mails and Frantic Phone Calls
Picture of Teacher at a Computer (hair frazzled and talking on the phone)

Slide #3:   (Point #2): Outlines and Visual Aids
Picture of the Textbook

Slide #4:   (Point #3): Speech Day Attire
Picture of Professionally Dressed Student/Picture of a Student in Jeans and Flip-Flops

Slide #5:   Picture—Champagne Glasses Raised in a TOAST with the word—CHEERS!

AUDIENCE RESPONSIBILITIES

Audiences have a responsibility, too! As the speaker enters the stage, please show appreciation for the speaker by giving your undivided attention and clapping until the speaker has taken his/her place on stage and is ready to begin the presentation! Your next task is to LISTEN to the speaker. Put away cell phones and electronic devices that would cause distractions and position your body to face the speaker. Using your nonverbal cues, show the speaker that she has your full attention and that you are anxious to hear her message. Smile at the speaker, nod your head in agreement, and show support with your face and body posture.

Prepare yourself to hear the speech. Listen carefully to identify the message delivered. Get plenty of rest and a good meal prior to the presentation. Just as the speaker has to prepare for you, it is your job to prepare yourself. Not enough sleep? You could be tempted to take a short nap during the presentation. YES, your speaker will know you are napping and that sends a negative nonverbal cue that you are bored and what the speaker is saying is of no consequence to you. If you are hungry, your stomach may growl or you could spend her speech thinking about what you might eat just as soon as the speech is over. Here are some tips to help you be a great audience member:

1. **Be an active listener** by showing appreciation for the speaker. Sending positive nonverbal cues such as smiling, head nods, leaning forward toward the speaker, and establishing eye contact, will show the speaker that you are glad to hear the speech. Just using the active listener posture will help you focus more on the speaker and become a better audience member.

2. **Resist distractions** and use your critical listening skills to focus in on the speaker and the message.

3. **Practice empathetic listening** and try to see the speaker's point of view, even if it differs from your own.

4. **Focus on verbal and nonverbal cues** being sent by the speaker. Are the speaker's verbal and nonverbal cues matching with the content of the speech?

5. **Take notes and create a presentation outline** during the speech. Informative listening is used during this time of the speech. Write down questions you may have so that you can ask them after the speech is over. Never interrupt the speaker to ask a question. Always save the questions to ask during a question and answer session or to pose privately to the speaker after she leaves the stage area.

© Monkey Business Images/Shutterstock.com

EVALUATING THE SPEECH

Communication Sharks Have THICK Skin

It's no secret, Communication Sharks have thick skin and will often ask others to evaluate or critique their speeches. As speakers work to improve stage presence, they will often video and audio record presentations then play the recordings over and over again searching for ways to improve. You need thick skin for this!

Speakers welcome evaluations and critiques that recognize their strengths, but also evaluations that offer specific suggestions and tips for overcoming weaknesses. **The purpose of an evaluation is to coach, help, build, mold, and encourage.** ALL of us can improve. Not only do Communication Sharks understand this concept, but they need thick skin to welcome feedback in all types of forms. Evaluations of presentations allow speakers to recognize and be prepared to capitalize on strengths and identify areas for improvement.

Generally, a one-page document is sufficient to evaluate overall speaking strengths and areas in need of improvement. In a learning environment, speakers may be asked to offer written or oral speech evaluations of their peers. **Written evaluations** are conducted during the presentation in the form of a rubric or guidelines. **Oral evaluations** are presented immediately following the speech and may be delivered by a member of the audience or by the speech coach. In any case, evaluations are an excellent tool to help us become better speakers.

Consider asking a friend or colleague to video record your speech. Plan to watch the video twice before completing a **self-evaluation**. The first time, watch the video without sound so that you pay careful attention to nonverbal cues that you may send: the way you are dressed, movements, gestures, eye contact, facial expressions, handling of visual aids, and referring to speech notes. The second time, watch the video with sound and pay careful attention to your vocal skills and to the content delivered. How was the attention step? Were your three main points supported by examples or research? Did you cite sources of research used? How was the conclusion of your speech? Did you use vocal variance? Could you hear passion for the topic in your voice?

Everyone benefits from speech evaluations. Obviously, the speaker benefits as he becomes aware of strengths and areas for improvement. The evaluator benefits and becomes a better speaker because the areas needed in a speech are accentuated by an evaluation. Not only is the evaluator reinforcing knowledge of areas needed in a speech, but is also using that knowledge to guide others. Audiences also benefit from hearing an evaluation because they are able to apply the lessons learned to their own speech presentations.

Before **peer-evaluating** a speaker, consider the skill level of the speaker. Is the speaker a novice or experienced speaker? Take advantage of evaluation tools in the form of rubrics or templates. Use audio or video recordings to play back and show the speaker as you offer a suggestion or praise. Be kind, but truthful with evaluations and be specific with areas that demonstrate speaking strengths or weaknesses. Here are explanations of things to consider.

Skill Level

If new to public speaking, the evaluator should use a less critical and more encouraging strategy for the evaluation, especially if the speaker is trying to overcome a fear of public speaking. First, compliment the speaker for stepping up to the stage to deliver a speech and then proceed with supportive and positive comments. Ask questions of the speaker. How did you feel as the speech was beginning? What strategies did you use to power through? What were you most proud of? What areas do you feel need to be improved? By having the speaker look inward, you might find their answers are delivered with less stress than the actual delivery of the speech. If that is the case, be sure to compliment their ease in speaking about the speech. It never hurts to offer evaluations that focus on the positive aspects of a speech for beginning speakers. It helps them to develop enough self-confidence to speak again. For a more experienced speaker, consider using some of the techniques and tips shown below.

Evaluation Tools

Using evaluation tools will help evaluators to do a more thorough job, which will be beneficial for the speaker and for those listening to the evaluation. In this chapter, you'll find rubrics, forms, and suggestions for evaluating a speech. Recordings are excellent tools. Whether you are using audio or video recordings, it is a great idea to play back sections of the speech as you offer evaluations. Not only are you telling the speaker about their strengths or weaknesses with presentations, but you can also show clips which add credibility to your evaluation.

Be Kind, But Truthful

Speakers usually know how they did and will know if it was a successful speech or if it wasn't successful at all. Be kind with your statements, but be truthful. Speakers can spot a dishonest evaluation a mile away and this will damage your credibility as an evaluator. In other words, don't say you liked something in their speech if you really did not like it at all. Preface the critique with, "It is my opinion that . . ." This allows the speaker to know that what you are sharing is your own perceptions of the performance. Kindness goes a long way when evaluating someone else's speech. Avoid being accusatory, rude, or insensitive with comments. Damaging the speaker's confidence and your own relationship with the speaker is not the purpose of an evaluation.

Be Specific

It takes skill to build an evaluation that motivates, encourages, and highlights areas to improve without making the new speaker feel defeated. Because of this, evaluators should provide specific examples and then offer suggestions for ways to improve. Avoid simply saying, "I liked your speech." Instead, tell the speaker why you liked the speech and give specific details regarding the areas you thought were outstanding. When offering critiques, avoid being vague. Give specific details regarding what areas need to be improved and provide suggestions for improving.

Sure, Communication Sharks have thick skin, but evaluators also need thick skin. With time and experience, evaluations can be delivered as a tender morsel to be savored, enjoyed, and appreciated! In the pages to follow, you will find explanations of the various methods and also rubrics that will help with the process. You'll find a rubric to give to the speech instructor prior to each speech, a self-evaluation rubric to be completed by you following each speech, and a series of peer evaluations that can be used as you evaluate the speeches of your classmates. Please be sure to check with your instructor to see which type rubric you are expected to use in the speech class.

SPEECH EVALUATION WORKSHEET
Instructor's Copy for Grading the Speech

Speaker's Name:_____   **Title of Speech:**_____

Time of Speech:_____   **Date:**_____

Speech Performance 100 possible points	Excellent 5 points	Good 4 points	Average 3 points	Fair 2 points	Poor 1 point	N/A 0 points

Introduction Step:
  Attention Step:
 	
  Establish Need/Relevance:
 	
  Establish Credibility:
 	
  Thesis (preview 3 points):						

Body: Point #1						
Body: Point #2						
Body: Point #3						

Transitions (4)
  To First Point
  To Second Point
  To Third Point
  To Conclusion						

Conclusion:
  Summary (review 3 points):
 	
  Closing Statements/Appeal:						

Use of Research
  Number of Sources Used:
  Clear Verbal Citations:
  Sources Supported Topic:						

Visual Aids
 	
  Types: _____
 	
  Setting up
  Handling of Visual Aids
  Design
  Visibility
  Management of Tech Team						

Handouts
  Design
  Distribution						

Speech Performance 100 possible points	Excellent 5 points	Good 4 points	Average 3 points	Fair 2 points	Poor 1 point	N/A 0 points

Language Skills
  Vocabulary
  Filler Words
  Sentence Structure
  Grammar Usage						

Vocal Delivery Skills
  Voice
  Volume
  Rate
  Vocal Variance						

Enthusiasm for Topic Passion/Energy						
Gestures						
Eye Contact						
Poise						
Confidence						
Professional Appearance						

Movement:
  Entrance to Stage
  Exit from Stage
  Movement while on Stage						

Time of Speech						
Handling of Notes/Note Cards						

Additional Comments and Suggestions:

SPEECH OUTLINE WORKSHEET
Instructor's Copy for Grading the Speech

Speaker's Name:_____ **Title of Speech:**_____

Time of Speech:_____ **Date:**_____

Outline Details	Possible Points	Points Earned
Standard Outline Format	20 points	
Typed	5	
Roman Numerals I, II, III	5	
ABCs	5	
123s	5	
Introduction:	20 points	
Attention Step	5	
Establish Need/Relevance	5	
Establish Credibility	5	
Thesis (Previews Main Points)	5	
Main Points	15 points	
Point #1	5	
Point #2	5	
Point #3	5	
Transitions/Links (4)	10 points	
Leads to Point #1	2.5	
Leads to Point #2	2.5	
Leads to Point #3	2.5	
Leads to Conclusion	2.5	
Conclusion	10 points	
Summary	5	
Closing Statement (Appeal)	5	
Research	25 points	
Required Sources Used	5	
Parenthetical Citations	5	
Works Cited Page	5	
Follows Citation Guidelines	5	
Copy of Research Included	5	

SPEAKER'S SELF-EVALUATION

This is an opportunity to evaluate YOUR speech.

Speaker's Name: _____ **Date of Speech:** _____

Speech Category: _____ **Title of Speech:** _____

After viewing the speech video twice, once to observe your nonverbal message and a second time to listen to the verbal message, please complete the self-evaluation worksheet. Be objective with responses and answer the questions asked with YES or NO.

Introduction Step:

When introducing the speech, did you:

_____ 1. Begin with an attention step?
_____ 2. Establish relevance for the topic?
_____ 3. Establish credibility by sharing your own experience with the topic?
_____ 4. Clearly state thesis and preview the main points?

Body:

In developing the body of the speech, did the speaker:

_____ 1. Identify and organize three main points?
_____ 2. Use well-chosen examples?
_____ 3. Effectively use research support materials such as statistics and quotations?
_____ 4. Properly cite sources (verbal citations)? How many sources did you hear? _____
_____ 5. Use transitions between each main point?

Conclusion:

When moving to finish the speech, did the speaker:

_____ 1. Signal the speech was concluding?
_____ 2. Review three main points?
_____ 3. End the speech with a BANG? How was this achieved? _____

Presentation and Visual Aids:

When using visual aids, did you:

_____ 1. Incorporate relevant and well-designed visual aids?
_____ 2. Effectively handle visual aids?

Delivery:

During the speech, did you:

_____ 1. Use voice appropriately by varying inflection, tone, and volume?
_____ 2. Speak words clearly with proper grammar and pronunciation?
_____ 3. Physically move and gesture with purpose?
_____ 4. Establish and maintain eye contact?
_____ 5. Appear confident, poised, and in control?
_____ 6. Dress professionally?

Overall Evaluation:

Considering the speech as a whole, did you:

_____ 1. Choose an appropriate topic?
_____ 2. Meet the assignment requirements, including time limits?

Add Specific Details and Comments:

BASIC PEER EVALUATION

Use a separate copy to evaluate each speaker.

Speaker's Name: _____ **Evaluator:** _____

Title of Speech: _____ **Date:** _____

Truthfully answer all areas with a simple YES, NO, or short answer.

Introduction Step:

When beginning the speech, did the speaker:

_____ 1. Use an effective attention step? What was used? _____

_____ 2. Establish relevance for the topic?

_____ 3. Establish credibility by establishing speaker's own experience with the topic?

_____ 4. Clearly state thesis and preview main points?

Body:

When developing the body of the speech, did the speaker:

_____ 1. Identify and organize three main points?

_____ 2. Use well-chosen examples or research support materials?

_____ 3. Verbally cite sources?

_____ 4. Use transitions between each main point?

Conclusion:

When moving to finish the speech, did you:

_____ 1. Signal the speech was concluding?

_____ 2. Summarize three main points?

_____ 3. End the speech with a BANG?

Presentation and Visual Aids:

When using visual aids, did the speaker:

_____ 1. Incorporate relevant and well-designed visual aids?

_____ 2. Effectively handle presentation aids?

Delivery:

During the speech, did the speaker:

_____ 1. Use voice appropriately by varying inflection, tone, and volume?

_____ 2. Speak words clearly with proper grammar and pronunciation?

_____ 3. Physically move and gesture with a purpose?

_____ 4. Establish and maintain eye contact?

_____ 5. Appear confident, poised, and in control of the presentation?

_____ 6. Dress professionally?

_____ 7. Speak passionately about the topic?

Overall Evaluation:

Considering the speech as a whole, did the speaker:

_____ 1. Choose an appropriate topic and purpose statement?

_____ 2. Meet the assignment requirements, including time limits?

Use the back of this page to add feedback/comments for the speaker.

KEY TERMS

- Adrenaline
- APA
- Aromatherapy
- Audience Analysis
- Breathing Exercises
- Block Indented Margin
- Cause-Effect
- Chronological
- Closed Questions
- Clustering and Webbing
- CMS
- Connectors
- CSE
- Ethos
- Figure/Ground
- General Purpose
- Gestalt
- Hanging Indentions
- Hierarchy
- Internal Previews

- Internal Reviews
- Interview
- Logos
- Meditation
- MLA
- Monroe's Motivated Sequence
- Noise
- Outline
- Parenthetical Citation
- Pathos
- Plagiarism
- Probing Questions
- Problem-Solution
- Public Speaking
- Research
- Spatial
- Specific Purpose
- Summary
- Topical
- Transitions

Chapter Ten

Group Communication

© TZIDO SUN/Shutterstock.com

In this chapter:

Small Group Development

Groups Defined

Types of Groups

The Nature of Groups

Group Decision-Making

Group Think

Until now, we haven't jumped into the deep abyss of group communication, yet I can already hear your thoughts surrounding groups and group work. Some of you enjoy working with groups, but many of you might have had less than positive experiences and dread the very thought of communicating with a group. The purpose of this chapter is to provide a deeper understanding of the way we communicate with others and to also offer opportunities to put your understandings to work.

Group Communication happens when the parameters of communication between individuals expand, but groups may vary in size and scope. *Dyadic Communication* happens when two people communicate and share their ideas, ideals, behaviors, interests, thoughts, and understandings. This type of communication can happen formally or informally. For example, if two people are communicating in an interview or a professional setting, they would be involved in **formal dyadic communication**. On the other hand, if the two people communicating are family or friends, they would be participating in **informal dyadic communication**.

Whether in professional or personal relationships, how we perceive others and how we perceive ourselves may be a factor in how we draw conclusions from what we see, hear, or feel during the **dyadic communication process**.

Verbal and nonverbal responses to each other may determine what we say or how we react to the message received from the other. If one member of the dyad is sending negative verbal and nonverbal cues, it is almost certain that the second member of the dyad will respond in kind. Tense situations often escalate to include moments of frustration and anger, yet can quickly be diffused if one member of the dyad is comfortable taking the high ground and bringing a positive note to the conversation. It is quite interesting to see the effect that just one person can make by adding a kind word, a smile, or a positive gesture.

SMALL GROUP DEVELOPMENT

The other day, I was volunteered to chair a committee. Has this ever happened to you? I'm sure at some point or another, you found yourself *voluntold* to do something that you really did not have a desire or the time to do. But, being the Communication Shark that you are, you decided to make the best of it only to find out that your committee was less than wonderful. As we find ourselves involved in group work of some sort, we realize there are various stages within the development of a small group. Through each stage, the group members will be aware of relationships and partnerships that develop. If you are lucky, you will have a full group of people who all work well together. More often than not, 90% of the group will have strong work ethics and will be group members anyone can count on.

Group communication is a hot topic of discussion among industry leaders. In the classroom and in the workplace, we find ourselves tasked with participating within a group environment to conduct research, make decisions, and establish policy. We will discuss various aspects in this chapter focused on group communication.

**GROUPS DEFINED

If small groups are an integral part of our lives, how then do we know if we are part of one? At the most basic level, *groups* are a collection of individuals with a common purpose. Burkhalter, Gastil, and Kelshaw (2002) indicated groups need at least three people, that the exact size of the group should be "manageable," and people in the group should be able to "see and hear one another" (p. 400). In today's world, seeing and hearing one another can be accomplished both face-to-face and virtually. In addition to having a collection of individuals, inherent to a group is the idea of mutual influence. The behaviors of one person create changes in others' behaviors. Mutual influence is like a tennis match. Both players in the match respond to the other's actions. Player A hits the ball to player B. Player B's movement is dependent upon what Player A does first. Player B's actions are in response to the previous actions by Player A. Player A then reacts to player B's actions and returns the ball.

© topten22photo/Shutterstock.com

Related to this idea is that of interdependence. Each group member has mutual influence on others because they are dependent upon the others in the group in some way. Think of the group as being like a family. You likely depend on certain people to perform certain functions. For example, one member of the family might make dinner, another takes out the trash, another might tease everyone, yet another member is the one who always checks in on the family. A group follows this model. You expect certain people to do certain things. When one person is not present, the group (just like the family) is different and individuals may need to adjust their behaviors to assume responsibility for the missing behaviors.

Another key component of group life is that of a common purpose or goal. All group members are working together toward the completion of some task. That is, they share in the achievement of a common end state. Without this common goal or purpose, they are simply individuals interacting without an end mission in mind. It is the common purpose or goal that helps to solidify the group and bring individuals together to focus on one project.

TYPES OF GROUPS

As evidenced by the scenarios at the beginning of this chapter, there are different types of groups. These include the people you work with at school, the church groups to which you belong, the clubs and organizations in which you participate, and the people with whom you work at your jobs. As research suggests, your past group experiences will influence your future group behaviors such as commitment to the group (Forrest & Miller, 2003). That is, if you have had a terrible group experience in the past, it could impact how you work with others in the future. Based on that negative experience, you probably said to yourself, "Never again will I do this!" Thus, your past experiences influence your perception of working in groups in the future.

Do you enjoy working in groups? When asked this question, students are often divided in their response, with some indicating they like working in groups and others reporting that they despise group assignments. You will be part of a number of different types of groups throughout your life. In some instances, you will have the opportunity to choose to be part of a group while other groups will be forced upon you. While this might sound a little intimidating, understanding the different types of groups and the factors that impact group communication will enhance your effectiveness when working in a group. The following are examples of groups that you are likely to encounter in your personal, professional, and public lives. It is important to note that some of these groups are voluntary while others are involuntary. Voluntary groups are those that we self-select to be part of, whereas involuntary groups are those in which group membership is assigned.

A *peer group* is one that is "composed of members who consider one another to be equals, in terms of abilities, background, age, responsibilities, beliefs, social standing, legal status, or rights. Not all group members agree about the equality of all other members at all times, but there is overt consensus that members of the group are primarily equal" (SunWolf, 2008, p. xii). Reflect on the number of peer groups that you have been a member of throughout your life. Most likely, you are part of many peer groups in your own life. Examples of these include a group of friends, a troop of scouts, or a congregation of worshipers.

A *purposive group* is a group "that has a goal" (Poole et al., 2004, p. 6), that is, working toward the completion of some task. You will be a member of numerous purposive groups throughout your professional and public lives. Examples of purposive groups include work project teams, a school board committee that will give a formal presentation to the board of trustees, support groups that raise awareness of a specific cause, or groups at school that work together to complete an assigned project.

Factional groups are defined as those "in which members are representatives or delegates from social entities" (Li & Hambrick, 2005, p. 794). That is, individuals from divergent areas of expertise are brought together to work toward the completion of a common goal. Especially prevalent in your professional life, for example, are individuals from two different parts of a company (e.g., those in marketing and sales) who combine to find a solution to a problem.

Finally, a *social group* is a collection of individuals focused mainly on relationship-building that gives members a place to develop self-esteem and have a sense of unity. This is different from a peer group because a social group does not necessarily contain the equality or sameness as shared by members of a peer group. An example of this type of group would be a family or a social club, as these types of groups provide for our need for solidarity.

THE NATURE OF GROUPS

Groups may take on a life of their own. Individuals collect and blend unique personalities and members of a group travel through a series of stages in which they "come together." Recall that groups work together to achieve a common goal. These stages help group members orient toward the task or goal at hand. Communication that takes place among members of groups can include interpersonal interactions among group members, but the overall group dynamics are inherently different from interpersonal, dyadic interactions. As a result, special consideration needs to be given to what makes group communication unique from other types of interactions.

Groups develop and "come together" in stages. One popular way to explain this process is by exploring the five stages of group development: forming, storming, norming, performing, and adjourning (Tuckman, 1965; Tuckman & Jensen, 1977). In the ***forming stage***, individuals gather together and assemble the group. During this period, members of the group begin orienting to the task, search for a leader, and determine the purpose of the group. Communication tends to focus on polite interactions to ensure we don't "step on others' toes" and small talk to learn more about one another. In the ***storming stage***, the group may experience conflict as a result of individuals' emotional responses to completing tasks. Members of the group may have different approaches toward accomplishing the goal, multiple people may want to fulfill the same role (e.g., be the leader), and arguments may ensue about how the group should proceed. It is not uncommon for group members to clash during this period; in fact, this is typically the stage where most of the conflict occurs. Once the group works through the conflicts, they reach the ***norming stage***. Group members have calmed the rough seas of storming and determined how best to work with one another. Individuals begin to adopt roles and share ideas with others. Rules are created for interaction and performance. In the ***performing stage***, the roles that were adopted in the norming stages become cemented. In essence, the "kinks" have been worked out and the group is able to address both the completion of tasks and the social demands of working with others. In essence, the group becomes a "well-oiled machine." Once the tasks are completed or the goal is accomplished, some groups cease to exist. During the ***adjourning stage***, individuals have performed their duties and reached the conclusion of the group experience. During this time, emotional changes such as sadness or excitement as members leave the group may occur. During this stage, there should be critical reflection of individual and others' performance.

To effectively perform groupwork during each of these stages, Hawkins and Fillion (1999) argued that several communication skills are essential. First, they emphasize the importance of effective listening. Remember that listening is a skill that requires effort. Working with others provides a unique opportunity to attend to and comprehend their messages. Additionally, everyone should understand each person's role as part of the larger work group. That is, all members of the group need to know how they "fit" with the others in the group. Building from this idea, Hawkins and Fillion also indicate that all members of the group should contribute actively to the group. Each person should be sure to perform his or her roles and duties. In addition, members should ask questions, use clear and concise language, and convey nonverbal professionalism. By picking the most efficient verbal and nonverbal behaviors, we can be sure that our communicative efforts are easily understood. Efficient verbal communication could entail summarizing each person's responsibilities before concluding a meeting. Nonverbally, it is unlikely that rolling your eyes or raising your voice would be appropriate and well received by others in your group. Given the global world in which we live, it is argued that we also need to devote attention to respecting cultural differences. Simply put, our culture influences our behavior. What is considered professional in one culture might not be regarded the same in another culture. For example, a handshake is a standard greeting of introduction in the United States whereas Chinese cultures may bow or nod instead. When working with diverse individuals, care should be taken to learn about others and attempts made to understand practices.

While somewhat intuitive, these skills are not only necessary for a group to be successful, but they can also be the easiest to forget when working with individuals who are different from us or when conflict emerges. Have you ever worked with a group and someone suggested an outlandish idea? It might have been something you thought was so off the wall that you rolled your eyes or made a facial expression similar to that of disgust. Similarly, when conflict emerges, have you ever lost your temper or perhaps attacked a person and not the idea? While we carefully monitor our verbal response in these situations, we sometimes neglect to consider our nonverbal reactions. Keeping communication concepts such as effective verbal and nonverbal communication and cultural differences in mind, we now look at other factors that impact group life and our ability to be a successful group member.

Size

The size of a group is important to consider. Scholars seem to agree that the ideal group size is three to seven members to ensure effective communication. Remember, a group is a collection of individuals who influence one another.

Have you ever attended a large dinner party? Perhaps you sat at a table that was so long you could not speak to the people at the far end. We would not consider that a group because your verbal and nonverbal behaviors cannot be effectively interpreted by all of the people at the table. Ultimately, group size should manageable so all individuals in it can consider themselves a part of the group.

Task versus Social Dimensions within Groups

Once individuals begin to gather and membership in the group is established, two types of communication occur. Communication can focus on the group's task dimension or the social dimension. The *task dimension* is characterized by messages that focus on solving problems, completing a task, or achieving a goal (Fujishin, 2001), while the *social dimensions* are those conversations among group members that focus on their relationships and feelings for one another. The social dimension can dictate how individuals approach the task. For example, what if you dislike a member of your group? If that person takes over the group and becomes the leader, you now have to "report" to him and "check in." If you do not like this person, the social dimension—your negative feelings—can affect how you approach the task. You could produce lower quality work, miss deadlines, or avoid communicating with the person, if possible. Thus, both task and social dimensions must be considered when working in groups. It is important for a group to maintain effective relationships in order to accomplish its goals. This does not mean that individuals need to be best friends or even like one another. They do, however, need to establish and manage their social interactions to ensure that they don't derail the group from its purpose.

Roles

Individuals offer unique contributions to groups through the types of roles they fulfill. One popular definition of *roles* is "that set of common expectations shared by the members about the behavior of an individual" (Bormann, 1969, p. 184). Roles are labels placed on individuals based on their function within a group. These labels have a set of expected behaviors that the individual playing that role or having that label must then perform. Roles can be formal and assigned. However, roles can also be informal and emerge as a result of group interaction. For example, when preparing for the first group meeting, you might know that someone needs to be in charge and create an agenda for the meeting or perhaps send emails to make sure all group members are doing their work. This would be a formal role. Perhaps one group member is self-assigned the role of leader. However, during your interactions with the other group members, it becomes evident that the group needs someone to take notes during meetings because members have difficulty recalling the previous meetings' proceedings. As a result, another group member takes on the role of note-taker. This role would be an informal role because it

© Andresr/Shutterstock.com

became evident through interactions among group members that someone needed to provide the function of note-taker. The role of note-taker could be formally elected or appointed through an election process while others can evolve more informally.

Benne and Sheats (1948) proposed a typology of group roles, organizing them into three categories. In a group, your role could be task, relational, or individually focused (Table 10.1).

Task roles focus on the group's assignment. A task role would include an evaluator-critic. This person focuses on setting standards and meeting goals. This individual will question the logic of others when unsure about the accuracy of a proposed idea.

Relational roles focus on building and maintaining connections among group members. A relational role includes that of the harmonizer. This group member produces communication that strives to bring the group members together and achieve cohesiveness. *Individual roles* are those in which individuals focus on self-achievement and not the efforts of the group. An individual role would include that of recognition-seeker. This individual attempts to bring light to his personal accomplishments and will likely take on more work in an attempt to gather more praise. In Table 10.1, many of the common roles within each of the categories are presented along with examples of how these specific roles are enacted in a group setting.

The roles in Table 10.1 may be present in every group. Task and relational roles are needed and critical to successful group life. Some members of the group need to focus on achieving task completion while others take care of the individuals in the group. Individual roles, however, can prove challenging as they are typically thought of as something that detracts from the group. They focus more on individual achievement rather than the collective achievement of the group.

TABLE 10.1

Typology of Group Roles

Type of Role	Description
Task roles	Focus on the group's goals and tasks
Evaluator-critic	Focuses on setting standards and meeting goals. Questions others' logic when unsure about accuracy
Coordinator	Focuses communicative efforts on who in the group accomplishes what tasks and when tasks should be done
Opinion-giver	Expresses opinions and possible interpretations associated with all tasks
Information-seeker	Collects information related to tasks and completing tasks.
Relational roles	Focus on building connections among members
Encourager	Offers praise to others and wants to hear others' opinions and ideas
Harmonizer	Focuses communicative efforts on bringing group members together to achieve cohesiveness
Compromiser	Avoids conflict and admits any mistakes; works to incorporate all ideas presented
Gatekeeper	Ensures participation by all group members and that they are listened to and considered during group processes
Individual roles	Focus on self-achievement
Recognition-seeker	Likes taking on a lot of work because it means he or she will get extra attention because of it
Dominator	Focuses communicative efforts on being heard; works to control the group and their efforts
Joker	Uses light-hearted, humorous communication that is often off topic in attempts to be perceived as funny
Withdrawer	Fails to connect and interact with the group; offers few opinions and may have issues

How are roles typically adopted in groups? Cragan and Wright (1999) suggested that groups should include "leaders" who are in charge of certain aspects of the group when assigning roles. These include a *task leader* who focuses group members on completion of assignments or a *social-emotional leader* who serves as the voice of the group members in terms of the affective orientation to the group.

One theory used to explain and predict roles that individuals perform is *Role Theory*, which concentrates on the ways in which individuals enact different social positions (i.e., roles) in their lives (Biddle, 1979). Role Theory offers five claims. First, individuals create and adopt roles based on their surrounding contexts; that is, the situation is important to consider when determining which roles are needed in the group. For example, if at a school board meeting, it is determined that all happenings should be video recorded, someone will be in charge of technology. Second, roles are commonly associated with individuals in social positions who share a common identity; that is, a role is something that individuals enact when working with others. Inherent to having a role is the idea that others must be present and you are in a group setting. Third, roles are governed by individual awareness of and expectations for each role; that is, how individuals perform a role is based on their knowledge of the role and the ideas of how the role should be enacted. For example, if you are assigned as group motivator, but are unclear of what that entails, such as motivating and reaffirming verbal communication, your ability to perform that role is diminished. Fourth, roles remain because of the consequences and functions associated with them and also due to the fact that roles are often imbedded within a larger social system; that is, groups need roles to be able to function. Roles may change over time, but the idea there is still a role to perform remains. The job duties of the note-taker may shift, but someone needs to record the happenings of the group. Finally, the fifth claim indicates that individuals must be taught the behaviors associated with each role and they must be socialized by others to properly perform a role. There is a learning curve associated with performing the role effectively. In order to play the role of family caregiver, you must first know what that role entails and the essential job functions. For example, a caregiver may be expected to clean the house, prepare meals, and pay bills.

Role Theory assumes that individuals learn the behaviors that correspond with their role. They remain in that role because that role is necessary for proper group functioning. Regardless of the type of role and how one learns the expectations associated with that role, there are some considerations to be made. As you read the list of role types, you probably thought, "I could perform a lot of these roles." If so, you experience something called *role flexibility*. This occurs when individuals have the ability to play a variety of roles and adapt according to the demands of the situation. In some instances, an individual could alternate between being the note-taker and being the emotional leader, depending on the situation. However, sometimes individuals are required to fill two or more conflicting roles simultaneously. *Role conflict* occurs when you have to perform multiple roles with seemingly contradictory behaviors. If you refer to Table 8.1, you can see by the descriptions that it would be difficult to be both a harmonizer and a dominator. A harmonizer works to bring the group together whereas the dominator is focused solely on advancing his or her position. A harmonizer tends to lighten the mood of the group, whereas a dominator may use communication that detracts from the task. Imagine working with a group of your peers on a class project. As your group works on its tasks, the harmonizer of the group would attempt to bring the group together by highlighting common interests, while the dominator of the group would try to showcase differences of other group members and pull the conversation to focus on these differences. The final consideration is called *role strain*. Have you ever been asked by others in the group to perform a role that you did not necessarily want to do? For example, if you did not want to be the leader of the group, yet the other individuals in the group encouraged you to do so, you may experience role strain. This occurs when an individual is required to assume a new role that he or she is reluctant to perform.

Collectively, there are a number of important and necessary roles that must be filled for groups to work efficiently. Because so many roles are necessary for a group to function, everyone in the group should have an active part in the group.

Rules

Do you remember when your parents told you to clean your room and they stated that if you did not do it, there would be a punishment? Throughout our personal, professional, and public lives, we encounter a number of rules associated with the roles we fulfill. *Group rules* refer to the notion that group members are expected to engage in specific behaviors, and if they do not do so, there are consequences. Rules can be both explicit and implicit. *Explicit rules* are formalized rules that are discussed and sometimes recorded in a document that all group members can access. For example, explicit or formal rules can be considered a company's bylaws or an organization's constitution. These are rules for what should happen in the group. *Implicit rules* are the unspoken expectations that everyone in the group seems to know and adhere to, although they are not formally documented. For example, members of the group understand that being on time for meetings is important.

Norms

Have you ever been part of a group where you were expected to act and behave in a certain way? These expected behaviors are called norms. *Norms* are standardized behaviors across all group members that focus on expected or anticipated behaviors. Homans (1950) argued that norms are behaviors that individuals in the group ought to perform under any circumstance. For example, if you are working in a group that has a treasurer, you would assume the treasurer would have reports of money spent and money paid and that this person could update the group on any financial happenings. These are norms. We expect

© luminaimages/Shutterstock.com

certain behaviors given particular positions. In a group, your norms will largely be dictated by your group role. For example, if you volunteered to be the secretary during group meetings, you would take notes, ask others to speak loudly so you can record information accurately, and provide the group members with a written recap of the meeting. Norms for behavior can be seen in a variety of situations, and we each have expectations for how others should communicate based on certain factors. Thus, if we expect people to adhere to specific norms for behavior and they do not, it can make group life difficult. Overcoming these difficulties can be accomplished through open communication where all group members share ideas about anticipated behaviors.

Power

Power refers to our ability to influence the behavior of others. Exercising power over others is contingent upon there being someone to control. Say you are part of a softball team. Each member of the softball team decides to skip an optional preseason workout. The only person that attends the workout is the team captain.

When the team captain arrives and sees no one on the field, who will the team captain be able to influence? That is right—no one. Power typically requires the presence of an interdependent relationship among group members. Thus, individuals are dependent upon one another for the transaction of power. Members of the softball team need to be present in order for someone to enact power.

Five different power bases have been identified (Table10.2). According to French and Raven (1960), the relationship between at least two people allows for power to be displayed.

As you can see from Table 10.2, some of these types of power are positive, whereas others are negative. You probably like receiving rewards for your behavior or completion of tasks, and it is safe to say you do not enjoy having your work criticized, especially if it occurs in front of others. Additionally, having someone in your group who has a level of expertise, knowledge, or past experience with the topic can also make for a smoother group process because that individual can offer insights others may not know.

TABLE 10.2

Typology of Power (French & Raven, 1960)

Type of Power	Description	Example of Power
Reward power	Refers to the ability to give out positive benefits or rewards	One who ensures all tasks are completed and gives group members tangible goods once the work is done
Coercive power	Refers to the ability to give out punishments	One who scolds, reprimands, criticizes, or offers other negative outcomes
Referent power	Refers to an individual's positive regard for/personal identification with the leader. Can be manifested in perceptions of similarity or interpersonal affinity.	When others do as they are told because they find the leader likeable and socially attractive
Expert power	Refers to the knowledge or expertise one has	When individuals in a group listen to what someone says about a task because of his or her skillful mastery of a topic or expert understanding
Legitimate power	Refers to the power that is associated with a certain position. Because of his or her position in the group, an individual has a certain right to influence/oversee others' behaviors.	When a group elects a "leader" (i.e., someone to oversee the completion of tasks), this person is said to have legitimate power because social norms indicate those designated as leaders have the inherent right to exert control or influence

When we exert power over others, we influence their behavior. In other words, we get them to do what we want. This is called ***compliance-gaining***. Wheeless, Barraclough, and Stewart (1983) suggested that compliance-gaining is the implementation of power. You get others to do what you want (compliance-gaining) because you put your power to work. The authors stated, "Compliance is not only the manifestation of exercised power, it is the very reason for the existence of power" (p. 121). Marwell and Schmidt (1967b, pp. 360–361) created a typology of 16 types of compliance-gaining tactics (Table 8.3) or behaviors that can be used to get others to go along with what we want.

TABLE 10.3

Typology of Compliance-Gaining Tactics (Marwell & Schmidt, 1967b)

Type of Compliance	Description	Example
Promise	Offering a reward for compliance	"Because we all agreed to the proposed idea, we can leave the meeting early!"
Threat	Threatening with punishment	"If we do not agree to a plan, the meeting will last at least another hour."
Expertise – positive	Telling others they will comply and be rewarded because that is just how things work	"If you go along with the plan now, you will be rewarded by the company later because the company likes a team player."
Expertise – negative	Telling others that, if they do not comply, they will be punished because that is just how things work	"If you fail to agree to the proposed idea, the team will punish you in the future by not listening to your ideas."
Liking	Acting friendly and open to get the receiver in a good frame of mind	"I really like your idea and think your insights are valuable. Would you mind supporting my group's proposed plan?"
Pregiving	Offering a reward before compliance is gained	"I like your group's ideas and in the future I plan to vote in favor of any of your group's ideas. Will you consider listening to my group's work now?"
Aversive stimulation	Engaging in continuous punishment until the recipient of the message gives in	"Like I've told you before, your group's ideas will not be supported by anyone. You need to really consider alternative solutions."
Debt	Making others feel indebted; the recipient of the message has to comply because of past favors he or she has received	"Remember when my group helped your group with that large project? The one we had to work extra hours to complete? My group now needs your group's assistance to complete a task."
Moral appeal	Telling others they are immoral people if they do not comply	"It is the right thing to help my group; a good person would do it."
Self-feeling – positive	Informing the recipients that they will feel better about themselves when they comply	"My group really needs some assistance. I know you will feel better about yourselves if you all agree to help us."
Self-feeling – negative	Informing the recipients that they will feel worse about themselves for not complying	"If your group does not agree to help us, you will probably feel bad about yourselves when the group fails."
Altercasting – positive	Telling others that a "good" person would comply	"A good person, a person of quality, would help the group."
Altercasting – negative	Telling others that a "bad" person would not comply	"Only a bad person would not help the group."
Altruism	Sharing with others that you need compliance very badly and asking them to "do it for me"	"Please help the group this time. Do it for me, because of our relationship and friendship."
Esteem – positive	Informing the recipient of the message that people he or she values will think better of him or her for complying	"Your help is much needed and you will feel good about yourself knowing that you motivated and encouraged this group to achieve its task."
Esteem – negative	Informing the recipient of the message that people he or she values will think poorly of him or her for not complying	"Everyone will think poorly of you if you do not go along with what we want."

You probably read through the list in Table 10.3 and said, "Some of these would never work on me." Existing research on compliance-gaining would agree with you. Not surprisingly, individuals respond more to positive or socially rewarding techniques than negative compliance-gaining strategies (see Marwell &

Schmitt, 1967a; Miller, Boster, Roloff, & Seibold, 1977; Williams & Untermeyer, 1988). How you deliver a compliance-gaining message is important as well. Individuals need to be mindful of tone, such as, for example, those who speak too softly are less likely to gain compliance (Remland & Jones, 1994). Overall, when it comes to working in groups and using power to gain compliance, it is best to approach it from a positive angle and not a negative one. The focus should be on creating a smooth road to goal completion.

Cohesiveness

Cohesiveness is defined as an individual's feeling of belonging to a given group. That is, cohesiveness is the extent to which group members feel like they are part of a group. There is a sense of "togetherness" when groups experience cohesion. In groups, cohesiveness, in general, is a positive characteristic. Generally, we want to feel like all members of the group are "in it" and that these members feel good about being part of the group. When group members feel cohesive, they participate in group processes such as goal-setting (Brawley, Carron, & Widmeyer, 1993) and experience satisfaction with the group (Tekleab, Quigley, & Tesluk, 2009). Thus, when you experience cohesiveness with members of a group, you feel as though you are working well with others.

You can help others feel like part of the group by listening. Have you ever told someone a story and they interrupted you? Maybe even changed the subject? Have you ever offered a solution that no one took into consideration? When people listen, they do more than hear. Hearing refers to having the physical ability to make sense of noise. It means you have the physical capacity necessary to perform the function. Listening goes beyond that. Not only do you hear the noise, but you also interpret and carefully consider the meaning behind the verbal and nonverbal messages. Feeling valued in the group and wanting to remain in the group often comes from being viewed as a competent source of information. This viewpoint is manifested when we listen to others.

Productivity

When individuals work together well, they are more likely to accomplish their goals. *Productivity* refers to a group's ability to complete tasks that ultimately lead to accomplishing the group's overall mission that brought them together in the first place. Productivity in a group can be considered at both the macro and micro levels. *Macro productivity* is bigger; it is completing the task that brought the group together. *Micro productivity* refers to the smaller activities that contribute to the completion of the overall task. Consider a class project. Your teacher assigns a task—the writing of a research paper that you will submit at the end of the semester. Completing the paper and submitting a final product is macro productivity. The work that you do along the way, including the collection of research and refining ideas, is micro productivity. Micro productivity contributes to macro productivity. If a group cannot focus on what needs to be accomplished, divide work appropriately, and make thoughtful decisions, it is far less likely they will achieve group productivity.

In addition to productivity, groups must work toward efficiency and effectiveness. *Efficiency* means that group members maximize what they do to complete the necessary tasks as correctly as possible. For example, rather than all members of a group trying to tackle each part of a project or task, they might decide to divide the labor among the individuals within the group and work on tasks that fit specific individual skill sets. *Effectiveness* means that the group meets all of its requirements and completes all of its tasks. That is, they accomplish what was asked of or assigned to them. Productive groups work toward being efficient and effective.

Overall, productivity in groups is important and can be enhanced in a number of ways. For example, groups can use technology (McFadzean, 1997) to enhance efficiency and effectiveness. For example, if a group has weekly, brief "check-in" meetings, the group may decide to hold these meetings in an online forum, rather than in a face-to-face meeting. Group roles (Rambo & Matheson, 2003) can also be used. Consider the nature of roles. Implied in the assignment of roles is that everyone has a portion of work to do, such as the note-taker keeping record of all meetings and decisions, and the leader setting the agenda and determining when work should be completed. A final technique that can be used to create a productive, efficient, and effective group is building cohesion among group members (Podsakoff, MacKenzie, & Ahearne, 1997). For example, making sure all group members contribute to ideas, are aware of one another, and can share in the work will make the group perform better.

© MonkeyBusinessImages/Shutterstock.com

Conflict

Just as we experience conflict in our interpersonal relationships, we are also likely to experience conflict when working in groups. Our personalities, unique communication styles, and different approaches to accomplishing goals may cause us to experience communication issues that need to be resolved. Keep in mind that *conflict* can be both a positive and a negative experience. A key element of conflict is that a struggle between individuals has been expressed verbally or nonverbally. Could you experience conflict with a group member if you don't let them know that you disagree or are upset with them? While you may experience the negative emotions, if you haven't made your feelings known to the other person, conflict may not exist.

There are two types of conflict you may experience while working with others. *Emotional conflict* refers to relational differences among group members and can include a lack of trust, feelings of dislike or animosity, and frustration (Evan, 1965). A second type of conflict is called *task conflict*, which refers to inconsistencies regarding how group members perceive the best way to complete the tasks being performed (Pelled & Adler, 1994).

As the group works toward a deadline or goal, you may become frustrated, experience personality clashes with a group member, or have differing opinions on how best to complete a task. While some conflict is beneficial because it encourages the group to consider alternate viewpoints and solutions, too much conflict can tear a group apart. Consider your own response to conflict when it occurs. Do you shut down, stop working with the group, or yell at others? While you may experience one or more of these reactions, it's not likely that they will help the group accomplish its goal.

Each of us has our own reaction to conflict, known as one's *conflict style*. According to Kuhn and Poole (2000), "An individual's conflict style is a behavioral orientation and general expectation about one's approach to conflict" (p. 559). While conflict in a group setting may be similar to interpersonal conflict, your style or approach to conflict may differ as you add more individuals to the interaction. Working in a group requires us to combine the personalities, opinions, and experiences of group members. Because of the multiple people you interact with in a group setting, you may respond to conflict differently than when you are simply engaging in dyadic or interpersonal communication. Your conflict style dictates the types of behaviors you display to others in the group. Three common responses that individuals apply to conflicts experienced in groups include avoidant, distributive, and integrative strategies (Sillars, Colletti, Parry, & Rogers, 1982). *Avoidant* strategies are used in an attempt to minimize or ignore the conflict. When asked if something is wrong, a group member who is avoidant will likely indicate that everything is fine. *Distributive* strategies require group members to give in to the wishes or ideas of other group members. Members of the group may adopt one solution rather than discussing all viable options. Finally, an *integrative* approach seeks to incorporate the opinions of all members of the group in order to evaluate options and arrive at the best solution.

As you can see from Table 10.4, some conflict styles lend themselves to positive conflict resolution. It is important to deal with conflict situations when they arise in groups. Allowing the conflict to go unresolved may cause relationships within the group to deteriorate and will likely deter the group from accomplishing its goal. Ignoring a conflict does not make it disappear. Identifying potential conflicts and working toward resolution can assist the group in making effective decisions by considering a variety of options or solutions proposed by group members.

TABLE 10.4

Typology of Power (French & Raven, 1960)

Conflict Style	Description	Example
Avoidant	Minimize or ignore conflict or move to another issue	When a group member brings up a topic you do not want to address, you change the subject.
Distributive	Involves one person giving in to another	A group member continuously argues for one solution until finally everyone in the group gives in and agrees to the solution.
Integrative	Individuals work together to find the best or most workable solution	Individuals in the group brainstorm, discuss, and combine ideas in order to achieve the most viable solution.

GROUP DECISION-MAKING

It seems clear from our previous discussion of groups that group members must work collaboratively to make a decision. However, this collaboration might be one of those things that is easier said than done. When working in a group, have you ever felt like no one listened to your opinion, that your input was of little value to other people, or that your ideas were not taken seriously? If you answered "yes" to any of these, you may not like working in groups. It *can* be challenging to get other people to listen to you. Effective and efficient groups consider the opinions and ideas of all members.

Group decision making requires thoughtful communication and the exchange of information between members (DeSanctis & Gallupe, 1987). This open exchange of ideas that contributes to group decision making can include several steps (Kuhn & Poole, 2000):

1. *Be open to alternatives.* All members of the group have important opinions and these should be given thoughtful consideration.

2. *Answer others' objections to alternatives.* When solutions are questioned, it is important to answer any objections or questions that arise.

3. *Blend ideas and work out compromises among alternatives.* Consider integrating suggestions from a variety of group members; the best possible solutions will likely be the result of incorporating a number of ideas.

4. *Coordinate the division of labor.* To make all members of the group feel important, it is paramount to divide the labor. In other words, everyone should have a job.

This process should also consider two key components: subjective outcomes and performance outcomes. Have you ever been part of a group in which a solution was proposed and, even though you may have used proper decision-making techniques, you still did not like or feel comfortable with the decision? McGrath (1984) labeled this feeling a **subjective outcome**. It can be thought of as a feeling that is associated with the group members' level of satisfaction with the proposed plan. For example, if you are part of a group that is working on a class project and the group uses the previously identified group decision-making behaviors, but you still do not think the agreed-upon decision is the correct one and instead feel disappointed, this is a subjective outcome. In addition to feelings associated with the decision, there are also **performance outcomes**. These outcomes focus on

© Goodluz/Shutterstock.com

productivity and the measurement of goal achievement. Imagine you and a group of others have been asked to improve parking on your campus. During your brainstorming sessions, your group's communication focuses on the task; communication is centered on the generation of ideas and questioning those ideas to determine the most appropriate outcome. Once a solution has been selected, it is then implemented and a plan for monitoring its success is also put into place. Through the monitoring of this solution, it is determined that the proposed solution does indeed improve parking on campus. Effective decisions take both subjective and performance outcomes into consideration. In other words, decisions that meet goals and represent something that the group feels positively toward are preferred.

GROUPTHINK

A key consideration to the group decision-making process is the idea of groupthink. Have you ever been part of a group where one person suggests an idea and everyone in the group goes along with it? If no one offers other ideas or solutions and the entire group seems to "jump on the bandwagon" and agree to the proposed idea, you may have experienced *groupthink*. Groupthink occurs when all of the group members go along with an idea without engaging in thoughtful discussion or careful analysis. Janis (1972) argues that groupthink minimizes disagreement or recognition of alternative options. Your group may be experiencing groupthink if:

- ▹ Group members pressure others to conform to the group's ideas.
- ▹ Group members and their ideas are considered stupid or bad if they go against the group, or if members try to negotiate.
- ▹ Group members self-censor and fall silent and their silence is considered agreement.
- ▹ Group members perceive the group to be invulnerable or "untouchable," that nothing can bring them down, which can result in an overly optimistic perception of ideas.
- ▹ Group members discount others' warnings or ideas and do not reconsider their positions.

As you may be thinking, groupthink is largely characterized as a negative group experience. Groupthink has occurred a number of times in our culture. For example, consider the 1986 explosion of the space shuttle *Challenger*. While a flaw in the design of an important part of the spacecraft, an O-ring, officially caused the explosion, there were several instances of groupthink leading up to the takeoff. For example, some engineers were concerned about the functioning of the O-ring, but these concerns were silenced and not shared with those higher in the chain of command. Other examples of groupthink in our culture include the Bay of Pigs invasion during President John F. Kennedy's tenure and the Nazi control of Germany. In all of these instances, voices of dissent were marginalized and group members failed to consider options. Groups can work to overcome this negative characteristic by working toward the best solutions, considering alternatives, not agreeing too quickly to one idea, and by asking all group members for input.

This chapter has defined groups, discussed the nature of groups, and highlighted the communication issues with which groups deal. While you may or may not enjoy working with groups, it is important to remember that it will likely be something you have to do and it can be a better process when thoughtful attention is given to communicative behaviors. It is a process that can be enhanced with clear communication and a discussion of the roles and rules relevant to groupwork. Remaining open to the insights of others, combining these insights, dividing the labor, and maintaining positive relationships will help groups achieve goals efficiently and effectively. Throughout goal completion, it is important to note that groups can experience both task and relational strain. If left unspoken, the strain can interrupt group processes. Open communication in which all group members are able to provide input will ultimately contribute to the most successful group functioning.

Understanding what a group is, the characteristics that compose group life, and how groups work together to make decisions will enhance your success when encountering group work. While depending on others to complete tasks can prove difficult and sometimes uncomfortable, working with others is a necessary part of your professional, public, and personal lives. Once everyone in a group understands how he or she "fits" in the group, it is easier to complete tasks and manage the social aspect of group life. **

Group Presentation

The task of presenting a Group Presentation is not always met with enthusiasm. That is because most of us have had the experience of working with a group and doing a majority of the group work on our own to make sure the project was completed on time and in good shape. We often think of group projects gone south when we think of group work in college. However, I can assure you that group work can also be a struggle in the corporate world. We wanted to cover Group Presentations in this book because you will be met with this task more often than you would like and it is a good idea to understand what is involved with a Group Presentation!

Everyone in a group is unique. That can be a bonus for your presentation, if you are able to use the strengths present within your group. As with any presentation, you should conduct an audience analysis, consider the purpose of the presentation and develop a topic that will enhance the knowledge of your audience members.

© Pressmaster/Shutterstock.com

There are advantages for presenting a project as a Group Presentation. First, realize that you cannot possibly know everything. Working with a group will allow the opportunity to expand the knowledge base and will cause you to add to your own knowledge of the subject your group will be covering.

Avoid disagreements regarding the division of labor by verbally acknowledging the value brought to the group by your group members. This also builds a feeling of teamwork among group members and fosters collaboration for the project.

Brainstorming is always much more effective when you can include more brains! This will also cause more active discussions to erupt which in turn will spark more ideas for the topic. Since each group is unique and there are many diverse cultures and thoughts present in a group, this will allow the group to incorporate different speech styles during the presentation.

Finally, speakers who are a bit shy usually feel more confident when they realize they are not alone on the stage making a presentation, but surrounded by their peers who are working together for a positive result.

Use this checklist when planning a Group Presentation:

Things to Consider	Explanation
Know Group Members	☐ Introduce yourself to the group. ☐ Exchange names and contact information. ☐ Discover strengths and weaknesses of group members. ☐ Determine a meeting schedule that works with everyone. ☐ Record information and distribute it to group members.
Discuss Group Expectations	☐ Ask questions. Answer questions. ☐ Divide tasks equally among group members. ☐ Be realistic with due dates and job responsibilities. ☐ Indicate group member responsibilities. ☐ Exercise accountability/responsibility duties. ☐ Establish consequences if a group member does not follow through.
Understand the Task	☐ Research the topic. ☐ Learn the time requirement for the presentation. ☐ Know what is expected. Do you need a visual aid? ☐ Do you need handouts? ☐ Create a timetable for responsibilities. ☐ What order will group members speak? ☐ Is there a Question/Answer segment during the presentation? ☐ Will you have a group moderator to introduce and conclude the speech? ☐ How will you be evaluated?
Respect Diversity	☐ Keep an open mind for other ideas. ☐ Encourage members to speak without reservation. ☐ Allow opportunities for members to interject opinions for the project.
Communicate Effectively	☐ Use effective listening skills. ☐ Speak clearly and make yourself heard. ☐ Ask for clarification, if you do not understand something. ☐ Use positive communication skills with group members.
Rehearsals	☐ Plan rehearsal dates. ☐ Rehearse together as a group. ☐ Assign a Tech Team member to manage the visual aids. ☐ Assign a Tech Team member to distribute handouts. ☐ Rehearse using visual aids for the presentation.

During the presentation, there is a protocol that should be followed. Here is the plan to follow for a Group Presentation:

1. **Moderator:** The moderator will open with an attention step, establish a need/relevance for the group presentation topic, establish speaker credibility for the group by introducing each speaker (first name and last name) and provide a clear thesis and list a brief description of each main point identifying the group member designated to cover. The moderator will then transition to the first speaker by again stating the speaker's first and last name along with the topic they will cover. *One thing to note: the moderator will be responsible to keep the presentation flowing. If at any time there is an awkward moment, the moderator has the responsibility of keeping the presentation advancing in a positive direction.*

2. **Speaker #1:** The first speaker will thank the moderator for the introduction and then will proceed to cover the main point. This will include an introduction, body, and conclusion of the point. Speaker #1 will then transition to the second speaker by stating the speaker's first and last name along with the topic the second speaker will cover.

3. **Speaker #2:** The second speaker will thank Speaker #1 for the introduction and then will proceed to cover the next main point. This will include an introduction, body, and conclusion of the point. Speaker #2 will then transition to the third speaker by stating the speaker's first and last name along with the topic the third speaker will cover.

4. **Speaker #3:** The third speaker will thank Speaker #2 for the introduction and then will proceed to cover the next main point. This will include an introduction, body, and conclusion of the point. Speaker #3 will then transition to the fourth speaker. If there is not a fourth speaker, then Speaker #3 will transition back to the Moderator using his or her first and last name.

5. **Moderator:** The Moderator will thank the last speaker and will proceed to summarize the three main points covered listing each Speaker's first and last name with the summary. Next, the Moderator will open the floor for a question and answer session. During the Q & A, the Moderator is responsible for keeping the conversation flowing, directing questions to different group members, and making sure that not one member monopolizes the conversation. If questions from the audience are all directed to one or two members, the Moderator can call for the audience that may have a question for the Speaker who has not been questioned. After a few questions and answers, the Moderator can then close the Q & A and thank the audience for their attention as they discussed the topic and participated in the Q & A session. Finally, the Moderator will again thank the group speakers, one at a time before closing the speech with a prepared Appeal to Action, which should be designed to keep the audience thinking about the group presentation topic.

NOTE: Research will be needed to support the individual points. The Moderator and each of the Group Speakers are responsible for conducting research to provide credible support of the points covered. Personal stories and personal experiences are also very helpful to support the points and to bring in a personal touch regarding the topic.

For a Group Presentation to be successful, the group needs to work together as a cohesive unit to make one presentation. They should choose a topic with the audience in mind, make a plan to achieve the purpose, decide on tasks and work divisions, create visual aids and handouts, set times for completion dates, individually work on identified tasks which includes research for the point to which the group member is assigned, evaluate progress, rehearse as a group and then of course, present the Group Presentation.

© racorn/Shutterstock.com

Group Presentations may not be the easiest presentations on the schedule, but they can be very effective because the group has different levels of knowledge about the topic and can also bring diverse thoughts and ideas to the table for discussion.

How Does the Moderator Handle the Question and Answer Sessions?

The way the Moderator handles the Q&A session will have a direct impact on the success of the group presentation. First, ask the audience members who want to ask a question to stand, identify themselves by first and last name, and then direct the question to a specific group member. The audience member should remain standing while the question is answered. Following the delivery of the answer, the audience member should thank the group member and then take a seat.

Group members should make sure the audience member has finished asking the question before they begin to answer the question. A good rule of thumb is to thank the audience member for the question and then repeat the question as mental preparation before answering. This step is important because it will mean that the group member will be answering the question that was asked. It also gives the speaker a moment to formulate the answer that will be given. After the question is answered, the speaker should say to the audience member, "I hope this has answered your question." The audience member can give a verbal or nonverbal response prior to sitting down so that the next question can be asked. Depending upon the time allotted for the Group Presentation, the Moderator can choose to take three to five questions or more.

The Question and Answer (Q & A) Session takes on the model of an impromptu speech. As the group member responds to unrehearsed questions and attempts to further add knowledge regarding the point, it is great to use the PREP model that is reserved for impromptu speeches and interview type situations. Here is how you PREP to prepare for any question!

P.R.E.P.

P = Point. Restate the question asked because that is the POINT. As you restate the question, it helps you to hear the question again and formulate the answer in your mind. Before you answer the question, be sure to follow the next step!

R = Relevance. Thank the person who asked the question for asking the question. Then, explain why the question is important because that is the RELEVANCE. After you cover the importance, then it is time to answer the question.

E = Example. Give a clear EXAMPLE as a follow-up to the answer of your question to make sure the audience has an understanding of the POINT. There is only one thing left to do, now!

P = Point. All good speeches will offer a summary and an impromptu speech requires the same. As you conclude, be sure to restate the question because that is the POINT and ask if you completely answered their question. If you get a head-nod or an affirmation, then you are good to go!

Group Presentations will use a different type of outline than other speeches because it involves information that will be covered by several people. We suggest using a One Point Outline for this type of presentation.

Here is a Brainstorming Worksheet to help you plan and an example of a One Point Outline for the Group Presentation.

Brainstorming Worksheet

Speech Category: Group Presentation

Identify Group Members:

Moderator: _____

Group Member #1: _____

Group Member #2: _____

Group Member #3: _____

Speech Title: Give your speech a clever title _____

Specific Purpose: Write a full sentence to show the purpose of your speech.

_____

Introduction—This will be covered by the Moderator: _____

Attention Step: Consider how you will get your audience's attention. Write all you plan to say using full sentences.

Establish Need/Relevance: Explain why this topic should interest the listener. Write all you plan to say using full sentences.

Establish Credibility: Explain why the group is credible to speak about this topic. Write all you plan to say using full sentences. Introduce each group member and establish their credentials.

Thesis (Preview) Statement: Write a full sentence that clearly states the three points you will cover:

_____

Point #1: Name of Group Member and The Point to be Covered: _____

Point #2: Name of Group Member and The Point to be Covered: _____

Point #3: Name of Group Member and The Point to be Covered: _____

Body:

Transition Sentence: Write a full sentence to transition from the Introduction Step to the first main point.

_____

     I. First Main Point (Covered by Name of Group Member):
         A. Sub-Point.
         B. Sub-Point.

Transition Sentence: Write a full sentence to transition from the first main point to the second.

_____

     II. Second Main Point (Covered by Name of Group Member):
         A. Sub-Point.
         B. Sub-Point.

Transition Sentence: Write a full sentence to transition from the second point to the third point.

_____

     III. Third Main Point (Covered by Name of Group Member):
         A. Sub-Point.
         B. Sub-Point.

Transition Sentence: Write a full sentence to transition from the third main point to the conclusion.

_____

Conclusion—This will be covered by the Moderator

Summary: Write in full sentence format a summary of your three main points. Identify the name of each Group Member covering each point.

Point #1: _____

Point #2: _____

Point #3: _____

Moderator: Opens the floor for the Question and Answer Session.

Moderator: Concludes the speech with Appreciation and a Wrap-Up: _____

(NOTE: Place the Works Cited Page on a page separate from the outline).

Works Cited

*Note: If you use visual aids, please include a Visual Aid Explanation Page
as a separate page following the Works Cited page.*

Visual Aid Explanation Page

Outline Template

Group Name 1

List All Group Members' Names Alphabetically
First Name/Last Name
Group Presentation
Day Month Year

Speech Category: Group Presentation
Title:
Purpose:

Introduction:
Attention Step:
Establish Need/Relevance:
Establish Speaker Credibility: Introduce each group member by first and last name.

Thesis: Today, I want to share three points about (Topic): (1) _____,

(2) _____, and (3) _____.

Body:
Transition/Link: First, I will start at the beginning by sharing a little about (Point #1).
    I. First Main Point—Presented by _____
        A. Sub-point
        B. Sub-point

Transition/Link: I've shared (Point #1) with you, now I'd like to tell you about (Point #2).
    II. Second Main Point—Presented by _____
        A. Sub-point
        B. Sub-point

Transition/Link: You've heard about (Point #1 and Point #2), now I'll cover (Point #3).
    III. Third Main Point—Presented by _____
        A. Sub-point
        B. Sub-point

Transition/Link: My purpose today was to (insert purpose and add a statement about the topic).
Conclusion:
Summary: Today, I shared with you three points—include each group member's name:

(1) Point #1_____, (2) Point #2 _____, and

(3) Point #3 _____.
Appeal to Action: As I conclude this speech, (End with a BANG).

(NOTE: Place the Works Cited Page on a page separate from the outline).

Works Cited

*Note: If you use visual aids, please include a Visual Aid Explanation Page
as a separate page following the Works Cited page.*

Visual Aid Explanation Page

Example Outline

Group #5

Ruth Joyner, Charles Hardnett, Bonnie Smith, Penny Waddell, Cassandra West
Group Presentation
1 August 2020

Speech Category: Group Presentation
Title: Preparing Students for Success
Purpose: The purpose of this group presentation is to provide the audience with useful tips to prepare students for the workplace.

Introduction: (Presented by the Moderator: Ruth Joyner)
Attention Step: Would you like to take your students from stress to success? How about from scared to prepared?
Establish Need/Relevance: Student success is a relevant topic as we all work to prepare students for the workforce. It is important, as educators, that you hear this presentation and learn tips for student success.
Establish Speaker Credibility: Realizing that experience is the best teacher, we have compiled a group of instructors with practical and experiential knowledge from elementary, middle, high school, and college settings.
Thesis: Today, I want to share four points about preparing students for success: (1) Charles Hardnett will share information about Time Management Skills, (2) Bonnie Smith will talk about Teamwork, (3) Penny Waddell will be covering Effective Communication Skills, and (4) Cassandra West will explore Cooperation.

Body: (Each point will be covered by an assigned group member)

Transition/Link: First, Charles Hardnett will share tips for Time Management Skills.
  I. **(Presented by Charles Hardnett) Time Management Skills**
      A. Managing Time
      B. Setting Priorities

Transition/Link: I've shared tips to encourage Time Management, now Bonnie Smith will tell how to foster Teamwork.
  II. **(Presented by Bonnie Smith) Teamwork**
      A. T.E.A.M. Acronym
      B. Tips for Teams

Transition/Link: You've heard about Teamwork, now Penny Waddell will cover effective Communication Skills.
  III. **(Presented by Penny Waddell) Communication Skills**
      A. Verbal Communication Skills
      B. Nonverbal Communication Skills

Transition/Link: Verbal and Nonverbal Communication Skills are essential for success, now Cassandra West will cover tips to encourage Cooperation.
  IV. **(Presented by Cassandra West) Cooperation**
      A. Respect Peers and Management
      B. Develop a "Do Whatever It Takes" Attitude

Transition/Link: Our purpose today was to share information with you to help you prepare students for success. At this time, I will relinquish the stage back to our Moderator, Ruth Joyner.

Conclusion: (Presented by the Moderator: Ruth Joyner)

Summary: Today, we shared with you four important work ethic skills to help your students find success: (1) Charles Hardnett shared information about Time Management Skills, (2) Bonnie Smith talked about Teamwork, (3) Penny Waddell covered Effective Communication Skills, and (4) Cassandra West helped us explore Cooperation.

Question and Answer Session: At this time, we would like to invite the audience to participate in a Question and Answer Session. Please stand to be recognized, provide your full name, address the group member by name and ask your question. (The Moderator will call on audience members one at a time and will conclude the session according to an established time by saying…) That is all the time we have for questions tonight. Thank you for attending. If you have further questions, please contact any of our group members by using the contact information supplied in your program. We challenge you to take your students from scared to prepared and from stress to success by encouraging strong work ethic skills in the classroom and in the workforce!

> NOTE: For this outline example, research was not used; therefore, a Works Cited page is not included. However, if you do use research for your own group presentation, please add parenthetical citations in the outline and a Works Cited page following the outline on a separate page.

The same is true if you use visual aids for a group presentation. Add a separate page that details the visual aids you plan to use and a description of each.

During Chapter Nine, you learned about individual speech presentations and evaluated the speeches of others. The same opportunity is available through group presentations. Evaluation rubrics are available to help make this process a bit easier.

As you evaluate others' speeches, consider each speaker's individual skills and provide kind, yet productive evaluations. Using the scoring rubrics will help document details needed for a thorough evaluation. Speakers usually want to know points well received and opportunities for improvement. Be specific with details. For example, don't just say you enjoyed the speech. Tell us why you enjoyed the speech and tell us what types of feelings or emotions you experienced while listening to their presentation. Communication Sharks have thick skins, but it will take an accomplished evaluation to deliver critiques as a tender morsel to be savored, enjoyed, and appreciated.

SPEECH EVALUATION WORKSHEET
Instructor's Copy for Grading the Speech

Speaker's Name: _____ **Title of Speech:** _____

Time of Speech: _____ **Date:** _____

Speech Performance 100 possible points	Excellent 5 points	Good 4 points	Average 3 points	Fair 2 points	Poor 1 point	N/A 0 points

Introduction Step:
  Attention Step:
 	
  Establish Need/Relevance:
 	
  Establish Credibility:
 	
  Thesis (preview 3 points):						

Body: Point #1						
Body: Point #2						
Body: Point #3						

Transitions (4)
  To First Point
  To Second Point
  To Third Point
  To Conclusion						

Conclusion:
  Summary (review 3 points):
 	
  Closing Statements/Appeal:						

Use of Research
  Number of Sources Used:
  Clear Verbal Citations:
  Sources Supported Topic:						

Visual Aids
 	
  Types: _____
 	
  _____
 	
  Setting up
  Handling of Visual Aids
  Design
  Visibility
  Management of Tech Team						

Handouts
  Design
  Distribution						

Speech Performance 100 possible points	Excellent 5 points	Good 4 points	Average 3 points	Fair 2 points	Poor 1 point	N/A 0 points
Language Skills Vocabulary Filler Words Sentence Structure Grammar Usage						
Vocal Delivery Skills Voice Volume Rate Vocal Variance						
Enthusiasm for Topic Passion/Energy						
Gestures						
Eye Contact						
Poise						
Confidence						
Professional Appearance						
Movement: Entrance to Stage Exit from Stage Movement while on Stage						
Time of Speech						
Handling of Notes/Note Cards						

Additional Comments and Suggestions:

SPEECH OUTLINE WORKSHEET
Instructor's Copy for Grading the Speech

Speaker's Name:_____ **Title of Speech:**_____

Time of Speech:_____ **Date:**_____

Outline Details	Possible Points	Points Earned
Standard Outline Format	20 points	
Typed	5	
Roman Numerals I, II, III	5	
ABCs	5	
123s	5	
Introduction:	20 points	
Attention Step	5	
Establish Need/Relevance	5	
Establish Credibility	5	
Thesis (Previews Main Points)	5	
Main Points	15 points	
Point #1	5	
Point #2	5	
Point #3	5	
Transitions/Links (4)	10 points	
Leads to Point #1	2.5	
Leads to Point #2	2.5	
Leads to Point #3	2.5	
Leads to Conclusion	2.5	
Conclusion	10 points	
Summary	5	
Closing Statement (Appeal)	5	
Research	25 points	
Required Sources Used	5	
Parenthetical Citations	5	
Works Cited Page	5	
Follows Citation Guidelines	5	
Copy of Research Included	5	

SPEAKER'S SELF-EVALUATION
This is an opportunity to evaluate YOUR speech.

Speaker's Name: _____ **Date of Speech:** _____

Speech Category: _____ **Title of Speech:** _____

After viewing the speech video twice, once to observe your nonverbal message and a second time to listen to the verbal message, please complete the self-evaluation worksheet. Be objective with responses and answer the questions asked with YES or NO.

Introduction Step:

When introducing the speech, did you:

_____ 1. Begin with an attention step?
_____ 2. Establish relevance for the topic?
_____ 3. Establish credibility by sharing your own experience with the topic?
_____ 4. Clearly state thesis and preview the main points?

Body:

In developing the body of the speech, did the speaker:

_____ 1. Identify and organize three main points?
_____ 2. Use well-chosen examples?
_____ 3. Effectively use research support materials such as statistics and quotations?
_____ 4. Properly cite sources (verbal citations)? How many sources did you hear? _____
_____ 5. Use transitions between each main point?

Conclusion:

When moving to finish the speech, did the speaker:

_____ 1. Signal the speech was concluding?
_____ 2. Review three main points?
_____ 3. End the speech with a BANG? How was this achieved? _____

Presentation and Visual Aids:

When using visual aids, did you:

_____ 1. Incorporate relevant and well-designed visual aids?
_____ 2. Effectively handle visual aids?

Delivery:

During the speech, did you:

_____ 1. Use voice appropriately by varying inflection, tone, and volume?
_____ 2. Speak words clearly with proper grammar and pronunciation?
_____ 3. Physically move and gesture with purpose?
_____ 4. Establish and maintain eye contact?
_____ 5. Appear confident, poised, and in control?
_____ 6. Dress professionally?

Overall Evaluation:

Considering the speech as a whole, did you:

_____ 1. Choose an appropriate topic?
_____ 2. Meet the assignment requirements, including time limits?

Add Specific Details and Comments:

GROUP PRESENTATION PEER EVALUATION
Use a separate copy to evaluate each speaker.

Speaker's Name:_____   **Evaluator:**_____

Title of Speech:_____   **Date:**_____

Truthfully answer all areas with a simple YES, NO, or short answer.

Introduction Step:

When beginning the speech, did the speaker:

_____ 1. Use an effective attention step? What was used? _____

_____ 2. Establish relevance for the topic?

_____ 3. Establish credibility by establishing speaker's own experience with the topic?

_____ 4. Clearly state thesis and preview main points?

Body:

In developing the body of the speech, did the speaker:

_____ 1. Identify and organize three main points?

_____ 2. Use well-chosen examples?

_____ 3. Effectively use research support materials such as statistics and quotations?

_____ 4. Properly cite sources (verbal citations)? How many sources did you hear? _____

_____ 5. Use transitions between each main point?

Conclusion:

When moving to finish the speech, did the speaker:

_____ 1. Signal the speech was ending?

_____ 2. Review three main points?

_____ 3. End the speech with a BANG? How was this achieved? _____

Presentation and Visual Aids:

When using visual aids, did the speaker:

_____ 1. Incorporate relevant and well-designed visual aids?

_____ 2. Effectively handle presentation aids?

Delivery:

During the speech, did the speaker:

_____ 1. Use voice appropriately by varying inflection, tone, and volume?

_____ 2. Speak words clearly with proper grammar and pronunciation?

_____ 3. Physically move and gesture with a purpose?

_____ 4. Establish and maintain eye contact?

_____ 5. Appear confident, poised, and in control of the presentation?

_____ 6. Dress professionally?

_____ 7. Speak passionately about the topic?

Overall Evaluation:

Considering the speech as a whole, did the speaker:

_____ 1. Choose an appropriate topic and purpose statement?

_____ 2. Meet the assignment requirements, including time limits?

Use the back of this page to add feedback/comments for the speaker.

KEY TERMS

- Adjourning Stage
- Cohesiveness
- Conflict
- Conflict Style
- Dyadic Communication
- Efficiency
- Emotional Conflict
- Explicit Rules
- Forming Stage
- Factional Group
- Group
- Group Communication
- Group Rules
- Groupthink
- Implicit Rules
- Individual Roles
- Maco Productivity
- Micro Productivity
- Norms

- Peer Group
- Performing Stage
- Power
- Productivity
- Purposive Group
- Relational Roles
- Role Conflict
- Role Flexibility
- Role Strain
- Role Theory
- Roles
- Social-emotional Leader
- Social Dimensions
- Social Group
- Storming Stage
- Task Conflict
- Task Dimension
- Task Leader
- Task Roles

REFERENCES

Benne, K. D., & Sheats, P. (1948). Functional roles of group members. *Journal of Social Issues, 4,* 41–49.

Biddle, B. J. (1979). *Role theory: Expectations, identities, and behaviors.* New York: Academic Press.

Bormann, E. G. (1969). *Discussion and group methods: Theory and practice.* New York: Harper & Row.

Brawley, L. R., Carron, A. V., & Widmeyer, W. N. (1993). The influence of the group and its cohesiveness on perceptions of group goal-related variables. *Journal of Sport and Exercise Psychology, 15,* 245–260.

Burkhalter, S., Gastil, J., & Kelshaw, T. (2002). A conceptual definition and theoretical model of public deliberation in small face-to-face groups. *Communication Theory, 12,* 398–422.

Cragan, J. F., & Wright, D. W. (1999). *Communication in small groups: Theory, process, skills* (5th ed.). Belmont, CA: Wadsworth.

DeSanctis, G., & Gallupe, R. B. (1987). A foundation for the study of group decision support systems. *Management Science, 33,* 589–609.

Evan, W. (1965). Conflict and performance in R&D organizations. *Industrial Management Review, 7,* 37–46.

Forrest, K. D., & Miller, R. L. (2003). Not another group project: Why good teachers should care about bad group experiences. *Teaching of Psychology, 30,* 244–246.

French, J. R. P, & Raven, B. (1960). The bases of social power. In D. Cartwright (Ed.), *Studies in social power* (pp. 150–167). Ann Arbor: University of Michigan Press.

Frey, L. R., & SunWolf. (2005). The communication perspective on group life. In S. A. Wheelan (Ed.), *The handbook of group research and practice* (pp. 159–186). Thousand Oaks, CA: Sage.

Fujishin, R. (2001). *Creating effective groups: The art of small group communication.* San Francisco: Arcada.

Gastil, J. (1993). *Democracy in small groups: Participation, decision-making, and communication.* Philadelphia: New Society.

Hawkins, K., & Fillion, B. (1999). Perceived communication skill needs for work groups. *Communication Research Reports, 16,* 167–174.

Homans, G. C. (1950). *The human group.* New York: Harcourt Brace Jovanovich.

Janis, I. L. (1972). *Victims of groupthink.* Boston: Houghton-Mifflin.

Kuhn, T., & Poole, M. S. (2000). Do conflict management styles affect group decision making?: Evidence from a longitudinal field study. *Human Communication Research, 26,* 558–590.

Li, I., &Hambrick, D. C. (2005). Factional groups: A new vantage on demographic faultlines, conflict, and disintegration in work teams'. *Academy of Management Journal, 48,* 794–813.

Lott, A. J., & Lott, B. E. (1965). Group cohesiveness as interpersonal attraction: A review of relationships with antecedent and consequent variables. *Psychological Bulletin, 64,* 259–309.

Marwell, G., & Schmitt, D. R. (1967a). Compliance-gaining behavior: A synthesis and model. *Sociological Quarterly, 8,* 317–328.

Marwell, G., & Schmitt, D. R. (1967b). Dimensions of compliance-gaining behavior: An empirical analysis. *Sociometry, 30,* 350–364.

McFadzean, E. (1997). Improving group productivity with group support systems and creative problem solving techniques. *Creativity and Innovation Management, 6,* 218–225.

McGrath, J. E. (1984). *Groups: Interaction and performance.* Englewood Cliffs, NJ: Prentice-Hall.

Miller, G. R., Boster, F., Roloff, M. E., & Seibold, D. (1977). Compliance-gaining message strategies: A typology and some findings concerning effects of situational differences. *Communication Monographs, 41,* 37–51.

Pelled, L. H., & Adler, P. S. (1994). Antecedents of intergroup conflict in multifunctional product development teams: A conceptual model. *IEEE Transactions on Engineering Management, 41,* 21–28.

Podsakoff, P. M., MacKenzie, S. B., & Ahearne, M. (1997). Moderating effects of goal acceptance on the relationship between group cohesiveness and productivity. *Journal of Applied Psychology, 82,* 974–983.

Poole, M.S., Hollingshead, A. B., McGrath, J. E., Moreland, R. L., & Rohrbaugh, J. (2004). Interdisciplinary perspectives on small groups. *Small Group Research, 35,* 3–16.

Rambo, E., & Matheson, N. (2003). *Enhancing group-work productivity through coordinator roles.* Retrieved from http://jalt-publications.org/archive/proceedings/
2003/E059.pdf.

Remland, M. S., & Jones, T. S. (1994). The influence of vocal intensity and touch on compliance gaining. *Journal of Social Psychology, 134,* 89–97.

Sillars, A. L., Colletti, S. F., Parry, D., & Rogers, M. A. (1982). Coding verbal conflict tactics: Nonverbal and verbal correlates of the "avoidance–distributive–integrative" distinction. *Human Communication Research, 9,* 83–95.

SunWolf. (2008). *Peer groups: Expanding our study of small group communication.* Thousand Oaks, CA: Sage.

Tekleab, A. G., Quigley, N. R., & Tesluk, P. E. (2009). A longitudinal study of team conflict, conflict management, cohesion, and team effectiveness. *Group and Organization Management, 34,* 170–205.

Time crunch: Breakdown of CEOs' time in a 55-hour workweek. (2012). *Wall Street Journal.* Retrieved from http://si.wsj.net/public/resources/images/MK-BS273B_CEOTI_NS_20120213203917.jpg

Tuckman, B. W. (1965). Developmental sequence in small groups. *Psychological Bulletin, 63,* 249–272.

Tuckman, B. W., & Jensen, M. A. C. (1977). Stages of small group development: Revisited. *Group and Organization Studies, 2,* 419–427.

Wheeless, L. R., Barraclough, R., & Stewart, R. (1983). Compliance-gaining and power in persuasion. *Communication Yearbook, 7,* 105–145.

Williams, M. L., & Untermeyer, N. K. (1988). Compliance-gaining strategies and communicator role: An analysis of strategy choices and persuasive efficacy. *Communication Research Reports, 5,* 10–18.

Communication SH⬛RK™

Unit #4

Workplace Communication

Soft Communication Skills

Professional Communication

Public Communication

Organizational Communication

Mass Communication

Communication SH🦈RK™

NOTES

Chapter Eleven

Soft Communication Skills

© ibreakstock/Shutterstock.com

SOFT SKILLS

The new buzz term in industry is soft skills. Employers use this when they are describing the type of employee they want to hire. As an instructor in a technical college, I can tell you that institutions of higher education also like to recruit students that have effective soft skills.

To have *soft skills* means that you have a nice mixture of communication skills, people skills, social skills, career knowledge, social and emotional intelligence, self-motivation along with impressive character traits and strong work ethics. Hard skills involve job specific knowledge which comes from training and experience. It's the hard skills noted on your resume that will get you in the door for a job interview. However, it is the soft skills that will help you get the job! But don't let the term, soft skills, cause you to think the person is a pushover. It also takes someone with a thick skin and a sharky attitude to keep the job once they have it.

Industry leaders are more interested in hiring candidates with soft skills than hard skills because someone with soft skills will have a teachable nature and can learn the hard skills while on the job. Someone with soft skills will be adaptable, flexible, trustworthy, and will have the coveted problem solving and critical thinking skills that are needed in today's workplace environment. It is also the person with effective soft skills that gets along well with customers and co-workers while working toward a common goal.

Here are some details to let you know what employers are looking for and will help you determine if you have the soft skills needed to get your dream job.

APPEARANCE

Appearance is part of the Kinesics study of communication because it covers the physical cues we see. Whether you are in a public speaking environment or a social arena, be very aware of the cues you are sending. The clothes and shoes you wear, the jewelry you choose, the type briefcase or bag you carry all speak to your brand. Take a look at the way you see yourself. Does your appearance reflect your own self-awareness? Do you understand your conscious and unconscious nonverbal cues through your choice of clothing and accessories?

Truthfully, there are many sides of you. There is the playful and casual side that is evident in the way you dress and behave when you are with your family and close friends. When at work, you may dress a bit more conservatively and more in keeping with the culture of the workplace. There is a romantic side when you are with the love of your life. Attitudes, beliefs, and values are often reflected in the type clothing we choose. It is appropriate to change appearances for different occasions and circumstances, but it is equally important to realize when to dress and groom in a particular manner.

Appearance is not just about the clothing, shoes, jewelry, and accessories that you choose, but also about grooming. Ask yourself the following questions:

- ► How does your clothing fit?
- ► Are your shoes polished?
- ► What colors do you choose?
- ► What styles appeal to you?
- ► What type hairstyle do you have?

- ► Are your clothes ironed or wrinkled?
- ► Does your clothing complement your accessories?
- ► Is your hair clean and styled?
- ► Are your fingernails manicured?

A few months ago, I had the pleasure of interviewing the Director of Talent Procurement for a Fortune 500 Company. During the interview, I asked if she looked for a particular type of clothing when she was scouting for new employees. She told me that she looks for candidates who are well-groomed and conservative and not for a particular clothing type. Different businesses reflect the culture of the business through the type clothing worn. She mentioned that for her organization, the most expensive suit was not always a bonus; however, she did want to see candidates wear clothing that was clean, ironed, and tailored to fit. As far as accessories, she said that haircuts, jewelry, and accessories often tell a great deal about the personality of the candidate. The most interesting thing she told me had to do with what the candidate was carrying! She shared that candidates who walked in with huge bags bulging with papers gave her the impression of an employee who was unorganized and messy. Instead, she preferred to see candidates walk in with a simple black folder or an iPad or tablet for note-taking. In today's technological world, anything that the employer may require can be sent with the touch of a key on the iPad or tablet. In other words, less is more!

Physical appearance sends a positive or negative message about your credibility. For most occasions, it is important to dress as if you are going to a job interview. Business casual dressing is always preferred. Wearing blue jeans and a t-shirt may not be the best choice if you want others to take you seriously. Have you ever heard, "You only get one chance to make a first impression?" Always ask yourself what message you are trying to send. Dress the part, Communication Shark!

Posture sends a nonverbal cue about how you feel about yourself. Good posture lends itself to effective movements and gesturing. Have you ever heard someone to tell you to stand tall? Hold your chin up, keep your eyes focused on the person with whom you are communicating and remember that good posture show self-confidence.

Poise is displayed with how you carry your body. Are you comfortable in your own skin? Shoulders should be up and eyes looking at your audience to display positive self-confidence. Avoid looking at the floor and walking with shoulders drooped as this sends a negative nonverbal cue. Walk confidently and look at others, smiling at them and letting them know you are happy to be there. Avoid leaning on furniture, shifting from one foot to the other, adjusting clothing or hair, handling notes, or putting your hands in your pockets.

© michaeljung/Shutterstock.com

All of these negative behaviors send negative nonverbal cues to others and will be evidence of a poor self-image. When all eyes are on you, make sure you are showing cues that increase your credibility.

Gestures are the ways you use your hands, body, and facial expressions to communicate points. I've often had students ask me, "What should I do with my hands?" My advice is to get immersed in your topic and in your audience so that you do not think about your hands and body. When you do this, you will have more natural and meaningful gestures. Don't put your hands in your pockets, clench them in front of you, or hold them behind you. These movements send a negative nonverbal cue. Gestures should not seem rehearsed, but should enhance your delivery and make visual points about things you are describing. They should be natural movements. The important thing is to make sure your gestures mirror the message you are sending.

Handshakes enter into the haptics study of communication because it involves touch and sends a nonverbal cue regarding your credibility. This gesture was briefly covered in the chapter for nonverbal communication, but also needs to be mentioned here since it is an indication of effective soft skills.

In the United States, handshakes are often expected when interviewing for a job, greeting someone, showing appreciation, or parting from a meeting. Handshakes are also used to offer congratulations, indicate an agreement, or as a show of good sportsmanship before and after an event.

A soft handshake may mean that you are sending a cue of weakness, while an overly dominant handshake may send a negative cue. It is considered proper etiquette and the **ideal handshake** to use right hands grasped no tighter than the grip used to open a door and then moved in an up-and-down motion a couple of times lasting no more than two or three seconds.

Across cultures, handshakes take various forms which may include **fist bumps**. I'm sure during flu season, you might have noticed the occasional fist bump or elbow touch in an effort to avoid spreading germs. **Double-handed handshakes** send a message that is more personal or intimate. Shaking with right hands while placing the left hand on the upper right shoulder of a person sends a **dominant handshake** message that you are taking the upper hand. The opposite message is sent if using the **fingers only handshake** or **limp fish handshake**.

Do you remember the news story when Microsoft founder Bill Gates met South Korean President, Park Geun-hye, for a business meeting? He greeted her with a kind smile and a handshake, but the media brought to light the fact that his left hand was in his pocket during the handshake and noted how this contradicted the positive handshake gesture he meant to send.

Don't send the wrong message. Practice your handshake with someone and ask for their feedback to make sure you are ready when the next opportunity arises. Since this may be an important step in the first impression you make with a prospective employer, teammate, or friend, you will want to make sure you are sending a positive nonverbal cue that will get the relationship off on the right hand.

Facial expressions include eye contact, smiling, head nodding, and head tilting to send a nonverbal cue during communication. Thoughts, emotions, and attitudes are often seen through facial expressions. Since many of our nonverbal cues include what people see, you can be assured that facial expressions are communicating to your audience things you are not saying verbally.

Eye contact promotes goodwill and a connection with the audience. It also helps the speaker appear more credible and knowledgeable about the topic. Establish strong eye contact and keep strong eye contact. Take a deep breath and establish direct eye contact to develop a connection with the audience. Believe it or not, but the smiles and head nods of others will give you strength and self-confidence. You need them and they need you.

It might be hard sometimes to establish eye contact with larger groups. In this case, start looking toward one side for the group and pan the entire side as you move your gaze to the other side of the group. Good eye contact help others to feel valued, included, and invested in your topic. Avoid gazing at any one person or group of people for too long of a time. Share your eye contact and your attention.

Head tilting and head nodding is a non-verbal cue which lets you know if your audience comprehends your point or if they still might have questions.

Smiling is a nonverbal cue that says, "I am happy to be here!" A genuine smile will send a positive message. As you smile, you will be pleased to notice that they will also smile at you. This reciprocal smile will help you not be as nervous as you might be without positive cues.

AVOID AWKWARD SILENCE

People who have excellent soft skills know how to avoid awkward silence that often happens when meeting someone for the first time or attempting to answer an interview question. While this was discussed in an earlier section of the book, this tip for soft skills can be repeated. The awkward silence will be no-more when you use the P.R.E.P. model for answering questions without prior preparation.

Acronym	Stands for...	Description
P	Point	Restate the question asked and then clarify the point of the question.
R	Relevance	Thank the person who asked the question, explain why the question is relevant, and provide a brief answer to the question.
E	Example	Provide a clear example as a follow-up to your answer and to make sure the audience has an understanding of the answer.
P	Point	Summarize the impromptu speech by re-stating the point and affirm that you answered the speaker's question.

1. Anticipate impromptu speaking opportunities and be **PREP**ared.
2. Memorize the **PREP** model and be ready for anything.
3. Listen, so that you don't have to ask for the question to be repeated.
4. Don't rush! Take a moment to process the question before you begin to answer it. Restating the question before you answer the point of the question will help give you a little extra time to decide how to answer the question. Your audience members will just think you are establishing good eye contact with them, when in reality you are thinking of a clever answer. People who get in too big of a hurry are the very same people who forget the question and stumble over their answers. Take your time.
5. The **PREP** model calls for brevity. Answers that get directly to the point of the question, connect relevance of the question to the answer, and offer real-life examples will affirm your credibility as a speaker.

To take this one step further, think of questions to ask the person you just met. Usually, the person who is introducing someone will add a brief statement to start the conversation. This is where effective listening skills come in handy. Be sure to listen and that will help with ideas to keep the conversation moving forward.

LISTENING

Consider how sharks find their prey. They do this using sensory receptors found along the sides of their bodies. These receptors perform much like our ears. They feel vibrations or movement in the water around them with these receptors and respond to the message received.

Communication Sharks also use sensory receptors to navigate communication waters to detect and gather information from that which we hear. *We listen!* Some of us are better listeners than others. You will also find that at times you may be a better listener than you are at other times. What we hear is often influenced by the amount of distractions that interfere with content being delivered. Instead of hearing a full sentence spoken to us, we might only hear bits and pieces of that sentence and decode the message into something that is not what the speaker intended. It happens often. Business deals, marriages, and friendships can be broken because of this breakdown in communication. Become a better listener and you will be a more effective employee, a better marriage partner, and a more reliable friend.

Since listening is the most important communication activity, it is important to also recognize the benefits of effective listening skills. These include listening to learn about a topic, listening to relate to others and show concern, listening to influence others to change attitudes, and listening for enjoyment.

Listening is quite different from hearing. Without any effort, you can hear something; however, it takes a conscious effort to listen. Hearing is a physical process that occurs as sound waves vibrate against our eardrums. Then, that sound moves to our brain where it is decoded into a message or response. Perhaps this table will make this clearer for you:

Listening	Hearing
Activity	Process
Learned Skill: can be taught and learned	Response to stimuli: involuntary
Active: requires the listener to be engaged, encode/decode, and respond	Passive: requires no action on the part of the listener
Choice: requires focus and attention	Continuous: if no hearing loss, hearing is ongoing
Message or content is consciously received and gets a response	Sound is received, but will not always elicit a response

Effective speakers are great listeners! They must listen to discover what is needed by their potential audience and then they go the extra mile to research main points within the content to provide their audience with credible information.

In earlier chapters, you learned that *communication* is defined as a process in which ideas or information are transmitted, shared, or exchanged. In other words, we communicate through various methods that are verbal and nonverbal.

The speaker decides to send a message and encodes the message and content they plan to send. *Encoding* is a process by which a person derives meaning and understanding. It may involve finding a common understanding to develop a deeper understanding of the point or topic.

Once the speaker has a good understanding of the content, the speaker delivers the message to the audience. Each rhetorical situation is different; therefore, the speaker needs to consider many factors when deciding how to deliver the message. Finding common ground, emphasizing the sharing of an idea, and determining an effective approach, will help the speaker to achieve the intended goal.

The listener receives the message, but the message may be distorted according to distractions in the surrounding area or by preconceived ideas and opinions of each audience member. As the listener receives the message, he will decode what was heard and understood before sending verbal and/or nonverbal feedback to the speaker. *Decoding* is a process by which we translate or interpret the content into meaning. The decoding process can be altered depending upon "noise" in the environment. *Noise* can be defined as distractions in the speaking environment, but also can include preconceived notions, opinions, and ideas. Sometimes feedback is verbal, but many times the feedback to the speaker is nonverbal. Feedback helps the speaker to know if the content delivered has been effectively decoded and received. In order to have feedback, the receiver (audience) will need to listen.

The listening process will look a good bit like the communication process described earlier in the book and reviewed in this chapter, but we removed the speaker from the equation to focus on the individual's listening responsibilities. The listening process requires the listener to receive, understand, remember, evaluate, and respond. Let's look at how each of the steps in this process are needed for a person to listen effectively.

THE LISTENING PROCESS

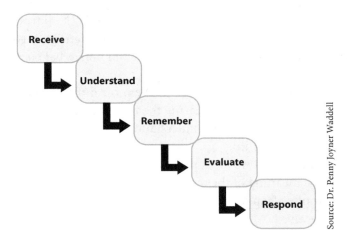

Source: Dr. Penny Joyner Waddell

Receive: There is a great deal of difference between listening and hearing. Listening is a choice we make. It is an active skill that requires the listener to focus on the message, receive content so that the message can be understood, remembered, and evaluated in order for the listener to elicit an appropriate and effective response.

To receive the full message being sent, the listener should resist distractions and devote complete attention to the message. Auditory signals account for verbal messages, but nonverbal messages often send a strong, clear message. As a rule, we believe what we see before we believe what we hear. The listener's challenge is to receive the message and avoid distractions that often change the meaning of the message. If distractions are prevalent, the listener can try to space himself closer to the speaker or remove the distractions. For example, the listener shows he is actively receiving the message by putting down the phone, turning off music, and positioning himself so that he is facing the speaker to show active listening skills.

Understand: Once the message has been received, the listener needs to confirm an understanding of the message. Verbal and nonverbal cues should be considered during this phase of the listening process.

The listener should first review verbal communication received and ask questions that are necessary to clarify understanding of the message. Avoid judging the speaker and try to see the message from the speaker's point of view. It is often necessary to paraphrase content heard in order to confirm a clear understanding between the listener and the speaker.

Nonverbal communication received will include vocal cues as well as visual cues. For example, you can often hear in someone's tone whether they are happy, unhappy, anxious, scared, or joyful. Visual cues will include how the speaker is standing/sitting, what they are doing with their hands and feet, how they greet you, what they wear, gestures, smiling, head nods, and postures.

Remember: Let's be honest, we do not all have memories like an elephant, but once we receive a message, it is important to remember the message. People have different strategies for remembering things. The old-fashioned way of remembering things was to take notes, but now that we have such incredible phones, we find ourselves opening the reminder or notes app on our phones and jotting down messages. We can also use the recording feature on our phones to record the entire conversation or speech in order to retrieve it at a later time.

If your phone isn't handy, you might try to identify key words or ideas that are received in the message, paraphrase (repeat to the speaker) the message, understood, and recount the message to someone else. As you repeat or recount the message, your brain will be hearing the message a second time through your own verbalization. This will also help you to remember key facts in order to reconstruct the message at another time.

Evaluate: When a message is shared, the speaker is usually trying to accomplish a particular purpose. The listener will evaluate the purpose while hearing the message. Is the purpose to inform, entertain, persuade, motivate, or is the speaker merely looking for approval, affirmation, or your opinion? We evaluate the message depending upon cues sent by the messenger. Verbal and nonverbal cues once again play a big part of our receiving, understanding, and remembering the message.

It is the evaluation part of this process that can be the most difficult as many listener's biggest mistake comes when we try to make judgments prior to hearing the full message. Resist the temptation to evaluate the message until there is a complete and thorough understanding of the message. Resist thinking ahead of the speaker to anticipate what may be upcoming.

Another challenge is realizing that we often make evaluations based upon our own prejudices, biases, or opinions that might change the meaning of the message.

Respond: Feedback can often happen as we are hearing the message and again later with a response made after the message was received.

During the receipt of the message, the listener should respond by using active listening skills: smiling, head nodding, and attention to the message. Empathetic listening involves seeing the other person's point of view. This also results in a response that shows the listener as responsive and supportive or not.

The listener can make verbal responses during the message delivery to show understanding or the lack of understanding. Questions sent in response to the message are used to seek clarification or to show agreement.

If you are looking for advice regarding how to respond to a message, Communication Sharks will tell you that it is always best to be honest. The person who is sharing a message deserves to expect honest responses from the listener, even if the listener does not agree with the message. Deliver the response in good taste and take the speaker's point of view into consideration.

What Keeps Us from Being Good Listeners?

In the beginning of the listening section we discussed "noise" that can be distracters during communication. Let's spend time now discussing these distracters in more detail. They include things we hear, see, do, know, and perceive/feel. These distracters are all prevalent whether we are in a public speaking situation or a private conversation. I'm sure you will be able to relate to all of these.

Things we hear: Have you ever tried to talk to someone in a crowded restaurant and the environmental noise surrounding you was so loud that you couldn't carry on a cohesive conversation? This could be anything from background music, other people's conversations, dishes rattling, glasses clinking, to chairs scraping on the floor. Extraneous noise can make it difficult to enjoy the person with whom you are sharing dinner. Do unusual accents cause you to reflect on how the speaker is pronouncing or saying a certain word resulting in misunderstanding content that was being shared? Perhaps you are visiting with friends during a "play date" with your children and you are trying to listen while your friend tells you about an issue she is having with her phone company, but you are also trying to tune in to the chatter going on with the children. Chances are you didn't hear your friend's entire story and you also did not gather the full meaning of the tug-of-war going on with the children. You may be hearing lots of sounds, but are you really listening?

Things we see: Often, we have trouble focusing on a message if things we see are interfering with the message. It could be a glare off the windshield of a car parked outside, the speaker's choice of clothing, decorations on the stage, or other people in the audience. I am sure this distraction is something with which all of you can identify.

Things we do: What are your own listening habits? Do you have a tendency to tune out of conversations while you check your text messages, Facebook, or Twitter? Are you completing a sentence on your computer while a colleague is trying to tell you about a problem they are having in their department? Does the heavy cologne worn by the speaker distract you from listening to the content? Do you anticipate how you will respond before your speaker finishes his/her sentence? What poor listening habits do you have that might keep you from actively listening?

Things we know/don't know: Have you ever been confused by meanings of words and spent the next few minutes trying to decide the meaning of the word or correct pronunciation of the word instead of listening to the message? Do you wonder, "How is that spelled?" or look up the meaning on your phone? Do you find yourself pondering over incorrectly cited research or questioning facts offered by the speaker? Too many facts presented during a speech can also cause us to miss the speaker's main point because we are too focused on details. These things can prevent us from active listening.

Things we perceive/feel: Illness, pain, hunger, anger, extreme happiness, or exhaustion can keep us from hearing all that is being said to us. Negative attitudes, prejudices, beliefs, or feelings toward a topic can cause us to lose our desire to actively listen as a topic is presented. We are more critical of speakers who have views which differ from our own. Consequently, we will receive less of the intended message that we would have heard if we listened with an open mind. Likewise, we might listen closer to those who speak about a topic with which we agree. To become better listeners, resist positive or negative distractions, focus on verbal and nonverbal messages, try to see the speaker's point of view, take notes, and concentrate on active listening.

What Are the Types of Listening Skills?

Active Listening: Listen to understand. Determine if nonverbal cues sent by the speaker mirror the speaker's message. Position your body so that your shoulders are facing the speaker, body posed forward, and use positive head nods and smiles to send a nonverbal cue that you are actively listening to the speaker.

Critical Listening: Resist outside noises and distractions to use critical listening skills. This involves looking past a speaker's distracting behavior and the environmental distractions that are around you. Avoid concentrating on yourself and your own feelings/perceptions. Instead, concentrate on the speaker and the message being delivered.

Empathetic Listening: Try to see the speaker's point of view, even if you do not share the speaker's views. We often find ourselves in diverse audiences and it is imperative that we actively try to understand the speaker's message and offer positive nonverbal cues in support for the speaker.

Informative Listening: Taking notes will help you use informative listening skills. Make notes of the main points or data presented and examples that are especially interesting to you. When your colleague or partner is speaking to you about an issue, take notes about the issue and show active listening skills with strong body posture.

Appreciative Listening: This is my favorite type of listening skill. As we show enjoyment of a speaker and their content, we exhibit appreciative listening. Send nonverbal cues that you are listening and enjoying the conversation. This is important and helps the speaker to be less anxious due to the positive nonverbal cues you send during conversation.

Would you like to find out what type listener you are? Please complete the worksheet on the following page and discuss your findings with a friend.

© DeeaF/Shutterstock.com

What Type Listener Are You?

Instructions: Evaluate the following by answering the question truthfully as you are at this time. Later, take the same evaluation to see if you can notice improvements. When finished, tally your score using the key found at the end of the evaluation.

Questions	Never 1	Rarely 2	Sometimes 3	Often 4	Always 5
1. I pay attention to the speaker.					
2. I can ignore distractions during the speech.					
3. I can listen to a speaker's ideas without letting my ideas/opinions get in the way.					
4. I can ignore distracting personal habits of the speaker (throat clearing, movements, note cards).					
5. I take notes to organize the speaker's main points.					
6. During the speech, I am thinking of questions to ask about ideas I do not understand.					
7. I can understand the meaning of unknown words from the balance of the speaker's message.					
8. I can separate fact from opinion, without it being verbally cited.					
9. I can tell the difference between important and unimportant details.					
10. I do not recognize unsupported points that a speaker makes.					
11. I agree and respect that others have differing points of view.					
12. I evaluate the speaker and the content of the speech.					
13. I identify specific words or phrases that impress me as I listen.					
14. I get caught up in the story or poem the speaker shares.					
15. I put what I hear into my own words so that I can recount it to others.					
16. I listen to what the speaker is saying and try to feel what the speaker feels.					
17. I find hidden meanings revealed by subtle verbal and nonverbal cues.					
18. I check my cell phone for text messages and e-mails while listening to a speech.					
19. In a casual setting, if the speaker is struggling to explain something, I step in and assist.					
20. When people speak to me, I give head nods and verbal confirmations like, "OK" or "Yes."					
Calculate Score by Adding Points					

Due to many different types of situations and speaker variables, responses to this questionnaire may not always reveal the same results. However, this assessment should give an idea of your average listening skills. Circle the evaluation that corresponds with your score.

15–30—POOR—Continue work to improve your listening skills; 31–70—AVERAGE—But, you need to set your goals higher; 70–100—GOOD—Never stop working to be a better listener

KEY TERMS

- Active Listening
- Appearance
- Appreciative Listening
- Critical Listening
- Communication
- Decoding
- Empathetic Listening
- Encoding
- Evaluate
- Eye Contact
- Facial Expressions
- Gestures
- Head Tilting or Head Nodding

- Informative Listening
- Listen
- Noise
- Poise
- Posture
- Receive
- Remember
- Respond
- Smiling
- Soft Skills
- Understand

Chapter Twelve

Professional Communication

© Peshkova/Shutterstock.com

In this chapter:

© GoodStudio/Shutterstock.com

Professional Communication Competence is expected from employees in every industry and involves multiple methods of communicating across various modalities. How are your skills? Are you able to compete in today's marketplace where professionals are communicating in writing, in person, and electronically? Do your skills reflect the industry knowledge and expertise that you have? Are you able to share messages with clarity to prevent misunderstandings? Are you open to constructive feedback so that you can improve the skills you have?

College campuses and the workplace are filled with many different types and cultures of people. Industry expects us to have excellent communication and collaboration skills. This is the reason that you are taking a Human Communication Course and the reason we are covering professional communication skills in this book.

Whether you are writing a letter to the governor, sending an e-mail to a colleague, conducting a business meeting with the board of directors, or chatting with your boss in the elevator, the way you communicate speaks volumes about you and your professionalism, or the lack thereof.

At this point in the course, you have a basic understanding of communication, how to make presentations, how to work with groups, the differences between verbal and nonverbal communication, intrapersonal, interpersonal, and international communication. You've also learned about the various types of communication we use in different settings. We've explored **kinesics, proxemics, chronemics, haptics, and olfactory** aspects that also communicate meaning. All these things work together to determine your communication competence. We will explore this further in the pages to follow.

**COMMUNICATION COMPETENCE

Have you ever interacted with someone and thought the person's behavior was inappropriate? Perhaps you found yourself pondering why the person said or did something or why their behaviors did not match the situation. Using effective communication and having successful interactions with others is an outcome we can achieve. Communication is something we can control. Your goal should be to strive for appropriate behaviors in all contexts and with all content. Successful navigation of the communication process is essential to becoming a competent communicator. Competence involves the capacity to alter verbal and nonverbal behaviors in creating appropriate and effective messages—messages that "fit" the situational demands of the interaction in addition to helping us reach shared meaning with the receiver of our message.

Communication Competence Defined

Communication competence is defined as an individual's ability to produce messages that are perceived as appropriate and effective. It is based on the understanding that communicators should possess three key elements in order to achieve competence: knowledge, skill, and motivation (Spitzberg & Cupach, 1984). **Knowledge** refers to our understanding of the appropriate messages or behaviors that should be used in a given situation or with a particular person. For example, in the United States, it is common to shake hands during an initial interaction. While we may have knowledge of what's appropriate or effective, it's also important to possess the ability to actually engage in those actions. *Skill* refers to the ability to produce or utilize the appropriate behaviors. For example, you may know that an effective oral presentation has an introduction, a body, and a conclusion, but you may lack the skills required to deliver a quality presentation. Finally, **motivation** refers to a desire to obtain results or accomplish a goal. We have to want to be competent communicators. Collectively, communication competence requires knowledge of what constitutes effective communication, the skills or ability to engage in those behaviors that are appropriate to the situation and effective in creating shared meaning, and a desire or motivation to be perceived as competent.

Achieving Competence

Competence involves considering the situation and the topic *in addition to* the person with whom you are communicating. Assessing situational elements is a key component to achieving competence. Chances are you have encountered situations that required you to complete a situational analysis without even realizing it. Have you ever adjusted your message based on the situation or the person with whom you were speaking? Have you ever told your parents about how you spent your evening but provided different details about the same evening to a friend? We collect information that guides our decisions regarding how to best proceed with conversations. Consider how you would ask your boss for a raise. You would likely address the situation by customizing your verbal and nonverbal behaviors to that specific situation. You might schedule a meeting with your boss and arrive early and dressed in a suit. The verbal message would be organized so that you first demonstrate how committed you are to the organization and then address why you believe you deserve a raise. How you communicate in this situation would likely be different from the verbal and nonverbal behaviors you would use while terminating a romantic relationship. Competence requires us to evaluate several different elements in determining what is acceptable in a given communication situation.

COMMUNICATION ETHICS

Our communication is often guided by personal standards of what we consider to be right or wrong, good or bad, and correct or incorrect. These guidelines serve as our personal ethics. *Ethics* are the standards, values, beliefs, and principles we use to help us determine what is acceptable or unacceptable behavior. It is important to note that there is no universal ethical standard. We each create and abide by our own ethical code of conduct. Some individuals view ethical behaviors as defined by laws or the legal system. If it is illegal, a behavior would be deemed unethical. Others evaluate ethical behaviors using a religious doctrine. If a religion believes it, then the behavior is acceptable or ethical.

Ethics and communication work together. When we think about the relationship between ethics and communication, we should take into consideration what behaviors will help us achieve our intended outcomes. As communicators, we do not want to mislead or manipulate our listeners. For example, suppose your friend begins to tell a personal story and asks you to keep the information secret, to not share the information.

An ethical communicator would respect the friend's request and keep the information private rather than violating the friend's wishes. Considering the ethical implications of our decisions when communicating with others and a commitment to achieving communication competence are things that we control. They are behaviors that we should use and strive to incorporate in all aspects of our lives.

BENEFITS OF COMMUNICATION

By now, we hope that you realize just how important communication is in all aspects of your life—personal, professional, and public. Communication is a skill that, when used appropriately, can benefit you in each of these areas. Consider the ways in which you currently adjust your communication when interacting with others. For example, you shake your boss's hand while greeting her, but you hug your romantic partner in greeting. A more formal communication style is used when speaking with your grandparents, while your interactions with friends include the use of slang and is more relaxed. Our communicative behaviors change depending on with whom we are interacting and the situation or setting in which we are communicating.

In Our Personal Lives

Personal relationships can be some of the most rewarding as well as the most challenging connections in our lives. When we use effective communication, we can experience a host of benefits, including *relational satisfaction*, which is feeling positive and content in our relationships, and *emotional closeness*, which is a perception or feeling of trust or solidarity with another individual. Improving your communication in personal relationships can contribute to these positive outcomes. Techniques you should consider using to enhance your communication:

1. *Understand yourself.* The more you understand your thoughts, the better you can communicate them to others. Knowing your own communication style and preferences can lead to more effective interactions. For example, you might prefer to address challenging conversations by sending text messages as opposed to confronting them face-to-face.

2. *Use honesty.* Being open and truthful with others can help create meaningful relationships.

3. *Take time to listen.* Active listening is a choice. By staying motivated and engaged in the conversation, you can enhance connections with others.

4. *Engage in meaningful conversations.* Even discussing topics we do not necessarily enjoy talking about, engaging in tough talk can help us learn about others' personal perspectives and their perceptions of a situation.

Successful relationships are the by-product of effective communication. Our personal lives are not the only area that will benefit from enhanced communication. Interactions in our professional lives can prosper as well if effective communication is used.

In Our Professional Lives

Fortune 500 executives indicate that the most sought-after skills when hiring new employees include effective oral and written communication (Hansen & Hansen, n.d.). By working to enhance communication in your professional life, you can experience a variety of positive outcomes including monetary gains, enhanced professional status, and more satisfying workplace relationships. Some suggestions for enhancing your communication in a professional setting include the following:

1. *Ask questions.* When you're unclear of a task or how to complete an assigned task, ask questions so you understand the other person or get clarification on a point.
2. *Include others.* Be sure to include others in dialogue, reach out to those you may not know.
3. *Offer your ideas.* When you have an idea about how to complete a project, offer it to others.
4. *Be direct.* Assign tasks in a direct manner.
5. *Use inclusive language.* Use language such as "we" and "us" to create team cohesion.

It is safe to say that we all want to be successful in our chosen careers. Effective communication can contribute to that success in terms of promotions and opportunities. Our public lives can also benefit from being able to successfully share our ideas with others.

In Our Public Lives

Communication can seem even more important when you are delivering a message to a large audience such as during an oral presentation. When our public speaking skills are strong and we deliver the message in a way that meets our audience's needs, we can experience increased perceptions of competence and credibility. Toastmasters, an organization dedicated to enhancing public speaking skills, provides the following suggestions for enhancing your public presentation skills:

1. *Know your material.* The topic matters.
2. *Practice.* Rehearse and revise as necessary.
3. *Know the audience.* Greet audience members and ask them questions.
4. *Recognize that people want you to succeed.* Audiences are rooting for you.
5. *Don't apologize for nervousness.* Audiences rarely notice a speaker's nervousness.
6. *Concentrate on the message.* Focus on content.

Our public lives not only include effectively presenting our ideas in a public context, but also our civic engagement and the images we portray to the public, such as posts to social media profiles such as Twitter, Instagram, or Facebook. Consider steps that you should take to carefully manage your public persona so as to avoid creating a negative perception.**

Using information learned about your personal communication competence will help you to become a more professional Communication Shark.

CONDUCTING MEETINGS

Last week I was asked to attend a meeting. My schedule was already very full, but I moved some things around in order to accommodate the time needed to attend the meeting. Additionally, I gave myself time to get to the meeting and arrived with an iPad ready for note-taking. As I arrived, there was a sign-in sheet on the table and a typed agenda of talking points that would be covered. I signed in, took a copy of the agenda, and found my seat just in time for the meeting to begin. The speaker took her place on stage and began to work quickly through the items on the agenda. As promised, the meeting was completed in a little less than an hour and those of us in attendance were able to get on with the rest of our day. Meetings are inevitable. If we are in business, we can expect to meet occasionally with our work groups so that we are all up to speed on impending projects and caught up on details that might affect the rest of our objectives.

Most professionals do not mind attending meetings because ultimately it helps us reach a common goal. However, we DO mind attending meetings that are unproductive and a waste of time. Professionals with excellent communication skills conduct more productive and effective meetings. This, in turn, adds to their credibility as a leader. What do you know about conducting effective meetings?

**ENHANCING THE MEETING PROCESS

Scheduling and coordinating group meetings can be quite difficult. An unproductive group meeting could leave group members feeling unmotivated to work and contribute to negative feelings toward working with others. There are, however, strategies to promote quality, efficient group meetings.

Manage Meeting Time

Time is valuable, and respecting the time of group members is important. The time allocated for group meetings should be carefully managed, perhaps by the leader of the group. The leader of the group could assign one person to serve in the role of timekeeper for the group to ensure that the group remains focused on accomplishing tasks within the specified time constraints. Remaining engaged and focused on group tasks can be challenging. Have you ever attended a meeting where the discussion went "off topic"? Meetings are often sidetracked due to conversations among members or discussions that are unrelated to the group's function. These unwanted discussions have an impact on the overall length of the meeting. In turn, this could affect people's commitment to the group. For example, you may think that being part of a group or a committee isn't important because "nothing gets accomplished" and so you stop attending meetings. Similarly, when members arrive late or leave early and expect time during the next meeting to be devoted to "catching them up" on what they've missed, productivity and commitment to the group diminishes.

Develop and Adhere to an Agenda

Few things are worse than a group meeting in which individuals feel negative about the group or its processes. An agenda can improve the quality of a meeting. The *agenda* is simply a list of the activities or tasks that need to be accomplished during a particular meeting. It may include what needs to be accomplished at the current meeting and also contain information about upcoming due dates or tasks. Organizing the agenda by specifying the amount of time devoted to each topic of discussion is another helpful way to ensure an effective meeting structure. *Time on task* is how much time the group will spend discussing a given topic. When writing the agenda, place items that require more time at the beginning of the agenda. By doing this, people in the group will feel productive as they move through the agenda items. It is best to tailor the agenda to fit the time allocated to the meeting. If the items that require more time are placed at the beginning of the agenda, and a meeting needs to end early, the important, necessary items have already been addressed. If you know the group will meet for only an hour, there is no need to place superfluous tasks on the agenda. Adjusting the agenda to fit the group members and goals is a process that takes refinement during the initial meetings. It is also helpful to get the agenda to the group before meetings. This way, group members are able to prepare thoughts and comments and time is not wasted trying to come up with answers or suggestions. Ultimately, when an agenda contains only the tasks to be addressed, it can help the group members feel as though they actually accomplish their tasks and ultimately can accomplish the group's purpose. This, in turn, could improve the overall quality and effectiveness during the meeting.

Demonstrating Respect for Others

Consider the following example:

> Your company has noticed that people seem indifferent about coming to work. No one seems overly excited to be there; people rarely come in on time and often are quick to leave. In addition, people do not interact while at work and the overall environment seems very isolated. As a result, your company has recently created a committee to address this issue. The committee was asked to create ways to boost or increase worker morale and propose solutions for improving relationships among workers. At the first meeting, however, the person who was asked to be in charge of the committee and serve as the leader is heard saying, "I hate working with others. Who cares about relationships with other people?"

If you heard this, how would you react? Would you want to continue working on a project with someone who doesn't seem interested? You're probably thinking that the person's language is quite counterproductive to what the group is trying to accomplish. Another tool for enhancing group meetings is demonstrating respect for others. This may be done by the type of language used. Most likely, you were told as a small child to "think before you speak" or "what you say to others matters." These old adages have some utility when working with others. Be sure to use inclusive language to reinforce the collective nature of the group. Terms such as "our project" and "we can accomplish this" help create a sense of cohesiveness.

Groupwork is difficult and you and the others in the group may want to take sides when determining solutions to problems. Nonjudgmental language and questions will demonstrate respect for others and enhance the group experience. Asking questions ensures that everyone is "on the same page." Using statements such as "What I think I hear you saying is …" is one example of paraphrasing what others have said to make sure that you have understood them correctly. It's important to note that paraphrasing doesn't necessarily mean that you agree with ideas or opinions. Rather, you are attempting to understand someone else's ideas. By doing so, you will make others in the group feel valued. Ask open-ended questions. **Open-ended questions** are those that cannot be answered with a one-word statement. They often start with who, what, why, or how. By using open-ended questions, others are encouraged to share and elaborate in discussing their ideas. When everyone is given a voice, all members feel valuable. If group members feel valued, they are more likely to be committed to accomplishing the group's goal.

In situations where confrontations occur, incorporate "I" statements to explain your perception. Statements such as "I feel frustrated when I feel like nobody is listening to my ideas" show personal ownership of the experience rather than the more accusatory, "You never listen to me."

Another way to demonstrate respect for the group is by arriving on time with all previously assigned tasks completed. If, at a previous meeting, you are given a task to complete, you should be able to report on the status of that task at the next meeting. During your update of the assigned task, your communication should stay focused and not drift into superfluous or unnecessary information.

Ultimately, group meetings can be quite productive. These simple and practical steps can ensure that a meeting achieves its goals and allows everyone an opportunity to express their ideas. By managing time and respecting others' boundaries and ideas, there is a greater chance of having a positive group experience.

There are many different approaches to leadership and leading a group. In fact, because of the different types of leaders, being an effective leader who guides group members to completing tasks can appear to be overwhelming. However, it is possible to tailor your leadership style to your particular group and task. This chapter provides tools and suggestions for determining an appropriate leadership style. These tools include considering the group's purpose, members, and potential obstacles. By doing so, you are likely to have a more positive leadership experience and a successful group. Ask yourself this series of questions:

- ► What is the group's purpose?
- ► With what type of individuals am I working?
- ► In what type of environment is the group working?
- ► What are the potential obstacles in the way of completing the task?
- ► Am I the best person for a leadership position?**

In asking and honestly answering these questions, you have begun to understand the group's dynamics and, as a result, will communicate more efficiently and effectively. Thus, it is important to think carefully about the important components to working in a particular group and tailor your communication accordingly. This will be beneficial in your personal, professional, and public lives. It is beneficial because all members of the group can have a clear understanding of what the tasks and challenges are, everyone can share insights about the group, and you, as the leader, can create messages that guide the group to successful completion of its tasks and goals.

While working with others can be daunting, there are simple strategies that can contribute to its overall effectiveness. It is important to keep in mind that there is no one right way to lead in a group. Oftentimes, you will experience individual differences and preferences for a certain leadership style over others. You must remember that these potential differences should not interfere with the group's overall functioning. If a problem arises, engaging in careful problem solving can efficiently minimize any difficulties. Ultimately, it is best to focus the group by using simple management solutions. With these ideas in mind, you and your group can successfully achieve the group's goals.**

ELEVATOR PITCHES

Every Communication Shark has had this experience in one way or another—or would like to. Some people call this the *one-legged interview* because it can happen at the water fountain, in the parking lot as you are walking into work, or in the elevator as you ride up to your stop with an executive. You know the scenario! For years you have been saying, "If I could just get two minutes with that guy, I would tell him . . .". In other words, the elevator pitch is your chance to provide a quick summary of your background and experience that could possibly help you get to the next level in your career. The *elevator pitch* is a very short speech that introduces yourself to someone in a compelling manner and can be delivered in the brief time it takes to ride an elevator to the next floor.

The elevator pitch is all about you and covers who you are, what you do, and what you want to do. Sharing your expertise and credibility with someone who has never met you isn't limited only to elevators. As mentioned above, you can use it at any number of events in which you have just a short time to share what you want others to know about your unique value and how the organization can benefit from having you on board. This activity requires you to think critically about your skills, knowledge, and experiences so the listener can relate your skill set to career paths in the organization.

I love assigning this in my Public Speaking class and also in the Human Communication course. In fact, the **purpose** for creating this type of speech is to give students the necessary tools and practice to have their own elevator pitch ready for job fairs, career expos, Facebook postings, or LinkedIn summaries. I also encourage students to use their pitch at networking events or when attending any type of function where someone might walk up and say, "Tell me about yourself."

Elevator Pitch Assignment Instructions:

Write a 2-minute elevator pitch. Smile and introduce yourself. Describe yourself, accomplishments, and goals to a potential employer. Share your skills. Mention your goals. Explain what you do or want to do and why you love it. Prepare and practice the pitch; however, it should sound unrehearsed.

The following elements are required:

1. **Introduction:** This will be a solid sentence of introduction
   A. Greeting, Name, job title, and a personal tagline
   B. Handshake
2. **Body:**
   A. Write a sentence discussing why you chose this line of work and how it fits in with your goals and values.
   B. List your top accomplishments. What have you achieved that you are proud of? Illustrate contributions you've made or the problems you've solved.
   C. List the ways people benefit from working with you. Include a brief story about a satisfied customer, team member, or supervisor.
   D. Write a sentence highlighting your strengths and experience. How do you bring value to an organization? What can you contribute?
   E. Write a sentence showing the interest(s) you have in the listener.
   F. Present a business card.
3. **Closing**
   A. Ask for an appropriate response to the pitch.
   B. Thank the listener and let him know you appreciate his time.
   C. Handshake

What is a tagline?
A *Personal Tagline is not* just your job title, but your main job and could answer one or all of the following questions: What do you do when you're doing your work? What's important about what you do? What change do you make for others? What do you do that's difficult to live without and worth paying for?

Here are Examples of Personal Taglines:

Job Title	Personal Tagline
App Developer	I write mobile apps that solve everyday problems.
Social Media Expert	I build Facebook pages to help companies engage with their customers.
Accountant	I help people create a path for comfort and wealth.
Customer Service	I change people from frustrated visitors to welcomed guests.
Cosmetologist	I show clients how to boost their confidence.
Sales Associate	I am a furniture sales associate with a track record to close sales.
Carpenter	I take drawings and measurements to create structures for people to use at home, work, and everywhere in between.
Health Care Provider	I keep people healthy so they can achieve their dreams.

ELEVATOR PITCH PEER REVIEW

Speaker's Name:_____   **Date:**_____

Reviewer's Name:_____

Area	Excellent 5	Good 4	Average 3	Fair 2	Poor 1	Missing 0
Introduction Sentence: • Greeting • Name • Job Position • Tagline • Handshake						
Body: • Covered what you want to do • Pitch was organized • Details were clear • Information focused • Business card presented						
Conclusion: • Restated name • Requested response to pitch • Shared appreciation for time • Handshake • Farewell						
Delivery: • Volume • Confidence and Enthusiasm • Appearance, Poise, Posture • Language Skills • Gestures						

Comments for the speaker:

PROFESSIONAL COMMUNICATION METHODS

Professional Presentations are covered in Unit 3 of this book, but it goes without saying that people who have **soft skills** know how to make professional presentations whether it is to a small group of board members or to an audience of hundreds. **Presentation skills** involve making sure that your message and content are designed with the audience in mind. Communication Sharks use the new SpeechShark app to craft and present speeches that leave their audiences engaged and informed. If you haven't started using the app yet, please be sure to visit our website at www.SpeechShark.com to see the features that can have you crafting speeches like a professional in no time at all!

Professional Communication Methods involve speaking and writing. These may be delivered in person or electronically. Regardless of whether it is communication delivered through various modalities, we need to keep in mind that all avenues of delivering content are quite different—and similar. This statement may seem confusing, but I'll explain.

In most instances, we use less formal and more conversational language styles with **oral communication**. This is true for speeches presented on a stage (in person) or through a YouTube video (electronically). Most of you will agree that your favorite speech will appear to be extemporaneous, unrehearsed, and spontaneous even though you can tell the speaker spent a great deal of time organizing the speech and artfully inserting data, research, or personal stories to support points. Oral communication often includes more details and repetition of points. In order to allow time for the audience to comprehend and retain information, the speaker will use shorter sentences, more contractions, and strategically placed pauses. Research is introduced by adding the author's name, the title of the work, when it was published, and who published the research. Then, you will hear the speaker insert the phrase, "and I quote" prior to including the information and ending with "end quote" to let you know the directly quoted information was complete.

Quite the contrary as we use more formal and less conversational language styles with **written communication**. If we are reading a passage and encounter difficult or unfamiliar content, we can always re-read the paragraph and take time to look up words to form a clearer understanding. We have time to figure out the unfamiliar content or determine the meaning of the content presented. A good book often challenges us by including words, experiences, and meanings that we have not previously explored. In either case, we need to remember that our purpose in producing professional communication is to use language that is clear, concrete, and specific.

Language, whether delivered orally or in writing, needs to be chosen with the listener or reader in mind. Using appropriate and ethical language skills are inherent with professional communication skills. Consider the audience and this will help you to know whether you should use familiar language or technical language. *Familiar language* involves using words that are familiar with the audience. Simple and direct language equates to a message easily understood and comprehended. *Technical language* should be reserved for a specialized audience who will understand the concepts you are sharing. Using technical terms for a general audience should always include an explanation or you risk excluding those who lack technical expertise in the content.

Last week, one of my students gave a speech about the use of reagents. As a communication major, the term *reagent* was not part of my normal vocabulary. Thankfully, this Chemistry student did an excellent job defining reagents in the introduction step prior to covering three main points. Because of this simple and clear definition, we were all able to follow the meaning of his speech and learned something we did not previously know.

Short and clear sentences are easier for listeners or readers to follow. *Defining modifiers* provide new and needed information and will include terms such as *innovative, brilliant,* or *antiquated*. This type of modifier is more important to communication than *commenting modifiers* which uses the words *very, most,* or *definitely* and adds little to the meaning that needs to be communicated.

Using *abbreviations* and *acronyms* as substitutions for longer words can also be a challenge in communication. It seems like the world of education revolves around acronyms. There are several members of our family who are instructors. Last Thanksgiving while several of us were having dinner and visiting, the conversation moved toward our work. We were throwing around acronyms like confetti and I quickly realized my soon to be son-in-law had no idea of what we were talking about. We went from a turkey dinner to alphabet soup in a matter of minutes. Halie was talking about IEPs for students with an ABA and Vina suggested that Halie take a look at AT that was recommended by the BOE. In this midst of this, I was lamenting over the LOs for my GE division that were not submitted by the due date. Of course, we never fully discussed the QEP review responsible for slowing things down for completion of the LOs. Oh my! Do you see what I mean? You don't have to be a Communication Shark to realize how the use of abbreviations and acronyms can make things simpler for the speaker, but more complicated for listeners who may have a challenge understanding the content. It begins to feel like you are trying to communicate with people who speak another language with which you are not familiar!

Simple and precise words and sentences result in more effective communication. Instead of using abstract language for professional communication, use concrete language. *Concrete language* will help the listener or the reader to receive clear and detailed content, whereas *abstract language* is often vague and open to misinterpretations. Precise wording will help communicate meaning accurately. Avoid using clichés that are overused because they don't add color or interest to communication.

Repetition of words is effective when delivering communication that you want your audience to remember and involves repeating, word-for-word, key elements of the message. *Restatements* involve rephrasing in a different way the key elements of the message. Public Speaking involves quite a bit of repetition and restatements. For example, in the introduction step, you will include a thesis to preview the main points you plan to cover in the body of the speech. Then you will restate each point as you transition to it and summarize the point as you conclude. This continues throughout the body, but in the conclusion what do you do? You are right! You will restate and summarize each of the main points again. This is a strategy we use to help the audience remember and retain the points covered.

Professional communication involves language use that is active and interesting. *Action language* will hold the interest and command the attention of the listener or reader. This dynamic strategy produces a livelier version of a speech or written document. Audiences and readers respond positively to language that gives a realistic and specific description of people, events, or concepts. Try to use *sensory language* that evokes one of our five senses: seeing, hearing, feeling, tasting, or smelling. Using the senses will help paint a picture the audience can visualize and internalize.

Language is a powerful force used to shape our knowledge, understanding, perceptions, and belief. *Gender-inclusive language* should be included in professional communications since our audiences are made of men and women. Throughout this book, you may have noticed the interchanging of terms between he and she. This is done because we are not in a one-gender society. Most audiences, whether present in a speech or as a reader of the written word, will expect the use of gender-inclusive or gender-neutral language. In choosing language, consider the audience's level of linguistic sophistication and their expectations. Is the occasion formal or casual? What is the nature of the event? What is the background of the audience's culture? Are there other expectations that might determine the type language you choose? A wise professional communicator will carefully consider audience expectations and make adjustments to design communication for the benefit and edification of the audience.

Rhetorical questions, metaphors, personification, alliteration, and oxymora are considered *figures of speech* which can heighten the color used in language making a concept clearer and more meaningful.

Rhetorical Questions are used quite often in professional communication as we ask questions but are not actually expecting an answer. Instead, this form of questioning is used as a way to pique the interest of the audience member or reader. Many of you might have used a rhetorical question as the attention step of a speech this semester. Caution should be used with this however, since poor timing or misuse of wording can thwart the best of intentions. This figure of speech is best used when you ask the question, allow a pause for the audience to consider the question, and then follow it with a solid statement. When we do this, we allow our listeners to think and to engage with the response. Here is an example: "What does poverty look like on our college campus?" After pausing for the audience to contemplate the question, follow with, "A student struggles to pay college tuition, purchase books and supplies, and provide transportation to the campus only to realize there isn't enough money left at the end of the month to cover food expenses."

Metaphors compare something that often has a dissimilar meaning. For example, if you are describing a student on campus who is always bright and positive, you might say she is like the sun that brightens your day.

Personification is used when we describe an inanimate form or thing as if it were human in order to enhance its emotional appeal. An example of this would be when students are complaining about accessing a test using the college's Learning Management System and will say, "BlackBoard wouldn't let me take the test." When actually, it is most likely user error or an Internet problem that is keeping the student from taking the test. After all, a learning management system, like BlackBoard cannot intentionally keep someone from taking a test.

Alliteration is a repetitive pattern of sounds used in a sequence of words to reinforce an idea. This happens if we use a common letter to begin the word for each point. An example of this would be if the three points for a speech are listed as: Plan, Prepare, and Persevere. The use of "P" for the beginning of each point is a way to reinforce key ideas and to make the points easier for the audience to remember after the speech is over. I'm sure you can remember seeing me use those three main points in this book.

Oxymoron patterns are used as we include expressions in combination with terms that are contradictory. Professional communicators use this to emphasize a contrast between two things or to offer a humorous twist of events. We see this often as we discuss *virtual reality* shows or describe the *organized chaos* found in our book bags.

As this chapter concludes and you have been able to see the many facets which surround the term *professional communication*, it is my desire that you have a clearer understanding of this industry expectation. Revisit this chapter often to make sure you have the skills employers desire. Remember, our industry leaders want Communication Sharks in the tank!

KEY TERMS

- ▶ Abbreviations
- ▶ Abstract Language
- ▶ Acronyms
- ▶ Action Language
- ▶ Agenda
- ▶ Alliteration
- ▶ Commenting Modifiers
- ▶ Concrete Language
- ▶ Defining Modifiers
- ▶ Elevator Pitch
- ▶ Emotional Closeness
- ▶ Ethics
- ▶ Familiar Language
- ▶ Figure of Speech

- ▶ Gender-Inclusive Language
- ▶ Metaphors
- ▶ One-Legged Interview
- ▶ Open-Ended Questions
- ▶ Oxymoron
- ▶ Personification
- ▶ Relational Satisfaction
- ▶ Repetition
- ▶ Restatements
- ▶ Rhetorical Questions
- ▶ Sensory Language
- ▶ Skill
- ▶ Technical Language
- ▶ Time on Task

Chapter Thirteen

Public Communication

© ImageFlow/Shutterstock.com

PUBLIC COMMUNICATION

To reflect the identification of a public presentation made in front of an audience, public communication was formed to showcase the balance of a speaker delivering remarks and responding to feedback. In the chapters describing public speaking, we covered the most effective ways to communicate, through careful preparation and delivery of information.

Public communication refers to *any* situation in which individuals and groups communicate a message in a public arena to an intended audience. Instead of treating the audience as a collection of separate people, the speaker(s) address the audience as a body brought together by a common interest or event. The purpose of the communication is to create a sense of unity and community in a large, diverse group of people. This could happen in a town hall meeting, a PTA meeting at your child's school, through public speaking events, online articles, blogs, brochures, or newspaper editorials. You might also experience public communication as you drive down an interstate and see large billboard advertisements along the way. It doesn't stop there! Facebook, Twitter, YouTube, Instagram, and many other social media platforms are examples of public communication.

The common denominator with public communication involves communicating to large audiences comprised of various types and cultures of people. Technology delivers audiences which are larger and more complex. Not to be confused with mass communication, public communication is characteristically formal, structured, and purpose-driven. For example, when enticing people to visit your restaurant, a billboard on a busy highway will get attention and communicate the type food you serve along with driving directions and hours of operation. This type of communication is less reciprocal than other modalities because the audience has limited opportunities for providing immediate feedback.

For Public Communication, the audience becomes the receiver of the message. This means their attention is focused on the source. For example, the attention would be focused on the speaker, billboard, brochure, or newspaper article. Feedback is restricted since the message communicated is being distributed to such a large audience.

When public communication takes the form of a public speaking event and the speaker is delivering a message to a crowd of a thousand audience members, the positive feedback could take on the appearance as smiles, head nods, or positive body posture. Negative feedback could be observed as audience members talk to neighbors, check their phones, or if they leave the auditorium. Question and Answer sessions following a large public address would give audience members the opportunity to question points or to offer verbal feedback.

The interesting thing about public communication is that we all have our own perception and interpretation of communication that we may hear or see. While we might all hear the same message delivered at the same time, we do not share identical experiences and that determines the interpretation we may take away from the message received.

Advances in communication technology are now expanding opportunities for audience participation through online comments, blogs, listener rating systems, and audience response systems. As an instructor, I use programs such as Padlet and KaHoot to incorporate students' smartphones and encourage audience participation. YouTube and Vimeo allow me to share messages delivered through video. Skype and Collaborate allow me to actually see my online students in a virtual classroom so that I can explain concepts verbally rather than in writing. Technology allows me to reach a wider audience, but in doing this, it becomes my responsibility to adapt the message to the various forms of technology and to also follow best practices with sharing information through this manner.

It is the public's role in the communication process that dictates public communication. People who tend to study public communication explore how individuals within a particular society contribute to social discourse and how they interact with this discourse. Those closest to public communication are often journalists or news commentators, but more often you will see educators taking up this mantel in order to reach more students.

© WAYHOME/Shutterstock.com

COMMUNICATION TRADITIONS AND TECHNOLOGY

As covered in Chapter One of this book, humans first began with an *oral tradition* of communicating. This culture involved verbally transmitting information through storytelling using the spoken word. Stories were told repeatedly until the *written tradition* evolved. It was during this time that hieroglyphics and later the alphabet progressed to the point where stories and words took shape in the form of a *print tradition*. With the emergence of a printed text, we ushered in the technology to develop a printing press which inked a surface resulting in a printed medium. It was at this point that we had the first mass production of books, newspapers, newsletters, magazines, and all manner of printed materials.

The *Electronic Tradition*, known as the First Media Age, included media which required us to use electronics to access the content through recordings, radio, telegraph, and television. With the emergence of the Internet, we moved to the *New Media Tradition*, known as the Second Media Age. It is during this stage of public communication that we have been able to incorporate oral, written, print, and electronic communication. Since all existing media fits into one or all of these categories, this is the age through which we now identify. Laptop computers, iPads, tablets, smartphones, smart watches, and everything in between refers to the *Digital Tradition* that we enjoy using on a daily basis. There are infinite possibilities of the way we can use this interactive media to produce unique, customized communication for any given audience.

As a young girl, I would visit my mailbox anxiously looking for a letter from a friend or relative. Now, I simply access my various e-mail accounts—we all have more than one—and can view communications from any number of people who might be contacting me for various reasons. It becomes easier and easier to think of our computers or our phones as an extension of ourselves because we use them interchangeably to communicate.

Do you remember the first time you began a Facebook (FB) page? How often do you check FB or use it to send messages (communication) to your family and friends? Do you find yourself sending a message on FB when you lose your phone?

Is it easier, more convenient, or more comfortable to text someone using your phone rather than calling them or making time to go see them? My daughter recently received over 200 birthday wishes. They weren't cards delivered to a physical mailbox at our house. Instead, they were messages on Facebook, LinkedIn, Twitter, or texts sent directly to her phone. Our way of public communication has certainly evolved through the years. In the past, 200 birthday wishes would have been considered **personal communication**; however, when it is sent out through a large audience it becomes **public communication.**

During a meeting this week with a dual enrolled student and his parent, the fifteen-year-old college student shared that he had already looked me up through LinkedIn and through the RateMyProfessor Web site.

In the past, students would use personal communication to ask friends which instructor was best. Now, they use public communication to decide which instructor to choose. Times are changing!

This New Media Tradition for which we are involved is more interactive and has resulted in our new classification as the *Communication Age*. Interactivity is the term used as we discuss communication at a distance through new media and involves sending and receiving communication in real time as it happens. Messages sent only two seconds ago are received immediately and can also be responded to in a matter of seconds.

If you are reading a newspaper article and decide that you would like to comment on the subject or the content covered, you can simply post a comment on the online version of the article for the editor and everyone else to see. Do you have a better understanding of how our communication has evolved to the public communication arena?

While new media is always changing and evolving, public communicators still have a responsibility to their audience. Ethical postings are more important now than ever. As an employer, I always look through a candidate's Facebook or LinkedIn page prior to requesting to meet them for an interview. Often, I've found things posted that will either encourage me to hire the candidate or keep looking. These forms of public self-presentation include interactions and communication styles that have shifted from face-to-face communication to computer-mediated communication. Do you know how proficient you are?

COMPUTER-MEDIATED COMMUNICATION

Computer-mediated communication is human communication through a massive range of technologies that include Facebook, LinkedIn, Tumblr, Twitter, Instagram, Snapchat, and Blogs. With more communication avenues come more responsibility.

Remember what you post or your history of viewing sites can be seen by any number of people. Some may even be a prospective employer. Being proficient and responsible with public communication is a valued and envied skill. Professionals who master ethical public communication usually find great success in their personal, professional, and public lives.

Complete the **Computer-Mediated Communication Competence Worksheet** to determine just how competent you are and note areas where improvement is needed. Ask a friend to read through your answers and indicate agreement or lack thereof.

COMPUTER-MEDIATED COMMUNICATION COMPETENCE

Name:_____ **Date:** _____

Peer Review:_____

Competency	Often	Sometimes	Never or N/A	Peer Agreement
I avoid saying things that are rude or offensive.				
I express my feelings without thought of others.				
I enjoy communicating using computer media.				
I use lots of emojis when communicating.				
I am competent using computer media.				
I post responses without checking accuracy.				
I am pleased with my computer media responses.				
I post weekly using computer media.				
I am skillful with posting interactions to others.				
I communicate with Gifs.				
I am competent using computer media.				
I post personal, religious, political, and personal views.				
I participate in heated computer media discussions.				
I am selective with whom I "friend" and communicate.				

Self-observations that need improvement:

Peer-observation that contradict posted self-observation:

KEY TERMS

- Communication Age
- Computer-Mediated Communication
- Digital Tradition
- Electronic Tradition of Communication
- New Media Tradition

- Oral Tradition of Communication
- Print Tradition of Communication
- Public Communication
- Written Tradition of Communication

Chapter Fourteen

Organizational Communication

© snapgalleria/Shutterstock.com

In this chapter:

Organizational Communication is a process through which members of an organization act together to create, sustain, and manage meanings. This type of communication is strategic in nature and has advantages above and beyond conducting business and preparing for career advancement. Whether you know it or not, we find that the same pressures and constraints that affect large corporations can also be present in the more personal and private areas of our lives. Being able to recognize, diagnose, and solve communication-related problems can help us to find success in the most advanced or simplistic organizations. Fortune 500 companies rely on effective organizational communication, but we also use these same skills in our work groups, classrooms, clubs, churches, and family units.

We communicate with people within our work groups because we like them, or our jobs require us to. It's nice when we also like the people with whom we work. Some of my best friends have been made through working relationships. As an instructor at a college level, I have had the pleasure through the years of teaching adults who have later become employees at the same college. We had the relationship of teacher/student at one time, but now we are peer employees and friends. As a matter of fact, one of my students attended a study and travel abroad program to Costa Rica with me. We enjoyed the trip and we have happy memories of zip lining through the tropical forests with monkeys and iguanas participating in our play. After the student graduated, she continued her education and has been working full-time for our college in institutional advancement and now as part of our college's internship placement program. Communicating with others on a professional level can often lead to a friendship or at the very least an appreciation of the gifts and talents that others can bring to the work environment.

© G-Stock Studio/Shutterstock.com

Work relationships are interpersonal relationships, but they are different from relationships with friends and family. Just as we create relationships through conversation, we also create organizations through conversation. It is more than simply a transfer of knowledge, but a multidimensional process through which organizing takes place, thus it becomes organizational communication. Perhaps the following pages will help you to better understand this concept.

**ORGANIZATIONAL COMMUNICATION DEFINED

Chances are that you have decided to pursue a college degree as the next step in your journey toward your professional career. While classes required in your major field of study typically focus on content specific to your chosen profession, the knowledge and skills directly related to communication effectiveness with your superiors, coworkers, and clients will be valuable in virtually any career. For example, if you've completed an accounting or biology class it is unlikely that much attention was devoted to the communication expectations in careers focusing on these fields. Once you complete your academic studies and pursue your professional career, knowledge about how to effectively interact with your supervisor, your colleagues, and your clients will be important in your daily workplace interactions.

Organizational communication is a subfield of human communication that focuses on the messages exchanged between members of an organization. Richmond and McCroskey (2009) define organizational communication as "the process by which individuals stimulate meaning in the minds of other individuals by means of verbal or nonverbal messages in the context of a formal organization" (p. 20).

Scholars in the field continue to explore issues encountered in organizations. Kassing (1997) has studied *organizational dissent* to better understand how employees express dissatisfaction with their supervisors or their jobs. Kassing helped organizational members recognize "how" members communicate their dissatisfaction and with "whom" they share these messages of discontent as they express their frustration. He identified three primary strategies that employees use to express their dissatisfaction. *Upward dissent* is one tactic in which employees directly communicate their frustrations with their supervisors. If you have a good relationship with your boss, you may be more comfortable going to him or her directly and confronting situations that frustrate you as opposed to avoiding or ignoring them. When employees vent their dissatisfaction to their coworkers, *lateral dissent* occurs. Caution and trust need to be given careful consideration when expressing dissent to coworkers. Information that you think is confidential may end up shared with others. If you vent frustration to a coworker, what could happen if he or she is interested in a job opportunity that you are also interested in pursuing? It is possible that the coworker could strategically disclose the things you shared in order to gain an advantage in the interview process. Since expressing one's dissatisfaction in the workplace can be risky at times, some members choose the communication strategy of *displaced dissent*. Displaced dissent occurs when frustrations are shared with nonworkplace friends and family members. While this approach may seem the safest of the three, it does little to help resolve the issue at hand. Why is research on employee dissent relevant? The answer is quite simple: It can help organizational leaders, human resources managers, and even employees recognize when dissatisfaction is being communicated and enable them to address the issue directly, thereby maximizing organizational efficiency. Otherwise, venting about issues as opposed to seeking solutions may waste too much time.

Another area that has generated significant attention in organizational communication is research that focuses on power and how it is communicated in the workplace. French and Raven (1968) initially conceptualized five core power bases that impact our professional interactions. Understanding how organizational members influence one another to accomplish goals is essential to one's professional success. We introduced the concept of French and Raven's five power bases. Figure 14.1 on the following page provides a review of these concepts. In our professional lives, we need to be aware of the influence of these power bases on our interactions with our supervisors and our colleagues. Understanding why we give power to others is an important step to becoming more effective in our professional and personal interactions in the workplace.

Other scholars have built on the work of French and Raven and explored how communication in the workplace influences employee motivation (e.g., Adams, Schlueter, & Barge, 1988) and how organizational leaders use power and strategies to gain employee liking and support to increase employee satisfaction (Richmond, McCroskey, & Davis, 1986). Studies like these continue to generate new information to help organizations understand how perceived power is communicated and the resulting impact on employee motivation and satisfaction.

In the 21st century, new issues in the work context have expanded the scope of relationships studied in organizations. If you work full time, chances are that you will spend nearly one-third of your waking hours with your coworkers. Because we spend so much time with our colleagues at work, it should come as no surprise that many friendships and romantic relationships are formed here. Current studies of organizational communication focus on how we negotiate the balance between these personal and professional relationships. Sias and her colleagues explored workplace friendships and our communication with coworkers. Most recently, Sias, Pedersen, Gallagher, and Kopaneva (2012) found that as more people telecommute or work

FIGURE 14.1

French and Raven's (1968) five bases of power.

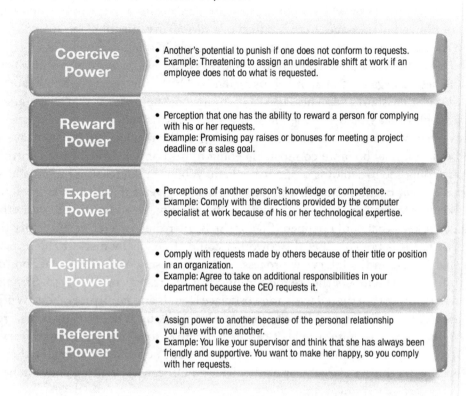

from home, the value or importance placed on being physically close to our friends at work decreases since we can rely on texting, cell phones, and email to stay connected even when we're not in the office.

A 2013 study by the Society for Human Resource Management found that 24 percent of employees report that they have had a romantic relationship with a coworker. Horan and Chory (2009) explored perceptions of coworkers as they studied the messages communicated by workplace romances. They found that coworkers feel less comfortable sharing information with colleagues who are involved in a romantic relationship with a supervi-

sor. When a coworker is dating someone of higher status in the organization, friends at work are less likely to trust him or her and are more likely to manipulate information. They may even avoid disclosing or sharing information for fear the coworker will "tell the boss."

Other studies have addressed some of the negative communication that interferes with productivity in the workplace. Cowan's (2011) research on workplace bullying has helped managers and employees better understand how verbal and nonverbal messages can cause distress in the workplace and her studies have helped human resources managers effectively deal with these issues. From superior–subordinate relationships to coworker or peer relationships, knowing how to communicate effectively may ultimately contribute to your success in your professional endeavors. The ability to interact with our clients or customers, to work effectively with our colleagues, and to exchange necessary information with our supervisors in order to accomplish the organization's goals and objectives is essential to our career success.

FAMILY COMMUNICATION

Consider the meanings that you attribute to family rituals. How have your family's customs for celebrating holidays and birthdays influenced your expectations for these rituals? Can you recall the last time you became discouraged when attempting to communicate with a family member? Have you ever become frustrated by sibling rivalry and competition? It's ironic how, when interacting with parents and siblings, we know one another's communication patterns so well that we can often complete one another's sentences, yet at other times it seems as if we struggle to be understood. Family communication is an area in which every student has a lifetime of experience. However, that does not mean that we are always successful in our interactions. Siblings can laugh together and share secrets one minute, and engage in bitter conflict the next. Parents can become frustrated if their teen is embarrassed when they post a "Happy Birthday" message on their Facebook page. Why is it sometimes so difficult to communicate effectively with those whom we love and know the best? These are just some of the questions that family communication scholars address in their research.

By examining patterns of communication in our family of origin, we may gain valuable insight into why we communicate the way we do. Many of the theories we use to explain and describe communication in interpersonal relationships can be directly applied to understanding our interactions with family members. Now consider the ways in which the same dialectical tensions function in the context of family relationships. Parents and children often identify with the dialectical tension of autonomy and connectedness. From a young age, children are taught to be independent. Parents begin encouraging toddlers to dress and feed themselves. As they grow older, they gradually take on additional responsibilities such as completing homework and chores. Children are expected to become more self-sufficient, thus fulfilling the desire to teach them autonomy and independence. As they approach the teenage years, however, teenagers start to identify more closely with their friends, start driving, and rely less on their family relationships. Parents' desire for connectedness may result in challenging conversations, particularly when social media is involved.

Family communication can be defined as the process of creating and sharing meaning through the exchange of verbal and nonverbal messages with those whom we consider to be family. A key element in this definition is your perception of *who* you consider to be a part of your family and *how* you define what it means to be a family. Increasing diversity in family composition has been a topic that communication researchers have turned their attention to in recent studies. Stereotypical perceptions of what it means to be a "family" have changed since the days of the traditional nuclear family portrayed by the Cleavers from *Leave It to Beaver* or Mike and Carol's blended family from *The Brady Bunch*. Various family types, such as single-parent families, foster care families, gay and lesbian families, sibling families, and interracial families, have redirected the focus beyond the traditional concepts of what it means to be a family. In addition, many people often describe close friends not related by blood or legal ties to be "like family" and form relationships that are closer than those formed with biological relatives. Television shows such as *Friends*, *The Big Bang Theory*, and *How I Met Your Mother* depict the closeness of these voluntary relationships in which friendships function in much the same way that family relationships do. Family communication scholars examine the dynamics of family relationships.

WHAT HAPPENS WHEN PARENTS AND CHILDREN COMMUNICATE VIA SOCIAL MEDIA?

Is it considered "uncool" to add mom or dad as a Facebook friend? Are parents who follow their children's Tweets spying on them? Family communication via social media might be more beneficial than you think. A 2013 study at Brigham Young University found that children and parents who connect with one another via Facebook, Twitter, and other social media sites report feeling closer in their relationships. Data collected from 491 families found that teens who "friend" their parents on Facebook or "follow" them on Twitter were less likely to experience depression or to engage in aggressive or delinquent behavior. Connecting online appears to increase feelings of connectedness in real life.

Source: Coyne, Padilla-Walker, Day, Harper, and Stockdale (2014).

One may gain valuable insight into the way their preferences for communicating evolved by examining the parenting styles experienced in families. Scholars have identified four different parenting styles. While the original research on parenting styles focused on how communication is used in the disciplining of children, later studies have applied these styles to understand the parent–child relationship better. Baumrind identified the first three categories of parenting styles in 1967, and a fourth style was added later.

Authoritarian parents adopt the philosophy that children should be "seen and not heard." It is expected that children will simply adhere to rules without asking questions. "Because I am the parent and I said so!" is a typical response to a child's inquiry or request for explanations. Very little responsiveness or clarification is provided, with the parent clearly in high control. At the opposite end of the spectrum are *permissive parents*. These parents are best described as being extremely supportive and nurturing to ensure that their child is happy and satisfied while exerting very little control or discipline. Children of permissive parents often report that there are few or no rules in the family, and the parents are often more focused on being the child's best friend than being an authority figure. *Authoritative parents* take a more democratic approach in their communication with their children. High levels of control accompany high levels of supportiveness. Parents make it a priority to listen to children, to encourage them to ask questions, and to offer explanations as to why rules are being enforced. Maccoby (1992) found that children of authoritative parents indicated that they were happier and ultimately more successful. As more dual-career families evolved, it was discovered that the demands of work sometimes interfered with one's ability to take an active role in parenting. In addition, some single parents struggle to provide for the basic needs of their children and often work multiple jobs while depending on siblings or other family members for assistance. As a result, a fourth parenting style was added to account for families in which parents offer little support or nurturing in their communication with their children and enforce little or no control in discipline. *Uninvolved parents* rarely engage in communication with their children. While these parents often make sure the child's basic needs are met, they devote little to no effort communicating or spending time together. An example of this may be seen in a family where

© Andresr/Shutterstock.com

a nanny is primarily responsible for disciplining or nurturing children due to a parent's busy work schedule. As a result of the low level of involvement, children may experience feelings of frustration and exhibit low levels of self-esteem and self-control.

Over the past 30 years, a growing number of women have pursued full-time careers to contribute to the family income. Taking on new roles in the workplace while caring for children and maintaining a household have resulted in additional stress. Television shows and movies portray the dilemmas faced by both working mothers and fathers who depend on effective communication with one another to coordinate childcare and family responsibilities.

Can you recall messages that your parents have shared with you regarding how they managed to balance work and family demands? A 2006 survey of 312 college students asked them to recall messages that their parents shared with them regarding how to effectively balance work and family life (Medved, Brogan, McClanahan, Morris, & Shepherd, 2006). The goal of these **balance messages** is to emphasize the importance of managing the demands associated with having both a career and a family. Students recalled four types of balance messages that their parents directly or indirectly shared with them as they offered insight into effectively managing a career and a family. **Work choice messages** discuss the various career options that enable parents to pursue a career while enjoying their children. Max's mother is an elementary school teacher, and as he contemplates what he should major in at college, she shares, "You've always been so good at math and you enjoy working with children, so you should think about majoring in education. Teaching is a great career because your schedule will be similar to your children's. You will be able to coach their sports teams and spend your summers and holidays with them." When parents emphasize the importance of prioritizing and organizing the personal versus the professional aspects of one's life, **life-planning messages** are being shared. Eliza's father encouraged her first to complete her medical internship and residency before adding children to her family. He pointed out that by doing so, she would be established in her career and later would be better able to devote attention to her children. **Combining messages** emphasize that both work and family can be enjoyed at the same time. Parents make comments such as "Don't let people tell you that you have to choose between a career and a family. You can have both! It may be stressful at times, but you'll figure it out." **Prioritizing messages** focus on the importance of placing family first and work second. When her daughter, a successful pharmaceutical sales representative, struggled with frequent traveling during the week, Jane advised her to "Consider your children. After all, they grow up so quickly. Career opportunities in the medical sales field will continue to grow. You should ask your boss if you can take some assignments closer to home while the children are young." By sharing this message, Jane emphasized the importance of placing family first while still maintaining a career.

In response to the changing composition of families in the 21st century, scholars are also attempting to help families effectively communicate about a number of issues that present new challenges. Today, parents not only need to be aware of the television shows that their children watch and have conversations with them about their viewing, but they also need to have discussions with their children about Internet safety and portrayal of the self on sites such as Facebook, Snapchat, and Instagram. In addition, subjects such as drugs and alcohol abuse, safe sex, school violence, and bullying require parents to talk with their children and reassure them about their safety. Researchers have examined a variety of contemporary issues facing families, ranging from how couples communicate with friends and family members about infertility issues (Bute & Vik, 2010) to how military wives choose to disclose and discuss stressful issues with their husbands who are deployed overseas (Joseph & Afifi, 2010; see box on following page).

Studies in family communication not only provide us with an opportunity to explore and explain our family's style of interaction, but they may also help us better understand our own communication preferences.

HEALTH COMMUNICATION

Recall your last visit to your primary care doctor. Did you feel comfortable sharing your health concerns? Did your doctor exhibit nonverbal indicators of listening as you explained your symptoms? Did you ask follow-up questions as your doctor provided instructions for enhancing your health? If your doctor prescribed medication or explained a treatment option, did you understand the information being shared? If you answered "no" to any of these questions, you are not alone. Many patients indicate that they are afraid to ask questions or share concerns when visiting their physician. The *Journal of the American Medical Association* refers to this fear as "white coat silence," and it often results from perceived barriers in interactions between physicians and patients. Such obstacles may include the status differential or doctor's authority, not wanting to be perceived as a "difficult" patient, and the perception of a doctor's time as being very limited. Thus, patients feel rushed during a visit.

The focus on health communication as an area of study gained momentum in the mid-1970s (Rogers, 1996) and the interest and demand in the field continues to grow. Communication scholars examine a variety of health-related topics including patient–doctor interactions, social support and caregiving, and health campaigns and initiatives. In 2013, the World Health Organization shared new data that indicates the average lifespan of humans has increased from 64 years in 1990 to 70 years in 2011. Advances in medical care options have contributed to this extended lifespan. With the

© Alexander Raths/Shutterstock.com

aging population, children are often involved in communication about healthcare issues for elderly parents. Now more than ever, individuals and doctors realize the important role that communication plays in promoting and providing quality healthcare. This focus on health spans a variety of communication contexts as we exchange messages about health-related issues. From political advocacy for health issues, such as legalization of medical marijuana and one's right to make decisions about his or her own health, to studying effective communication across the healthcare team of doctors, nurses, pharmacists, and insurance providers, the impact of messages and achieving shared meaning is undeniable. Watch one episode of *Grey's Anatomy* and you will come to realize the value of effective communication among the healthcare team that provides patient care.

It is estimated that U.S. citizens spent more than $2.3 trillion in 2008, or an average of $7,680 per person, focusing on health-related visits and resources (CBS News, 2010). While that estimate may seem high, consider the ways in which you focus on ensuring your own health. Visits to dentists and physicians, purchase of medications and vitamins, eating healthy and working out—these costs add up quickly. Patients no longer rely solely on their healthcare provider for information about diagnosis and treatment of ailments. Online sites, such as WebMD, and support forums for topics ranging from diabetes management to bereavement to what to expect during pregnancy provide a wealth of information that often leads to self-diagnosis.

Earlier we discussed the anxiety that patients encounter during medical visits. Recall our earlier discussions of communication apprehension. While these chapters focused primarily on apprehension in the public-speaking context, communication scholars have found that our apprehension also impacts our desire to share information in the health context. Communication apprehension is a potential barrier to effective communication between healthcare providers and their patients, and the lack of sharing information may result in additional problems. Consider the patient that is afraid to disclose that he has been experiencing severe indigestion because he is afraid that his doctor will require him to undergo tests for heart issues. Perhaps an individual fails to disclose her recent dental surgery with her personal trainer at the gym because she perceives that it is "not that big of a deal." This reluctance to share information can interfere with effective diagnosis and medical advice. What are some of the possible behaviors of patients who have a high level of communication apprehension? They may simply listen to the doctor's orders without asking questions, refrain from seeking second opinions because of their anxiety over further communication with new doctors, or even avoid visiting and communicating with healthcare providers altogether (Booth-Butterfield, Chory, & Benynon, 1997). It should come as no surprise that patients who have a high level of communication apprehension report lower levels of satisfaction with both their healthcare provider and their treatment (Richmond, Smith, Heisel, & McCroskey, 2001). Health communication scholars continue to examine the impact of this apprehension and to recommend strategies to encourage effective patient–physician interactions.

Another area that has gained the attention of researchers is how stress influences our interactions with others. Health-related issues, such as the diagnosis of a terminal disease or decisions regarding healthcare options, often produce stress and understanding how people communicate while coping with these situations may enable us to provide support. Three types of *coping strategies* identified by Kohn (1996) may assist healthcare providers and caregivers in recognizing the verbal and nonverbal signs of stress. **Emotional-focused coping** is exhibited when individuals openly express their frustrations, are sensitive to messages from others, or are very emotional when faced with stressful situations. Consider the different coping styles portrayed in the following scenario. Alonzo and Kourtney's son was diagnosed with leukemia at the age of 5. Each parent reacted to this news in very distinct ways. Kourtney exhibited signs of emotional-focused coping when they first heard the news. She spent hours blaming herself as she cried to her sister and her friends. Alonzo's reaction to the news was very different. He began actively researching the

Internet to educate himself about the disease, and he coordinated a team of coworkers and friends to participate in the Light the Night Walk to raise funds for leukemia research. Alonzo used **problem-focused coping** strategies to gain information and research opportunities to assist the family in adjusting to the stressful news. Alonso's parents chose to use **avoidance-focused coping** in response to the news of their grandson's illness. They mentally and physically disengaged in situations where their grandson's health issues were discussed. Often they would quickly change the subject or leave the room to refrain from talking about his illness. Increasing our awareness of how people differ in their responses to stressful situations can shed insight into how to discuss these difficult topics and assist them in the coping process.

As college students, you encounter a variety of situations in which you act as both a source and receiver of health-related messages. For example, you may find yourself in situations where you're required to talk to a friend or roommate about alcohol use. Lederman and her colleagues (2007) developed the LTAI (Let's Talk About It) simulation to encourage students to consider the types of messages that should be communicated about decisions related to drinking. In studies where the LTAI was used, college students reported that they would use a variety of communication strategies to help protect a friend who was intoxicated. These strategies ranged from "tricking" the friend to avoid potentially embarrassing or dangerous situations (e.g., telling them that they were leaving a party and going to someplace more fun) to communicating for their friend when it became evident that they were too impaired to speak for themselves (e.g., informing others that the friend was intoxicated and unable to make good decisions).

Chances are that, after college graduation, you will continue to encounter a variety of health-related messages. Organizations promote health awareness among their employees in an effort to decrease insurance claims, and the media constantly bombards us with messages about the latest diet, vitamin supplements, or exercise phenomenon that is guaranteed to give us the results we desire. The ability to process messages about health-related issues that are sometimes the subject of debate will better prepare you to engage in

---

WHEN SHOULD YOU "FIRE" YOUR DOCTOR?

A recent *Wall Street Journal* article encourages patients to consider the important role that physician–patient communication plays in their overall health. Primary patient complaints identified in the article include:

- Unclear or confusing instructions or explanations
- Disorganized staff
- Delays in communicating and receiving test results
- Difficulties in resolving billing issues
- Rushed office visits that interfere with having concerns addressed

The article recommends that patients consider their options when deciding to change care providers. Office managers and patient satisfaction surveys are two ways to communicate dissatisfaction with care. Consider switching to another physician if your doctor is part of a group practice. After all, you may find that your personalities and communication styles are a better match. If you ultimately decide to switch to another office, know your rights. Be sure to request a copy of your medical history that you are entitled to receive under the federal Health Insurance Portability and Accountability Act.

Your health is important, and patient satisfaction is essential to receiving the best care possible.

Source: Gerencher (2013).

conversations and express your opinions about health legislation. Health-related messages are everywhere, and identifying strategies for sharing and seeking information as well as communicating our decisions to others is an essential element in ensuring healthy living.

Communication occurs in a variety of contexts. Chances are you have already experienced interactions in the organizational, family, and health contexts. Understanding how we adjust our messages across communication settings is critical to ensure your success as a competent communicator in the personal, professional, and public aspects of your life.**

Hopefully, this explanation has provided you with a clearer view of organizational communication and how it affects our personal, public, and professional lives. At its very core, we have learned that how we communicate in an organizational setting will build trust, encourage cooperation, and influence shared responsibilities.

KEY TERMS

- Authoritarian Parents
- Authoritative Parents
- Coercive Power
- Coping Strategies
- Displaced Dissent
- Expert Power
- Family Communication
- Lateral Dissent
- Legitimate Power

- Organizational Communication
- Organizational Dissent
- Permissive Parents
- Referent Power
- Reward Power
- Uninvolved Parents
- Upward Dissent

REFERENCES

Adams, C. H., Schlueter, D. W., & Barge, J. K. (1988). Communication and motivation within the superior–subordinate dyad: Testing the conventional wisdom of volunteer management. *Journal of Applied Communication Research, 156,* 69–81.

Baumrind, D. (1967). Child-care practices anteceding three patterns of preschool behavior. *Genetic Psychology Monographs, 75,* 43–88.

Booth-Butterfield, S., Chory, R., & Beynon, W. (1997). Communication apprehension and health communication behaviors. *Communication Quarterly, 45,* 235–250.

Bute, J. J., & Vik, T. A. (2010). Privacy management as unfinished business: Shifting boundaries in the context of infertility. *Communication Studies, 61,* 1–20.

CBS News. (2010, January 5). *$2.3 trillion spent on health care in 2008.* Retrieved from www.cbsnews.com/2100-250_162-6057429.html.

Cowan, R. L. (2011). "Yes, we have an anti-bullying policy, but…": HR professionals' understandings and experiences with workplace bullying policy. *Communication Studies, 62*(3), 307–327.

Coyne, S. M., Padilla-Walker, L. M., Day, R. D., Harper, J., & Stockdale, L. (2014). A friend request from dear old dad: Associations between parent–child social networking and adolescent outcomes. *Cyberpsychology, Behavior and Social Networking, 17*(1), 8–13.

French, J. R. P., & Raven, B. (1968). The bases for social power. In D. Cartwright (Ed.), *Studies in social power* (pp. 150–167). Ann Arbor: University of Michigan Press.

Gerencher, K. (2013, June 30). When should you fire your doctor? *Wall Street Journal*. Retrieved from http://online.wsj.com/news/articles/SB10001424127887324328204578571640215952804

Horan, S. M., & Chory, R. M. (2009). When work and love mix: Perceptions of peers in workplace romances. *Western Journal of Communication, 73*(4), 349–369.

Joseph, A. L., & Afifi, T. D. (2010). Military wives' stressful disclosures to their deployed husbands: The role of protective buffering. *Journal of Applied Communication Research, 38*, 412–434.

Kassing, J. W. (1997). Articulating, antagonizing, and displacing: A model of employee dissent. *Communication Studies, 48*, 311–332.

Kohn, P. M. (1996). On coping adaptively with daily hassles. In M. Zeidner & N. S. Endler (Eds.), *Handbook of coping* (pp. 181–201). New York, NY: Wiley.

Lederman, L. C., Stewart, L. O., Bates, C., Greenberg, J., LeGreco, M., & Schuwerk, T. J. (2007). *Let's talk about it*. New Brunswick, NJ: Center for Communication and Health Issues, Rutgers University.

Maccoby, E. E. (1992). The role of parents in the socialization of children: An historical overview. *Developmental Psychology, 28*, 1006–1017.

Medved, C. B., Brogan, S. M., McClanahan, A. M., Morris, J. R., & Shepherd, G. J. (2006). Family and work socializing communication: Messages, gender and ideological implications. *Journal of Family Communication, 6*, 161–180.

Richmond, V. P., & McCroskey, J. C. (2009). *Organizational communication for survival: Making work, work* (4th ed.). Boston, MA: Allyn & Bacon/Pearson.

Richmond, V. P., McCroskey, J. C., & Davis, L. M. (1986). The relationship of supervisor use of power and affinity-seeking strategies with subordinate satisfaction. *Communication Quarterly, 34*, 178–193.

Richmond, V. P., Smith, R. S., Heisel, A. D., & McCroskey, J. C. (2001). Nonverbal immediacy in the physician/patient relationship. *Communication Research Reports, 18*, 211–216.

Rogers, E. M. (1996). The field of health communication today: An up-to-date report. *Journal of Health Communication, 1*, 15–23.

Sias, P. M., Pedersen, H., Gallagher, E. B., & Kopaneva, I. (2012). Workplace friendship in the electronically connected organization. *Human Communication Research, 38*(3), 253–279.

Workplace Romance. (2013). Retrieved from http://www.shrm.org/research/surveyfindings/articles/pages/shrm-workplace-romance-findings.aspx

Chapter Fifteen

Mass Communication

© Arthimedes/Shutterstock.com

Before we dive into the murky waters of mass communication, let's take a look at how we personally handle opportunities to communicate through various media avenues. Do you view mass communication like a Communication Shark or are you more like a piranha? Each of us is inundated daily with various means of mediated communication delivered in mass. Some of us use it occasionally while others are highly addicted to it. Some use it as a means to reach a goal while others are consumed in a frenzy that can overtake logic and common sense.

When messages are expanded to large audiences through a variety of contexts, including print, electronic, social media, and so forth, we define that form of communication as mass communication. Mass communication has the ability to provide information and disseminate messages in an expansive way to instantly connect with audiences.

Mass communication is the broadcast of information to a very large audience. It does not involve the exchange of ideas as most methods of communication do; instead, it is more of a delivery and receipt of a mass message. Audiences who receive this type of communication may agree or disagree with the message transmitted and although there is uniformity and universality of the message, it is not an outlet where the audience can instantly respond or refute the message presented. For this reason, we often refer to mass communication as mediated communication.

**MEDIATED COMMUNICATION DEFINED

You wake up in the morning to your favorite song, which you downloaded from the Internet. As your day begins, you catch up on the news on television then listen to sports talk radio in the car as you drive to work. During the day, you watch YouTube videos, read magazines, and research recipes for dinner. In the evening, you send emails to your family, catch up with a long-distance romantic partner via FaceTime, and spend a few moments reviewing your favorite blog. As a society, we are inundated with mediated forms of communication. Throughout the day, we encounter a wide variety of media. In 2013 Americans spent over half their day engaged with some form of media.

Not only are you bombarded with mediated forms of communication, but the messages communicated via these channels impact you in a variety of ways. Worsnop (1989) identifies several ways in which media impacts our lives. Specifically, media:

1. Helps us understand the workings of our immediate world. It gives us information about current events, locally, nationally, and internationally.

2. Serves as a source of stories. Media outlets serve as the authors of the stories we consume.

3. Requires us to learn and use critical thinking skills. When turning to the media for information, we should be examining what we consume for accuracy.

4. Defines how we communicate. Media can shape our communication with others by influencing the channels we use for communication and the topics of our conversations.

5. Helps us (mis)understand ourselves and others. It serves as a tool for helping us learn more about who we are and who we are not.

6. Explains how things work. Media can provide us with useful insights about the processes of events and gather explanations of how happenings occur.

7. Brings us pleasure. We can turn to media to view videos and articles that bring us joy or help us escape from the mundane routine of life.

Considering the amount of time we spend with media and the multiple types of information and impact it can have on us, it seems crucial to understand the role it plays in our lives. The scope of media and the constant consumption of mediated messages can affect nearly every aspect of our lives.

Mediated communication involves individuals utilizing technology as a channel of delivery for a message. Mediated forms of communication include cell phone calls, texts, and emails. Mediated communication includes both *mass media* and *social media*. When you watch television and listen to commercials, you are a receiver of mass media communication. "Mass" refers to the large audience that receives the message, and "media" refers to the technological channels used to communicate the message. **Mass media** utilizes technology to send messages to a large number of people. *Social media* are websites used to create an online identity and may include sites such as Facebook or Instagram that build communities of people.

Most mediated communication can be described as *lean communication*. This refers to a communication channel that can limit access to nonverbal communication cues such as facial expressions, tone of voice, and eye contact. Consider ways in which your ability to receive and interpret nonverbal cues is limited when you interact with others via telephone, email, text, or blog. Have you ever received a text message or an email and thought the message sounded abrupt or angry? Perhaps you were confused about how you were supposed to interpret and respond to the message. Nonverbal communication cues are valuable tools that assist us in understanding the intended meaning behind the message. We depend on both nonverbal and verbal communication in order to understand the intended meaning behind the message, as both dimensions of communication provide insight into how the message is interpreted. Some mediated channels of communication—for example, email or text messaging—reduce access to this nonverbal information. You may use emoticons (such as a smiley face) or acronyms (such as LOL) to help the receiver of the message understand the ways in which the message should be interpreted; however, it can still be difficult to interpret the message accurately.

DISTINGUISHING TYPES OF MEDIATED COMMUNICATION

At its most basic level, mediated communication involves the use of technology, such as a computer to send an email or a cell phone to call or text someone. However, these are not the only mediated forms of communication. Radio, television, magazines, billboards, and websites all provide us with channels to share messages with others. Communication scholars focus on specific types of mediated communication: mass media and social media. Mass media utilizes technology to send messages to a large number of people. Mass media can be useful in terms of shaping ideas, sharing culture, and influencing behaviors. For example, do you remember television shows such as *Friends* and *Jersey Shore*? Each of these shows was popular at one point in time, and both created social impact. For example, Rachel, a character on *Friends*, had a very popular hairstyle that influenced a number of women to ask their hairstylists for "The Rachel." Characters on *Jersey Shore* had a distinct verbal style and vocabulary. They wore glittery t-shirts designed by Ed Hardy and described not-so-attractive women as "grenades." These t-shirts soon became embraced by our society and their description of unfortunate women became a popular phrase.

Boyd and Ellison (2008) describe ***social media*** as websites that individuals use to create or portray profiles to a list of users with whom they interact. *Collaborative projects* focus on co-creating information with other individuals. These would include websites such as Wikipedia where individuals can add or delete information. *Blogs* are often more personal in nature and can be considered an online journal. They are typically written from a one-person perspective and shed light on any number of topics. Websites that aim to build both personal and professional connections with others are called *social networking*. Examples of social networking sites include Facebook, Instagram, and LinkedIn. *Virtual game worlds* and *virtual social worlds* create fictional lives. Game worlds focus on players following the rules of a game and include games such as *World of Warcraft*. Social worlds provide a space for individuals to create another life and interact with others and include games such as *Second Life*. While participating in virtual game worlds, people wear headsets that allow for verbal interaction with their opponents. Virtual social worlds allow for interaction in the game as characters can interact.

Mediated forms of communication—be it using a phone, playing a game online, or watching your favorite television show—are prevalent in our daily lives. Each form of mediated communication has unique qualities. We first explore mass media communication and then turn our attention to social media. Included in our social media discussion is an examination of texting, calling, and emailing. While distinct from social media, texting, calling, and emailing do aid in relationship initiation, maintenance, and termination. As a result, these channels of communication share many of the same properties as social media.

MASS MEDIA IN OUR LIVES

Mass media is noteworthy because you have choices and decide what you listen to and watch. It can be used as a tool to influence our interactions with others. A popular television show from 1998 until 2003 was *Dawson's Creek*. Actors on the show included James Van Der Beek and Katie Holmes, and the plot focused on their lives as teenagers. It was a favorite show of one of the authors, and she often watched it with her friends. The next day at school she and her friends would discuss the current week's episode. When other friends would join the group, they were often told the topic and asked to wait until they were finished discussing the show before starting a new topic of conversation. In this way, the television impacted the flow of interaction. It informed the topic of conversation (the topic was the current episode) and who could participate in the discussion (only those who had watched the episode).

Many times we have a choice about what media we consume (e.g., listening to the television at your home or the radio in your car); however, not all mass media consumption is by choice. The billboards you pass while driving are considered mass media, and the content shared on these signs is beyond your control. However, recall the perception process. You do not take in and comprehend every message to which you are exposed; rather, we make careful decisions about what we will be able to recall based on certain criteria. The same can be said of the decision-making process behind mass media consumption. You make careful decisions about the media you put into your life.

Selecting Media Sources

Suppose you have a favorite television show you never miss. You and your friends may discuss the characters or storyline. Perhaps you find yourselves "taking sides" and having emotional reactions to the characters' experiences (called *parasocial interactions*, an idea that is discussed later in the chapter). Additionally, you may have websites that you frequently visit. For example, for the latest news, you may only check *www.cnn.com*. Your decision to select specific media is often based on the utility of the information, the relevance of the message, or how similar the message is to your existing attitudes, beliefs, and values. Thus, you focus on mass media messages that hold value for you. Once you believe that the message is either helpful or has the potential to be of benefit in the future, you are likely to select it.

One theoretical lens used to understand how individuals use media is the *Uses and Gratifications Theory*. The uses and gratifications approach argues that media are strategically selected in order to meet our personal needs. This theory seeks to understand the relationship individuals have with the media. While it might seem odd to think of yourself as in a relationship with media, you use the media to fulfill personal needs and, in doing so, you are gratified or get something out of it. When selecting media, we may use it before we have a need for information, persuasion, education, or entertainment. Media can also be selected to meet cognitive needs, affective needs, personal integrative needs, social integrative needs, and/or entertainment needs (Katz, Blumler, & Gurevitch, 1974).

© Barone Firenze/Shutterstock.com

Suppose you have had a bad day at work, then you remember that your favorite television show airs that night. Once at home, you eagerly sit in front of the television as your show starts. For the next hour it is as if nothing else matters. You selected a favorite show and are now using it to get away from the bad day you had.

Uses and Gratifications Theory focuses on the audience—that is, it seeks to comprehend why individuals use media in an effort to explain the media choices individuals make and the consequences experienced.

Parasocial interaction covers perceived interpersonal or relational connections with individuals in the media. Have you ever heard a news report that details someone stalking a celebrity? For the person doing the stalking, in his or her mind a relationship is present with the famous person; the two individuals are connected. By using media, we gather information to discuss with others. This information can assist us in building relationships or serving as a starting place for potentially difficult conversations.

Retention of Media Info

Given that we are inundated with messages, recalling everything that we've been exposed to on a daily basis would be a daunting task. It would be nearly impossible to remember every message. Humans are limited-capacity processors. This refers to the fact that we can only retain so much information. When studying for a test, for example, have you ever thought there is no possible way you will be able to take in any additional information? It is almost as if your brain is "full." To retain or recall information, we need to perceive the information to have utility. If the information is viewed as being helpful, we can recall it. We also remember information if it is novel or new. When we say to ourselves, "Wow, that is interesting" or "Hmmm, I had no idea," it is likely information that we will be able to recall later. In our interactions with others, you have likely expressed statements such as "Guess what I heard today on television…?" Media informs our discussions and gives us new topics of conversation. This information is helpful for our personal, professional, and public lives. If, for example, you have ever been on a job interview and created a list of topics to discuss as you prepared for the meeting, you may have used something that you heard from mass media.

FUNCTIONS OF MASS MEDIA

The media fulfills a variety of functions. We look to mass media as a source of information, in addition to fulfilling the needs previously discussed. Katz et al. (1974) argues that we use media "to match one's wits against others, to get information and advice for daily living, to provide a framework for one's day, to prepare oneself culturally for the demands of upward mobility, or to be reassured about the dignity and usefulness of one's role" (p. 20). Mass media provides insight on a variety of topics. From gathering information about current events to understanding how families communicate, we often use mass media to gather information about the world in which we live that we then use to help us form ideas.

Information Gathering and Idea Formation

Consider the following example. Your friend encourages you to purchase a new car. You are open to suggestions, and your friend is eager to offer advice. She encourages you to buy a Ford. Since you have never driven a Ford, you have no previous knowledge about the company or its vehicles. You begin researching the Ford your friend wants you to purchase. Information is gathered from commercials, the Internet, radio, and television, and you notice that with every mass media message you take in, each has a different opinion of the product. From all of these messages, you begin to form an opinion about the product.

Mass-mediated messages can be a valuable resource for gathering information about the world in which we live. Turning on the television or surfing the Internet for insights about current events is easy. In fact, the media are often the primary source of information when we are gathering information, deciding on purchases, researching information on lawmakers and policies, and seeking entertainment. However, during this consumption, there are some key ideas to consider. According to the Center for Media Literacy (n.d.), all media have five core concepts that individuals should consider that center around authorship, format, audience, content, and purpose. First, authorship refers to the idea that all media messages are constructed, created, or produced by someone or some entity. It is important to note who created it as those individuals likely have a vested interest in it. Each person and the company he or she represents have allegiances, alliances, and values that impact what messages are conveyed. Additionally, all messages are created in a particular format, such as advertisements in a magazine, billboards on the highway, or banners that appear on a Web page. These messages are produced for an intended audience. A company, for example, may produce an advertisement for a magazine and the targeted audience is the consumer of the magazine. It is important to note that different people experience the same message differently. Our perception may cause each of us to react differently to the same message. Thus, even if we are exposed to the same media, each of us may interpret the messages in very distinct ways. You and your friend could be exposed to the same commercial yet create different impressions of the same content. The content used in the media is influenced by the audience who is being targeted and includes particular language or visuals that are used to grab the viewer's attention and it is important to pay attention to these cues. Finally, purpose refers to the idea that much of mass media is produced for the purposes of gaining attention, power, or profit. These motivations impact how a message is created. It is important to be a thoughtful consumer of mass media and check facts with multiple sources.

Hopefully by now you realize that mass media serves a significant purpose in our lives. It has a noteworthy impact on our beliefs, it informs our language system, and it ultimately impacts our interactions with others. Other forms of media impact and influence our knowledge and interactions too. We now turn our attention to social media.

SOCIAL MEDIA

Chances are either you or someone you know has used social media to either collect information about someone else or to connect with others. Perhaps you have logged on to Facebook, entered someone's name, and attempted to gather information about the person. Maybe you've reconnected with friends from high school that you have not spoken with for several years. Social media are unique tools with a wide variety of potential uses. Businesses use social media to connect and build relationships with customers, teachers use social media to remind students and parents about upcoming events and assignments, and you may use social media to share thoughts and opinions on recent events. Remember, these types of communication are intended to build communities of people. Previously, we identified a number of types of social media you could choose to use. You can decide what sites to visit or join, and you can also decide how you want to present yourself on these sites. Once you have joined these sites and decided how to present yourself, you will work to build relationships with others. Each social media outlet offers a unique opportunity for us to connect and build relationships with others.

Relationship Building

Social media can be valuable tools for building or enhancing relationships. According to boyd (2006), one of the primary reasons for investing time in social networking sites is to promote social connections. Chances are you use social media websites primarily as a way to connect with others. Websites such as Facebook have enhanced the individual's ability to connect and reconnect with others, and new relationships can be created where strangers discover that they share a common interest or activity. Quan-Haase and Young (2010) utilized Uses and Gratifications Theory to understand the gratifications individuals experienced when using Facebook versus instant messaging. They found that individuals perceived using Facebook as fun and a shared social activity. That is, if a friend suggested using Facebook, participants in the study were likely to listen to their friends and join the social networking site. Additionally, they found that college students view Facebook as an entertaining networking opportunity. Thus, your social networks play an important role in the types of social media you choose to use, and, because of their influence on your choices, you could gain a larger social network because you may connect with individuals you had not previously connected. While the study above addressed Facebook, there are many different types of social networking sites individuals can choose from when interacting with others. Sites such as Instagram, LinkedIn, and Pinterest are also social networking sites individuals can use to connect with others. According to boyd (2008), there are benefits in using social networking sites. These benefits include:

1. Outlets or opportunities for involvement with the community;

2. Enhancement and growth of individual creativity through sharing of art or music;

3. Growing or developing ideas from the creation of blogs, podcasts, or videos;

4. Expansion of one's online connections; and

5. Fostering of one's individual identity and unique social skills.

© Twin Design/Shutterstock.com

While social media can promote the creation of relationships, it too can diminish the quality of a relationship. Consider the following example posted on the website *www.thinkbeforeyousend.com*:

> "My wife was forwarding an e-mail from her father. She had made sarcastic comments about a friend in her email, and prior to forwarding the email, forgot to delete the sarcastic comments. That friend was one of the people who received the forwarded message. This situation seriously strained the friendship."

Communication cannot be reversed. While this concept is true of all communication, this idea becomes particularly salient to mediated communication because the message is written and recorded. Often the time and date of the message accompany it for later reference. Emails, text messages, or social media posts can be revisited and reread and used as evidence in conversations. Thus, it proves more difficult to deny or change communication and it could, as a result, hurt relationships.

Networking and Social Movement

Two particularly interesting aspects of social media are its networking and social movement abilities. First, online communities such as LinkedIn and Facebook provide opportunities to network with others. Organizations and companies may turn to social media sites such as LinkedIn when recruiting new employees. People can search sites and locate reputable talent to assist them in projects. Companies can promote their services and build their identities. These online relationships can supplement face-to-face relationships or serve as the primary medium of connection.

Additionally, social media sites can be used as a way to create a social movement. Unze (2010) describes how a 17-year-old boy used Facebook as a way to gather support for a skate park proposal. The plan needed to be approved by the city council. The teen created a Facebook profile describing the cause so users could follow and "like" the information. As a result of the Facebook support generated, the teen had evidence of the impact of the project and funding was eventually allotted for the park. Due to the widespread popularity of social media sites, many celebrities and political candidates have turned to Facebook, Twitter, and Instagram to share their opinions and messages.

© PiXXart/Shutterstock.com

Social media efforts connect individuals and companies alike. Moreover, they can be used strategically as a means of persuasive communication and to gather support for incentives. These powerful tools should be used with caution, however. Social media users should be mindful of what types of information they are disclosing. In fact, websites are dedicated to cautioning people about the uses of social media. For example, Microsoft cautions users to be careful when clicking on links, mindful of whom you allow to be your friend, and selective in deciding what social media websites you use.

ONLINE IDENTITIES

It is important to keep in mind that when we use social media, we often first create an online identity or person—a public image of ourselves that we share with others. One key concern for communication scholars investigating mediated forms of communication is that of identity or *impression formation*. Scholars refer to the sense-making of others' actions and disposition as impression formation. Typically, through our interactions with others, we form a general impression or idea about the other person's character or qualities and personality (Hancock & Dunham, 2001). For example, after meeting and interacting with someone for the first time, you may think to yourself, "He seemed polite," "I really liked her clothing," or "They seemed a little uncomfortable." All of these are possible impressions that we form of others and that others form of us. Impression formation is a two-way street with us forming impressions of others and others forming impressions of us. If everything you do sends a message, it is important to consider the impressions created by words and photos that are posted online.

Social media profiles enable us to share a variety of information. All of this information is "up for interpretation" by the reader. Impressions are formed based on the information you choose to share. Perhaps you post the lyrics from a country music song and a coworker then invites you to attend a country music concert with her. In reality, you do not enjoy country music, you just appreciated the message behind the lyrics. In this example, we see then that the way you meant to send information, liking a song for meaning, can be interpreted differently, that you actually enjoy country music.

Hancock and Dunham (2001) found that after viewing a person's profile with whom you have no relational history, judgments made are more intense than if the people had met and communicated face-to-face. That is, interacting with a person's online persona (via their profile information) left viewers with stronger attributions and perceptions of the individual. Online representations often fail to incorporate a person's complete or true identity. Because of this, individuals who view your profile can make exaggerated explanations about your personal qualities. They may, for example, stereotype you based on some aspect of your persona. If you disclose online that you enjoy country music, a reader may assume that you are a conservative person too. Thus, individuals should use caution in online forums and work to manage the impressions they can elicit in others.

Self-Presentation and Decision-Making

Perhaps one of the most interesting aspects of social media is the fact that you are in control of the information that you share with others. You decide what material you disclose to others and what information you choose to keep private. Individuals often make careful decisions about what they post for others to see or read. These decisions are called *self-presentation* strategies. Goffman (1959) describes self-presentation as impression management. Self-presentation strategies are the choices about content (e.g., photos, quotes, or other demographic information) that we make when sharing with others. These choices guide the creation of the online personal profile. Individuals make a conscious effort to control how their audience perceives them. This effort becomes especially heightened in online mediums. In an online format, images are often carefully selected and perhaps even edited to convey physically

© Michael Tureski/Icon SMI/Corbis

attractive qualities. Quotes and phrases are chosen to reflect a person's attitudes, and friendships are created and maintained by sharing information about interests and hobbies.

Unfortunately, the anonymity of our online presence results in some instances of deception and dishonesty. The MTV television show *Catfish* follows individuals that have built relationships online. People meet and interact online without physically meeting one another, then television crews share their stories as they meet for the first time. The most notable aspect of the show is that oftentimes the individuals have been talking to a fake persona. Consider, for example, former University of Notre Dame linebacker Manti Te'o. Te'o, who was drafted to play in the National Football League in 2013, was duped into believing a woman he was communicating with and dating online was a real person. The person he thought he was communicating with, however, didn't exist. In fact, an acquaintance of Te'o's admitted to creating the fake profile. When using mediated forms of interaction and building online relationships, it is possible to experience deception, that the creator of the profile may have strategically altered information or photos.

While the source or creator of a profile can control the content posted on social media sites, when it is viewed by others, the responses they may acquire cannot be controlled. While you may be able to post a specific photo, you are not able to control how people will perceive that post and respond to it. In fact, individuals can perceive, react, and respond to the same post in a variety of ways. Determining how to respond to others' social media presence is an important component in the decision-making process. Remember that using social media is not just about creating responsible profiles, but it is also deciding how to respond to others' profiles. Shea (1995) crafted rules of etiquette for the Internet to provide guidelines for appropriate online interactions. Her book *Netiquette* summarizes some best practices for Internet use:

Rule 1: Remember that there is a human component. There is a real person on the other side of the social network site. Use caution and treat others as you would prefer to be treated.

Rule 2: Adhere to the same standards of behavior online that you follow in real life. Most people tend to follow laws and rules. Use an ethical compass to guide your behaviors.

Rule 3: Know where you are in cyberspace. Much like the public speaking process, which calls for audience analysis, you too should analyze a website before you begin posting. Standards of conduct vary from website to website.

Rule 4: Respect other people's time. Your message is important, but so too is the reader's time. Make sure to create efficient and effective communication.

Rule 5: Make yourself look good online. The content and quality of your message will be judged. Take care in the tone, spelling, and grammar of your message.

Rule 6: Share your expertise. If you know the answer to another's question, offer your insights.

Rule 7: Help keep flame wars under control. Flaming occurs online when individuals attack one another or offer insults. When individuals "flame," they are freely sharing emotions and not "pulling any punches." While flame wars can be entertaining initially, they can lose value quickly.

Rule 8: Respect others' privacy. It seems likely that you would not invade someone else's space by examining the contents of a man's wallet or a woman's purse. The same should be true of someone's email.

Rule 9: Do not abuse your power. If you have access to another's private information, respect the person and do not read materials.

Rule 10: Forgive others' mistakes. All users start somewhere. A lack of experience on websites or blogs could contribute to errors. Give others a break.

Because mediated communication appears to be only increasing in popularity, individuals need to use caution when determining how to convey themselves in online settings. Remember, because you cannot control the reader's perceptions, you should take care to create a thoughtful profile. Esterline (2009) offers guidelines to create positive personal, professional, and public social media identities. These tips can be used when creating your online identity, specifically when creating a profile online and subsequently updating the profile information.

Tip 1: Status updates. Do not update your status with information an employer may not want to know.
Tip 2: Photos. Post photos with caution. Avoid posting photos that compromise your image.
Tip 3: Groups and applications. Avoid joining groups, fan pages, and applications that are not relevant to your
    field.

As you can see from the above list, a number of considerations should be taken when creating an online profile. Online personas should reflect carefully thought-out and planned communication. In many instances the positive connections you form online can "spill over" or be continued in face-to-face relationships. For example, you may post a status or an article that other people enjoy reading and can discuss in face-to-face interactions.

© dolphfyn/Shutterstock.com

THE IMPACT OF SOCIAL MEDIA ON FACE-TO-FACE RELATIONSHIPS

Given the nature and prevalence of social media, it makes sense that it would impact your face-to-face relationships. You can probably recall a time when social media helped you learn information about someone that caused you to feel emotionally close to the person. Perhaps you discovered new information that you had not known previously. Just as social media may be useful in forming relationships, it may also be helpful in maintaining existing relationships and promoting feelings of closeness and relational satisfaction. However, some also indicate that social media can be used as a replacement for face-to-face interactions and contribute negatively to relationships.

Lickerman (2010) argues that the overuse of social media may serve to isolate a person. Data suggests that we spend approximately 16 minutes out of every hour engaged in online social media sites (Finn, 2013). This isolation takes time away from face-to-face interactions and may diminish the quality of a relationship. The author argues for using a balance of mediated and face-to-face communication. Thus, not all interactions should occur on social media channels. Face-to-face communication does allow for important elements of nonverbal communication, such as the use of touch, that social media does not allow. Consider, for example, asking your relationship partner to marry you. You may determine that face-to-face communication is better for this communicative exchange because it allows you to hear your partner's response.

Kearsley (1998) recommends the following rules for communicating via mediated channels. These recommendations will likely be useful when communicating professionally, personally, and publicly. These tips are useful when sending email communications, building websites, or using chat functions, all of which are part of the relationship-building function of social media sites. First, being brief is likely best. All messages, files, and photos should have focus. For example, do you have a friend that updates his or her Facebook status multiple times a day? What impression does that create in your mind? Over-posting could be perceived negatively. It could make someone think that you do not have anything better to do with your time or that you are scattered and cannot decide on one status you like. Also, remember these are public domains. Think carefully about what you write. If, for example, in an email you indicated to a coworker that you do not like a policy that your boss is enforcing and your coworker forwards the message to your boss, this communicative act cannot be undone. Always assume that anything you post could be made public.

Additionally, remember to be kind. There is no need to make social network sites a negative place where people attack one another. Presenting different opinions and discussing issues is very different from attacking someone's character and competence. Finally, you should provide structure in your messages. When you send an email, for example, take a moment to create a subject line or description that your receiver will not only understand but that will help orient him or her to the purpose/context of the information.

Hopefully, throughout this chapter, you have been thinking about your own social media use. Social media can be a helpful tool in building relationships and it provides us with a unique method of communication with its own strengths and weaknesses. Much like mass media, we get to make decisions regarding our social media use. Because we are in control of the content, it is important to select content that is representative of us as individuals and creates a positive impression on our receivers. **

COMMUNICATION AND SOCIAL MEDIA

Social Media consists of the use of digital technology and channels to interact with a limited group of receivers. In a world where social media rules the communication game, we should understand why we use this form of communication. Some use it for information while others use it to keep up with friends and family members, establish an online identity, or simply for entertainment.

In a world where social media rules the communication game, we have to ask why we use it. Some of us simply use it for information access. Others use it to keep up with friends, family members, or to initiate romantic relationships. There is also the aspect of establishing our professional identity online. And lastly, we simply utilize social media for our own enjoyment.

Reasons We Use Social Media	Details
Information	To gain knowledge or content
Personal Relationships	To maintain connections with others
Identity Management	To observe behaviors to validate personal choices
Entertainment	To share interests or activities

How do you use social media? Do you find yourself Facebook messaging your friends to ask them to meet you for dinner or do you still text or call them on the phone? If you are using social media outlets as a way to maintain or grow personal relationships, you might find that it is hard to truly connect with a screen between the two of you. Often words written may be misunderstood without the nonverbal cues that go along with a personal conversation. According to Albert Mehrabian's theory of communication, the written word only compromises 7% of the total communication we use. I guess that is why so many people include emojis along with their texts and Facebook posts! Does this look familiar?

Hi Friend!☺ I haven't heard from you in a while.☺ Does this mean you are mad at me?☹ Would you mind if I gave you a call ☎ to say Hello!✋ Check one: ☒ or ☑

A *competent communicator* is a person who has the knowledge, skill, and motivation to do what is appropriate, effective, and ethical in any situation. Having the ability to communicate does not always parallel with the way we actually communicate. Are you a competent communicator when it comes to social media? If you are not sure, you might ask yourself these questions:

- ▹ Do you take measures to keep yourself and others safe?
- ▹ What channel is most appropriate for the communication you need?
- ▹ Do you post, like, or share information that may cause problems for you or others?

With constant updates and changes made to social media technology, revisit privacy settings regularly to ensure that you and the content you post is protected. Develop skills to deliver messages in an ethical and appropriate manner.

Through the years, I have noticed friends, family, and students of mine who found themselves in a frenzy to take down posts that could potentially cost a friendship or perhaps their job. It's time we got serious about how we use social media and how often we use it. If you are unsure about your use, start by completing the worksheet on the next page:

HOW DO YOU USE SOCIAL MEDIA?

Name:_____Date:_____

Answer the following areas truthfully to evaluate your own use of social media. If you don't recognize the icon, chances are you are not using that form of social media.

Social Media	Twice a Day	Once a Day	Twice a Week	Once a Week	Twice a Month	Once a Month	Almost Never	Never
Facebook								
Twitter								
Instagram								
Pinterest								
YouTube								
Snapchat								
LinkedIn								
WhatsApp								
(star)								
Messenger								
D								

Mass media and social media provide us with opportunities for including information-gathering, entertainment, and relationship creation and maintenance. There are many strategies for successfully using mass and social media in your personal, professional, and public lives such as using caution with photos and posts. Ultimately, you need to make careful decisions about the types of media you consume. Each mass media outlet comes with its own biases and viewpoints. It is important to consider these when determining how to use the messages you receive. Social media, in all its forms, can contribute to relationships. It allows us to initiate contact to build relationships, maintain the status of those relationships, and diminish relationships and quality. Ultimately, we need to remember to be cautious in our online personas, as communication in this format can leave a lasting record. Remember, once something is posted, it cannot be undone.

KEY TERMS

- Blogs
- Collaborative Projects
- Competent Communicator
- Impression Formation
- Lean Communication
- Mass Communication
- Mediated Communication
- *Netiquette*
- Parasocial Interaction
- Self-Presentation
- Social Media
- Social Networking
- Uses and Gratifications Theory
- Virtual Game Worlds
- Virtual Social World

REFERENCES

boyd, d. m. (2006, December). Friends, Friendsters, and MySpace top 8: Writing community into being on social network sites. *First Monday*. Retrieved from http://131.193.153.231/www/issues/issue11_12/boyd/index.html.

boyd, d. m. (2008). *Taken out of context: American teen sociality in networked publics.* Retrieved from www.danah.org/papers/TakenOutOfContext.pdf.

boyd, d. m., & Ellison, N. B. (2008). Social network sites: Definition, history, and scholarship. *Journal of Computer-Mediated Communication, 13*, 210–230.

Center for Media Literacy. (n.d.). *CML's five key questions and core concepts of media literacy for deconstruction.* Retrieved from www.medialit.org.

Esterline, R. M. (2009). *8 tips to building and maintaining a professional online image.* Retrieved from http://bizzywomen.com/2009/8-tips-to-building-and-maintaining-a-professional-online-image/.

Finn, G. (2013, April). *Study: 27% of time online in the U.S. is spent on social networking.* Retrieved from http://marketingland.com/study-27-of-time-online-in-the-us-is-spent-on-social-networking-40269.

Goffman, E. (1959). *The presentation of self in everyday life.* New York: Doubleday.

Hamilton, N. T. (1998). Uses and gratifications. *Theories of Persuasive Communication and Consumer Decision Making.* Retrieved from http://www.ciadvertising.org/studies/student/98_fall/theory/hamilton/leckenby/theory/elements.htm.

Hancock, J., & Dunham, P. (2001). Impression formation in computer-mediated communication revisited: An analysis of the breadth and intensity of impressions. *Communication Research, 28,* 325–347.

Kaplan, A. M., & Haenlein, M. (2010). Users of the world unite!: The challenges and opportunities of social media. *Business Horizons, 53,* 59–58.

Katz, E., Blumler, J., & Gurevitch, M. (1974). Utilization of mass communication by the individual. In J. Blumler & E. Katz (Eds.), *The uses of mass communication: Current perspectives on gratifications research* (pp. 19–34). Beverly Hills, CA: Sage.

Kearsley, G. (1998). *A guide to online education.* Retrieved from http://home.sprynet.com/~gkearsley/online. htm#rules.

Lickerman, A. (2010). The effect of technology on relationships. *Psychology Today.* Retrieved from www.psychologytoday.com/blog/happiness-in-world/201006/the-effect-technology-relationships.

Palmgreen, P., Weener, L. A., & Rayburn, J. D. II. (1980). Relations between gratifications sought and obtained: A study of television news. *Communication Research, 7,* 161–192.

Quan-Haase, A., & Young, A. (2010). Uses and gratifications of social media: A comparison of Facebook and instant messaging. *Bulletin of Science, Technology and Society, 30,* 350–361.

Shea, V. (1995). *Netiquette.* San Francisco: Albion.

Temkin Group. (April, 2013). *American's daily media consumption, 2012 vs. 2013.* Retrieved from http://trends.e-strategyblog.com/2013/04/04/americans-daily-media-consumption/10074.

Unze, D. (2010, March). Facebook helps spark movements. *USA Today.* Retrieved from www.usatoday.com/news/nation/2010-03-25-facebook_N.htm.

Worsnop, C. M. (1989). *Media literacy through critical thinking: Teacher materials.* Retrieved from http://depts.washington.edu/nwmedia/sections/nw_center/curriculum_docs/teach_combine.pdf.

Communication SH▲RK™

Glossary

Abbreviations: used as a substitute for longer words

Abstract Language: vague language used in communication

Accommodation: one party concedes or gives in to resolve things

Acronyms: used to shorten names or phrases by using the first letter of each word

Action Language: movements used to supplement words and share emotion; language use that is active and interesting

Action Model of Communication: communication shown as a motion or action sent and meaning received

Active Listening: listening to understand

Active Strategies: process which involves soliciting information by asking third parties about another person

Adaptors: unintentional forms of nonverbal communication such as straightening clothing or moving hair from our eyes

Adjourning Stage: a stage in which a low performing group will disband

Adrenaline: a physiological impulse which involves increased heart and respiration rate as a result of a situation perceived to be frightening or exciting

Affect Displays: obvious use of our faces for smiling and frowning as a nonverbal cue

Agenda: list of activities or tasks that need to be accomplished during a meeting

Albert Mehrabian: developed the 7%-38%-55% Verbal/Nonverbal Communication Model

Alliteration: a repetition of sounds used in a sequence of words to reinforce an idea

APA: the American Psychological Association style of citing research

Appearance: nonverbal cue communication about ourselves and our credibility

Appreciative Listening: showing enjoyment of a speaker or content while listening

Aromatherapy: process which involves the sense of smell and uses scents to overcome stress and improve overall mental health

Articulation: process by which a speaker sounds out words so the audience can understand what is being said

Artifactual Communication: the use of object language, such as our own appearance, as a way to communicate

Attitudes: learned predispositions to respond favorably or unfavorably toward another person, group, or object

Attraction Theory: theory that we are initially drawn to others on the basis of attraction

Audience Analysis: process for determining who will be in your audience

Authoritarian Parents: parenting style in which low levels of support and high levels of control are exhibited

Autonomy vs. Connectedness: focuses on desires to maintain independence

Avoiding: stage in which a relationship begins to move apart and partners make a conscious effort to avoid one another

Barriers: language miscommunication which can create conflict; different views, accents, and word meanings may create barriers

Behavioral Familiarity: a strategy used to help identify dishonesty

Beliefs: personal convictions regarding truth or existence

Bias: refers to the potential for language to convey stereotypes, insensitivity, or negativity toward a group of people or about a topic

Block Indented Margin: process reserved for quotes that are longer than four lines

Blogs: personal in nature, but considered more of an online journal written from a one-person perspective regarding a target topic

Bonding: final stages of a relationship coming together

Breathing Exercises: process that can help affect your state of mind, lower heart rate, and bring stress under control

Cause/Effect: process of ordering points to show a relationship between a cause and the effect

Certainty Message: a message delivered in which the originator of the message believes only in his or her perspective

Channel: path through which the message is sent

Chronemics: the study of time and how it is used to communicate

Chronological: process of ordering points with a reference to time

Circumscribing: the stage in which couples begin to drift apart in the quality and quantity of their communication

Closed Questions: questions designed to be answered with a simple yes or no

Clustering and Webbing: visual process used for brainstorming, organizing, and mapping ideas in which ideas are clustered together

CMS: the Chicago Manual Style for citing research

Co-Culture: smaller cultures that comprise a larger culture

Coercive Power: assigning authority to another person based on their perceived ability to punish or deliver negative consequences for noncompliance

Cognitive Function: using language to gather information, to reason, and to make sense of the world

Cohesiveness: general sense of belonging among group members

Collaboration: strategy requiring both parties to communicate concerns while proposing solutions

Collaborative Projects: focus on co-creating information with other individuals

Collectivism: group is viewed as most important

Color: refers to energy, enthusiasm, feelings, and attitudes included in our message

Commenting Modifiers: using words that may add little meaning to the message

Communication Accommodation Theory: theory in which the speaker changes verbal communication during an interaction

Communication Age: communication at a distance through various media outlets in real time

Communication Barriers: any barrier that can keep effective communication from happening

Communication: a process by which we transmit, share, or exchange ideas or information through verbal and nonverbal methods

Competent Communicator: a person who has the knowledge, skill, and motivation to do what is appropriate, effective, and ethical in any situation

Competition: conflict when both partners have strong opinions and there is a control for power

Computer Mediated Communication: human communication through a range of technologies

Concealment: process of withholding important or relevant information

Concrete Language: detailed language used in communication

Conflict: expressed struggle between at least two interdependent parties who perceive incompatible goals, resources, and interference from the other party in achieving goals

Connectors: transitions or links used in a speech

Connotative Language: words used as an expression in language and is not used as defined in a dictionary

Context: the setting in which communication occurs; includes the environment where the message is delivered, the people who receive the message, and experiences with the topic of the message

Converge: refers to when individuals become similar with verbal choices

Coping: strategies regarding whether individuals can respond emotionally, through active research, or avoidance toward stressful situations

Critical Listening: resisting outside noises and distractions to concentrate on message being delivered

CSE: the Council of Science Editors style for citing research

Cultural: understanding and communicating with a sensitivity to others with various cultures

Culture Borrowing: occurs when one culture sees the benefits of aspects of other cultures

Culture: refers to common characteristics and shared perceptions that unify a group of people and shape their communication expectations

Decode: process by which we translate or interpret content into meaning

Defensive Message: communication produced in response to some kind of threat

Defining Modifiers: providing new and needed information which clarifies language or concepts

Denotative Language: words that are used as they are found in a dictionary

Dialect: regional differences in language usage; accents

Dialectical Tensions: contradictory pulls between opposing goals or desires in a relationship

Differentiating: stages couples may find in which they spend more time disagreeing or emphasizing differences

Digital Tradition: communication using all existing media

Discrimination: practice of denying others their equal rights

Displaced Dissent: communication strategy in which organizational members share dissatisfaction or frustration with family members and nonworkplace friends

Diverge: refers to when individuals become increasingly different in their verbal choices

Diversity: that which is different

Dyadic Communication: communication that occurs when two people communicate and share their ideas, ideals, behaviors, interests, thoughts, and understandings

Ego Defensive Function: provides a scapegoat to blame others for misfortunes

Electronic Tradition of Communication: communication distributed through recordings, radio, telegraph, and television

Elevator Pitch: a short speech that introduces yourself to someone in a compelling manner and delivered in the brief time it takes to ride an elevator to the next floor

Elocution: the sound of language; how words are produced and delivered

Emblems: movements or gestures that take the place of words

Emotional Closeness: perception or feeling of trust with another individual

Empathetic Listening: actively trying to understand the message and offer positive nonverbal cues in support for the speaker

Empathy: the ability to understand how someone else is feeling or thinking

Encode: process by which a person derives meaning and understanding

Entry Stage: first stage of a relationship in which individuals engage in small talk characterized by sharing of basic demographic information

Equivocation: used in situations to spare someone's feelings by using vague or ambiguous language to avoid speaking the truth

Ethical Communication: ability to be honest and use a set of standards to guide appropriate or positive behaviors

Ethics: standards, values, beliefs, and principles we use to determine whether something is acceptable or unacceptable

Ethnicity: refers to a common heritage, nationality, ancestry, or background

Ethos: an appeal to ethics

Evaluate: the process of determining if a purpose was met or not met

Exaggeration: process of stretching the truth or adding details to enhance a story

Exit Stage: involves making the decision to terminate or end the pursuit of a relationship

Expectancy Violation Theory: Burgoon's theory regarding how we perceive our territory and the way we react when our expectations are violated or not met

Experimenting: involves the exchange of multiple questions and answers in an attempt to gain more information and identify areas of commonality

Expert Power: assign power to another based on their knowledge or expertise

Explicit Learning: formalized instruction

Explicit Rules: formalized rules that are discussed and recorded in a document for all group members

Expressed Struggle: open expression of conflict

Eye Contact: nonverbal cue using eyes to promote goodwill and a connection with others

Facial Expressions: includes eye contact, smiling, head nodding, and head tilting to communicate

Factional group When group members are representatives or delegates from other social entities.

Familiar Language: using words that are familiar with the audience

Family Communication: process of creating and sharing meaning through the exchange of verbal and nonverbal messages with those whom we consider to be family

Feedback: helps the speaker to know if content delivered has been effectively decoded and received

Femininity: cultural values for nurturance, cooperation, and support among members

Figure of Speech: rhetorical questions, metaphors, personification, alliteration, and oxymora

Figure-Ground: design theory that allows the audience to see information that is most or least important

Filler Words: phrases, sounds, or words used to fill awkward pauses while communicating a thought

Forming Stage: a stage in which group members meet each other for the first time and learn the purpose for the group

Functional Group: group of representatives or delegates brought together for the completion of a common goal

Gender-Inclusive Language: language that includes all genders

Gender: understanding and communicating with a sensitivity to other genders

General Purpose: a purpose statement which defines the type of speech you will present

Gestalt: design theory that incorporates figure-ground and hierarchy and means the whole is greater than the sum of many parts

Gestures: the way you use your hands, body, and facial expressions to communicate

Group Communication: communication that occurs when the parameters of communication between individuals expand

Group Identity Function: focuses on the use of language as a signal of membership in a group

Group Rules: refers to the notion that group members are expected to engage in specific behaviors

Groupthink: occurs when all group members go along with a proposed idea without thoughtful discussion or careful analysis

Group: collection of individuals with a common purpose

Hanging Indentions: the first line goes to the far left of the margin while additional lines are indented

Haptics: the study of touch and how it is used to communicate

Head Tilting or Nodding: nonverbal cue to communicate using the head

Hear: an involuntary response in which sound is received and meaning may or may not be established

Hierarchy: design theory that uses organizational tools to command the audience's attention

High Power-Distance: cultures that value status and power differentials in communication

High-Context: cultural orientation that prefers a more indirect style of communication

Ideograms: written communication as a picture or symbol used to represent a thing or idea

Illustrators: use of our bodies to gesture or indicate directions

Implicit Learning: acquiring information by observing

Implicit Rules: unspoken expectations that everyone in the group seems to know and follow

Impression Formation: sense making of others' actions and disposition

Individual Roles: When individuals focus on self-achievement and not group efforts.

Individualism: self is viewed as most important

Information Function: a prejudice which provides us with information to use in guiding our communication with others

Informative Listening: taking notes of main points or data communicated

Initiating: process when a relationship focuses on the initial communication that occurs

Integrating: lives of both partners begin to merge, and status is acknowledged personally and publicly

Intensifying: a more intimate expression of commitment by testing impressions that others have formed about the relationship

Interactional Model of Communication: illustrates how we use communication to exchange messages

Interactive Strategies: direct communication for uncovering information about others

Interdependent: both partners in the relationship are likely to experience frustration with each other, but not with strangers

Internal Previews: statements used to let an audience know what is coming next

Internal Reviews: statements used to summarize covered points for the audience

Interpersonal Communication: communication between two people in which one person stimulates meaning in the mind of the other

Interpretation The third phase of the perception process where we attach meaning to what we have selected and organized.

Interview: asking specific questions with the intent to gather information

Intimate Distances: involves touching the person next to you and is usually eighteen inches or less

Intrapersonal Communication: communication that occurs when we envision or have a conversation with ourselves

Jealousy: a negative or destructive communicative response to a perceived threat to a relationship

Kinesics: the use of facial and body language to communicate

Language: the words, their pronunciations, and the methods of combining them for use in communication

Lateral Dissent: expression of dissatisfaction or frustration to coworkers

Lean Communication: communication channels that reduce access to nonverbal communication such as facial expressions, touch, and eye contact (example: e-mail, texts, or blogs)

Legitimate Power: assign power to another based on their position or title within the organization

Lies: the process of falsifying information

Linguistics: another word for language

Listen: an activity which requires the listener to consciously receive a message and respond

Logographs: written communication using a letter, symbol, or sign to represent a word

Logos: an appeal to logic

Low Power-Distance: cultures that value equality among members

Low-Context: cultural orientation that emphasizes the spoken word and direct verbal expression

Masculinity: culture values for assertiveness, ambition, and achievement

Maslow's Hierarchy of Needs: a theory which categorizes needs from basic physiological needs to higher level needs

Mass Communication: utilizing technology to broadcast information to a very large audience

Mediated Communication: utilizing technology as the channel for delivery

Meditation: process which uses imagery and positive visualization to calm stress

Message: written, spoken, or unspoken content communication sent intentionally or unintentionally

Metaphors: language used to compare something that has a dissimilar meaning

Minimizing: process of downplaying the truth

MLA: the Modern Language Association style of citing research

Monochromatic: time as a commodity that must be carefully scheduled to do one thing at a time

Monroe's Motivated Sequence: a strategy for presenting a persuasive presentation which describes the problem, offers a realistic solution, and describes expected results

Netiquette: good manners when using the Internet

New Media Tradition: communication distributed through electronics which included the addition of computers, iPads, tablets, smartphones, smart watches, and other more advanced forms of technology

Noise: verbal or nonverbal distractions in the speaking environment that can include preconceived notions, opinions, and ideas

Nonverbal Communication: communication that does not involve words or sounds

Norms: standardized behaviors

Novelty vs. Predictability: addresses our need to experience things new and different while wanting routine and consistency

Object Language: intentional or unintentional use of objects to communicate

Olfactory Communication: the study of smell and how we use it to communicate

One-Legged Interview: another term used for an elevator pitch

Open-Ended Questions: questions that cannot be answered with a one-word statement

Openness vs. Closedness: reflects need to share information with others while keeping some areas private

Oral Communication: communicating verbally

Oral Tradition of Communication: verbal transmission of information through storytelling

Organization: the second phase of the perception process, organization of stimuli selected and categorizing what we have received

Organizational Communication: process through which members of an organization act together to create, sustain, and manage meanings

Organizational Dissent: method of reducing uncertainty that involves directly soliciting information about another person

Outline: tool which places related items together

Oxymoron: language patterns used as we include expressions in combination with terms that are contradictory

Pace: describes the rate at which we vocalize syllables in a word

Para-Social Interaction: perception of connection to individuals in the media

Paralanguage: the vocal part of speech that involves volume, rate, pitch, pace, and color

Paralinguistics: nonverbal aspect of communication that involves sound, but not words

Parental Messages: communication of importance of strategies as it relates to demands on both career and family as it regards balance, work choice, life planning, and combinations of all

Parenthetical Citation: citation process which includes the author's last name and the page number or date of the work surrounded by a parenthesis

Passive Strategies: implicit or unintended means to gather information during the initial stages of a relationship

Pathos: an appeal to emotion or passion

Pause: a break in speech rhythm for emphasis

Peer Group: a group of people composed of members with equal abilities, background, age, responsibilities, beliefs, social standing, legal status, or rights

Perceived Incompatible Goals: frustration due to partners focusing on different goals

Perception Checking: the process whereby we validate the accuracy of our perceptions

Perception process: a three-step process that includes selection, where we focus our attention on something and ignore other elements in the environment; organization, where we form what we have received into meaningful patterns; and interpretation, where we attach meaning to what we have selected and organized

Perception: a three-part process (select, organize, and interpret) used to make sense of messages we encounter

Performing Stage: a stage in which group members begin to focus on task completion

Permissive Parents: parenting style in which high levels of support and low levels of control are demonstrated

Personal Distances: area reserved for close friends and family and covers 18 inches to 4 feet

Personal Stage: characterized by the exchange of more personal or emotional information such as attitudes, beliefs, and values

Personification: language used when we describe an inanimate form or thing as if it were human

Petroglyphs: written communication through carvings or paintings into a rock surface

Physical Attraction: we seek in forming working relationships where we depend on others to accomplish a task or goal that cause us to be physically drawn to another

Pictograms: written communication through graphic elements of uniform size and arranged in sequence

Pitch: describes the high, medium, or low sounds produced by vocal cord vibrations

Plagiarism: the act of using someone else's ideas or work as if it is your own

Poise: how you carry your body

Polychronic: time is flexible and not viewed as important as relationship

Posture: nonverbal cue to show how you feel about yourself

Power: ability to influence the behavior of others

Prejudice: type of attitude in which we directly express negative reactions toward another individual or group

Primary Territories: things or spaces we own or possess

Print Tradition of Communication: communication distributed through a printed medium

Probing Questions: questions designed to encourage the interviewee to elaborate about a topic

Problem-Solution: the process of ordering points with the problem first and the solution to follow

Productivity: refers to a group's ability to complete tasks that ultimately lead to accomplishing the group's overall mission

Professional: communicating with others using appropriate verbal and nonverbal skills

Pronunciation: elocution and delivery of sounds in a word

Proxemics: study of special cues to show whether we are comfortable or uncomfortable with the space between us and others

Public Communication: any situation in which individuals or groups communicate a message in a public arena to an intended audience

Public Distances: occupying a space twelve to twenty-five feet from others

Public Speaking: the process of speaking in public to an audience

Public Territories: spaces that can be used and are open to everyone

Purposive Group: a group that has a goal toward completion of a task

Race: term used to refer to inherited biological characteristics

Rate: the method used to determine how fast or slow someone is speaking

Receive: active skill that requires the listener to focus on a message, receive, understand, remember, and evaluate content

Receiver: person who receives the message communicated and decodes the signal to make sense of the information

Reciprocal Self-Disclosure: refers to the notion that individuals will engage in a similar exchange in terms of the types of information shared and the amount of information disclosed

Referent Power: assign power to another person because of your personal relationship with them

Reflected Appraisal: perception of how we believe others see us

Regulators: unintentional or intentional cues used during communication with others to show interest or to motivate the speaker to continue speaking or to give room for you to speak

Relational Expectations: explicit and implicit anticipations for ideal verbal and nonverbal responses

Relational Roles: Focus on building and maintaining connections among group members.

Relational Satisfaction: feeling positive and content in our relationships

Relational: use of nonverbal and verbal communication skills to establish relationships with others

Relationship Dissolution: occurs when one or both partners perceive the relationship as being dissatisfactory and make a decision to end their connection

Remember: retain information received

Repetition: words used in communicating that includes repeating words as a key element of the message

Research: process for finding support materials and credible information to be used as support

Respond: verbal or nonverbal feedback to show understanding or lack of understanding

Restatements: rephrasing things in a different way to emphasize key elements of a message

Reward Power: assign power to another person based on their perceived ability to deliver benefits or incentives as a result of compliance with their request

Rhetoric: use of effective speech and study of how we use language to share knowledge

Rhetorical questions: the process of asking a question, but not expecting an oral response

Rhythm: poetic placement of words combined with artfully placed pauses

Roles: labels placed on individuals based on their function within a group and are differentiated as task, relational, or individual roles

Secondary Territories: spaces you occupy or to which you have been assigned, but do not own

Selection: selection of stimuli that we feel are significant

Self-Concept: perceptions or beliefs we have about ourselves

Self-Disclosure: refers to the sharing of personal information with others in an attempt to build or maintain a relationship

Self-Esteem: a subjective evaluation of our worth

Self-Fulfilling Prophecy: something we believe is true about ourselves

Self-Perception: understanding how we perceive something prior to communicating it

Self-Presentation: influences how we want others to perceive us; choices about content that individuals share when crafting an online profile

Self-Serving Bias: the tendency for us to interpret the things we do in the most positive way or deny personal responsibility for the negative things that happen to us

Semantics: the meaning of a word

Sender: source or originator that encodes the communication sent

Sensory Language: language use that evokes one of our five senses: seeing, hearing, feeling, tasting, or smelling

Sign Language: gestures used to replace words

Skill: ability to produce or utilize the appropriate behaviors

Slang: words used in a cultural situation

Smiling: a nonverbal cue that shows approval

Social Attraction: characteristics that we seek in forming relationships with those whom we enjoy spending time and socializing

Social Dimensions: conversations among group members that focus on relationships and feelings

Social Distances: Usually four to twelve feet and is the space that most people are comfortable with when working with others

Social Group: a collection of individuals focused on relationship building

Social Media: Web sites that allow for individuals to create a profile to build communities

Social Networking: sites that aim to build both personal and professional connections with other individuals

Social Penetration Theory: process of how individuals share information with one another as relationships develop and move from one stage to another

Soft Skills: having a mixture of communication skills, people skills, social skills, career knowledge, social and emotional intelligence, self-motivation, impressive character traits, and strong work ethics

Solid Reality Function: focuses on how language is used to reflect the reality of the world around us

Spatial: process of ordering which involves location or direction

Speaker: person who communicates

Specific Purpose: a purpose statement which indicates a goal

Stagnating: phase in which the relationship becomes stale

Stereotypes: generalizations we hold about a group or category of people that may affect our perceptions

Stereotyping: refers to tendency to view individuals as possessing characteristics assigned to a group

Storming Stage: a stage in which group members become familiar and comfortable with each other

Storytelling: communicating as a result of writing, telling stories, or relating anecdotes

Summary: internal review of points in a speech

Supportive Communication: occurs when an individual feels as though he or she has little reason to have anxiety or concern about communication being received

Task Attraction: characteristics we seek in forming working relationships where we depend on others to accomplish a task or goal

Task Dimension: tasks characterized by messages that focus on solving problems, completing a task, or achieving a goal

Task Roles: Includes all roles that focus on the group's assignment.

Technical Language: using words reserved for a specialized audience who will understand concepts shared

Telecommunications: communication which involves transmitting signals over a distance

Terminating: the process in which a relationship dissolves

Territoriality: the way we view our own space and our own objects

Time on Task: process of determining how much time the group will spend discussing a given topic

Topical: ordering process used when order is not critical

Transactional Model of Communication: model that shows communication that transfers between sender and receiver

Transitions: links, connectors, internal previews, signposts, signals, or internal reviews used to help audiences follow the order of a speech

Truth Bias: interferes with our ability to see deception with close friends, romantic partners, or family members

Uncertainty Reduction Theory: how we use communication in the initial stages of a relationship to decrease our uncertainty about the other person

Understand: processing and internalizing messages received

Uninvolved Parents: parenting style in which low levels of support and low levels of control are exhibited

Upward Dissent: directly communicating one's dissatisfaction or frustration with an organization's upper management or administration

Uses and Gratifications Theory: theoretical lens through which relationships individuals have with media is understood with relation to information seeking, decisional utilities, entertainment, or interpersonal utilities

Values: personal philosophy that guides actions and behaviors and assists us in evaluating ethical situations

Verbal Abuse: process of engaging in verbal comments, name-calling, or jokes that are insulting or demeaning to others

Verbal Modeling: consciously using the same dialects, words, or phrases that others use

Verbal: communication that is delivered using words or sounds

Virtual Game Worlds: online games that include a created reality

Virtual Social World: provides a space for individuals to create another life and interact with others

Visual Literacy: the ability to understand and make visual statements through nonverbal communication

Volume: the level at which sound is heard

Written Tradition of Communication: written transmission of information using the written word